ne & Hana

14

STORY AND ART BY

Yuki Shiwasu

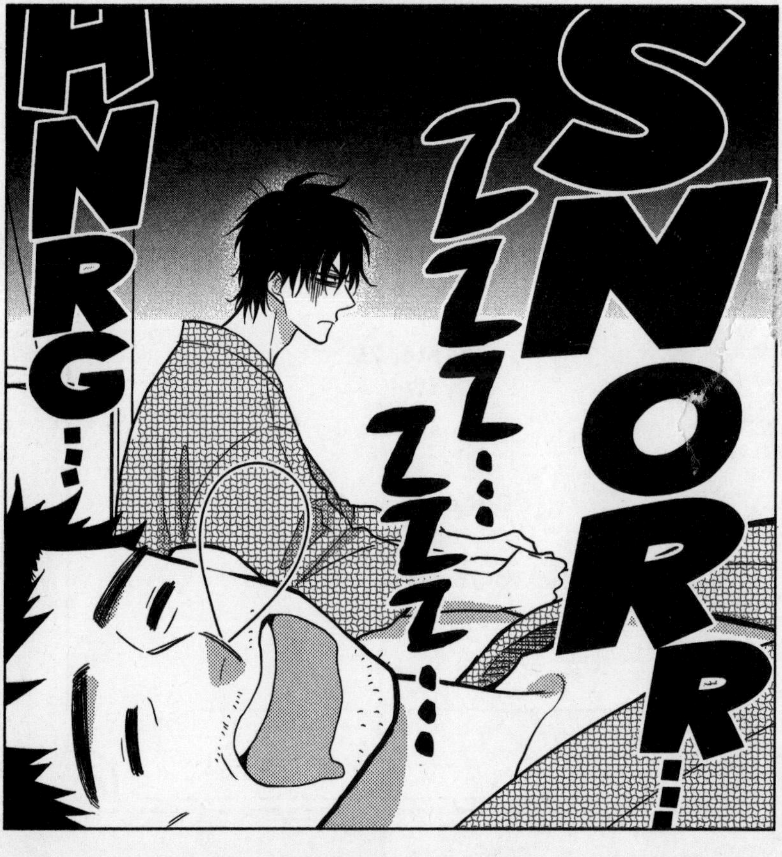
SNORR...
ZZZZ...
ZZZZ...
HNRG...

Takane & Hana

14

Chapter 75
~003~

Chapter 76
~033~

Chapter 77
~065~

Chapter 78
~095~

Chapter 79
~127~

Bonus Story 1
~157~

Bonus Story 2
~165~

Bonus Story 3
~183~

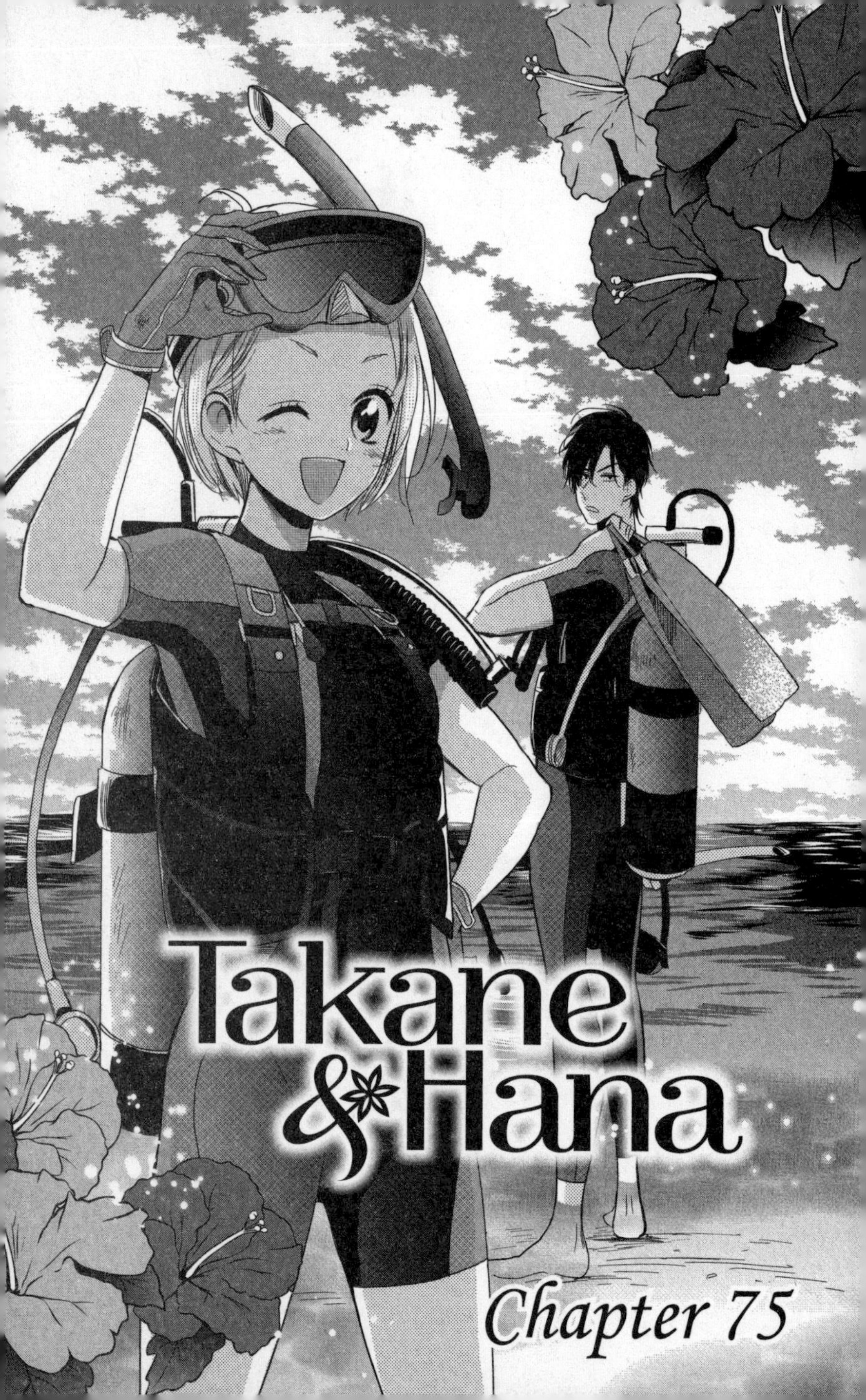
Takane & Hana
Chapter 75

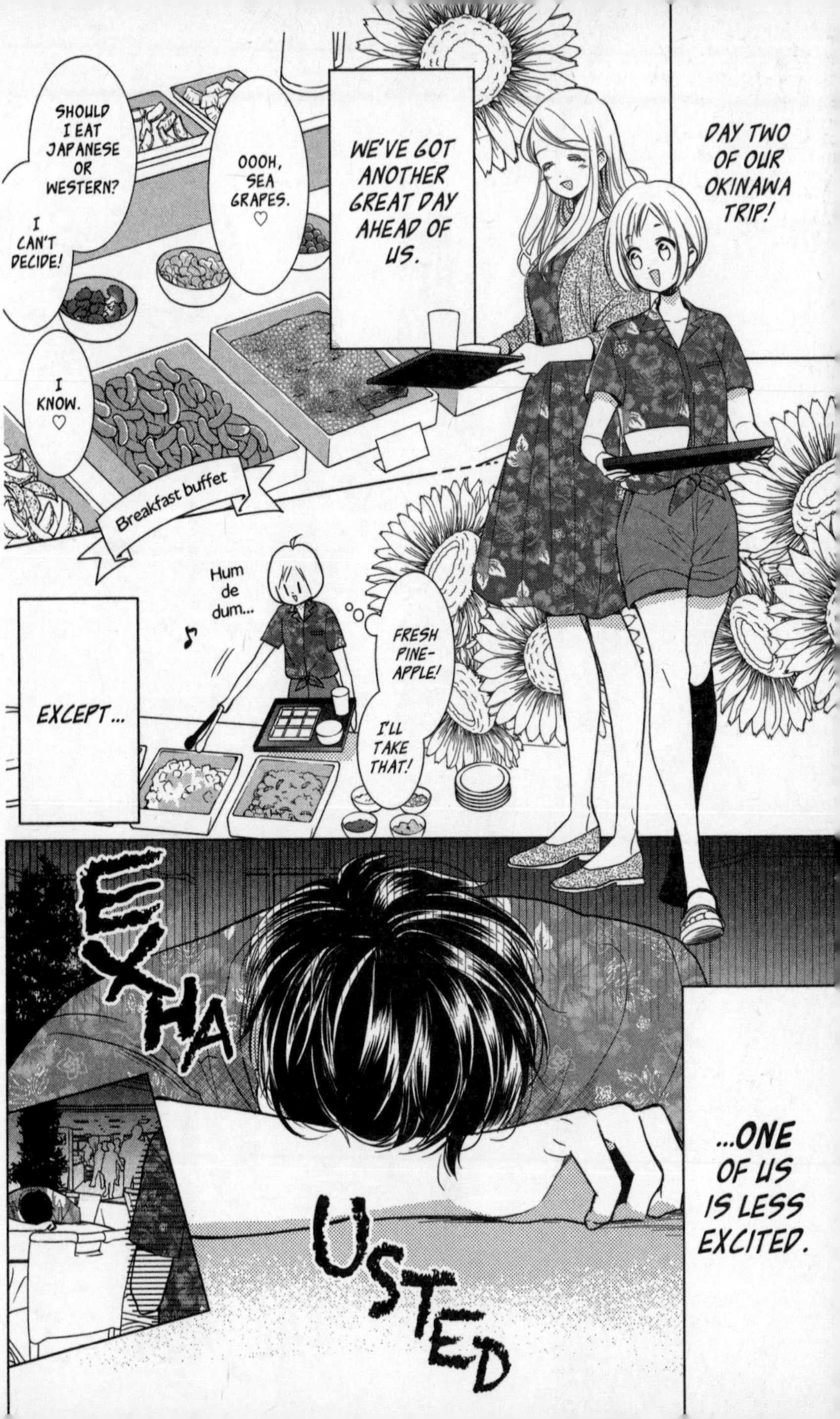
DAY TWO OF OUR OKINAWA TRIP!
WE'VE GOT ANOTHER GREAT DAY AHEAD OF US.
OOOH, SEA GRAPES. ♡
SHOULD I EAT JAPANESE OR WESTERN?
I CAN'T DECIDE!
I KNOW. ♡
Breakfast buffet
FRESH PINE-APPLE!
I'LL TAKE THAT!
Hum de dum...
EXCEPT...
...ONE OF US IS LESS EXCITED.
EXHAUSTED

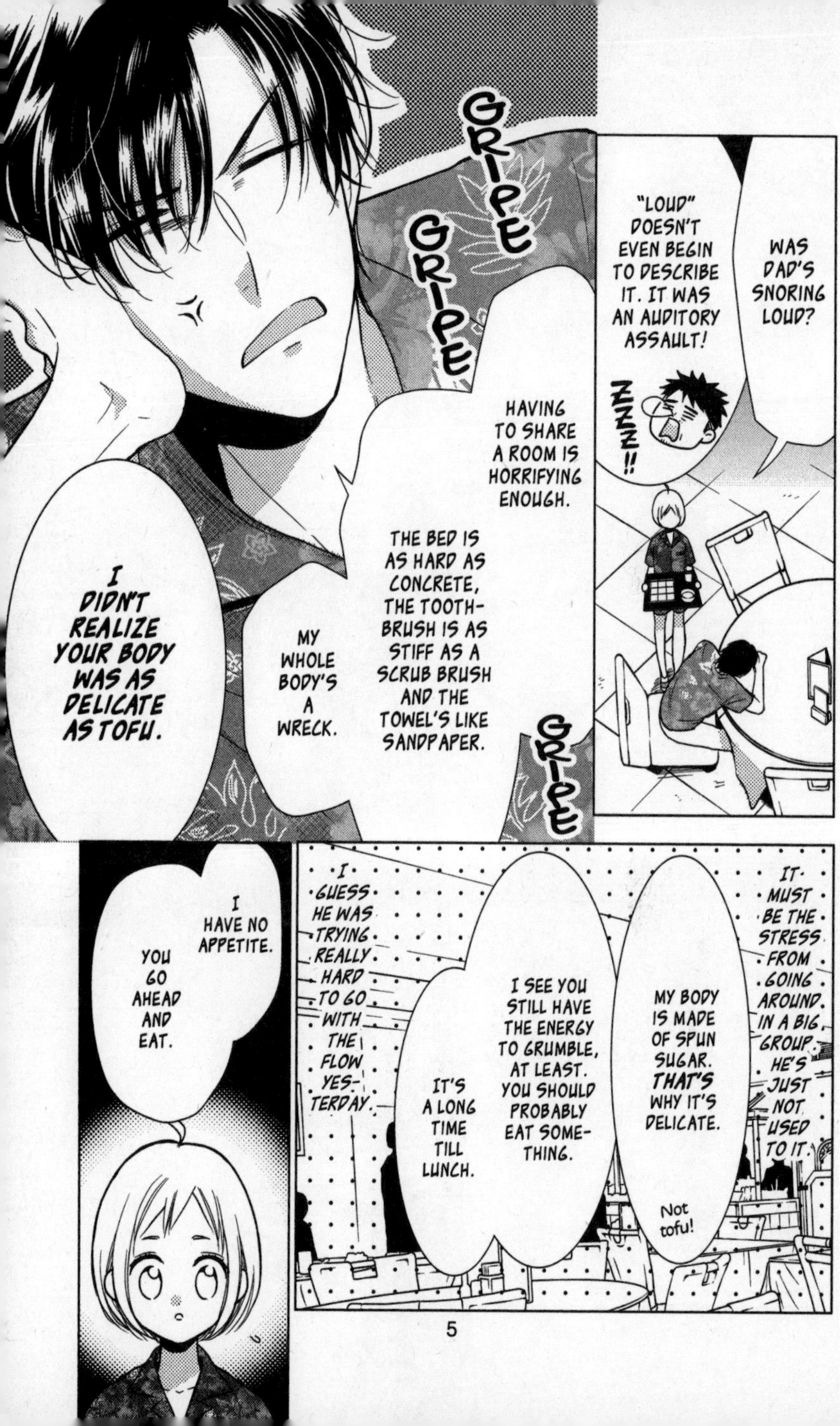
WAS DAD'S SNORING LOUD?
"LOUD" DOESN'T EVEN BEGIN TO DESCRIBE IT. IT WAS AN AUDITORY ASSAULT!
ZZZZ!!
GRIPE
GRIPE
HAVING TO SHARE A ROOM IS HORRIFYING ENOUGH.
THE BED IS AS HARD AS CONCRETE, THE TOOTH-BRUSH IS AS STIFF AS A SCRUB BRUSH AND THE TOWEL'S LIKE SANDPAPER.
MY WHOLE BODY'S A WRECK.
GRIPE
I DIDN'T REALIZE YOUR BODY WAS AS DELICATE AS TOFU.
IT MUST BE THE STRESS FROM GOING AROUND IN A BIG GROUP. HE'S JUST NOT USED TO IT.
MY BODY IS MADE OF SPUN SUGAR. THAT'S WHY IT'S DELICATE.
Not tofu!
I SEE YOU STILL HAVE THE ENERGY TO GRUMBLE, AT LEAST. YOU SHOULD PROBABLY EAT SOME-THING.
IT'S A LONG TIME TILL LUNCH.
I GUESS HE WAS TRYING REALLY HARD TO GO WITH THE FLOW YES-TERDAY.
I HAVE NO APPETITE.
YOU GO AHEAD AND EAT.

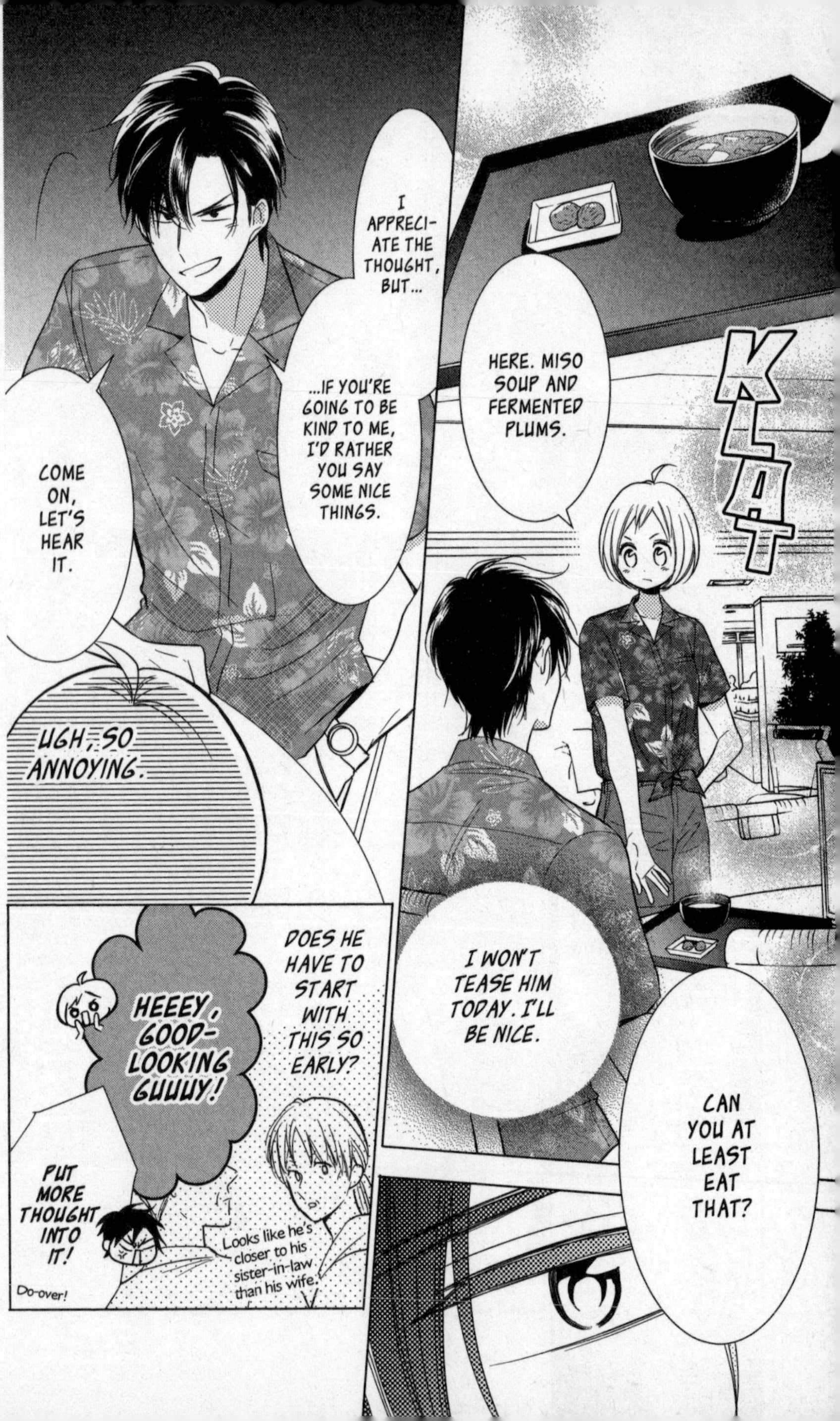
KLAT
HERE. MISO SOUP AND FERMENTED PLUMS.
I WON'T TEASE HIM TODAY. I'LL BE NICE.
CAN YOU AT LEAST EAT THAT?
I APPRECIATE THE THOUGHT, BUT...
...IF YOU'RE GOING TO BE KIND TO ME, I'D RATHER YOU SAY SOME NICE THINGS.
COME ON, LET'S HEAR IT.
UGH, SO ANNOYING.
DOES HE HAVE TO START WITH THIS SO EARLY?
HEEEY, GOOD-LOOKING GUUUY!
Looks like he's closer to his sister-in-law than his wife.
PUT MORE THOUGHT INTO IT!
Do-over!

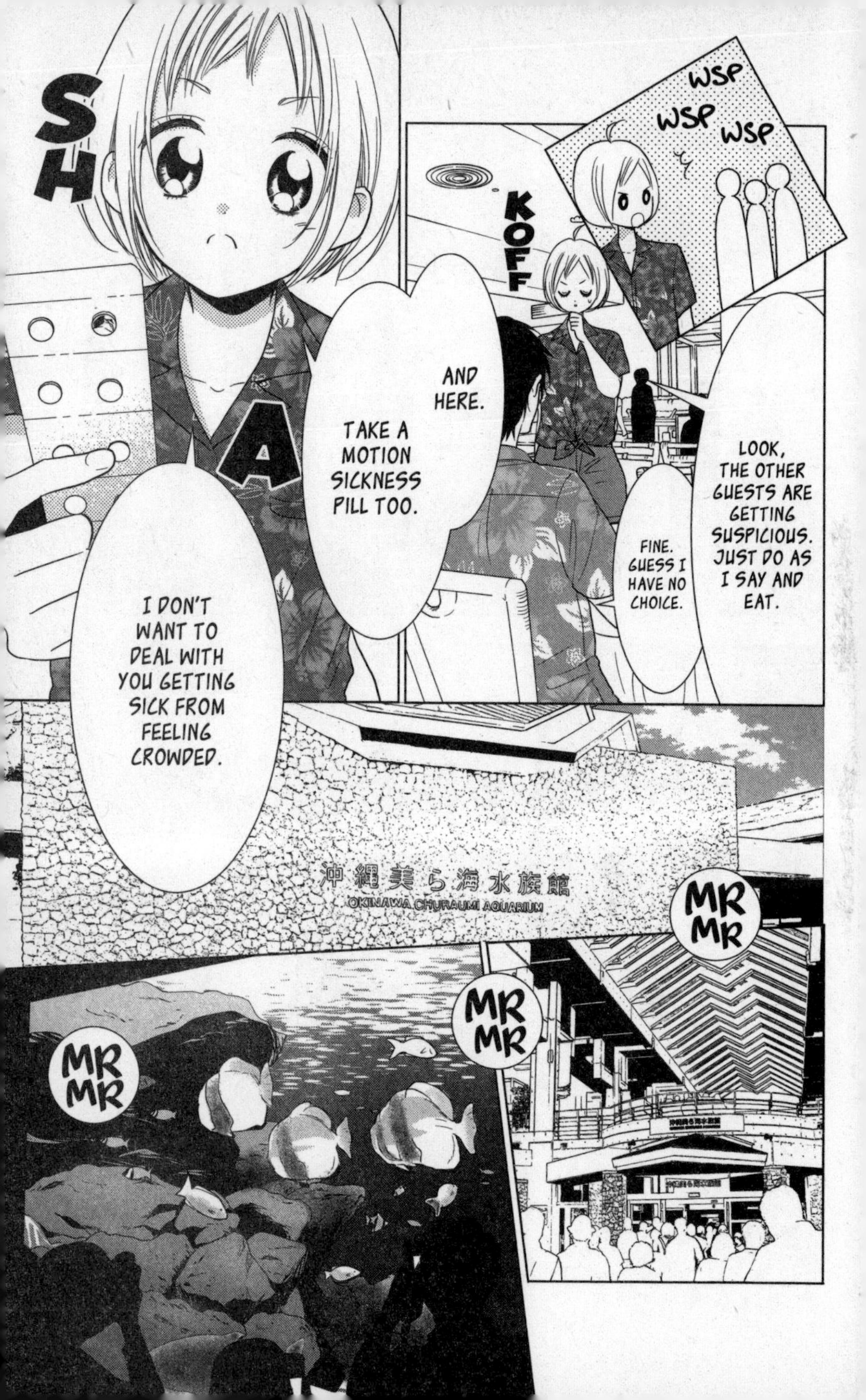
WSP
WSP
WSP
KOFF
LOOK, THE OTHER GUESTS ARE GETTING SUSPICIOUS. JUST DO AS I SAY AND EAT.
FINE. GUESS I HAVE NO CHOICE.
SH
A
AND HERE.
TAKE A MOTION SICKNESS PILL TOO.
I DON'T WANT TO DEAL WITH YOU GETTING SICK FROM FEELING CROWDED.
沖縄美ら海水族館
OKINAWA CHURAUMI AQUARIUM
MR MR
MR MR
MR MR

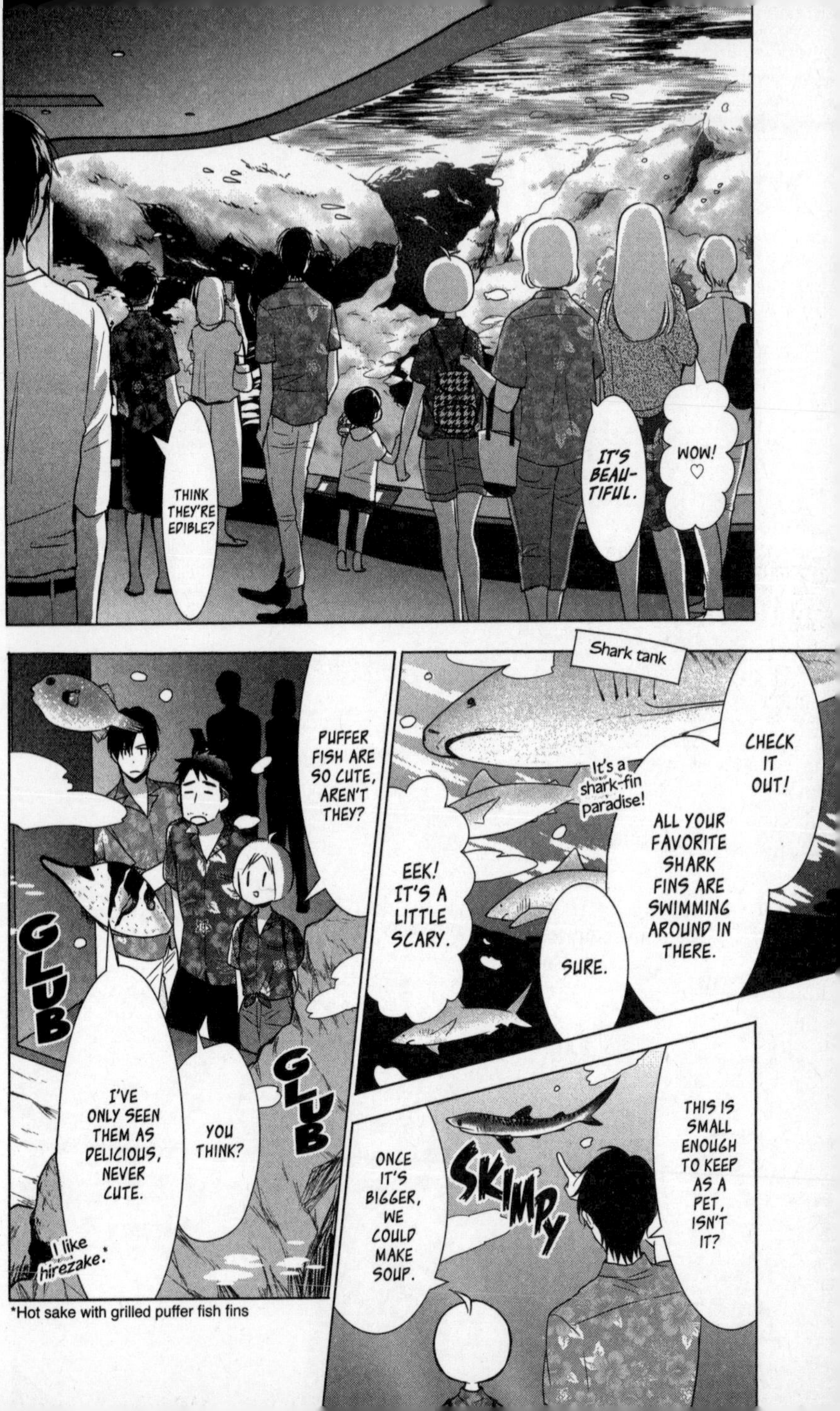
WOW! ♡
IT'S BEAU-TIFUL.
THINK THEY'RE EDIBLE?
Shark tank
CHECK IT OUT!
ALL YOUR FAVORITE SHARK FINS ARE SWIMMING AROUND IN THERE.
It's a shark-fin paradise!
SURE.
EEK! IT'S A LITTLE SCARY.
THIS IS SMALL ENOUGH TO KEEP AS A PET, ISN'T IT?
SKIMPY
ONCE IT'S BIGGER, WE COULD MAKE SOUP.
PUFFER FISH ARE SO CUTE, AREN'T THEY?
GLUB
YOU THINK?
GLUB
I'VE ONLY SEEN THEM AS DELICIOUS, NEVER CUTE.
I like hirezake.*

*Hot sake with grilled puffer fish fins

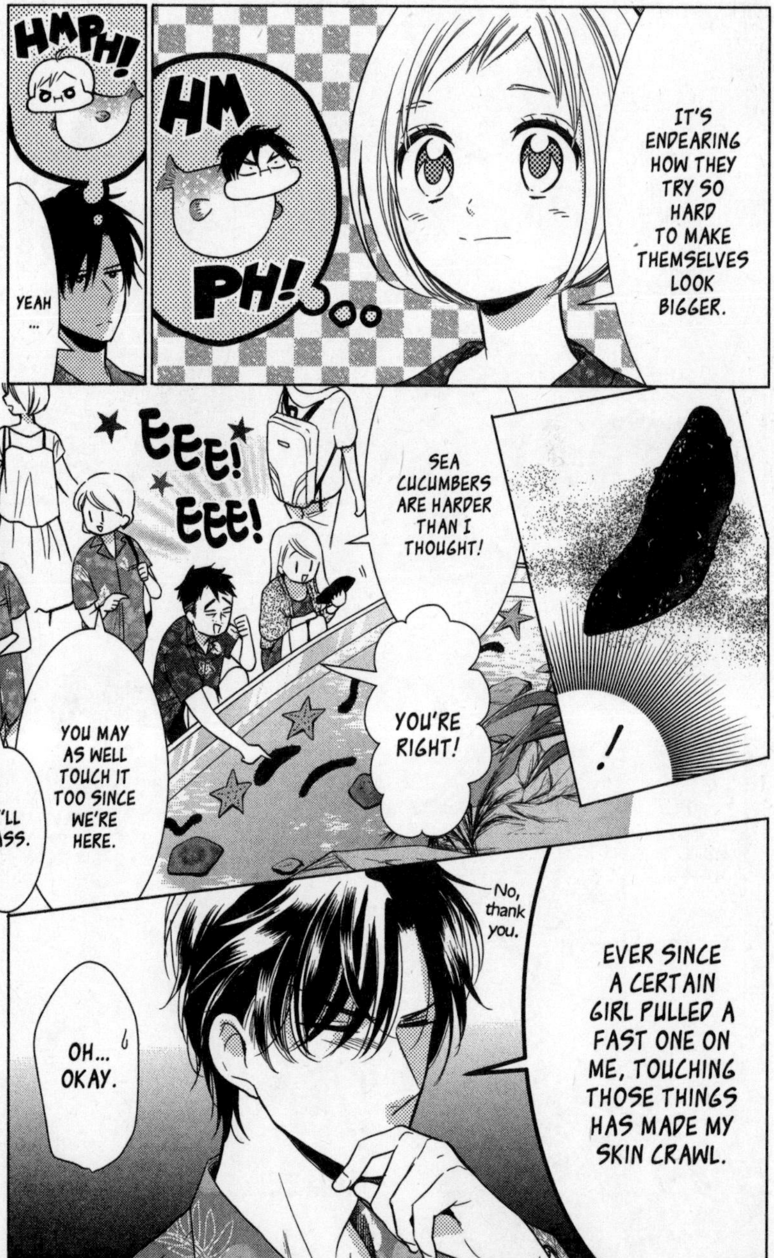
IT'S ENDEARING HOW THEY TRY SO HARD TO MAKE THEMSELVES LOOK BIGGER.
HMPH!
HMPH!
YEAH ...
!
SEA CUCUMBERS ARE HARDER THAN I THOUGHT!
EEE! EEE!
YOU'RE RIGHT!
YOU MAY AS WELL TOUCH IT TOO SINCE WE'RE HERE.
I'LL PASS.
EVER SINCE A CERTAIN GIRL PULLED A FAST ONE ON ME, TOUCHING THOSE THINGS HAS MADE MY SKIN CRAWL.
No, thank you.
OH... OKAY.

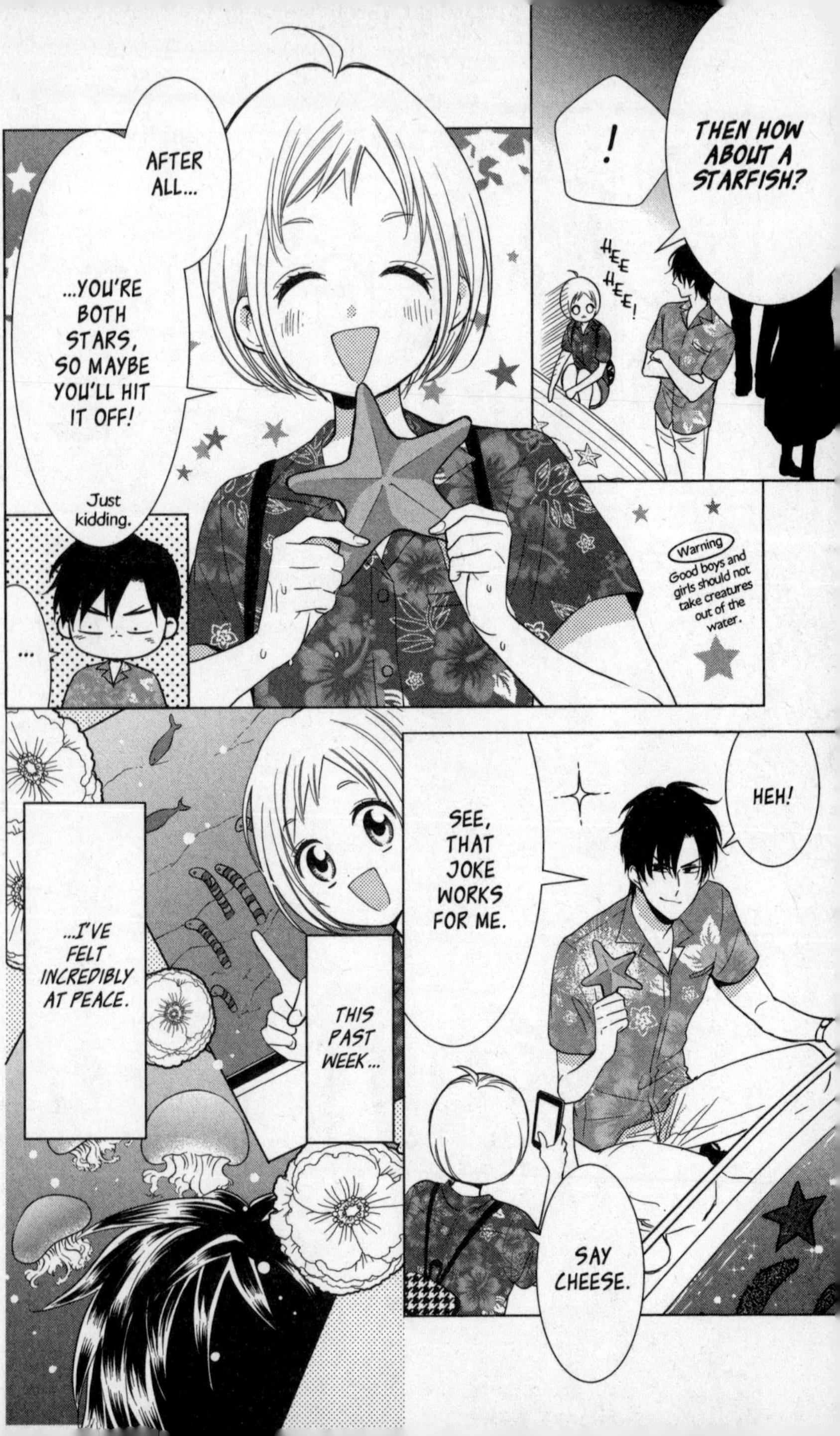
THEN HOW ABOUT A STARFISH?
!
HEE HEE!
Warning
Good boys and girls should not take creatures out of the water.
AFTER ALL...
...YOU'RE BOTH STARS, SO MAYBE YOU'LL HIT IT OFF!
Just kidding.
...
HEH!
SEE, THAT JOKE WORKS FOR ME.
SAY CHEESE.
THIS PAST WEEK...
...I'VE FELT INCREDIBLY AT PEACE.

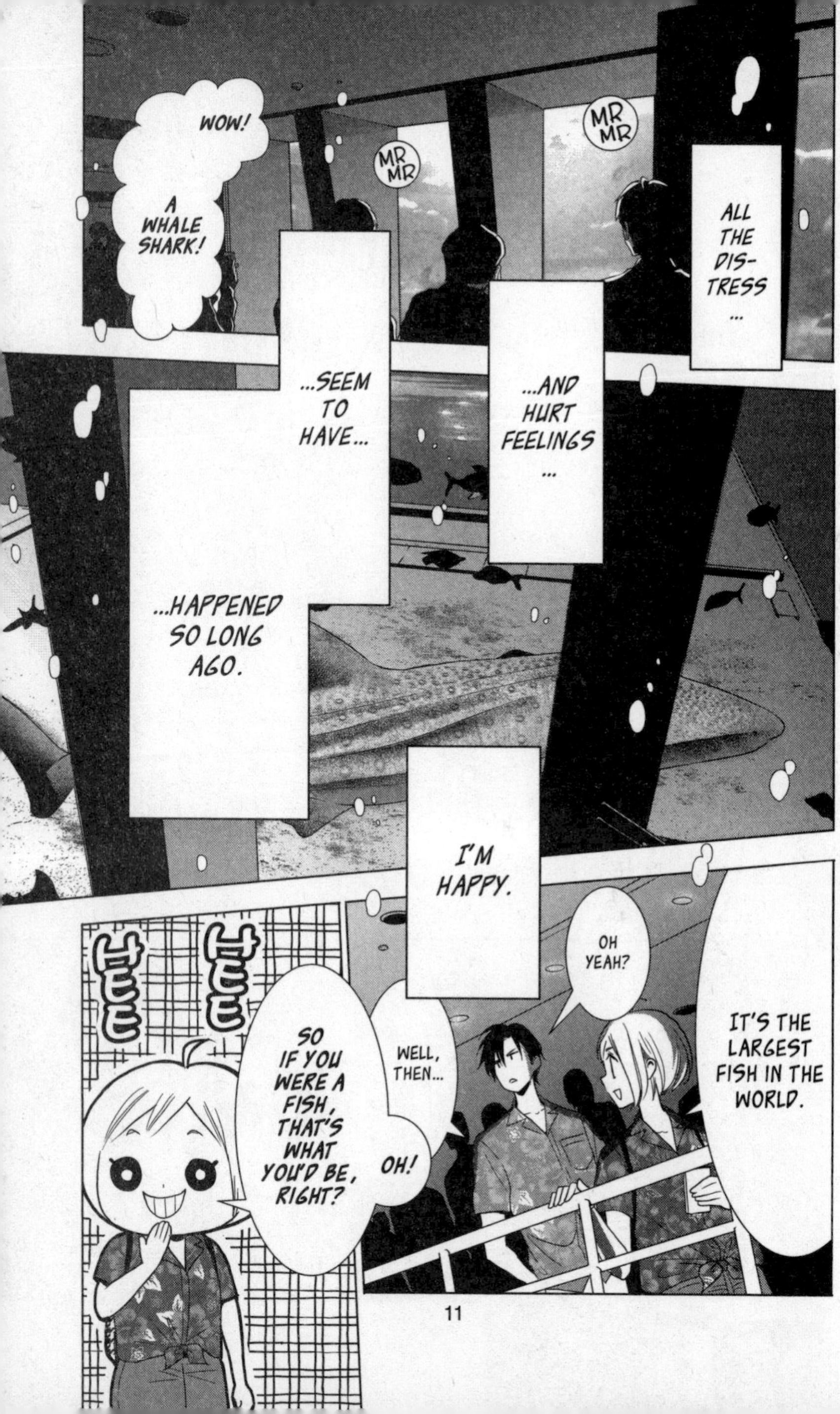
MR MR
MR MR
WOW!
A WHALE SHARK!
ALL THE DISTRESS...
...AND HURT FEELINGS...
...SEEM TO HAVE...
...HAPPENED SO LONG AGO.
I'M HAPPY.
IT'S THE LARGEST FISH IN THE WORLD.
OH YEAH?
WELL, THEN...
OH!
SO IF YOU WERE A FISH, THAT'S WHAT YOU'D BE, RIGHT?
HEE
HEE

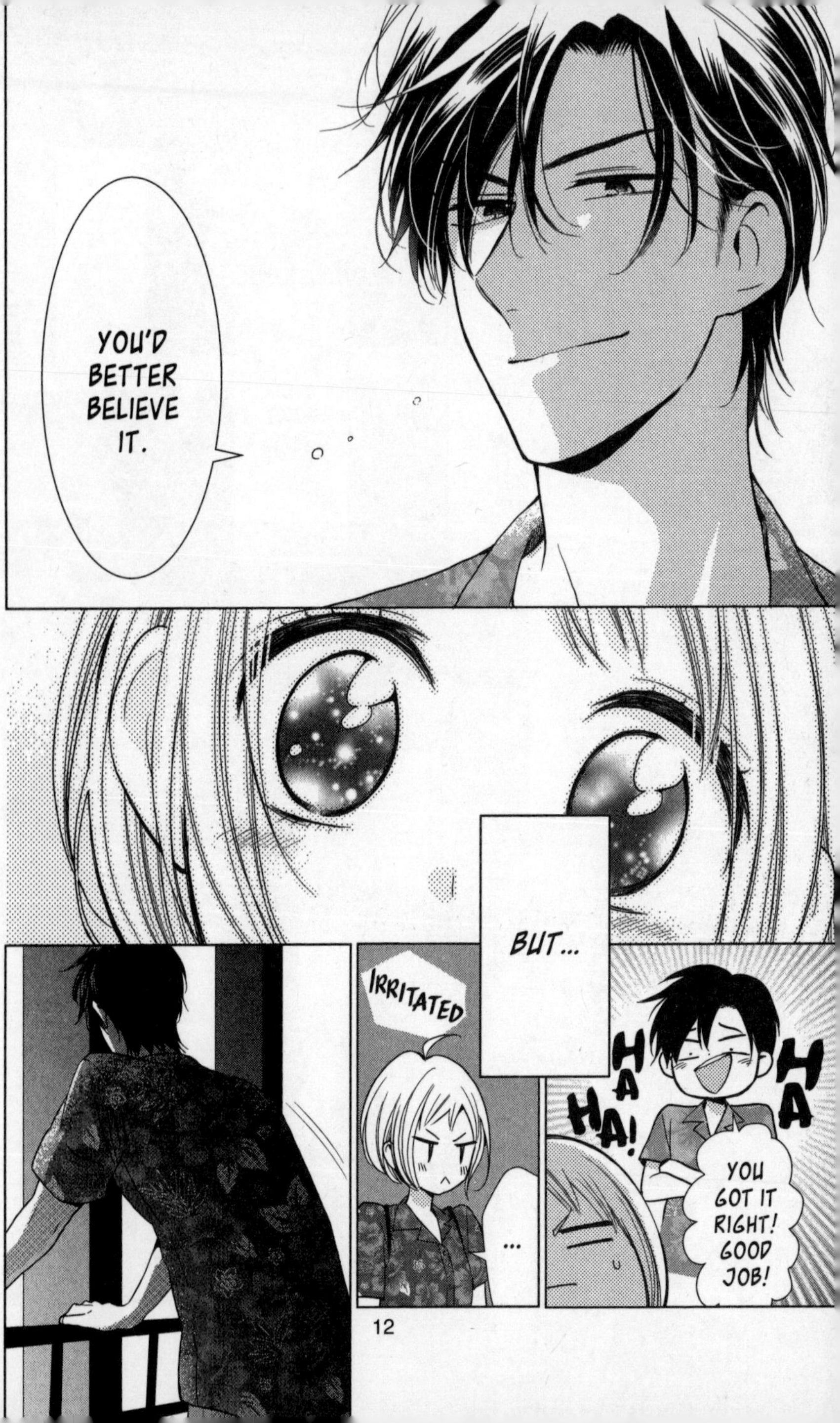
YOU'D BETTER BELIEVE IT.
BUT...
HA HA HA!
HA HA
YOU GOT IT RIGHT! GOOD JOB!
IRRITATED
...

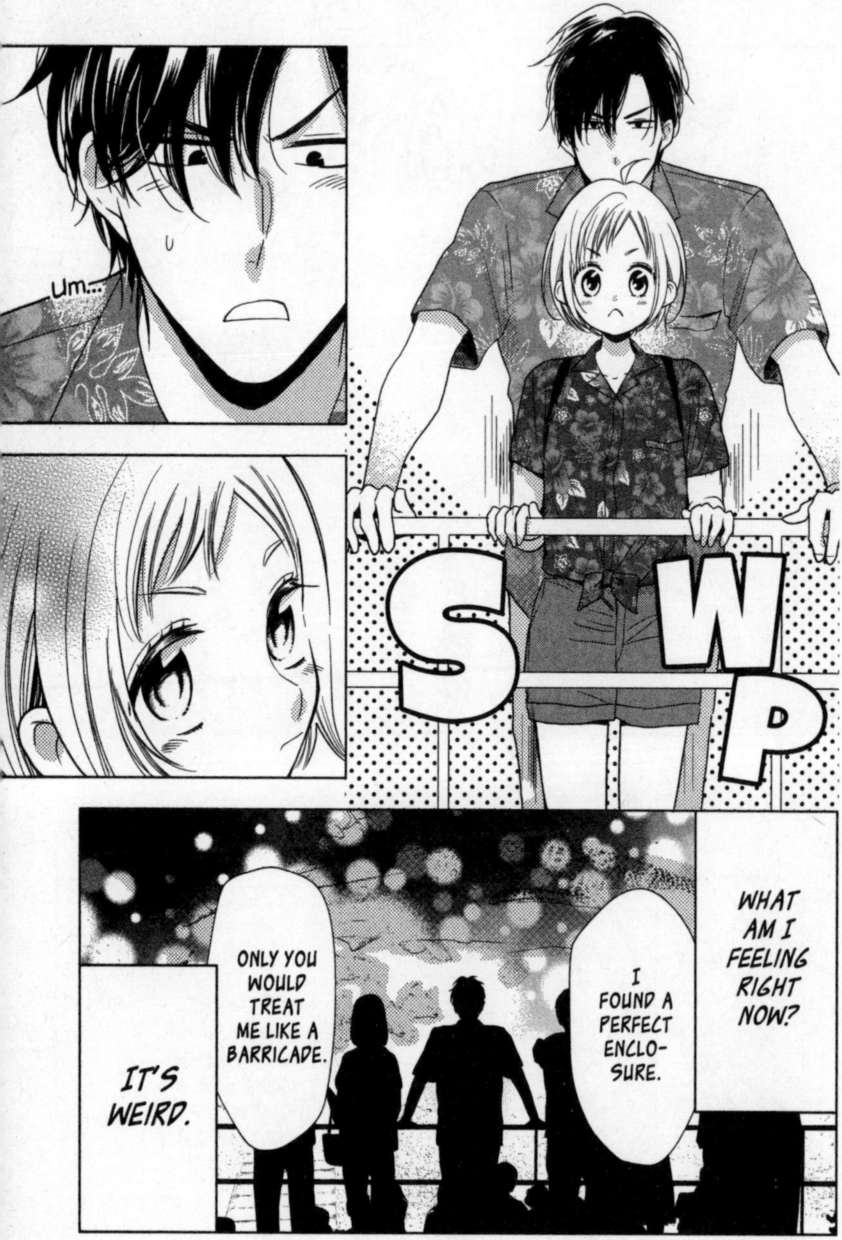
SWP
Um...
WHAT AM I FEELING RIGHT NOW?
I FOUND A PERFECT ENCLO-SURE.
ONLY YOU WOULD TREAT ME LIKE A BARRICADE.
IT'S WEIRD.

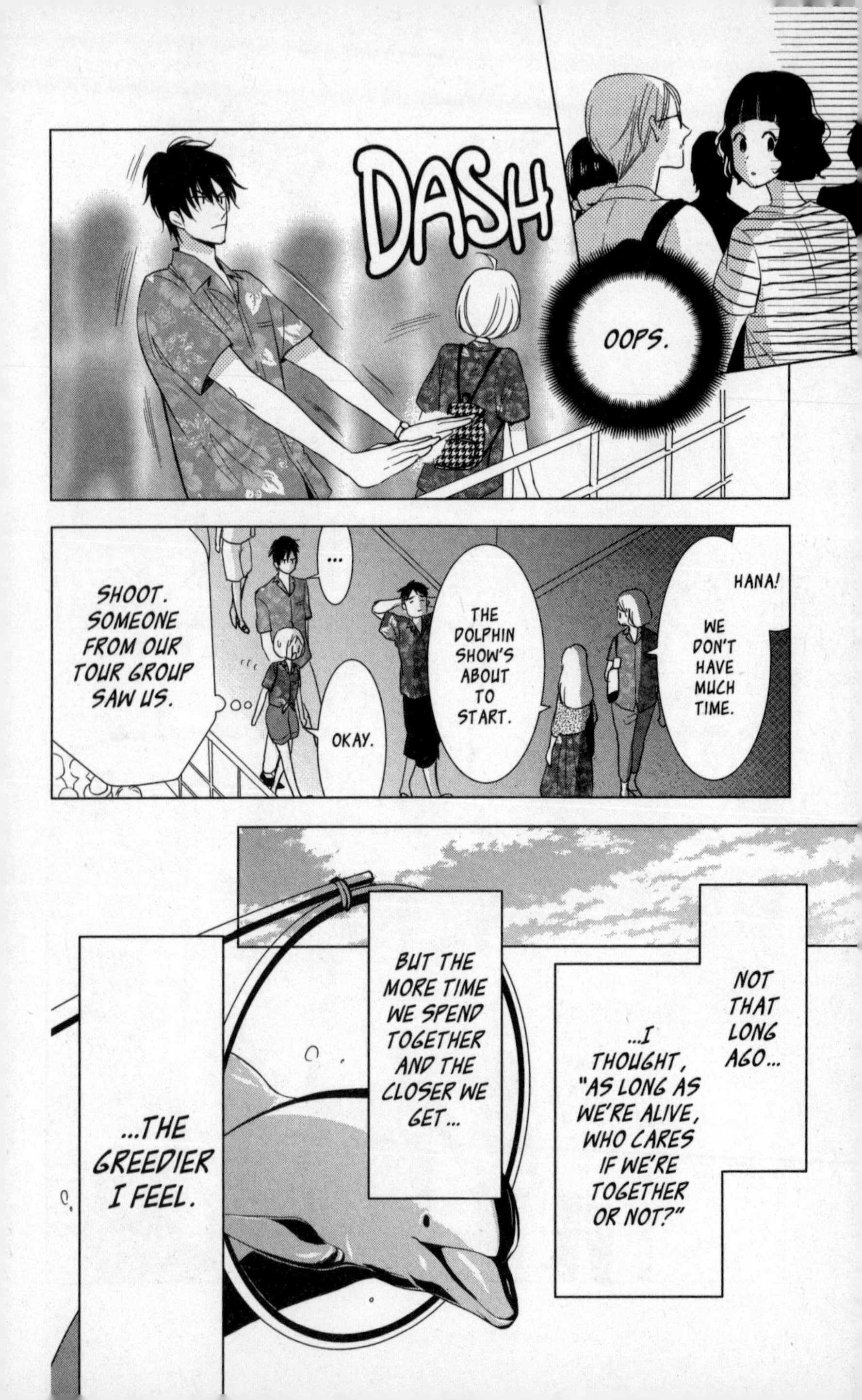
OOPS.
DASH
HANA!
WE DON'T HAVE MUCH TIME.
THE DOLPHIN SHOW'S ABOUT TO START.
...
OKAY.
SHOOT. SOMEONE FROM OUR TOUR GROUP SAW US.
NOT THAT LONG AGO...
...I THOUGHT, "AS LONG AS WE'RE ALIVE, WHO CARES IF WE'RE TOGETHER OR NOT?"
BUT THE MORE TIME WE SPEND TOGETHER AND THE CLOSER WE GET...
...THE GREEDIER I FEEL.

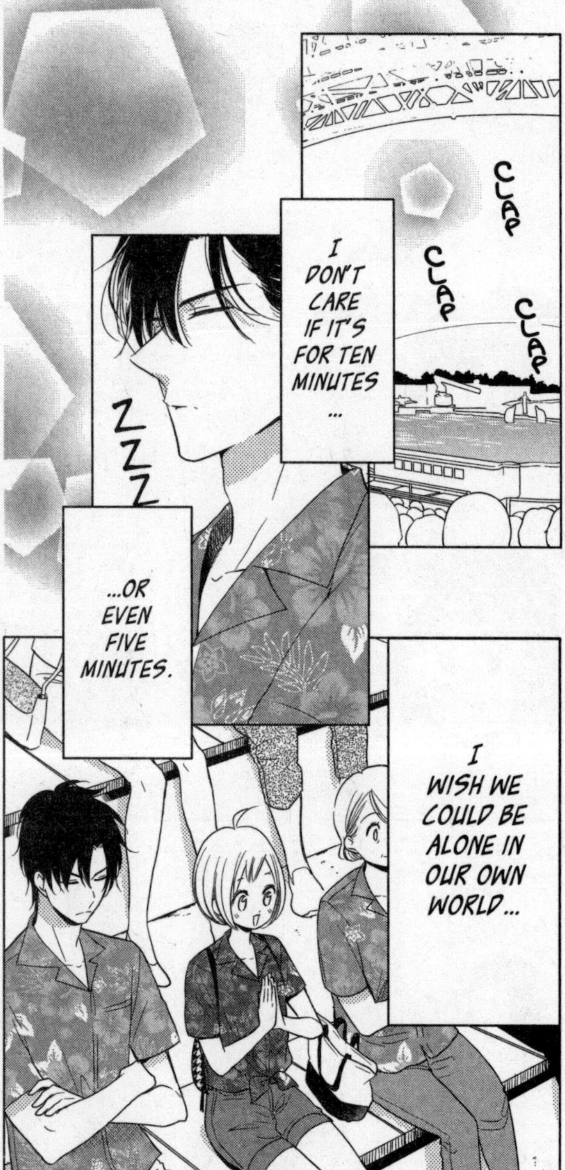
CLAP
CLAP
CLAP
I DON'T CARE IF IT'S FOR TEN MINUTES...
ZZZ
...OR EVEN FIVE MINUTES.
I WISH WE COULD BE ALONE IN OUR OWN WORLD...

• About This Space •

Up until the last volume, every chapter had this column space. But in this volume, it will only appear in half the chapters, and in the next volume, it'll be completely gone.

When the manga ran in the magazine, this space was used for advertising. Starting this year, they've decided not to run ads anymore, so there's no need to keep this space open. I feel a bit sentimental about it, but at the same time, it makes it easier for me since I don't have to keep coming up with things to say. (*Ha ha.*)

Before social media, this space was the only way you could get to know the manga creator, but times have changed so much. Social media means I can always reach out, so not having this space anymore won't be an inconvenience for me. That said, it's always a bit sad to lose something you're used to having.

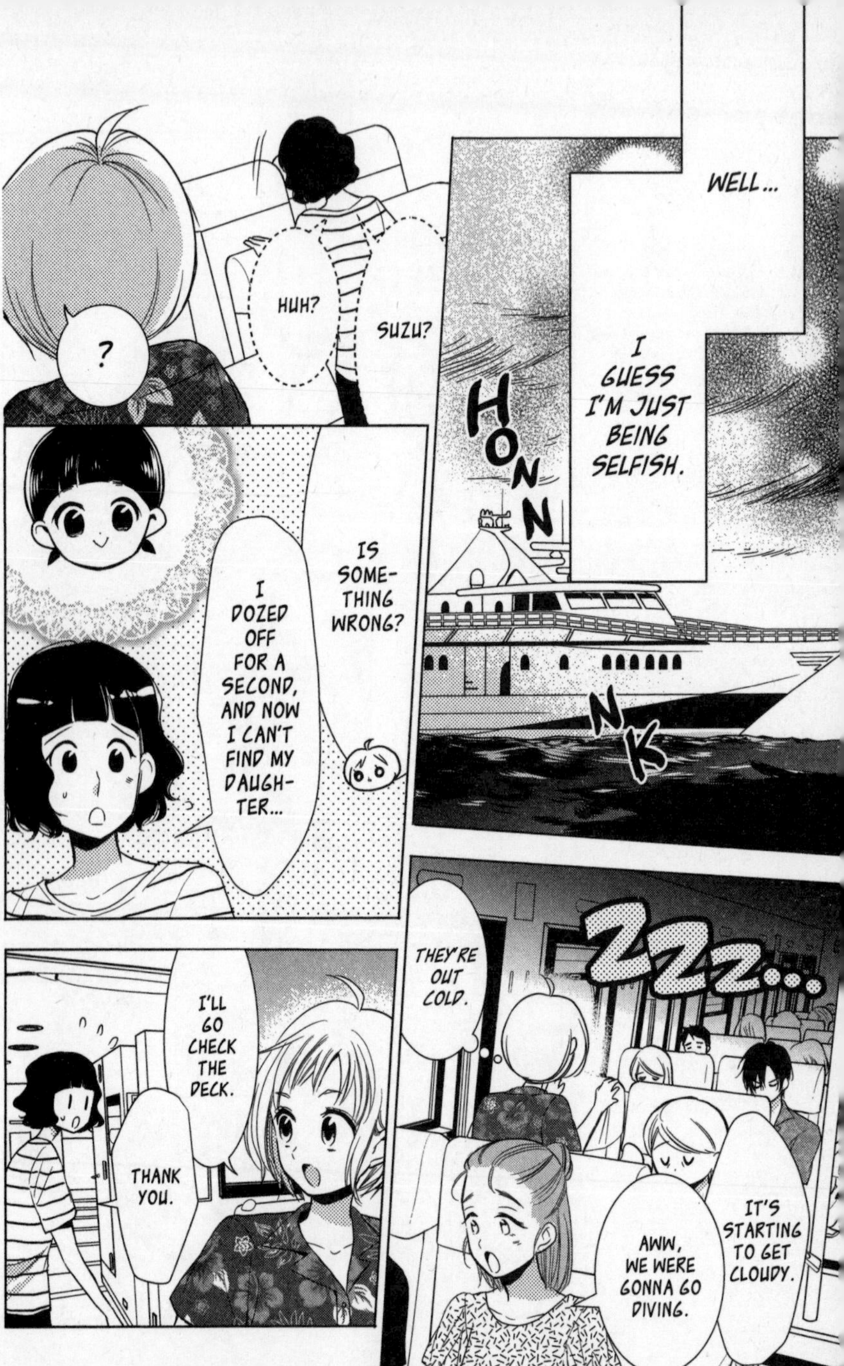
WELL...
I GUESS I'M JUST BEING SELFISH.
HONNNK
SUZU?
HUH?
?
IS SOMETHING WRONG?
I DOZED OFF FOR A SECOND, AND NOW I CAN'T FIND MY DAUGHTER...
ZZZ...
THEY'RE OUT COLD.
IT'S STARTING TO GET CLOUDY.
AWW, WE WERE GONNA GO DIVING.
I'LL GO CHECK THE DECK.
THANK YOU.

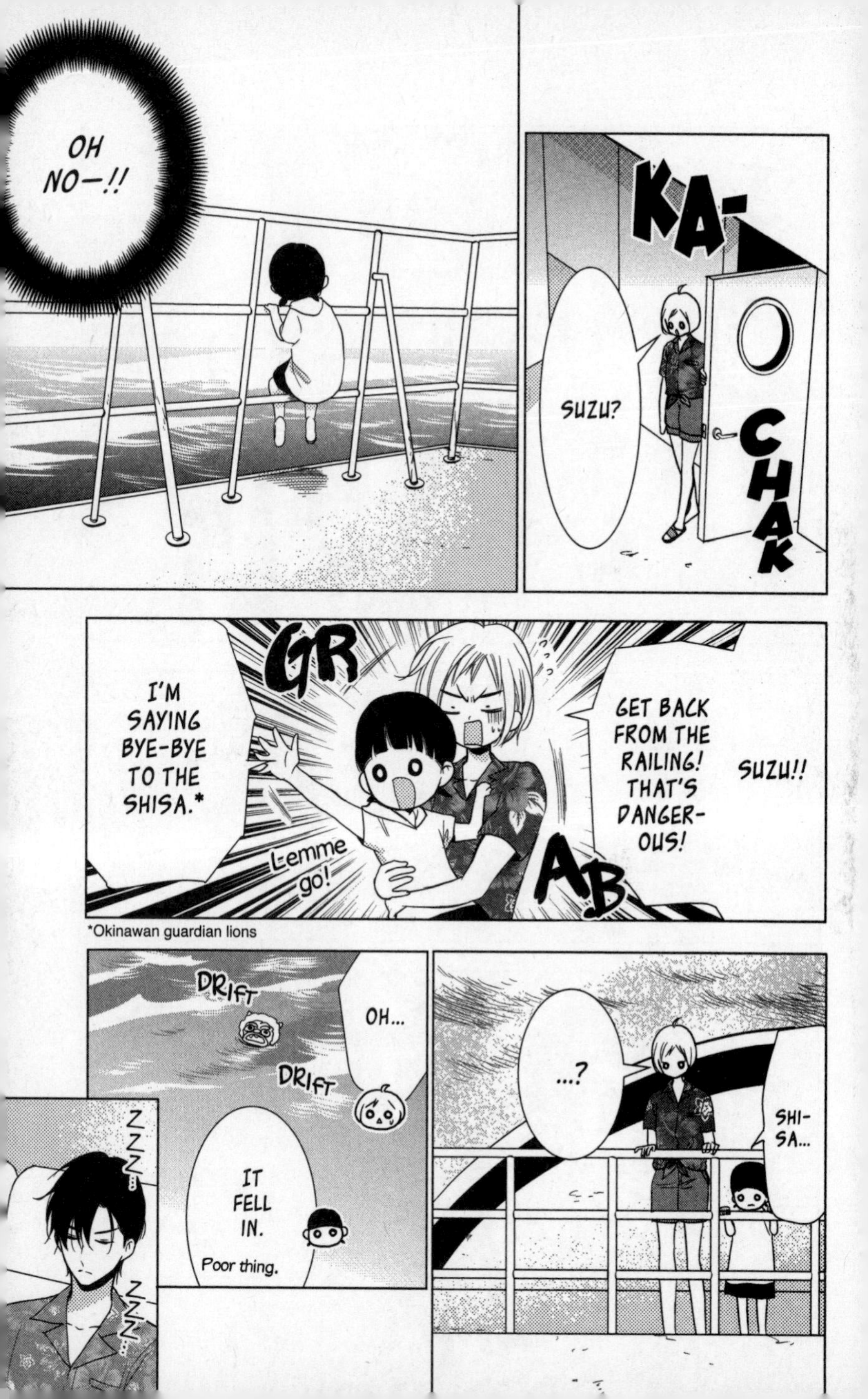
KA-
CHAK
SUZU?
OH NO—!!
SUZU!!
GET BACK FROM THE RAILING! THAT'S DANGEROUS!
GR
AB
I'M SAYING BYE-BYE TO THE SHISA.*
Lemme go!
SHI-SA...
...?
OH...
DRIFT
DRIFT
IT FELL IN.
Poor thing.
ZZZ...
ZZZ...
*Okinawan guardian lions

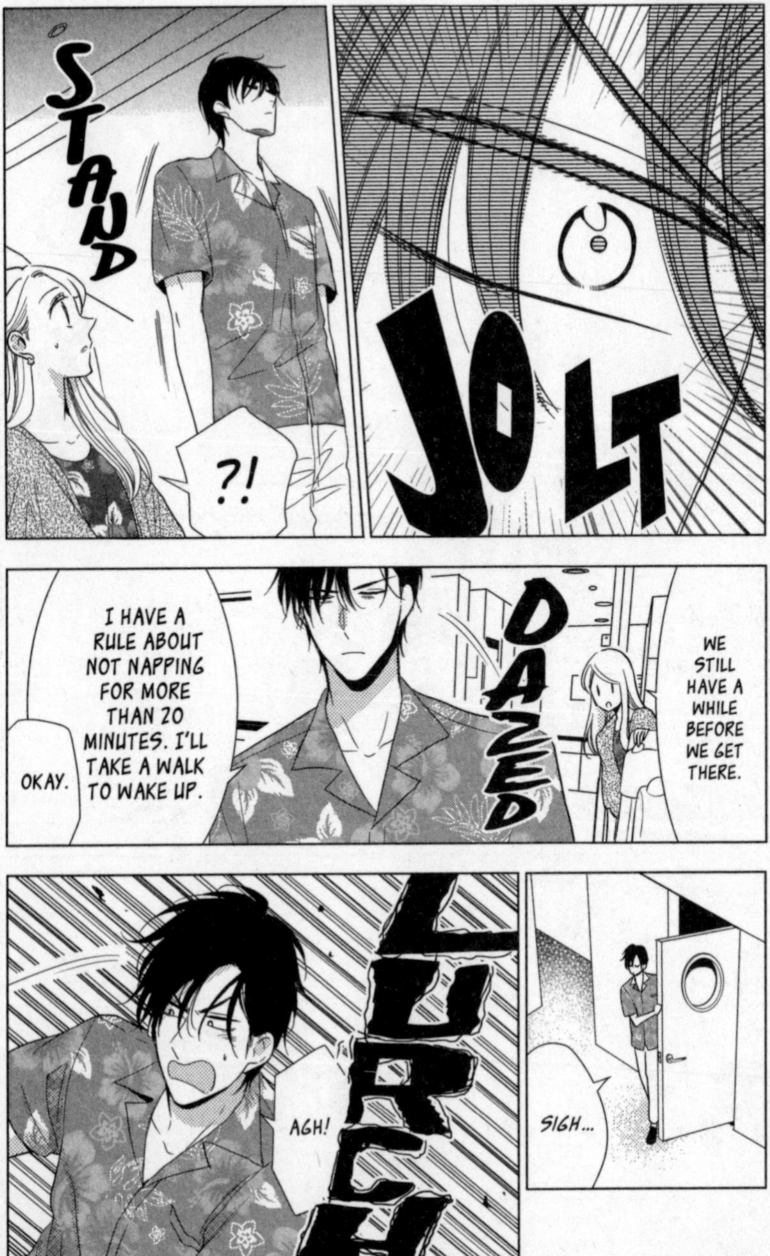
JOLT
STAND
?!
WE STILL HAVE A WHILE BEFORE WE GET THERE.
DAZED
I HAVE A RULE ABOUT NOT NAPPING FOR MORE THAN 20 MINUTES. I'LL TAKE A WALK TO WAKE UP.
OKAY.
SIGH...
LURCH
AGH!

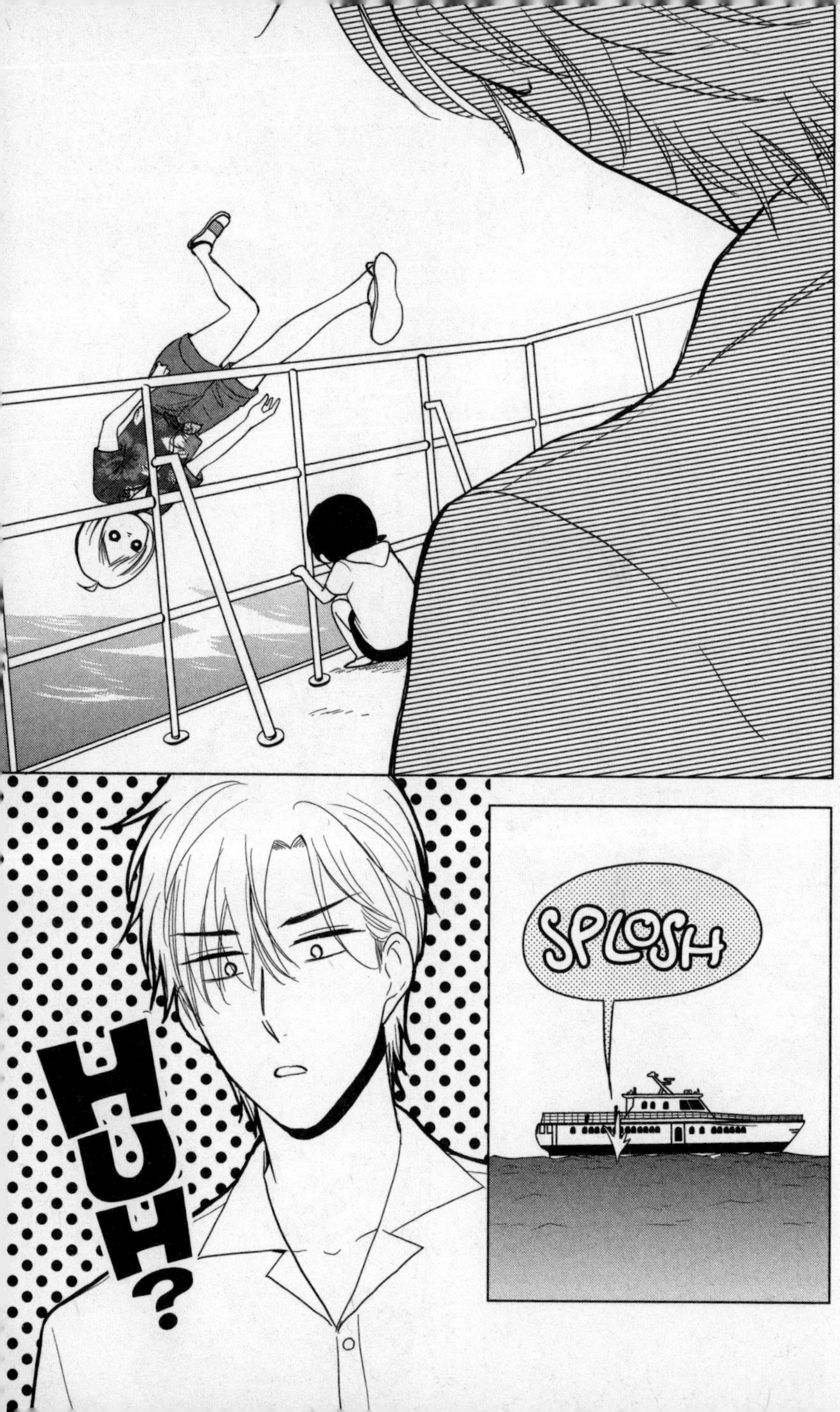
SPLOSH
HUH?

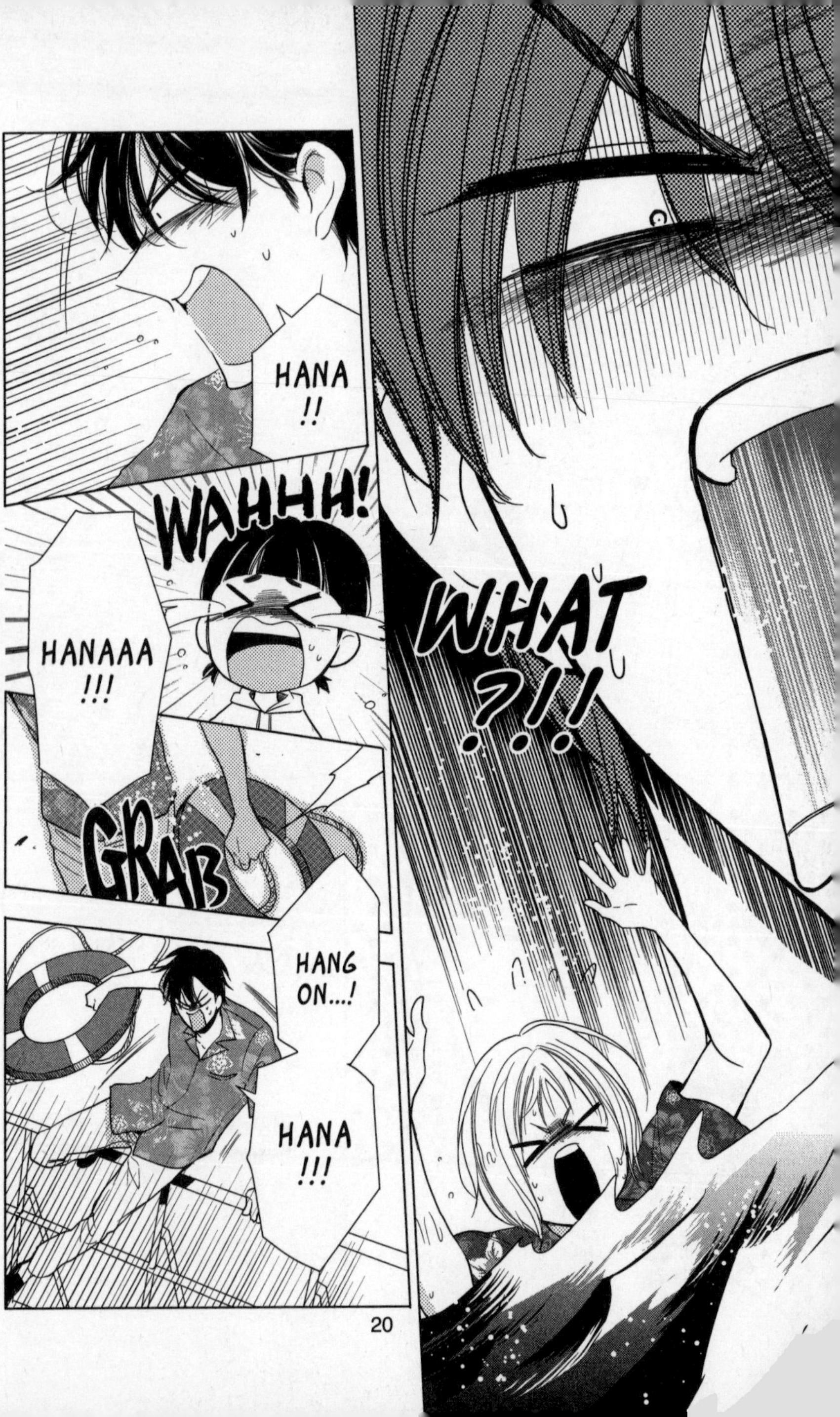
WHAT?!!
HANA!!
WAHHH!
HANAAA!!!
GRAB
HANG ON...!
HANA!!!

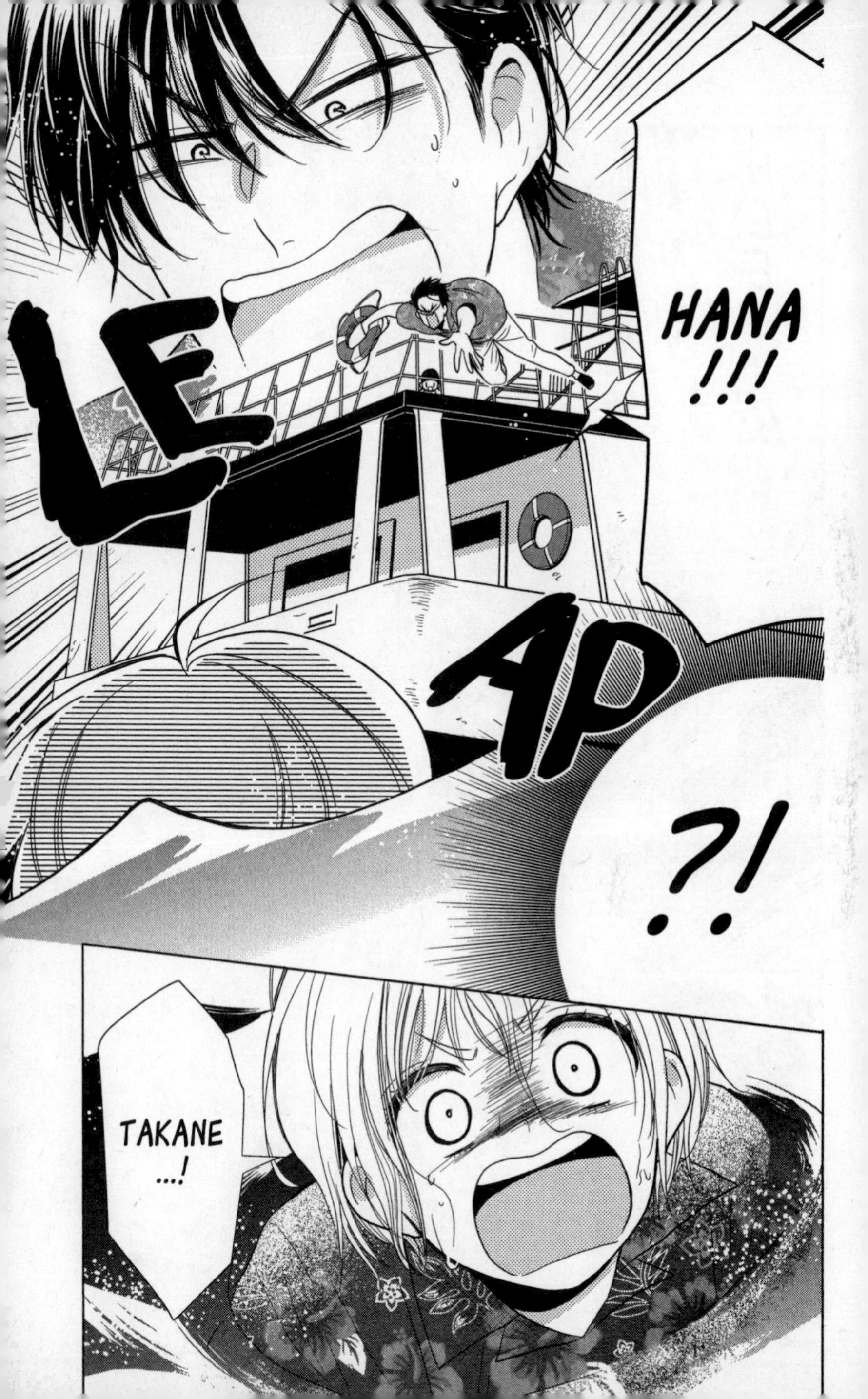
HANA !!!
LEAP
?!
TAKANE ...!

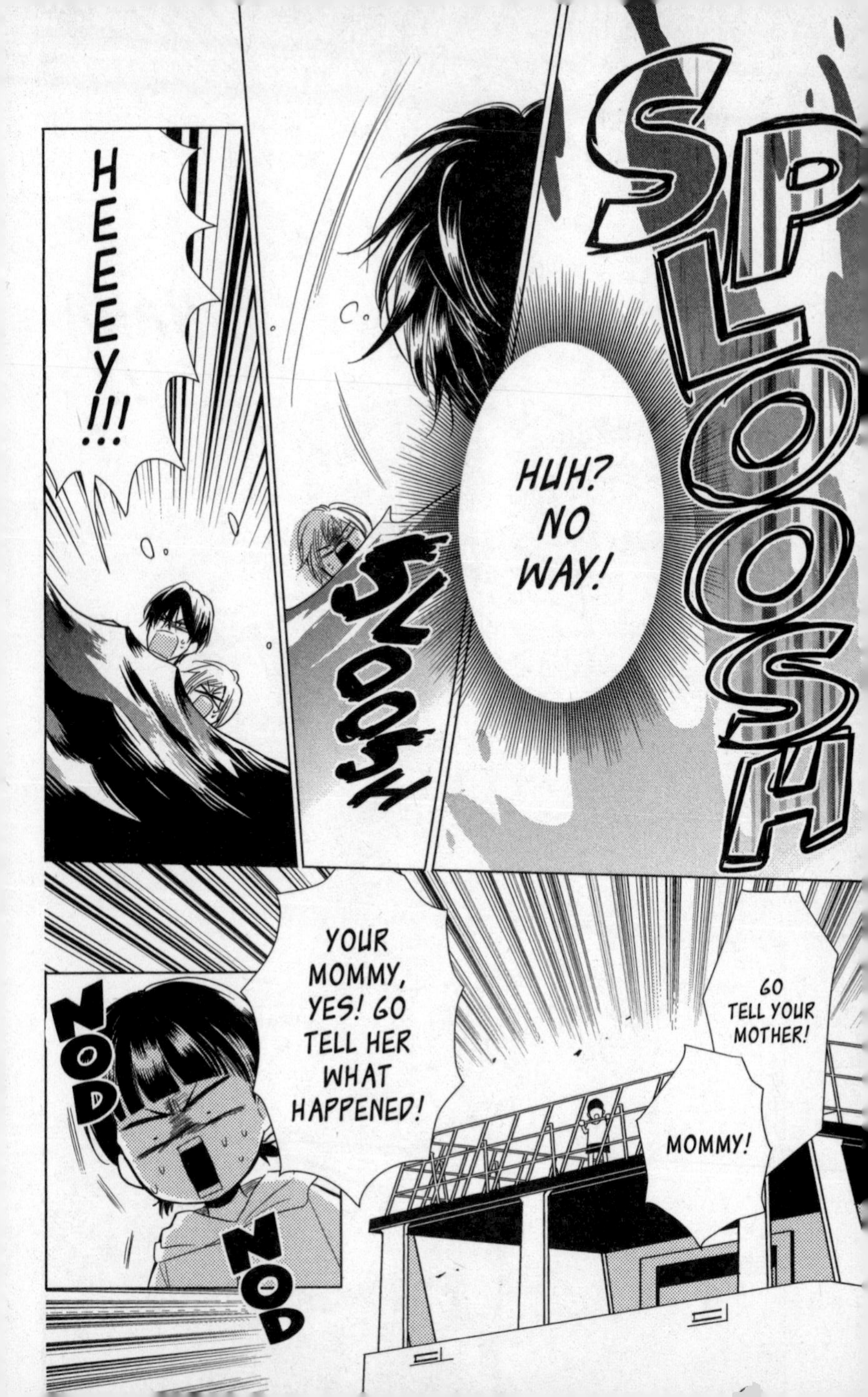
SPLOOSH
HUH? NO WAY!
SLOOSH
HEEEEY!!!
GO TELL YOUR MOTHER!
MOMMY!
YOUR MOMMY, YES! GO TELL HER WHAT HAPPENED!
NOD
NOD
NOD

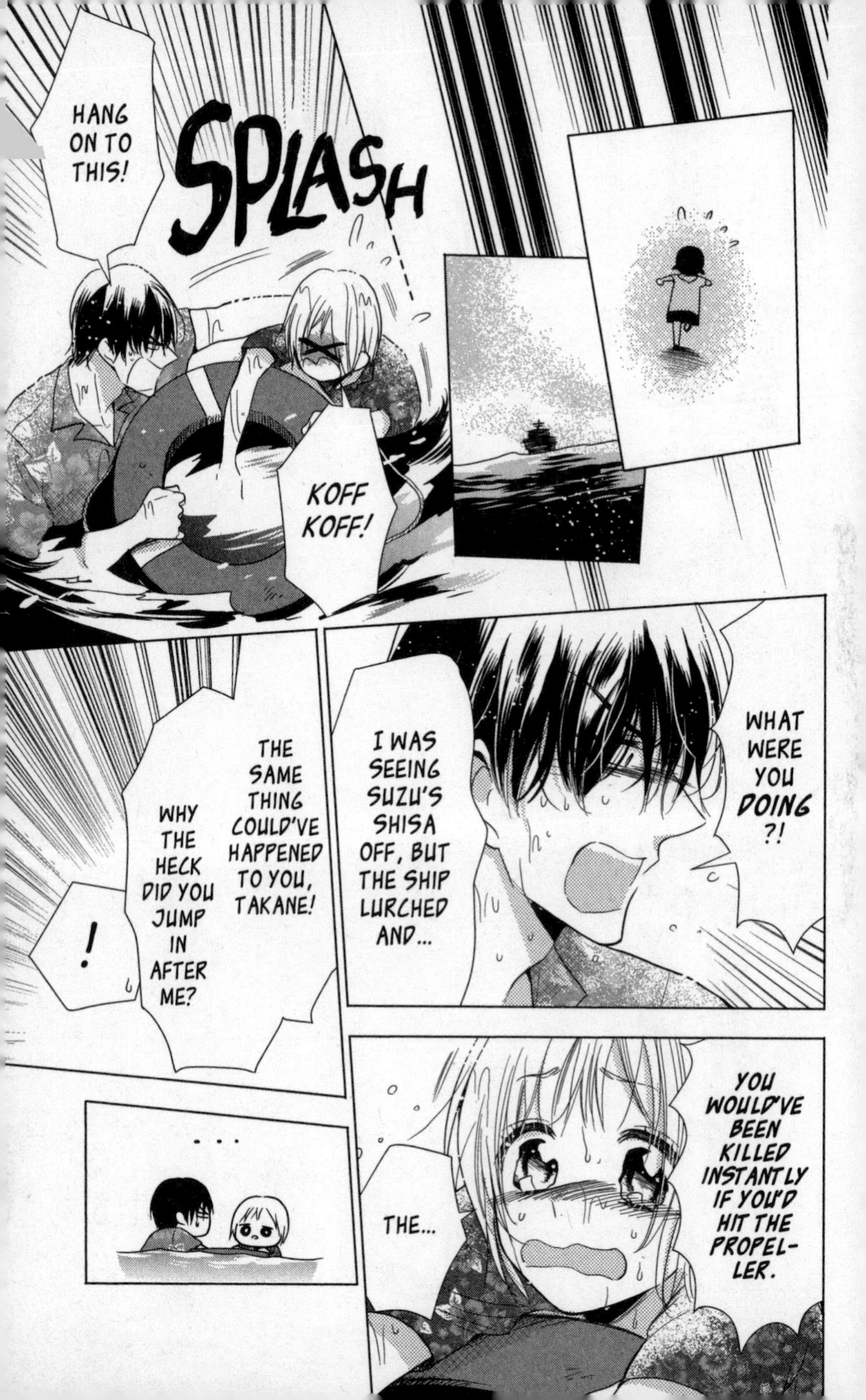
HANG ON TO THIS!
SPLASH
KOFF KOFF!
WHAT WERE YOU DOING?!
I WAS SEEING SUZU'S SHISA OFF, BUT THE SHIP LURCHED AND...
THE SAME THING COULD'VE HAPPENED TO YOU, TAKANE!
WHY THE HECK DID YOU JUMP IN AFTER ME?
!
YOU WOULD'VE BEEN KILLED INSTANTLY IF YOU'D HIT THE PROPEL-LER.
THE...
...

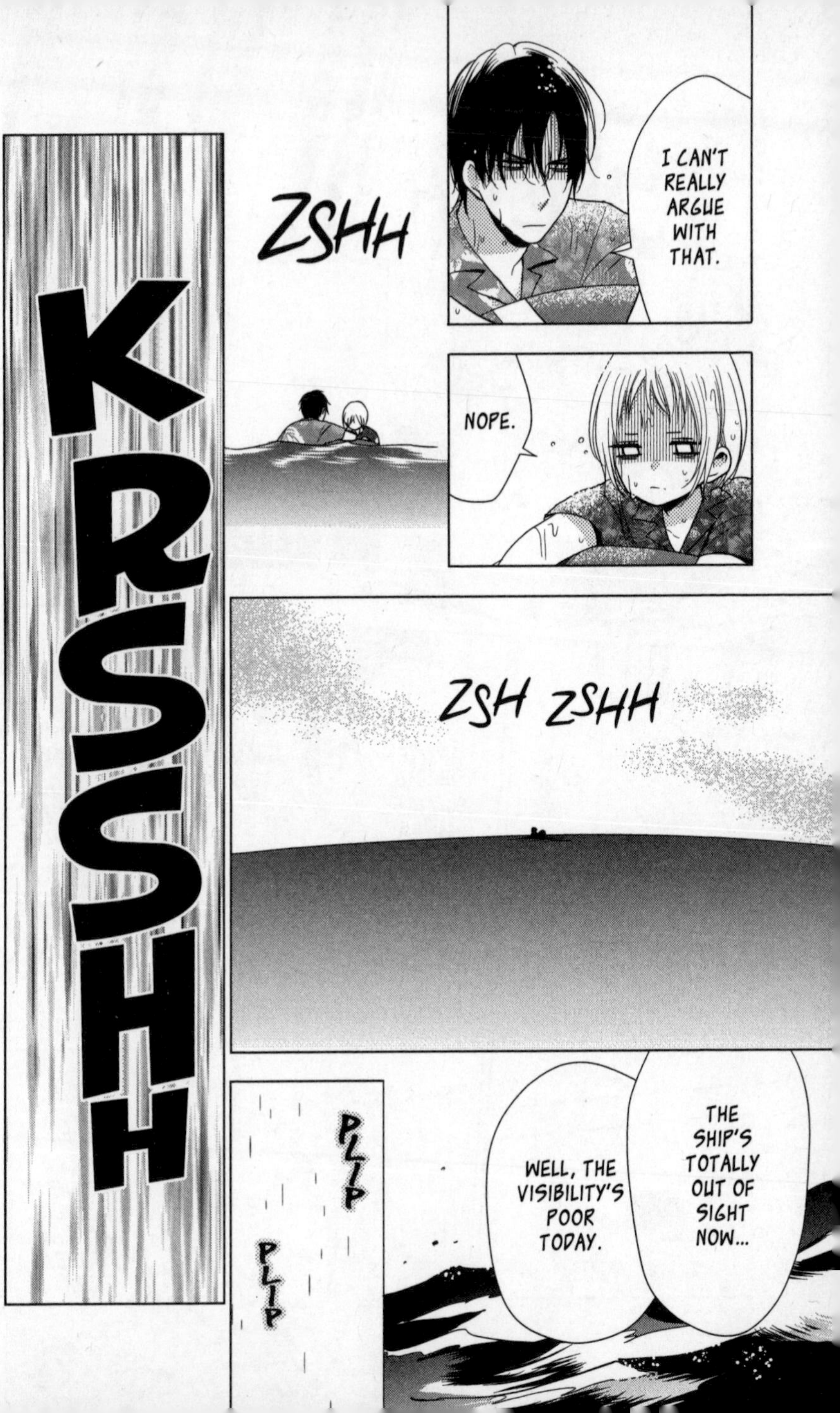
I CAN'T REALLY ARGUE WITH THAT.
NOPE.
ZSHH
ZSH ZSHH
THE SHIP'S TOTALLY OUT OF SIGHT NOW...
WELL, THE VISIBILITY'S POOR TODAY.
PLIP
PLIP
KRSHH

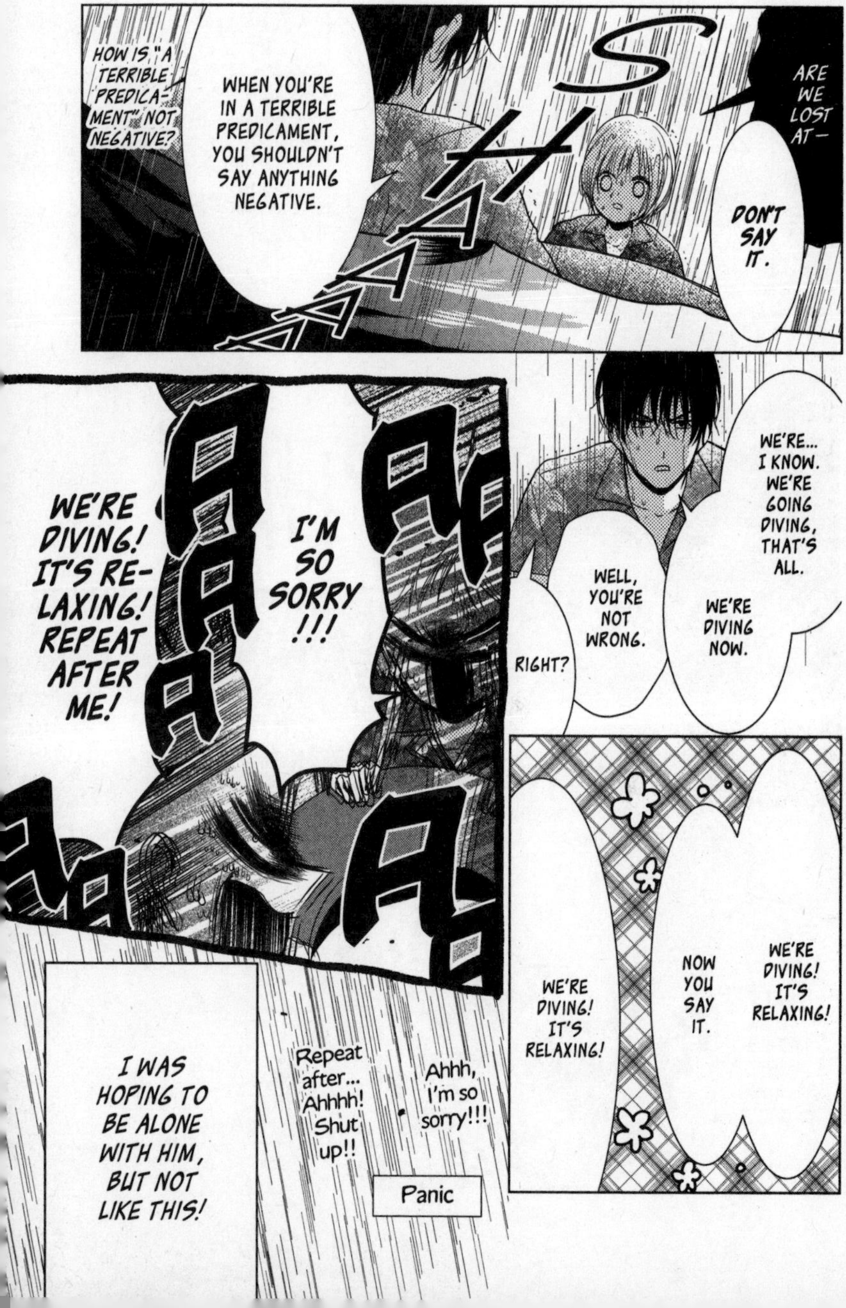
ARE WE LOST AT—
DON'T SAY IT.
WHEN YOU'RE IN A TERRIBLE PREDICAMENT, YOU SHOULDN'T SAY ANYTHING NEGATIVE.
HOW IS "A TERRIBLE PREDICAMENT" NOT NEGATIVE?
SHAAAAA
WE'RE... I KNOW. WE'RE GOING DIVING, THAT'S ALL.
WE'RE DIVING NOW.
WELL, YOU'RE NOT WRONG.
RIGHT?
WE'RE DIVING! IT'S RELAXING!
NOW YOU SAY IT.
WE'RE DIVING! IT'S RELAXING!
I'M SO SORRY!!!
WE'RE DIVING! IT'S RE-LAXING! REPEAT AFTER ME!
Ahhh, I'm so sorry!!!
Repeat after... Ahhhh! Shut up!!
Panic
I WAS HOPING TO BE ALONE WITH HIM, BUT NOT LIKE THIS!

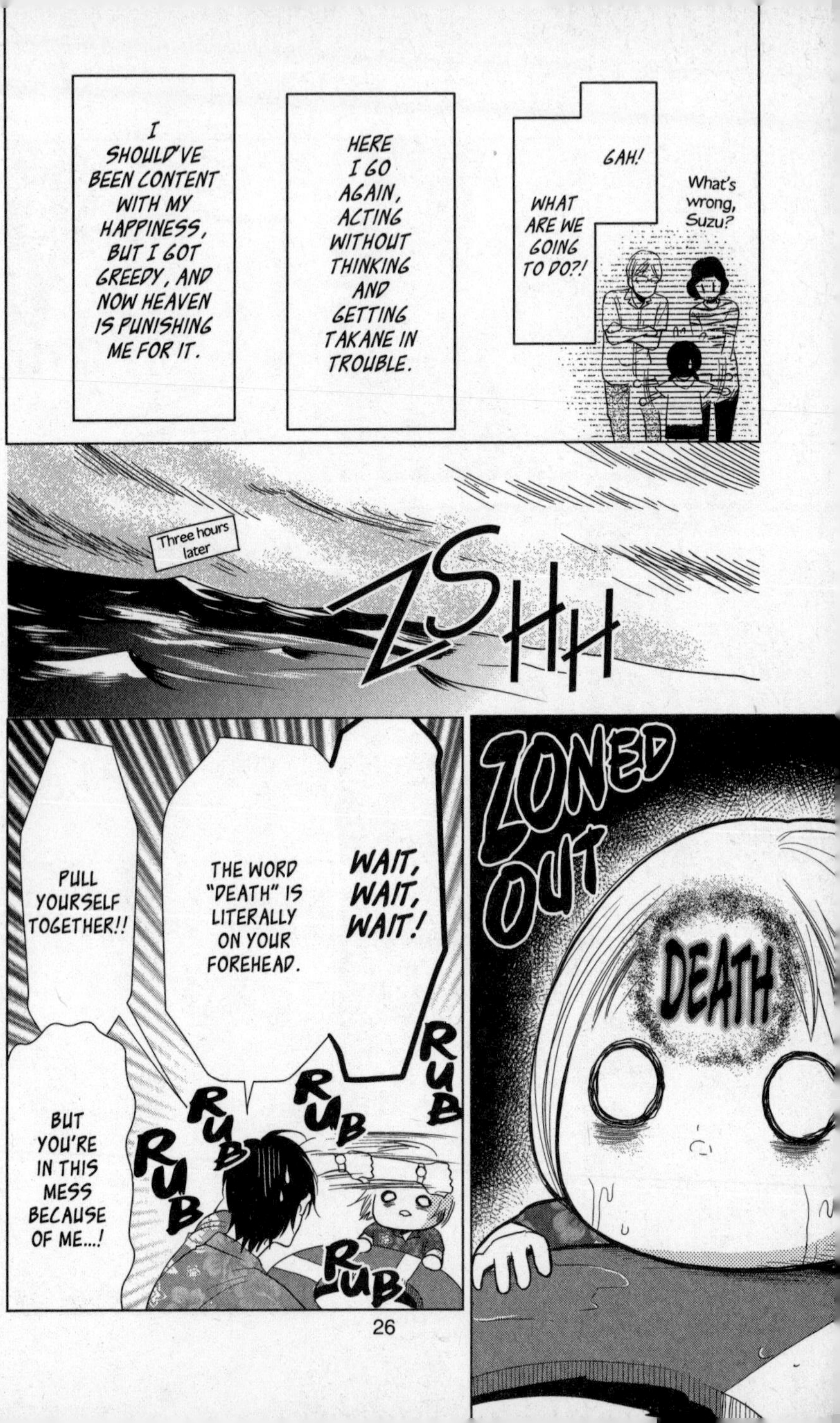

GAH!
WHAT ARE WE GOING TO DO?!
What's wrong, Suzu?
HERE I GO AGAIN, ACTING WITHOUT THINKING AND GETTING TAKANE IN TROUBLE.
I SHOULD'VE BEEN CONTENT WITH MY HAPPINESS, BUT I GOT GREEDY, AND NOW HEAVEN IS PUNISHING ME FOR IT.
Three hours later
ZSHH
ZONED OUT
DEATH
WAIT, WAIT, WAIT!
THE WORD "DEATH" IS LITERALLY ON YOUR FOREHEAD.
PULL YOURSELF TOGETHER!!
BUT YOU'RE IN THIS MESS BECAUSE OF ME...!
RUB RUB RUB RUB RUB

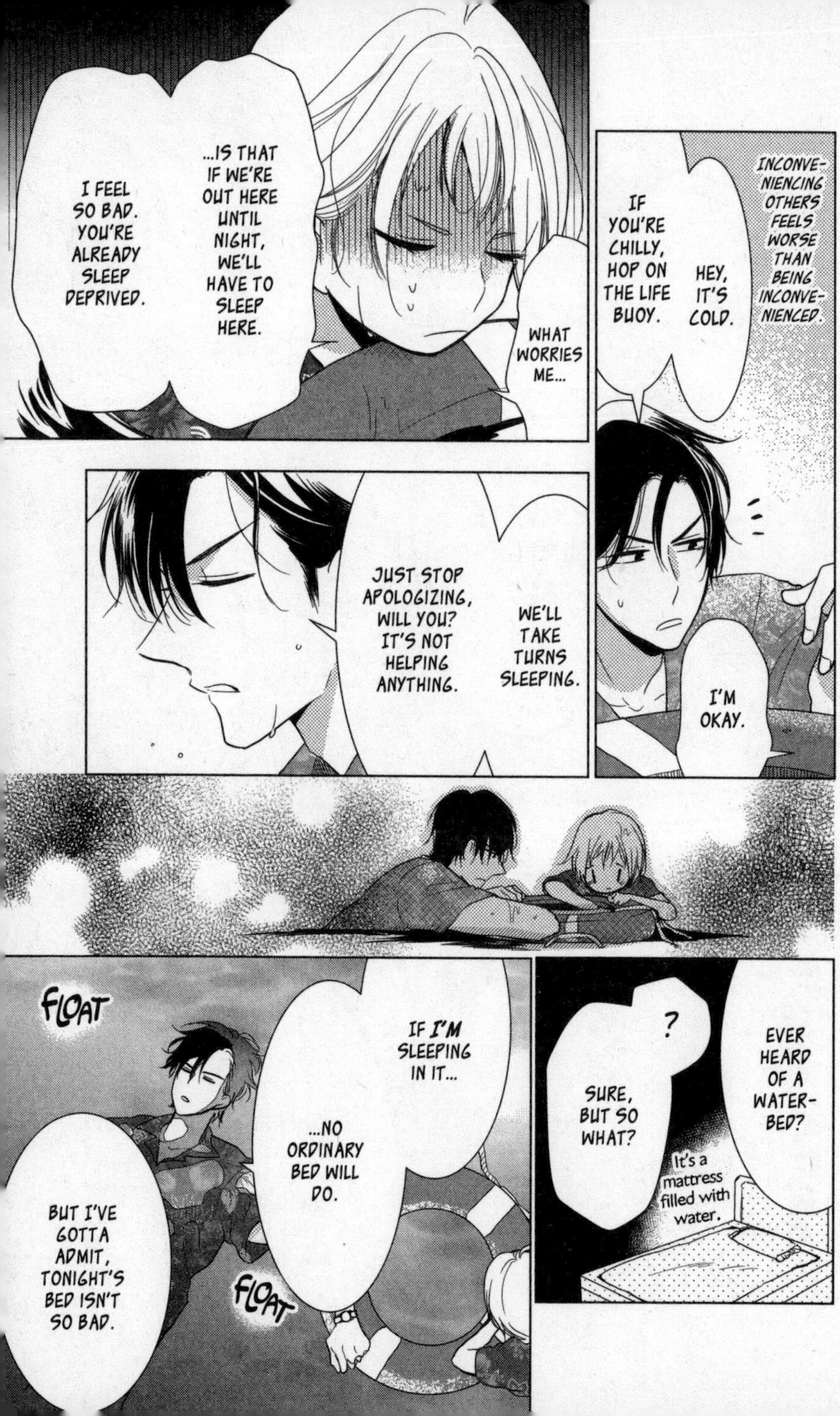
INCONVENIENCING OTHERS FEELS WORSE THAN BEING INCONVENIENCED.
HEY, IT'S COLD.
IF YOU'RE CHILLY, HOP ON THE LIFE BUOY.
I'M OKAY.
WHAT WORRIES ME...
...IS THAT IF WE'RE OUT HERE UNTIL NIGHT, WE'LL HAVE TO SLEEP HERE.
I FEEL SO BAD. YOU'RE ALREADY SLEEP DEPRIVED.
WE'LL TAKE TURNS SLEEPING.
JUST STOP APOLOGIZING, WILL YOU? IT'S NOT HELPING ANYTHING.
EVER HEARD OF A WATER-BED?
?
SURE, BUT SO WHAT?
It's a mattress filled with water.
IF *I'M* SLEEPING IN IT...
...NO ORDINARY BED WILL DO.
FLOAT
BUT I'VE GOTTA ADMIT, TONIGHT'S BED ISN'T SO BAD.
FLOAT

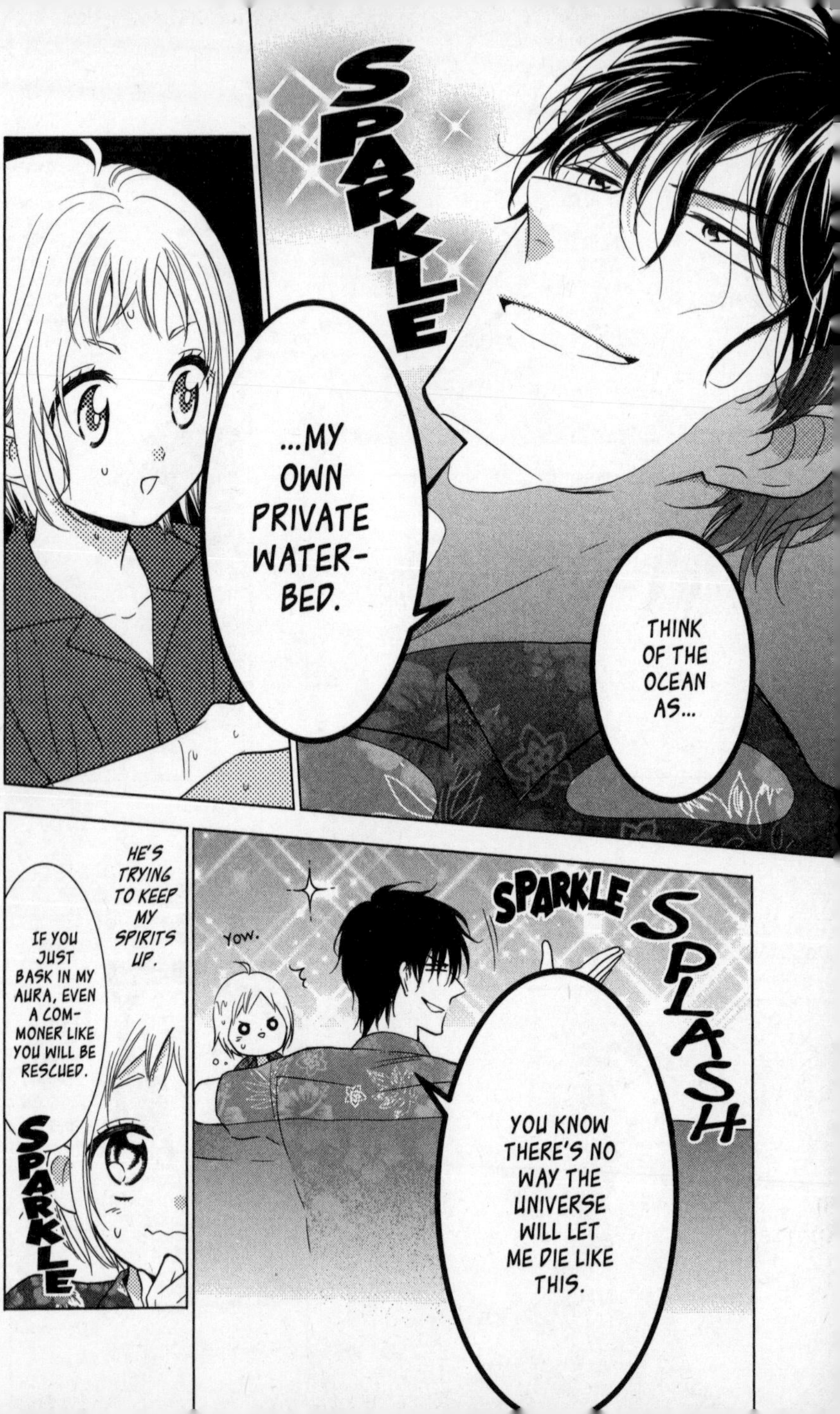
SPARKLE
THINK OF THE OCEAN AS...
...MY OWN PRIVATE WATER-BED.
SPARKLE
SPLASH
YOU KNOW THERE'S NO WAY THE UNIVERSE WILL LET ME DIE LIKE THIS.
YOW.
IF YOU JUST BASK IN MY AURA, EVEN A COM-MONER LIKE YOU WILL BE RESCUED.
HE'S TRYING TO KEEP MY SPIRITS UP.
SPARKLE

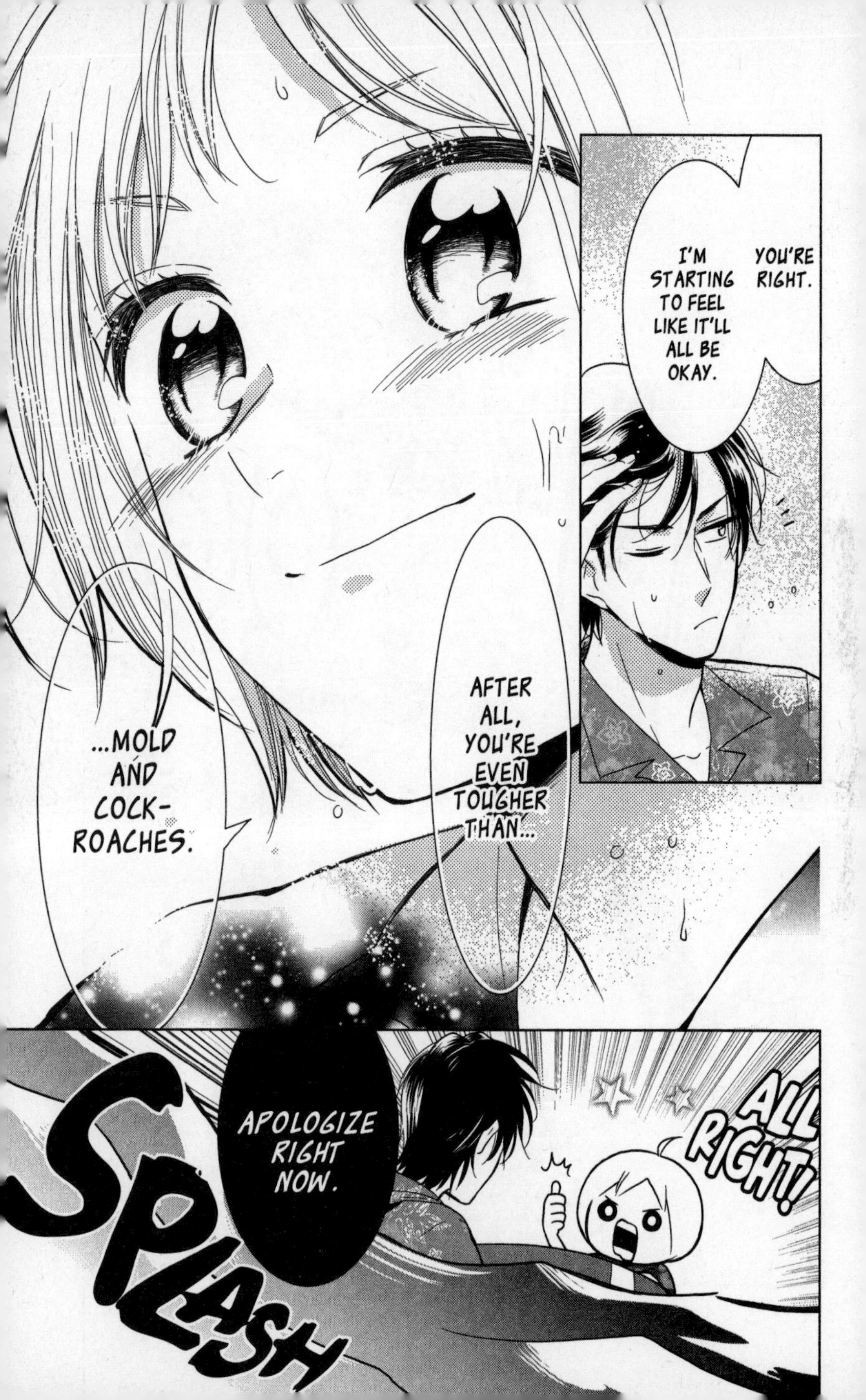
YOU'RE RIGHT.
I'M STARTING TO FEEL LIKE IT'LL ALL BE OKAY.
AFTER ALL, YOU'RE EVEN TOUGHER THAN...
...MOLD AND COCK-ROACHES.
ALL RIGHT!
APOLOGIZE RIGHT NOW.
SPLASH

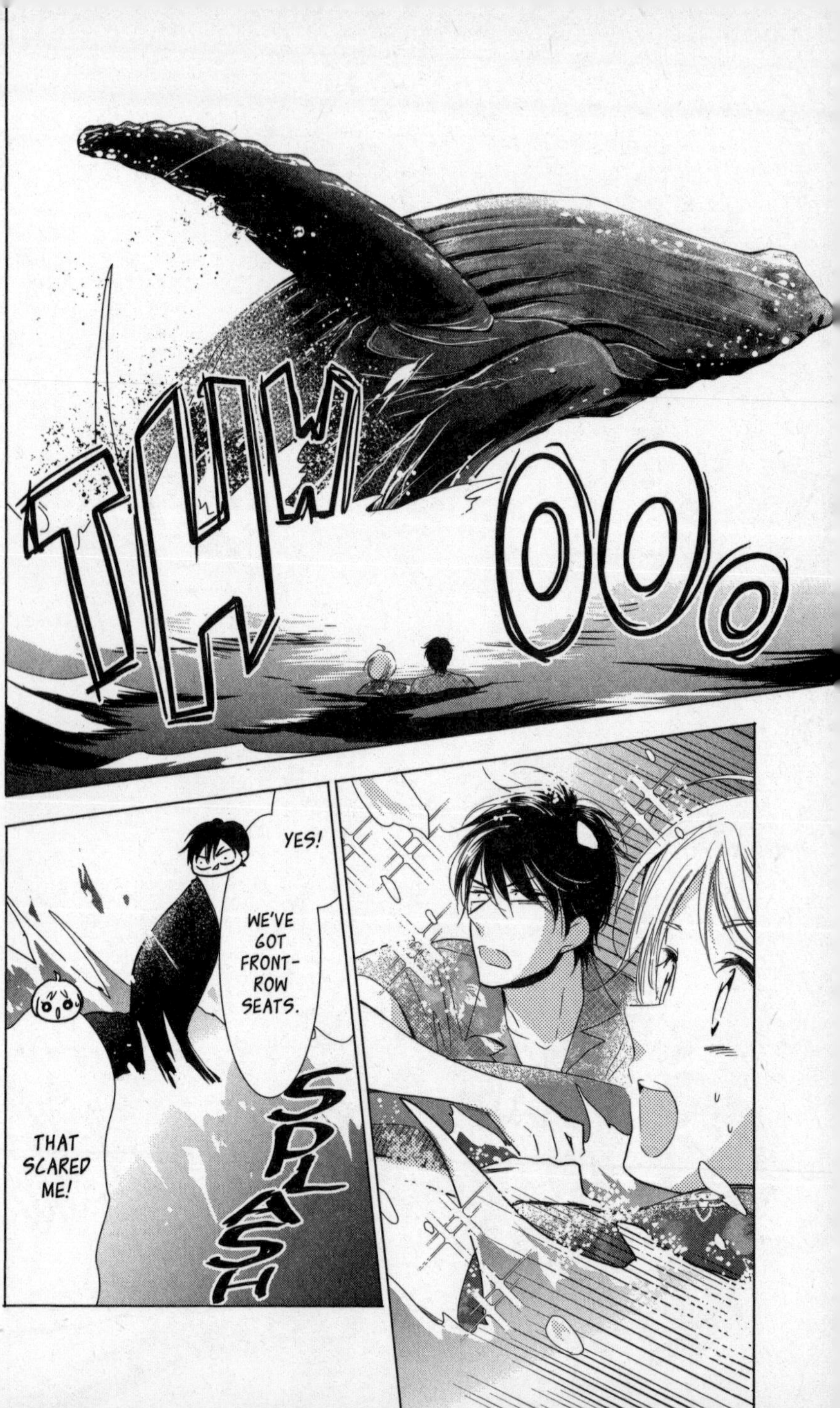
THWOOO
YES!
WE'VE GOT FRONT-ROW SEATS.
SPLASH
THAT SCARED ME!

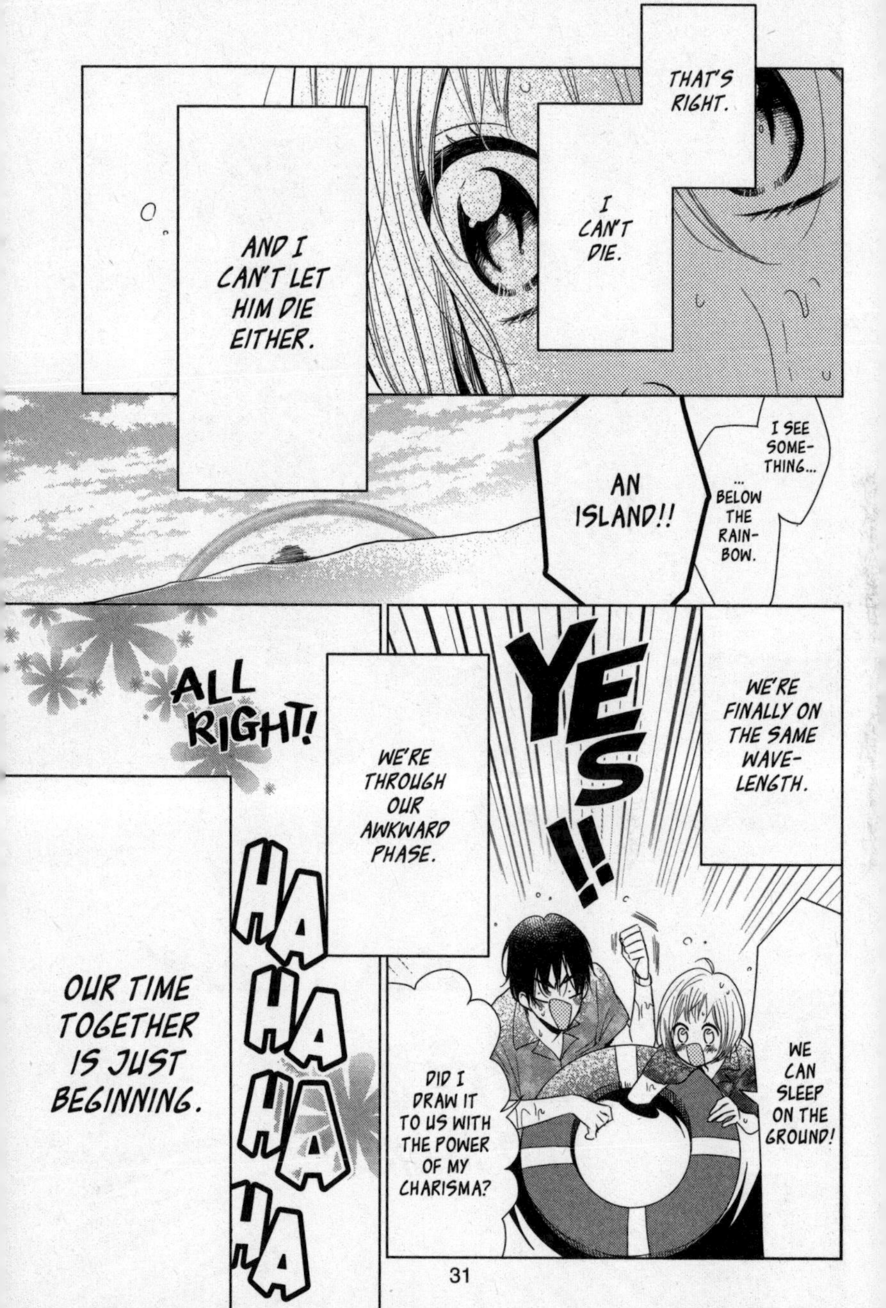
THAT'S RIGHT.
I CAN'T DIE.
AND I CAN'T LET HIM DIE EITHER.
I SEE SOME-THING...
...BELOW THE RAIN-BOW.
AN ISLAND!!
WE'RE FINALLY ON THE SAME WAVE-LENGTH.
YES!!
WE'RE THROUGH OUR AWKWARD PHASE.
WE CAN SLEEP ON THE GROUND!
DID I DRAW IT TO US WITH THE POWER OF MY CHARISMA?
HA HA HA HA HA
ALL RIGHT!
OUR TIME TOGETHER IS JUST BEGINNING.

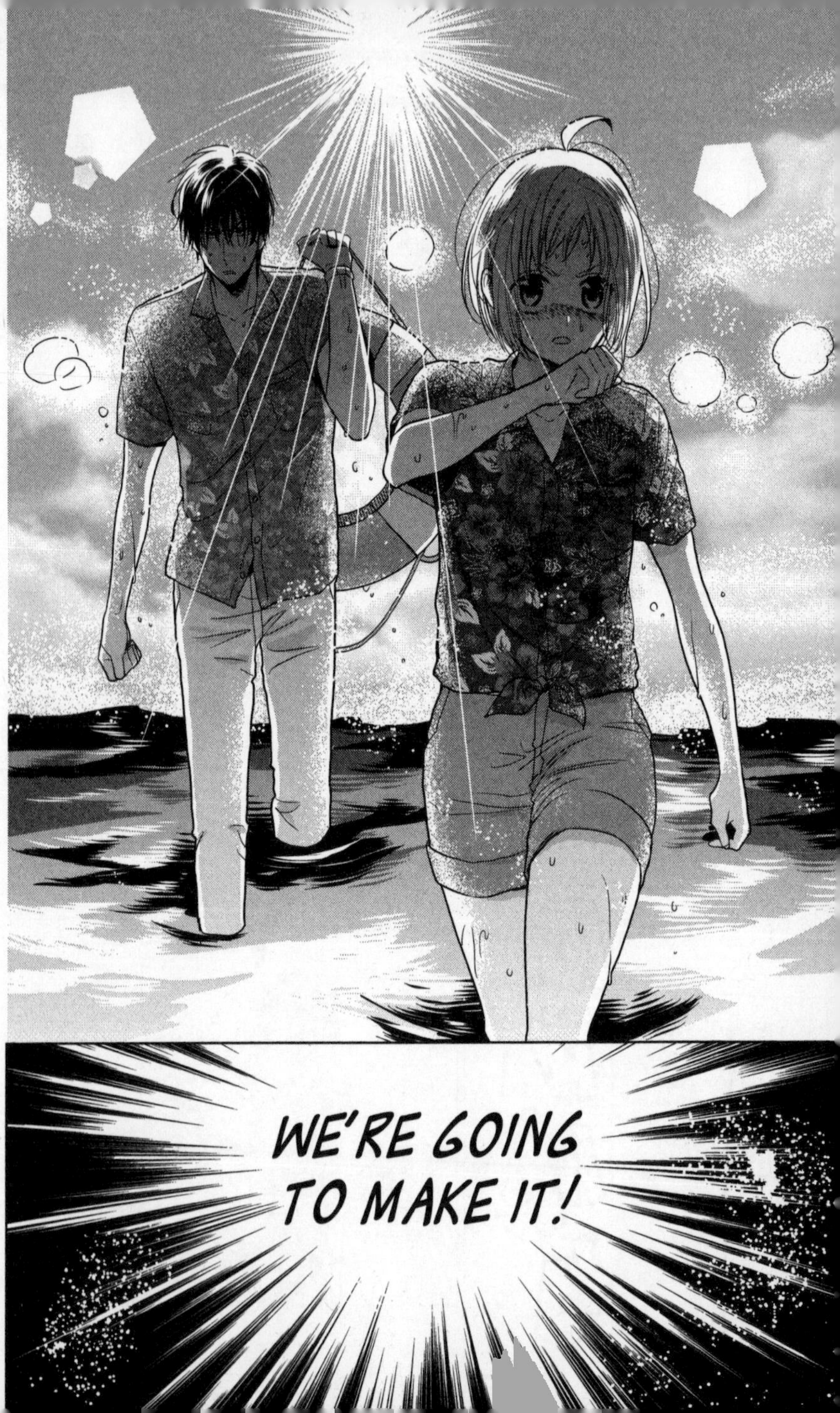
WE'RE GOING TO MAKE IT!

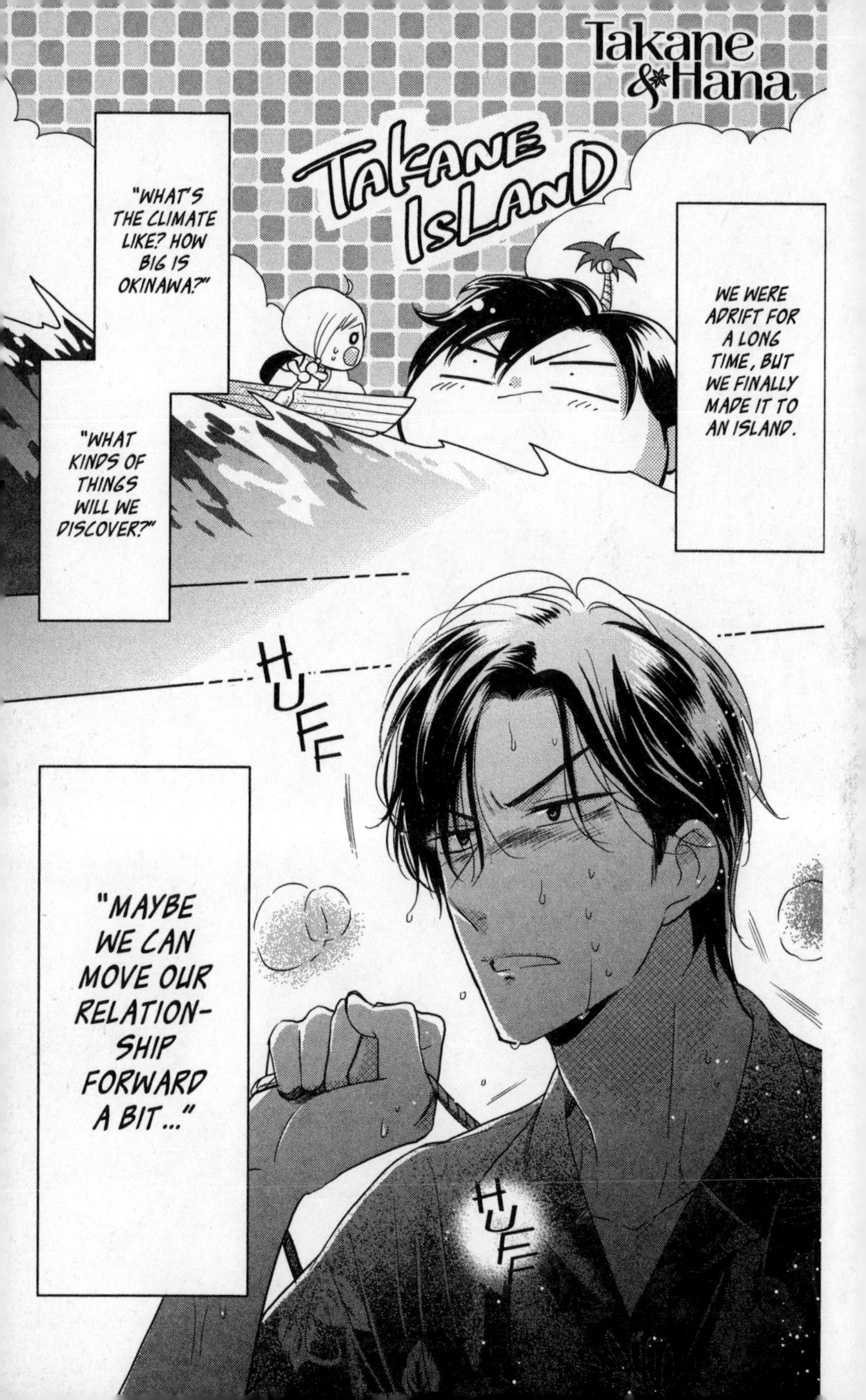
Takane & Hana
TAKANE ISLAND
WE WERE ADRIFT FOR A LONG TIME, BUT WE FINALLY MADE IT TO AN ISLAND.
"WHAT'S THE CLIMATE LIKE? HOW BIG IS OKINAWA?"
"WHAT KINDS OF THINGS WILL WE DISCOVER?"
HUFF
"MAYBE WE CAN MOVE OUR RELATION-SHIP FORWARD A BIT..."
HUFF

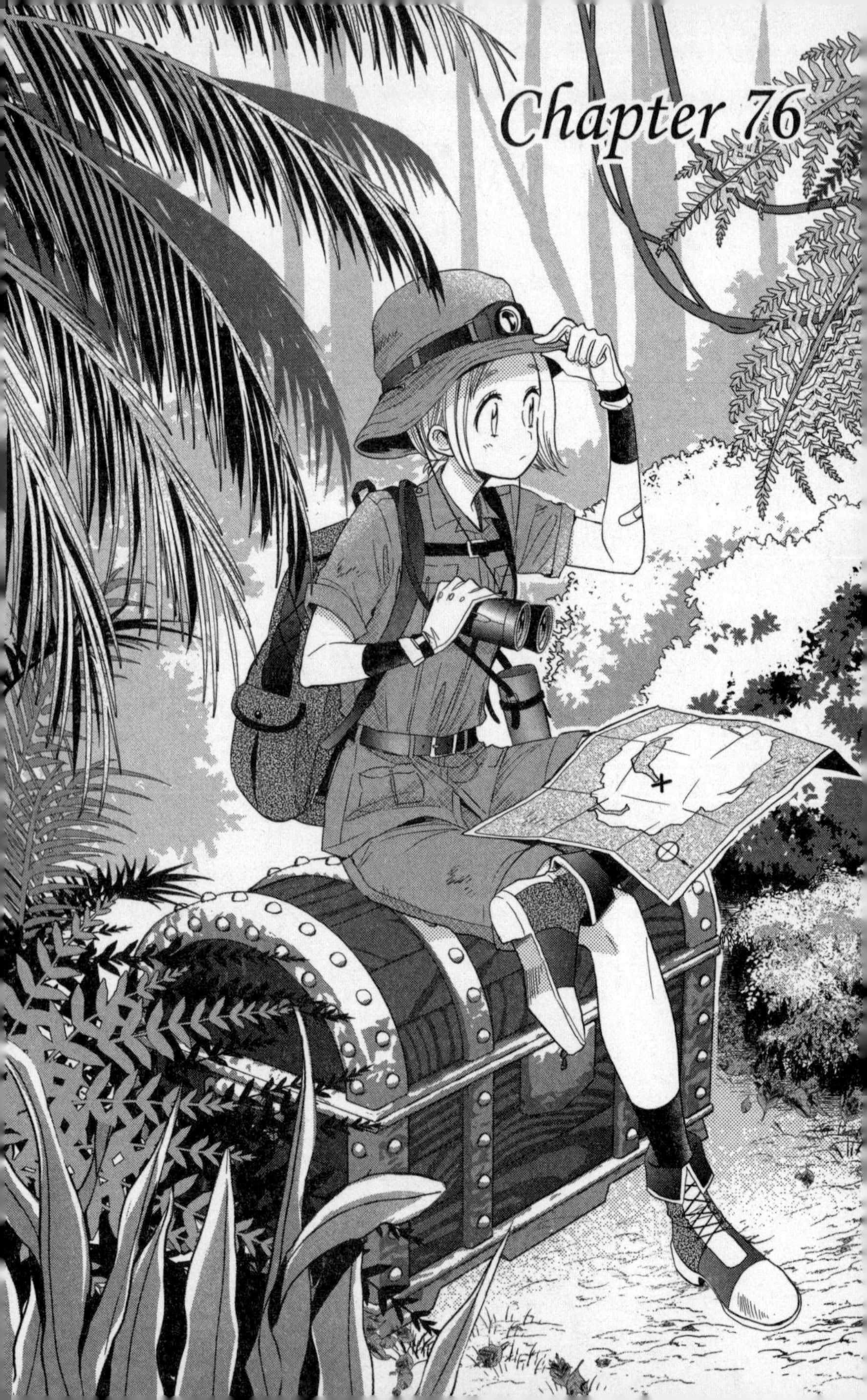
Chapter 76

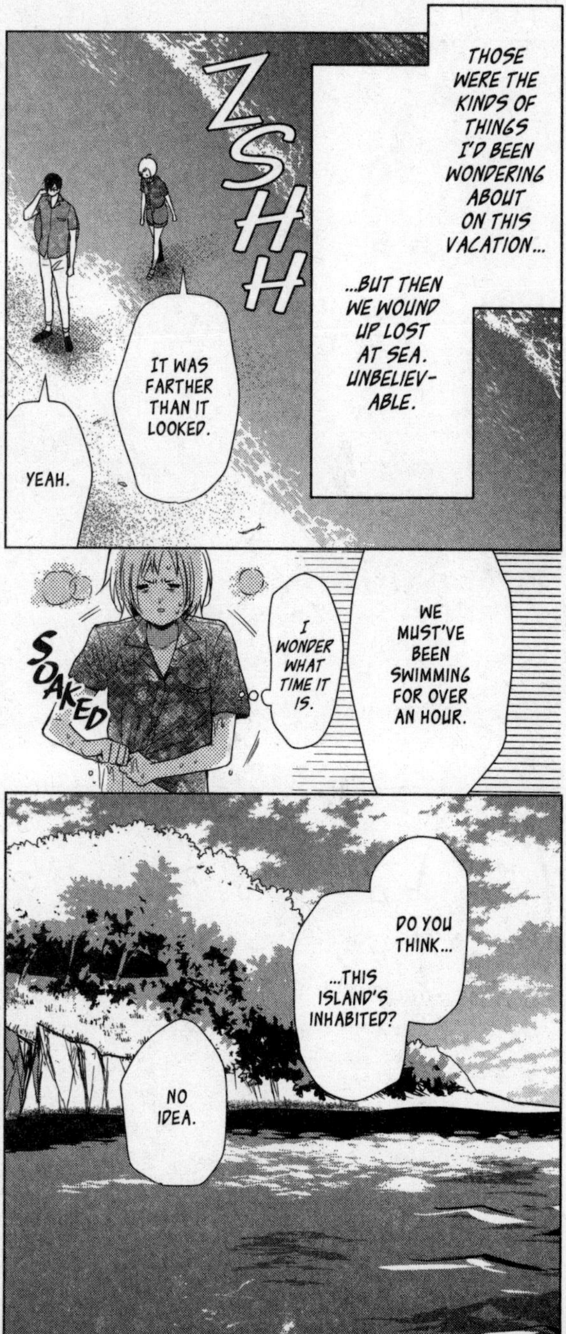
THOSE WERE THE KINDS OF THINGS I'D BEEN WONDERING ABOUT ON THIS VACATION...
...BUT THEN WE WOUND UP LOST AT SEA. UNBELIEV-ABLE.
ZSHH
IT WAS FARTHER THAN IT LOOKED.
YEAH.
WE MUST'VE BEEN SWIMMING FOR OVER AN HOUR.
I WONDER WHAT TIME IT IS.
SOAKED
DO YOU THINK...
...THIS ISLAND'S INHABITED?
NO IDEA.

• Cover Illustration •

Everyone, did you notice? The cover art for volume 14 is a big fake out! The main story in here is about them being lost at sea. But even if it was just for the cover, I wanted you to get a sense of the fun and brightness of Okinawa. That was my intention.

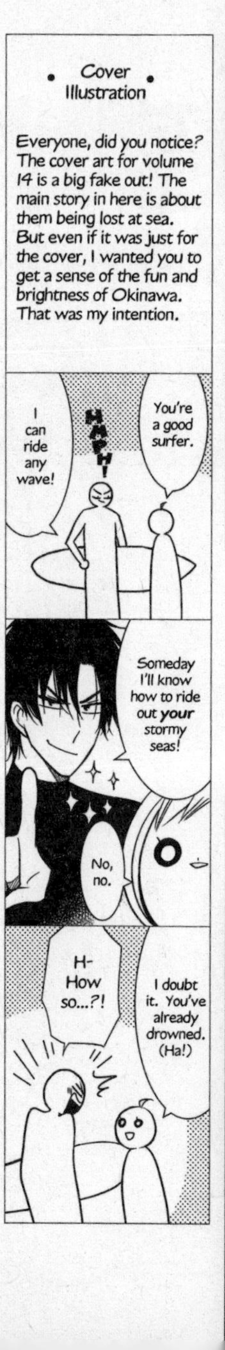
You're a good surfer.
HMPH!
I can ride any wave!
Someday I'll know how to ride out *your* stormy seas!
No, no.
I doubt it. You've already drowned. (Ha!)
H-How so...?!

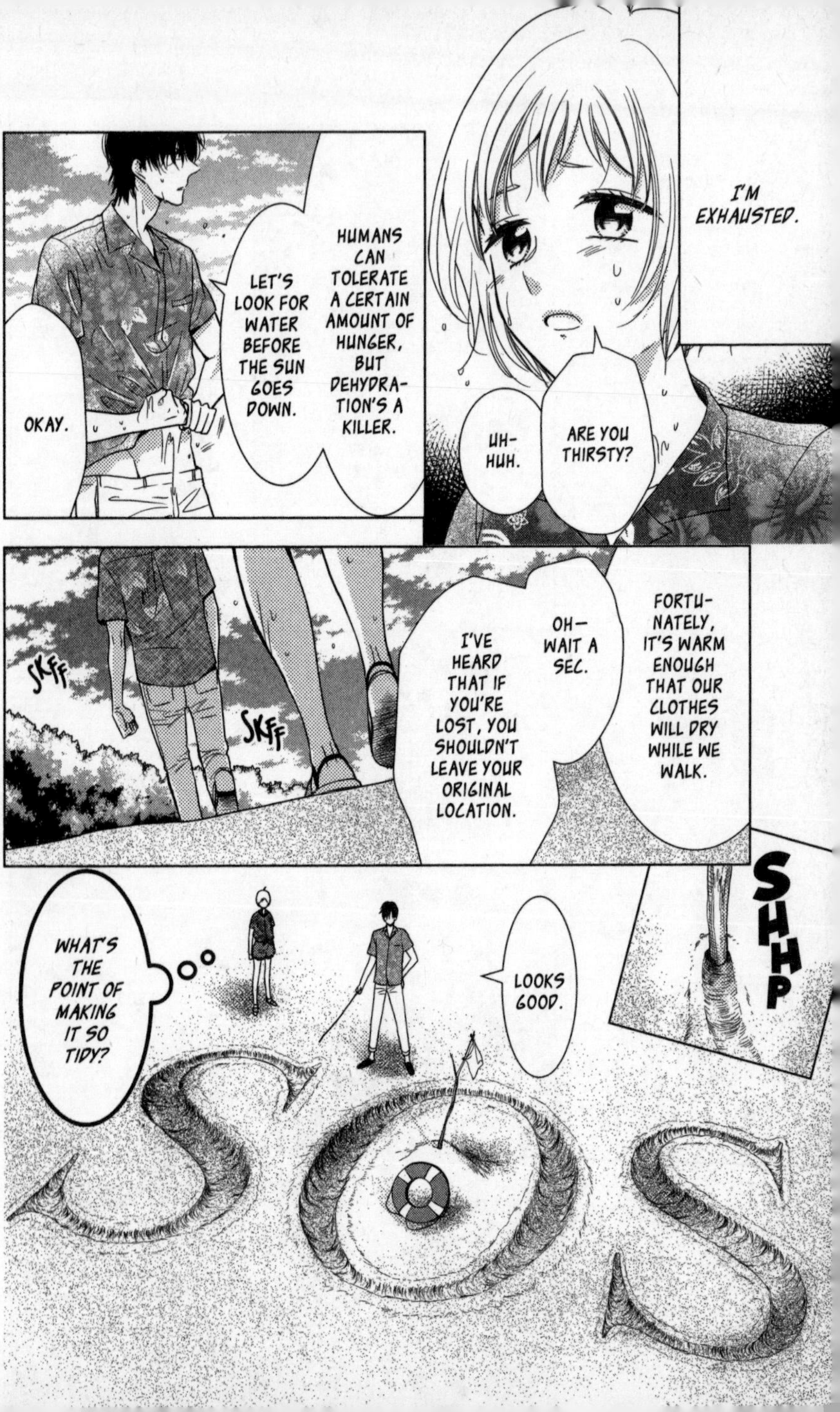
I'M EXHAUSTED.
ARE YOU THIRSTY?
UH-HUH.
HUMANS CAN TOLERATE A CERTAIN AMOUNT OF HUNGER, BUT DEHYDRATION'S A KILLER.
LET'S LOOK FOR WATER BEFORE THE SUN GOES DOWN.
OKAY.
FORTUNATELY, IT'S WARM ENOUGH THAT OUR CLOTHES WILL DRY WHILE WE WALK.
OH— WAIT A SEC.
I'VE HEARD THAT IF YOU'RE LOST, YOU SHOULDN'T LEAVE YOUR ORIGINAL LOCATION.
SKFF
SKFF
SHHP
LOOKS GOOD.
WHAT'S THE POINT OF MAKING IT SO TIDY?
SOS

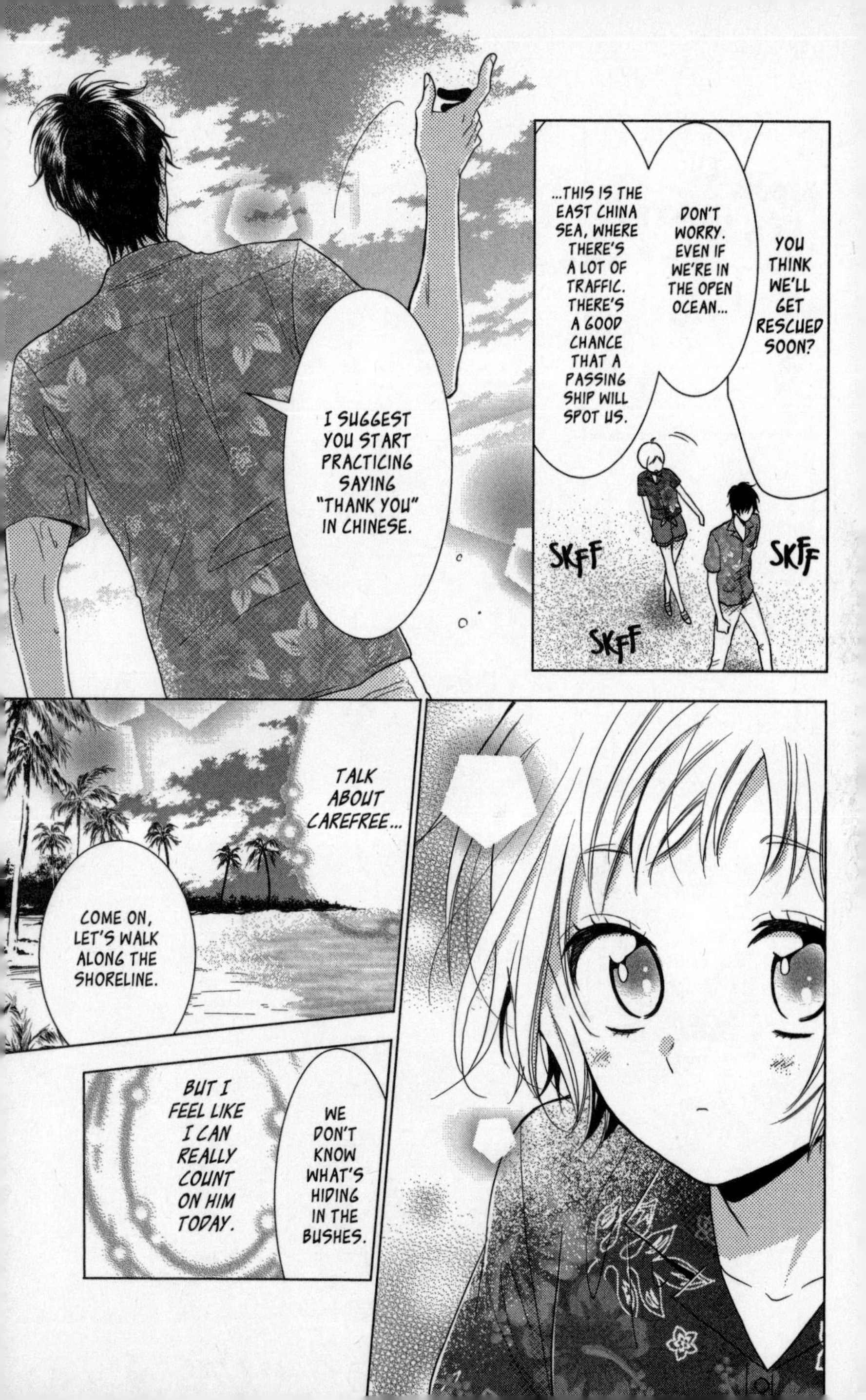
YOU THINK WE'LL GET RESCUED SOON?
DON'T WORRY. EVEN IF WE'RE IN THE OPEN OCEAN...
...THIS IS THE EAST CHINA SEA, WHERE THERE'S A LOT OF TRAFFIC. THERE'S A GOOD CHANCE THAT A PASSING SHIP WILL SPOT US.
SKFF
SKFF
SKFF
I SUGGEST YOU START PRACTICING SAYING "THANK YOU" IN CHINESE.
TALK ABOUT CAREFREE...
COME ON, LET'S WALK ALONG THE SHORELINE.
WE DON'T KNOW WHAT'S HIDING IN THE BUSHES.
BUT I FEEL LIKE I CAN REALLY COUNT ON HIM TODAY.

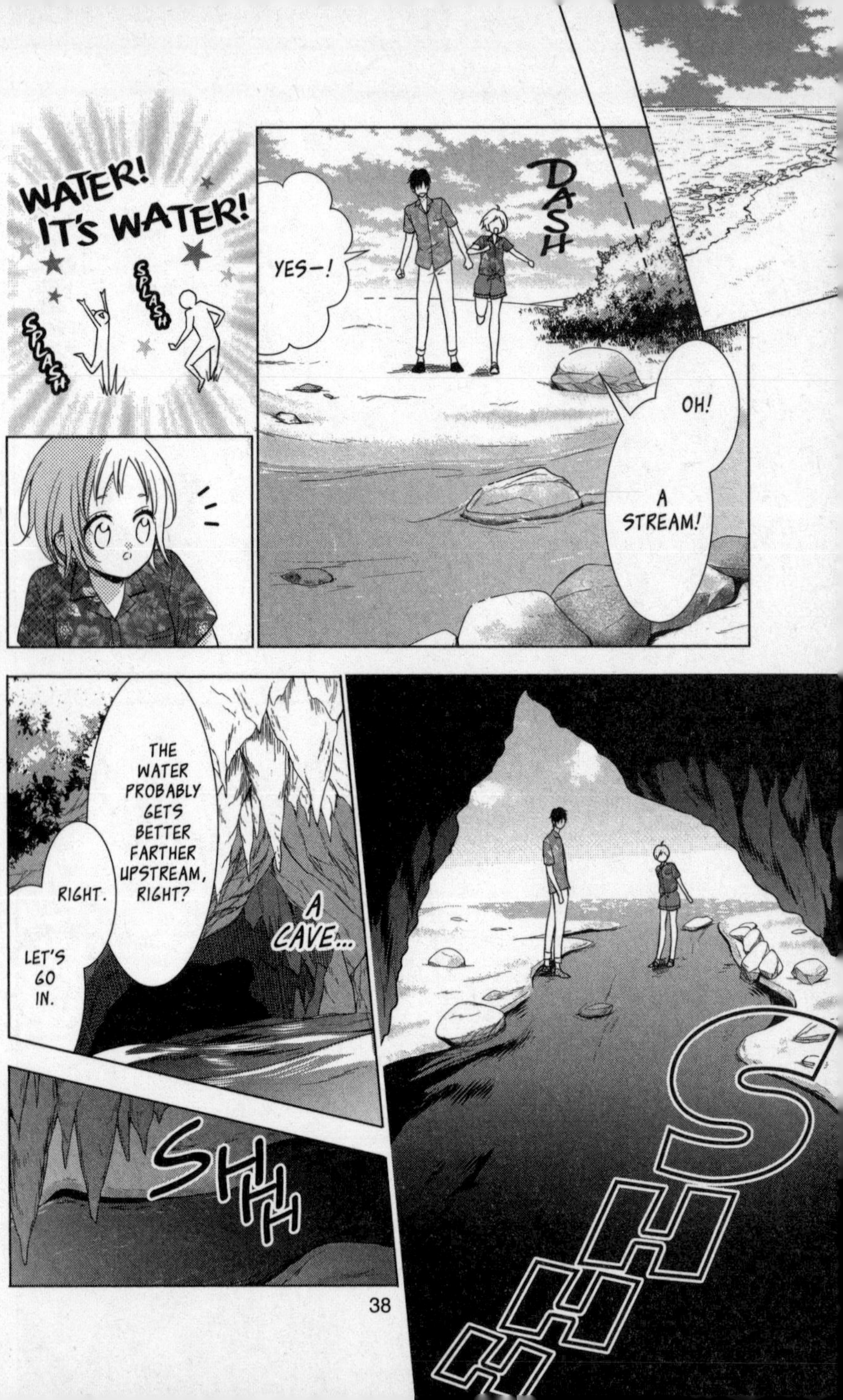

OH! A STREAM!
YES—!
DASH
WATER! IT'S WATER!
SPLASH
SPLASH
SHHHHH
A CAVE...
THE WATER PROBABLY GETS BETTER FARTHER UPSTREAM, RIGHT?
RIGHT.
LET'S GO IN.
SHHHH

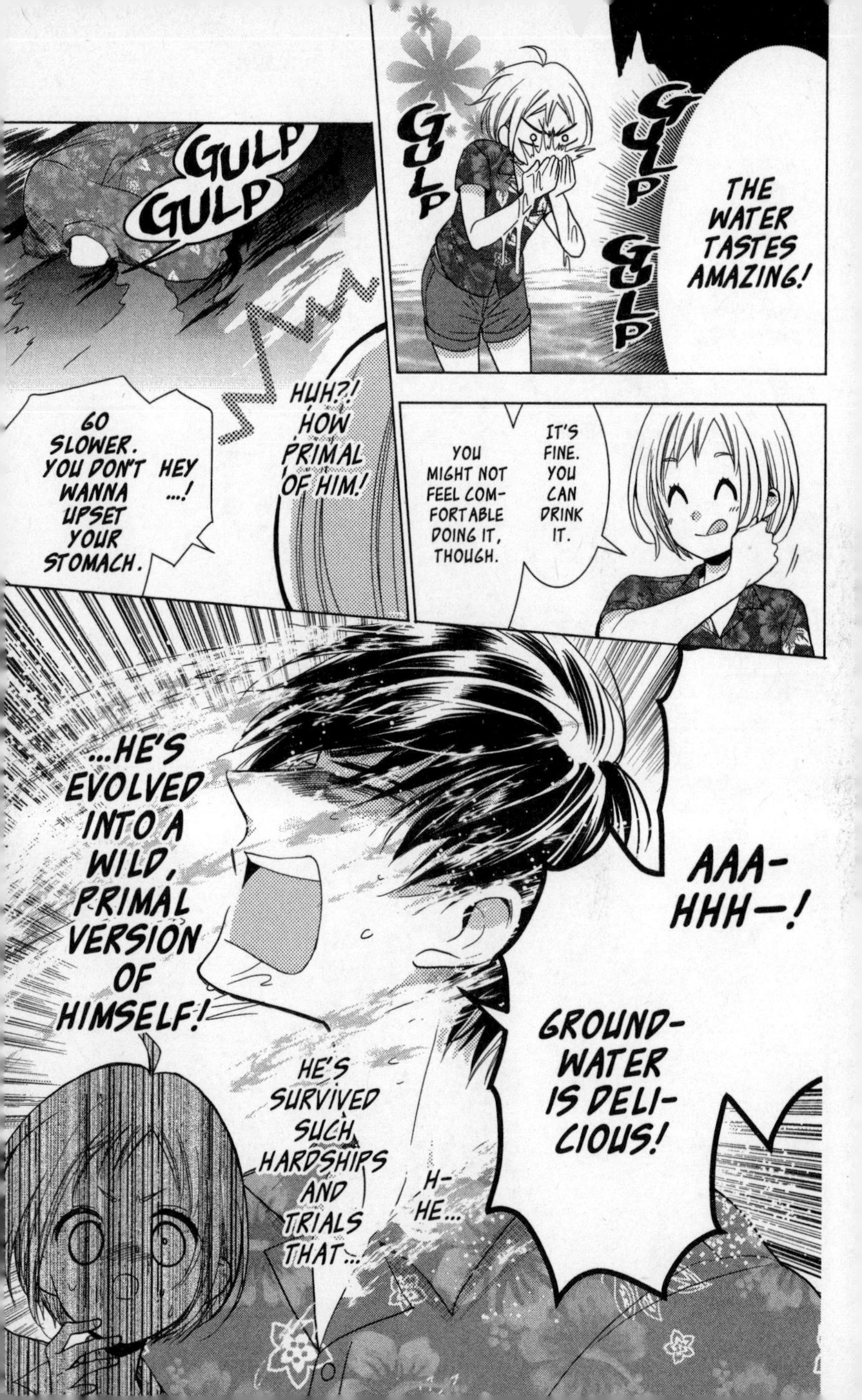
GULP GULP
GULP GULP
THE WATER TASTES AMAZING!
GULP GULP
IT'S FINE. YOU CAN DRINK IT.
YOU MIGHT NOT FEEL COM-FORTABLE DOING IT, THOUGH.
HUH?! HOW PRIMAL OF HIM!
HEY ...!
GO SLOWER. YOU DON'T WANNA UPSET YOUR STOMACH.
AAA-HHH—!
GROUND-WATER IS DELI-CIOUS!
...HE'S EVOLVED INTO A WILD, PRIMAL VERSION OF HIMSELF!
H-HE...
HE'S SURVIVED SUCH HARDSHIPS AND TRIALS THAT...

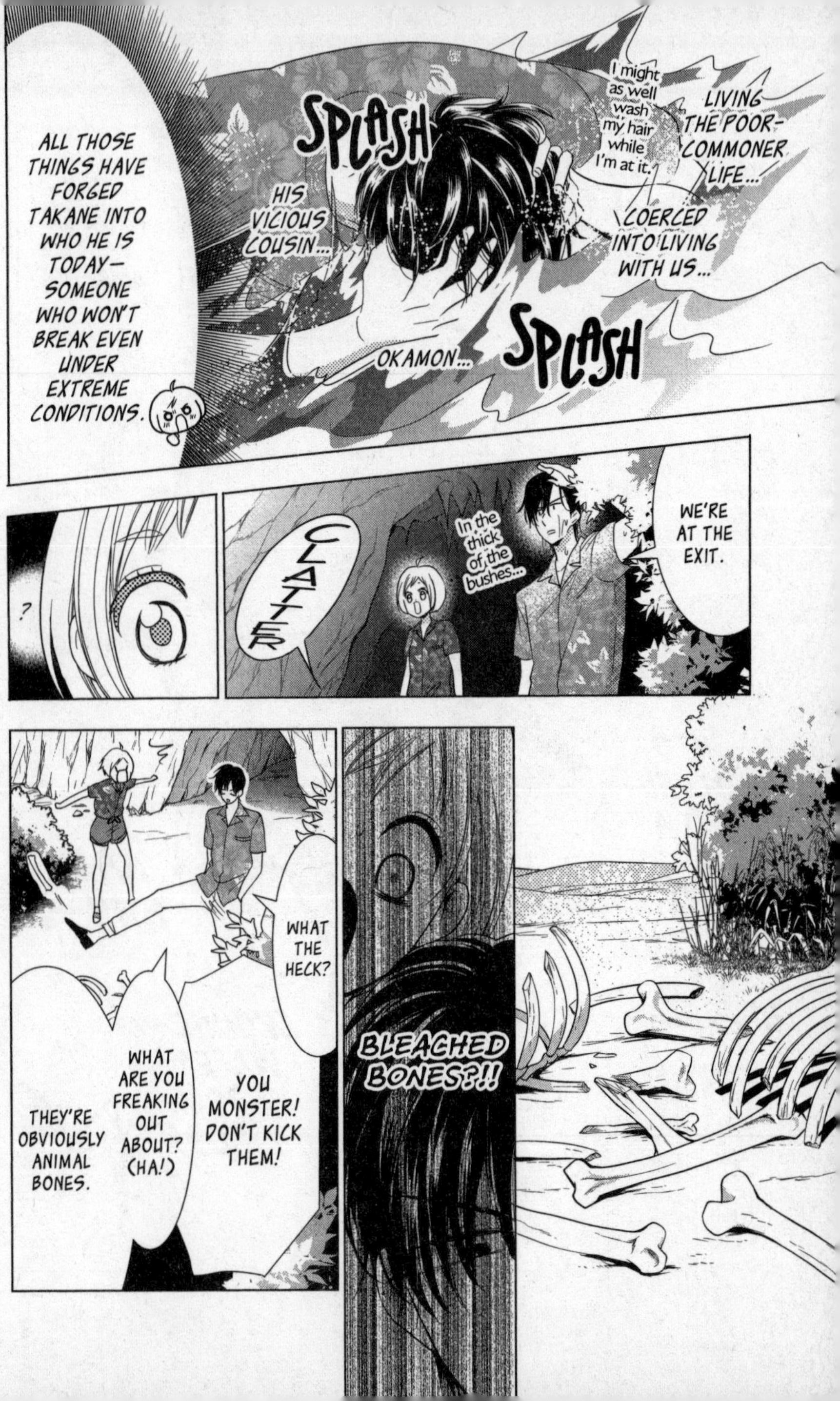
LIVING THE POOR-COMMONER LIFE...
I might as well wash my hair while I'm at it.
SPLASH
COERCED INTO LIVING WITH US...
HIS VICIOUS COUSIN...
OKAMON...
SPLASH
ALL THOSE THINGS HAVE FORGED TAKANE INTO WHO HE IS TODAY—SOMEONE WHO WON'T BREAK EVEN UNDER EXTREME CONDITIONS.
WE'RE AT THE EXIT.
In the thick of the bushes...
CLATTER
?
BLEACHED BONES?!!
WHAT THE HECK?
YOU MONSTER! DON'T KICK THEM!
WHAT ARE YOU FREAKING OUT ABOUT? (HA!)
THEY'RE OBVIOUSLY ANIMAL BONES.

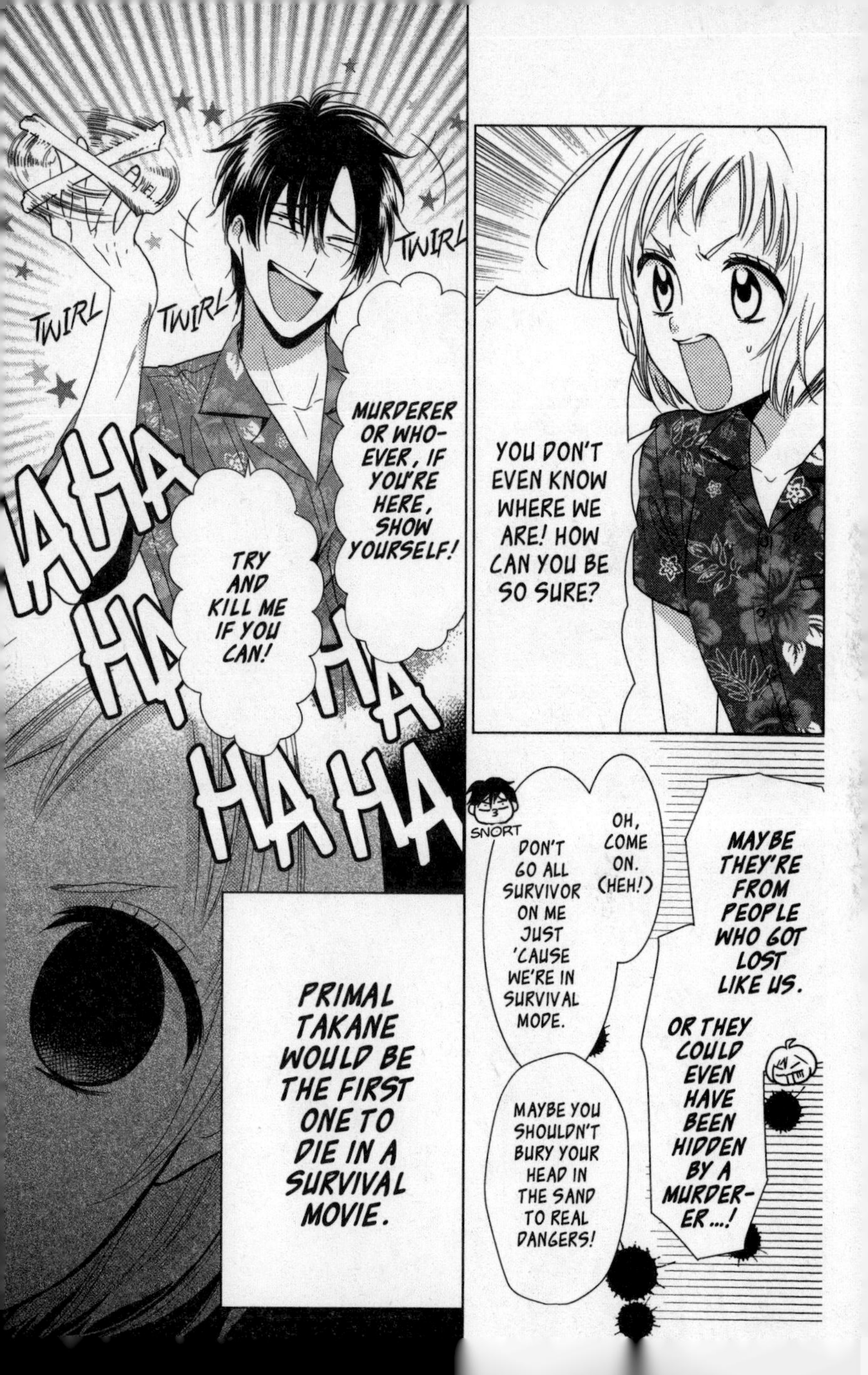
YOU DON'T EVEN KNOW WHERE WE ARE! HOW CAN YOU BE SO SURE?
TWIRL
TWIRL
TWIRL
MURDERER OR WHO-EVER, IF YOU'RE HERE, SHOW YOURSELF!
TRY AND KILL ME IF YOU CAN!
HA HA HA HA HA HA HA
MAYBE THEY'RE FROM PEOPLE WHO GOT LOST LIKE US.
OR THEY COULD EVEN HAVE BEEN HIDDEN BY A MURDER-ER...!
SNORT
OH, COME ON. (HEH!)
DON'T GO ALL SURVIVOR ON ME JUST 'CAUSE WE'RE IN SURVIVAL MODE.
MAYBE YOU SHOULDN'T BURY YOUR HEAD IN THE SAND TO REAL DANGERS!
PRIMAL TAKANE WOULD BE THE FIRST ONE TO DIE IN A SURVIVAL MOVIE.

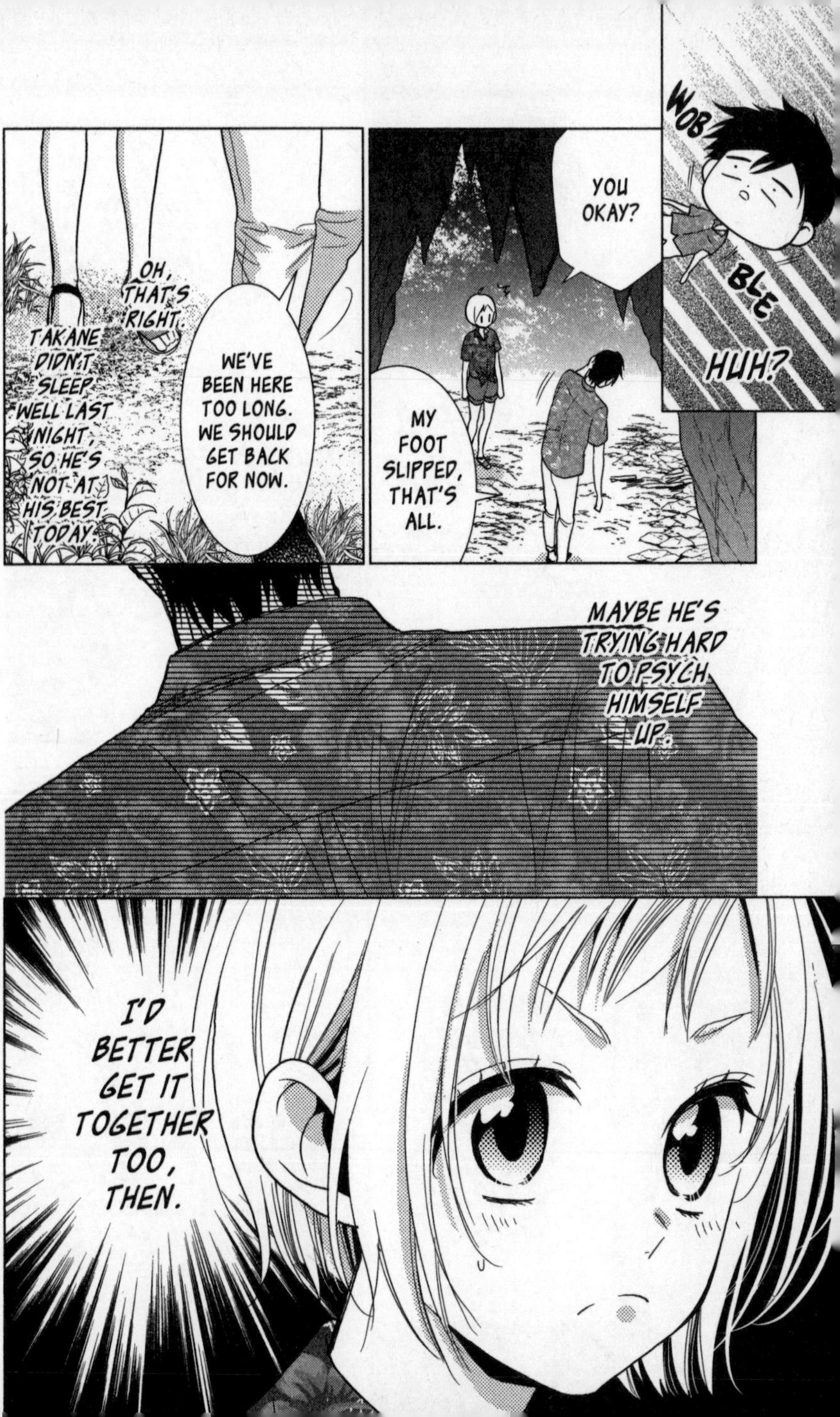
WOB
BLE
HUH?
YOU OKAY?
MY FOOT SLIPPED, THAT'S ALL.
WE'VE BEEN HERE TOO LONG. WE SHOULD GET BACK FOR NOW.
OH, THAT'S RIGHT.
TAKANE DIDN'T SLEEP WELL LAST NIGHT, SO HE'S NOT AT HIS BEST TODAY.
MAYBE HE'S TRYING HARD TO PSYCH HIMSELF UP.
I'D BETTER GET IT TOGETHER TOO, THEN.

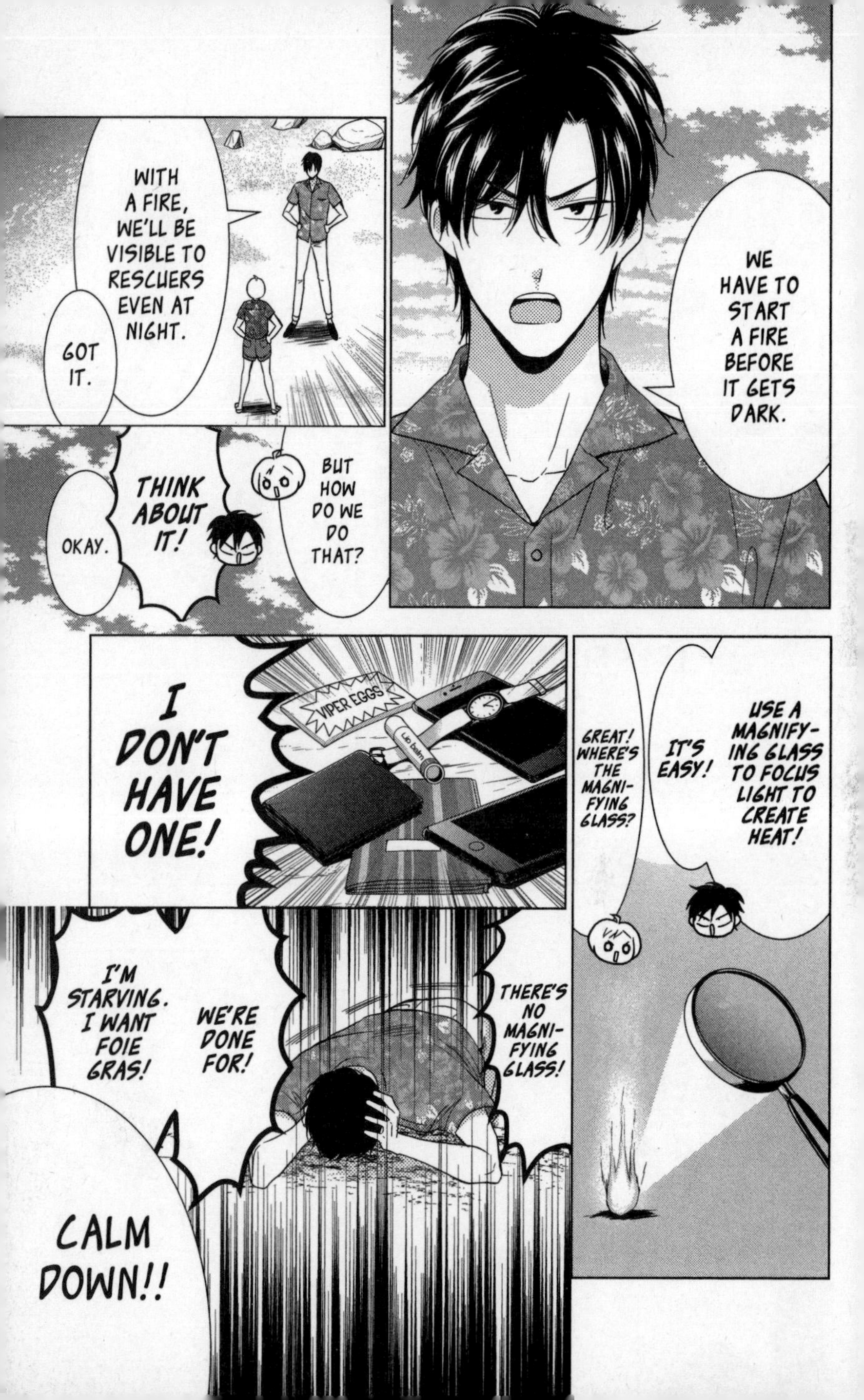
WE HAVE TO START A FIRE BEFORE IT GETS DARK.
WITH A FIRE, WE'LL BE VISIBLE TO RESCUERS EVEN AT NIGHT.
GOT IT.
BUT HOW DO WE DO THAT?
THINK ABOUT IT!
OKAY.
USE A MAGNIFYING GLASS TO FOCUS LIGHT TO CREATE HEAT!
IT'S EASY!
GREAT! WHERE'S THE MAGNIFYING GLASS?
VIPER EGGS
Lip balm
I DON'T HAVE ONE!
THERE'S NO MAGNIFYING GLASS!
WE'RE DONE FOR!
I'M STARVING. I WANT FOIE GRAS!
CALM DOWN!!

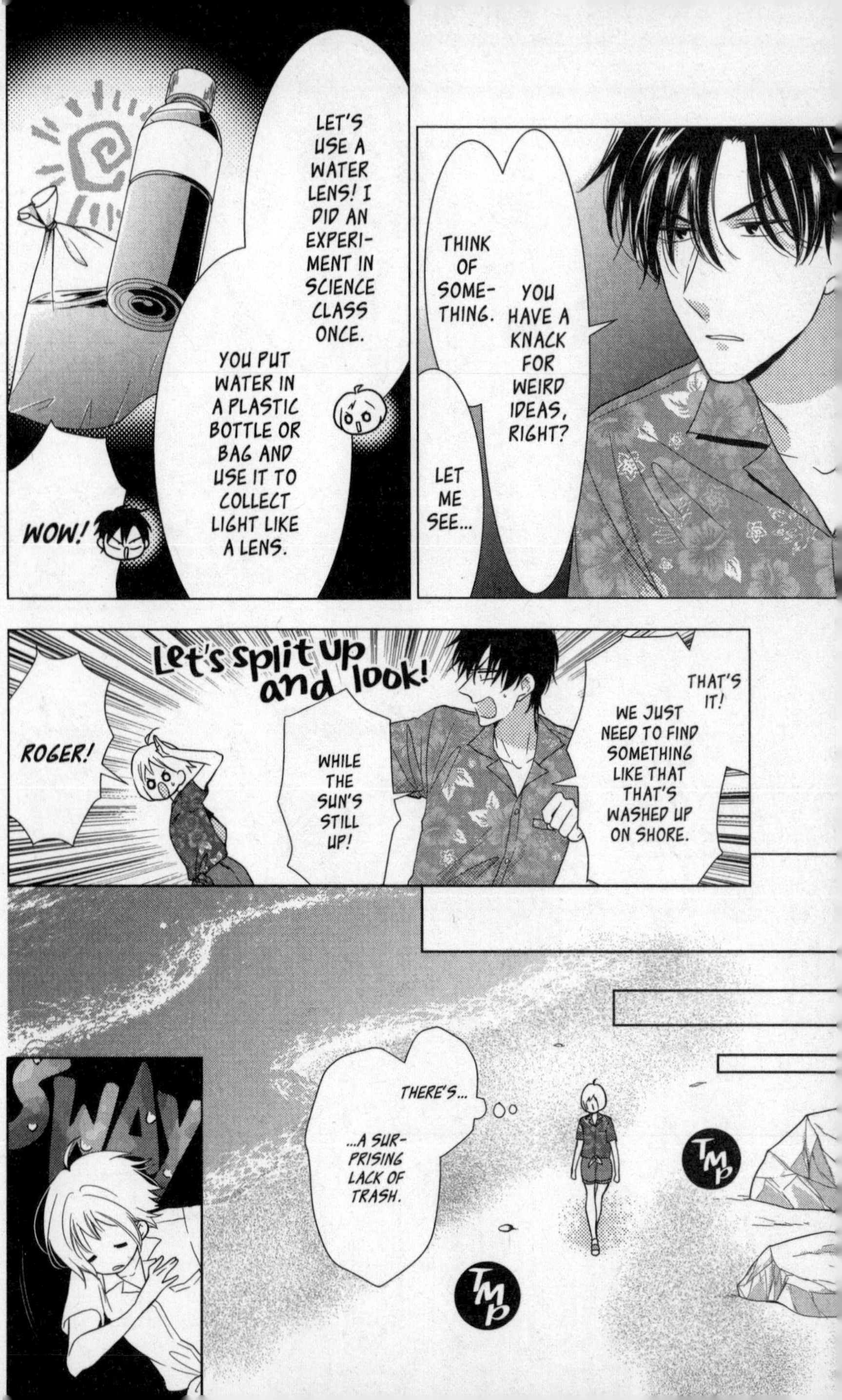
THINK OF SOME-THING.
YOU HAVE A KNACK FOR WEIRD IDEAS, RIGHT?
LET ME SEE...
LET'S USE A WATER LENS! I DID AN EXPERI-MENT IN SCIENCE CLASS ONCE.
YOU PUT WATER IN A PLASTIC BOTTLE OR BAG AND USE IT TO COLLECT LIGHT LIKE A LENS.
WOW!
THAT'S IT!
WE JUST NEED TO FIND SOMETHING LIKE THAT THAT'S WASHED UP ON SHORE.
WHILE THE SUN'S STILL UP!
Let's split up and look!
ROGER!
TMP
THERE'S...
...A SUR-PRISING LACK OF TRASH.
TMP
SWAY

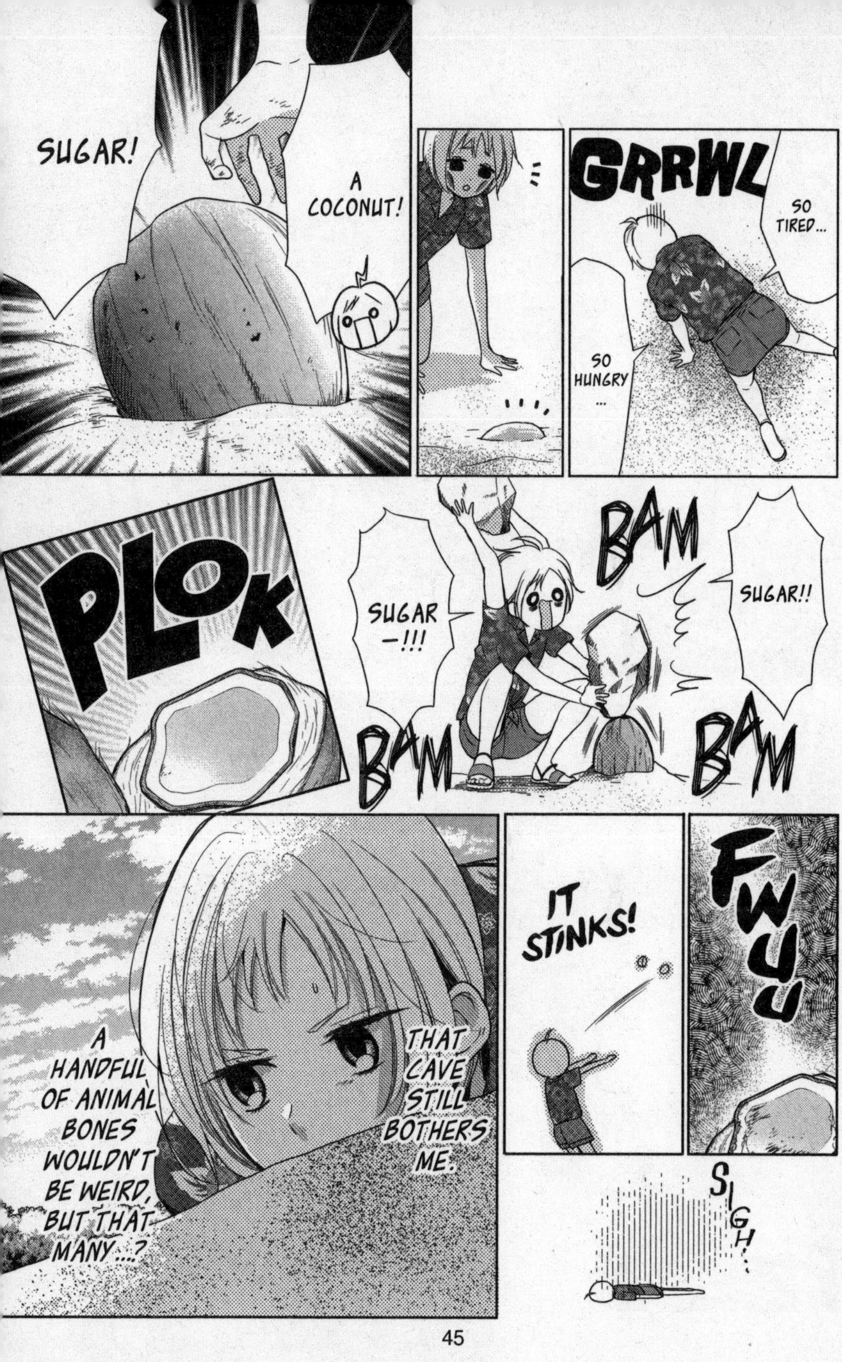
GRRWL
SO TIRED...
SO HUNGRY ...
A COCONUT!
SUGAR!
BAM
SUGAR!!
BAM
SUGAR—!!!
BAM
PLOK
FWUU
IT STINKS!
SIGH...
THAT CAVE STILL BOTHERS ME.
A HANDFUL OF ANIMAL BONES WOULDN'T BE WEIRD, BUT THAT MANY...?

FW SH

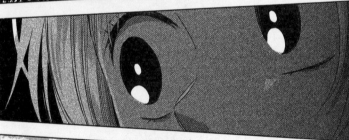

THERE WAS SOMETHING THERE...

TAKANE...? IS THAT YOU?

HUH ....?

ZWIP

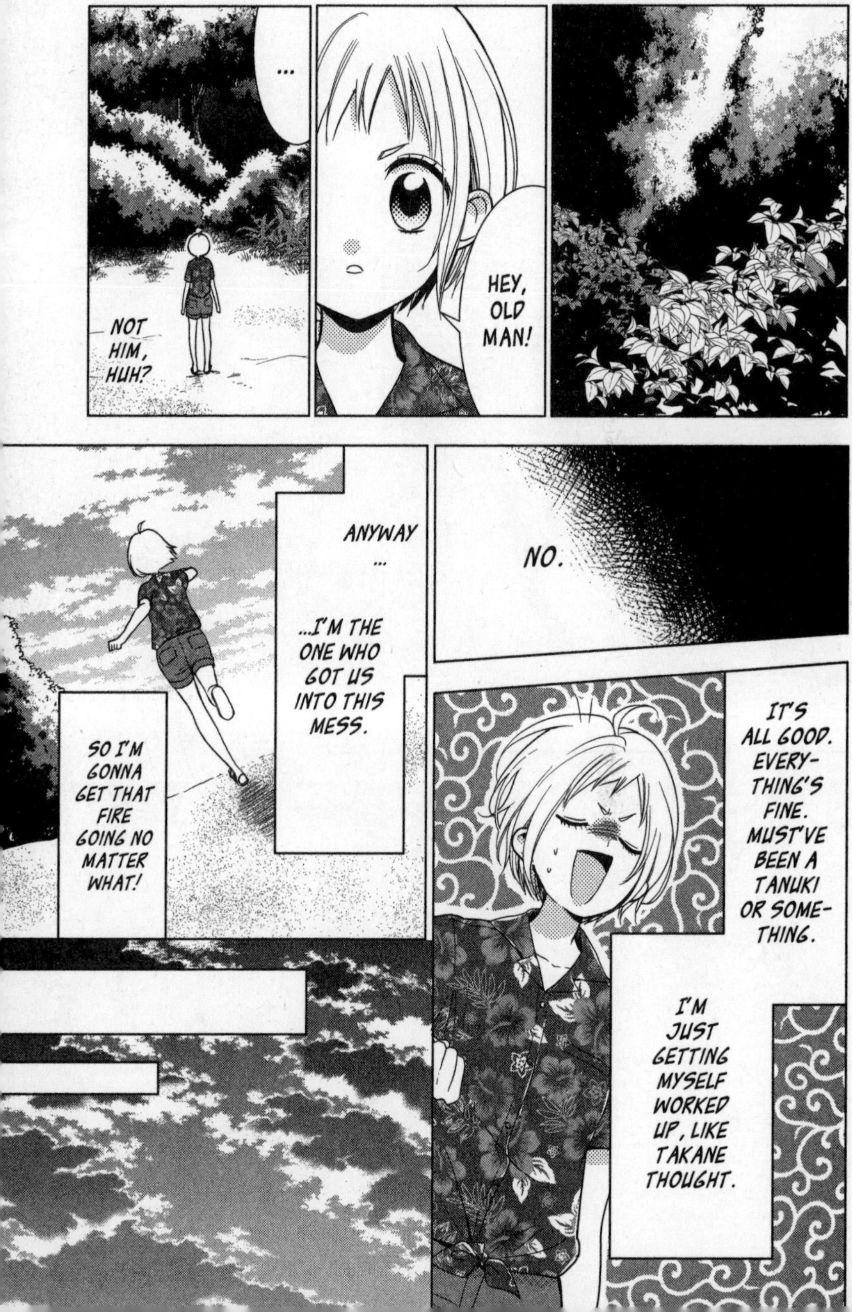
HEY, OLD MAN!
...
NOT HIM, HUH?
NO.
IT'S ALL GOOD. EVERYTHING'S FINE. MUST'VE BEEN A TANUKI OR SOMETHING.
I'M JUST GETTING MYSELF WORKED UP, LIKE TAKANE THOUGHT.
ANYWAY...
...I'M THE ONE WHO GOT US INTO THIS MESS.
SO I'M GONNA GET THAT FIRE GOING NO MATTER WHAT!

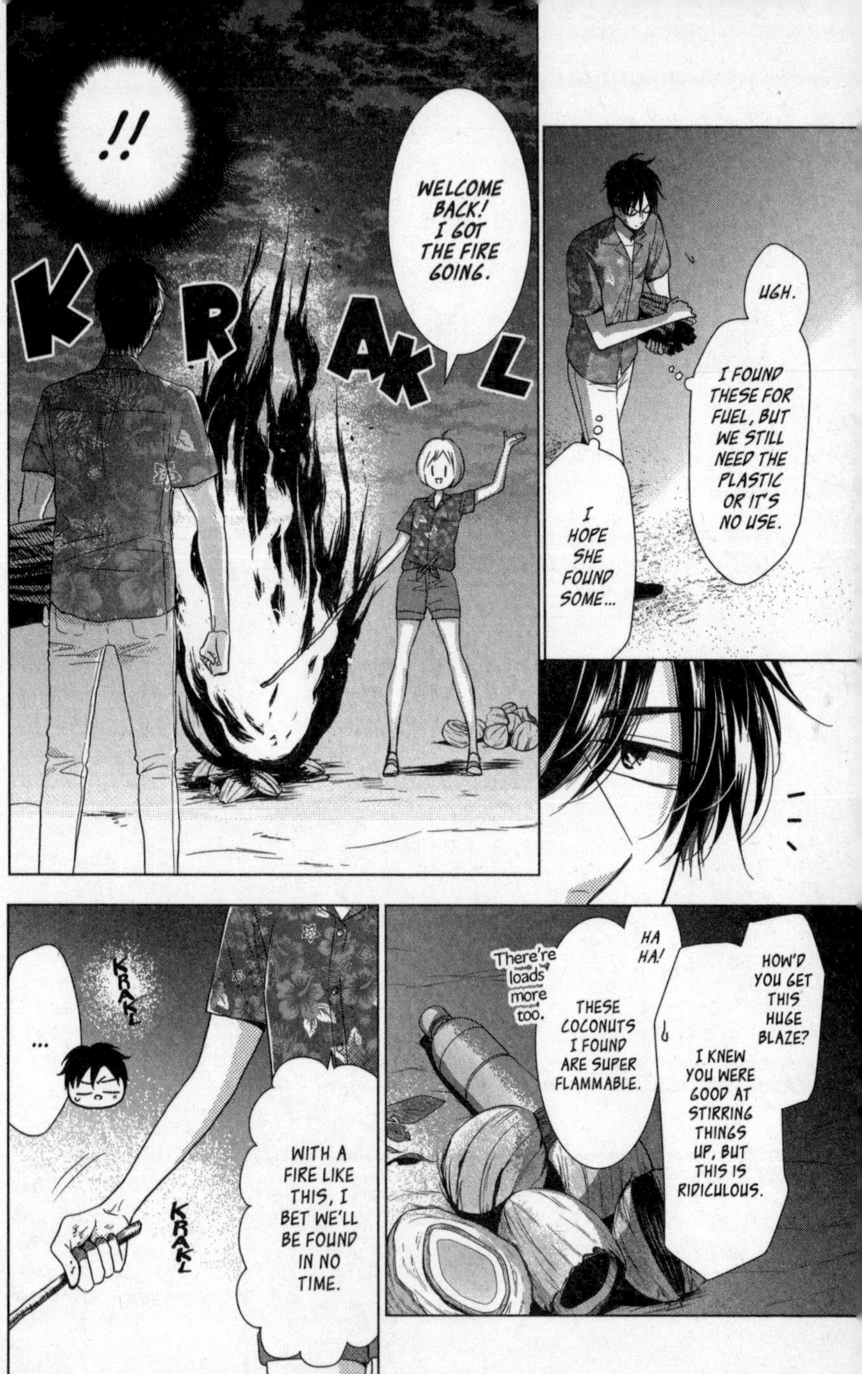
UGH.
I FOUND THESE FOR FUEL, BUT WE STILL NEED THE PLASTIC OR IT'S NO USE.
I HOPE SHE FOUND SOME...
!!
WELCOME BACK! I GOT THE FIRE GOING.
KRAKL
HOW'D YOU GET THIS HUGE BLAZE?
I KNEW YOU WERE GOOD AT STIRRING THINGS UP, BUT THIS IS RIDICULOUS.
HA HA!
THESE COCONUTS I FOUND ARE SUPER FLAMMABLE.
There're loads more too.
WITH A FIRE LIKE THIS, I BET WE'LL BE FOUND IN NO TIME.
KRAKL
KRAKL
...

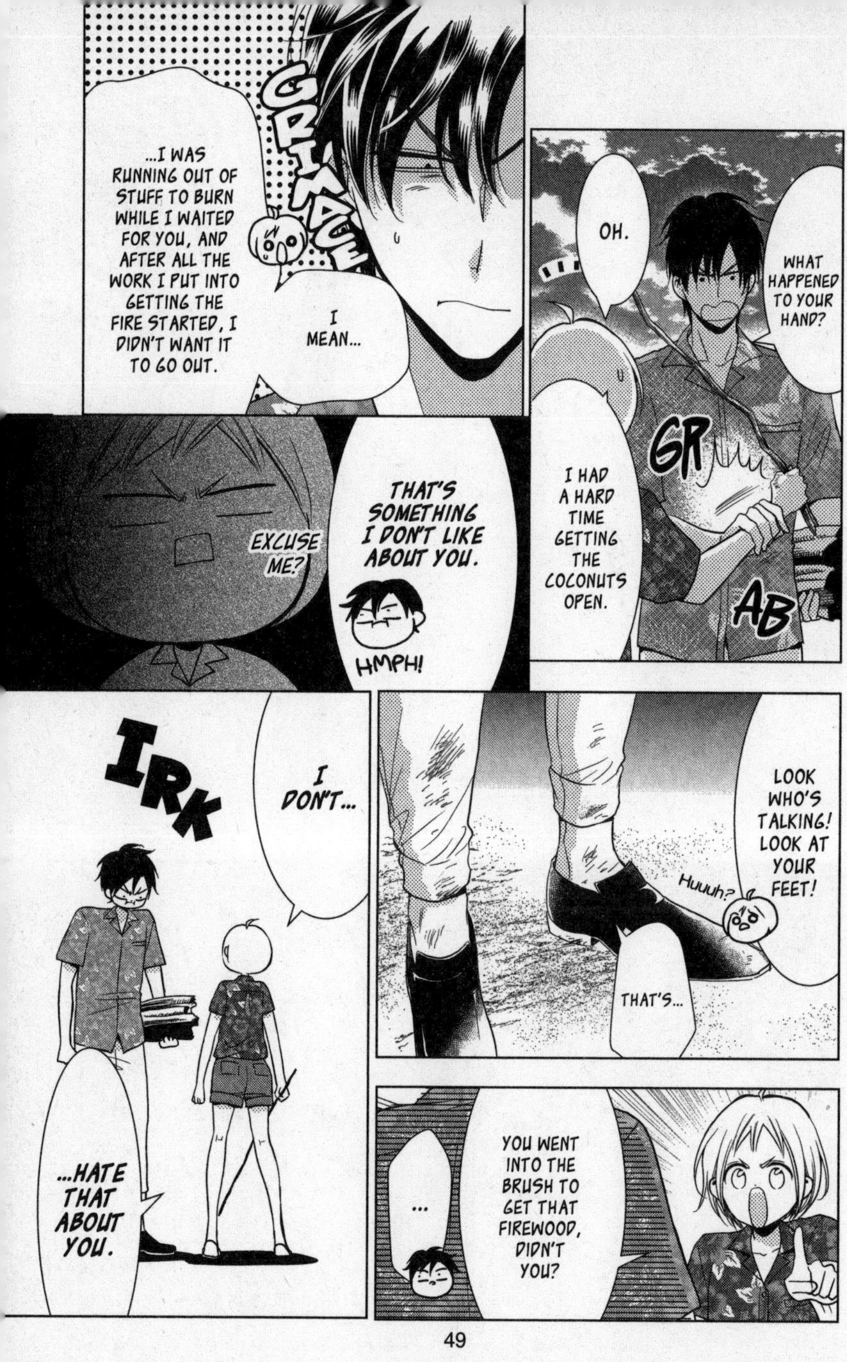
WHAT HAPPENED TO YOUR HAND?
OH.
GR
AB
I HAD A HARD TIME GETTING THE COCONUTS OPEN.
GRIMACE
I MEAN...
...I WAS RUNNING OUT OF STUFF TO BURN WHILE I WAITED FOR YOU, AND AFTER ALL THE WORK I PUT INTO GETTING THE FIRE STARTED, I DIDN'T WANT IT TO GO OUT.
THAT'S SOMETHING I DON'T LIKE ABOUT YOU.
HMPH!
EXCUSE ME?
LOOK WHO'S TALKING! LOOK AT YOUR FEET!
Huuuh?
THAT'S...
YOU WENT INTO THE BRUSH TO GET THAT FIREWOOD, DIDN'T YOU?
...
I DON'T...
IRK
...HATE THAT ABOUT YOU.

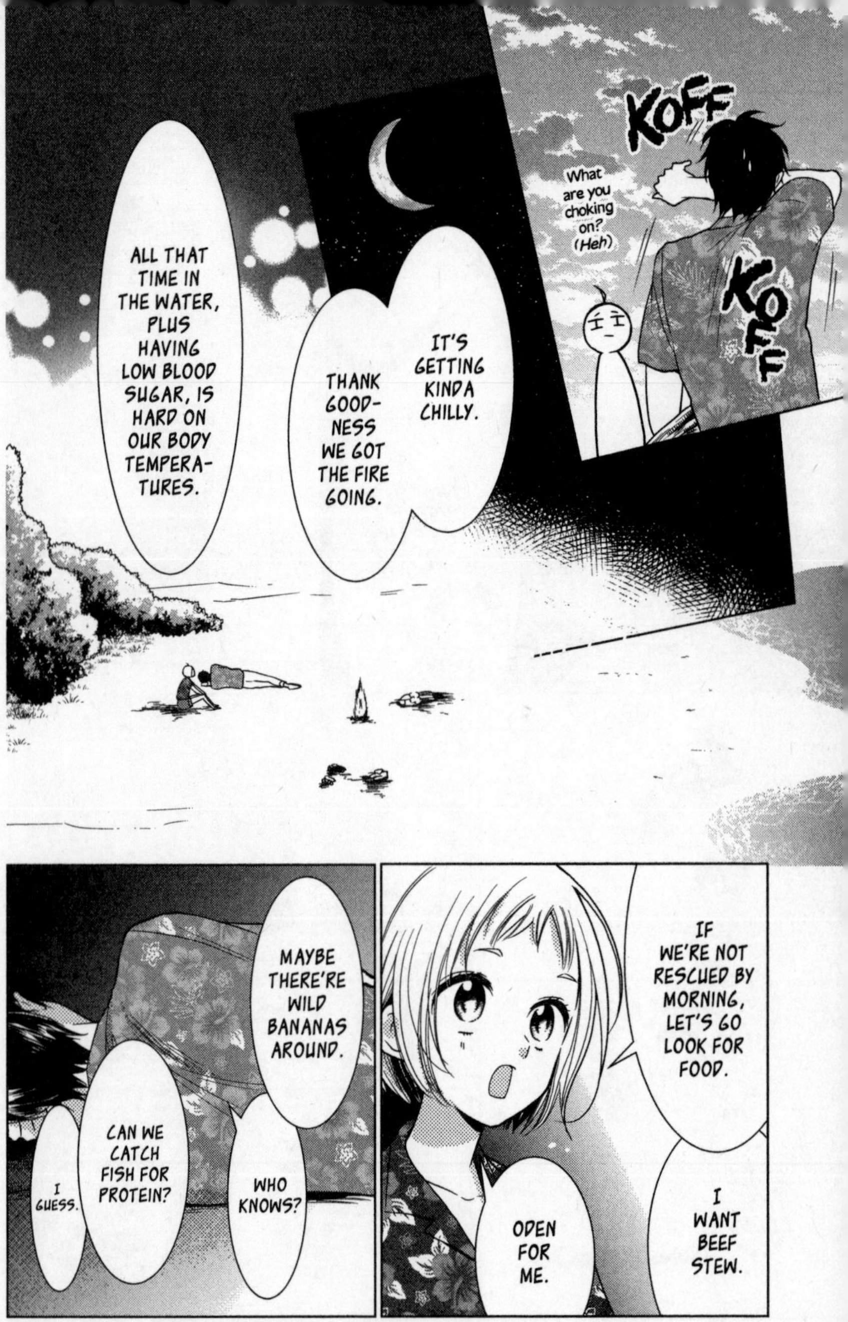
KOFF
What are you choking on? (Heh)
KOFF KOFF
IT'S GETTING KINDA CHILLY.
THANK GOODNESS WE GOT THE FIRE GOING.
ALL THAT TIME IN THE WATER, PLUS HAVING LOW BLOOD SUGAR, IS HARD ON OUR BODY TEMPERATURES.
IF WE'RE NOT RESCUED BY MORNING, LET'S GO LOOK FOR FOOD.
I WANT BEEF STEW.
ODEN FOR ME.
MAYBE THERE'RE WILD BANANAS AROUND.
WHO KNOWS?
CAN WE CATCH FISH FOR PROTEIN?
I GUESS.

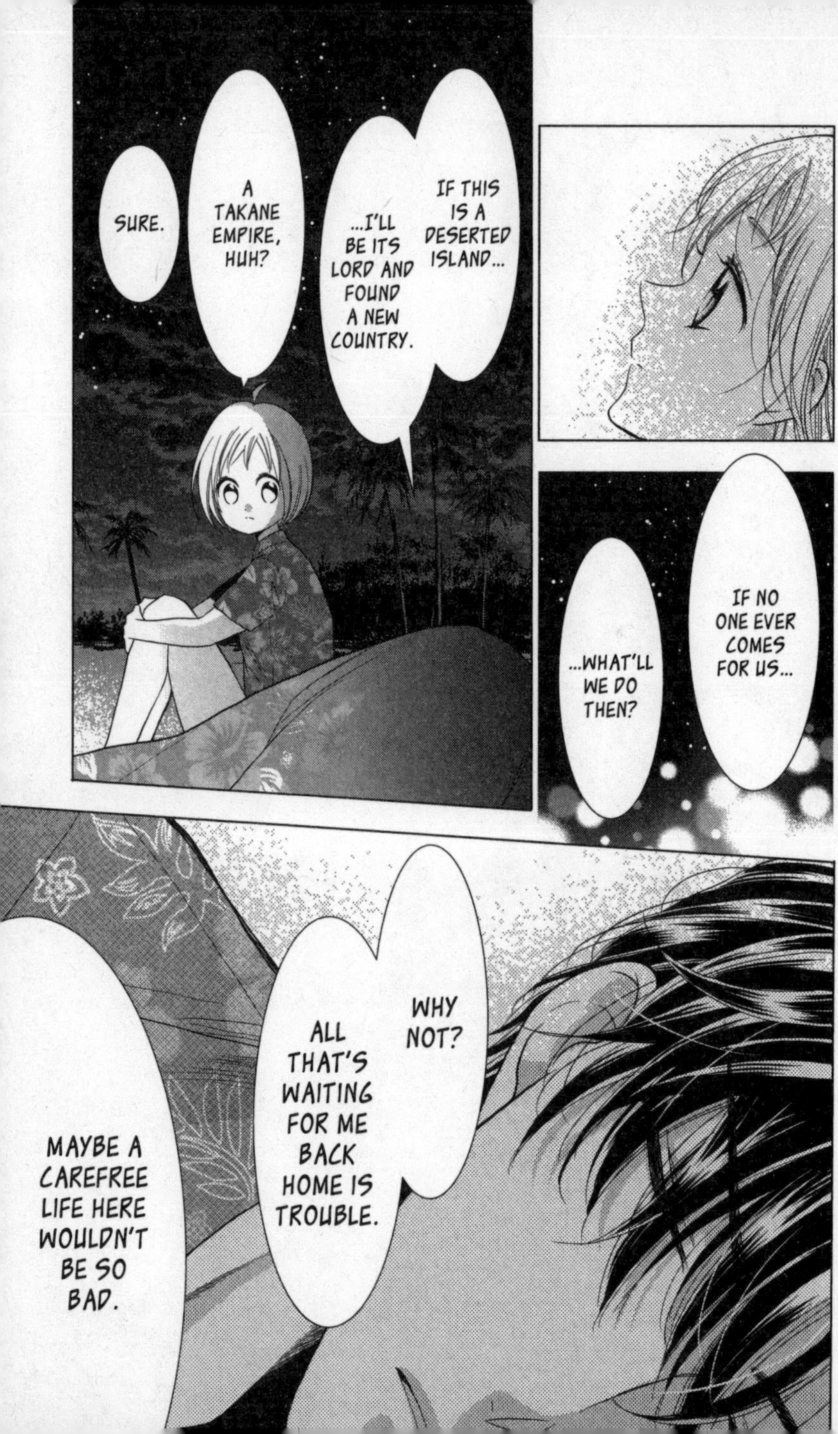
IF NO ONE EVER COMES FOR US...
...WHAT'LL WE DO THEN?
IF THIS IS A DESERTED ISLAND...
...I'LL BE ITS LORD AND FOUND A NEW COUNTRY.
A TAKANE EMPIRE, HUH?
SURE.
WHY NOT?
ALL THAT'S WAITING FOR ME BACK HOME IS TROUBLE.
MAYBE A CAREFREE LIFE HERE WOULDN'T BE SO BAD.

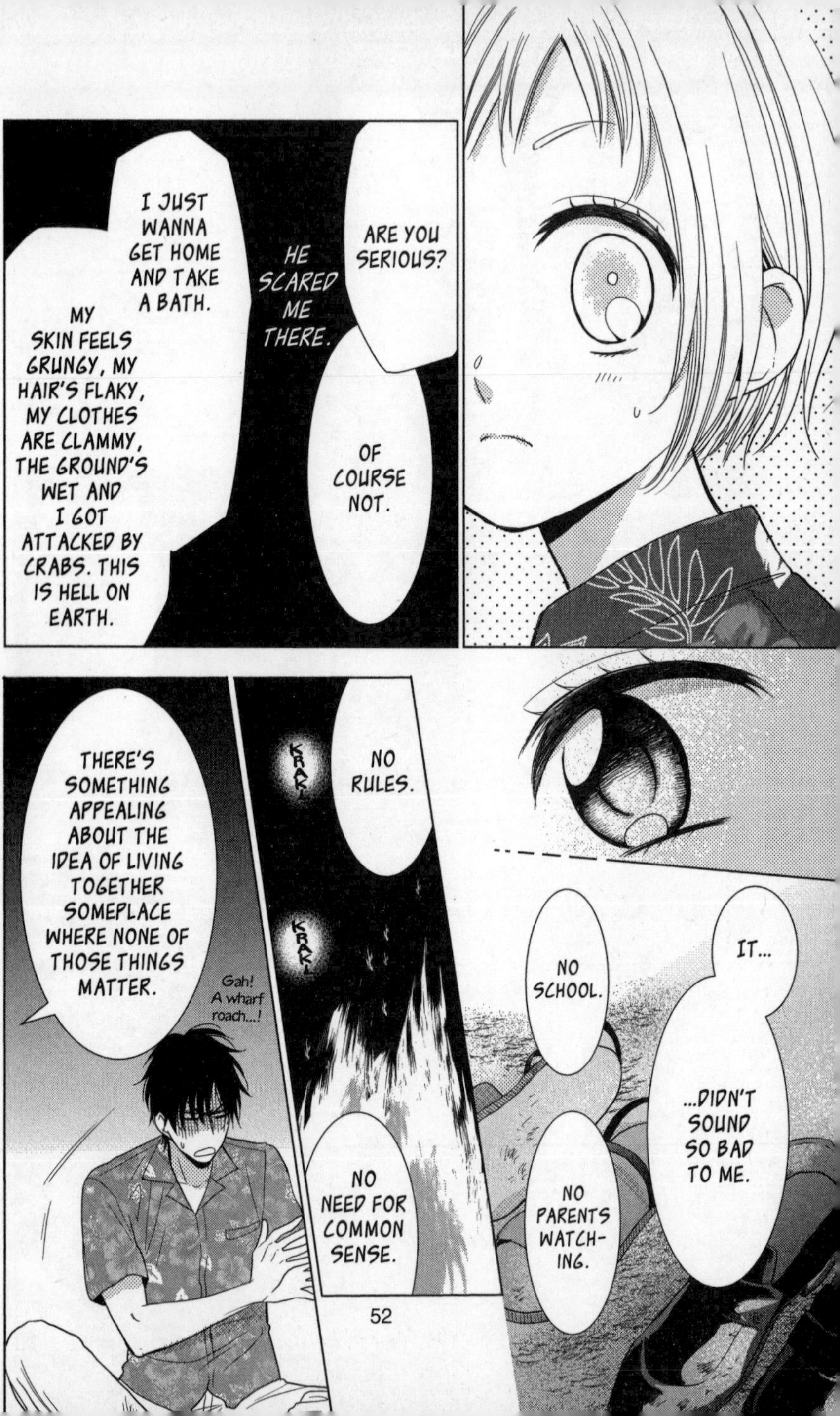
ARE YOU SERIOUS?
OF COURSE NOT.
HE SCARED ME THERE.
I JUST WANNA GET HOME AND TAKE A BATH.
MY SKIN FEELS GRUNGY, MY HAIR'S FLAKY, MY CLOTHES ARE CLAMMY, THE GROUND'S WET AND I GOT ATTACKED BY CRABS. THIS IS HELL ON EARTH.
IT...
NO SCHOOL.
...DIDN'T SOUND SO BAD TO ME.
NO PARENTS WATCH-ING.
KRAK
NO RULES.
KRAK
NO NEED FOR COMMON SENSE.
THERE'S SOMETHING APPEALING ABOUT THE IDEA OF LIVING TOGETHER SOMEPLACE WHERE NONE OF THOSE THINGS MATTER.
Gah! A wharf roach...!

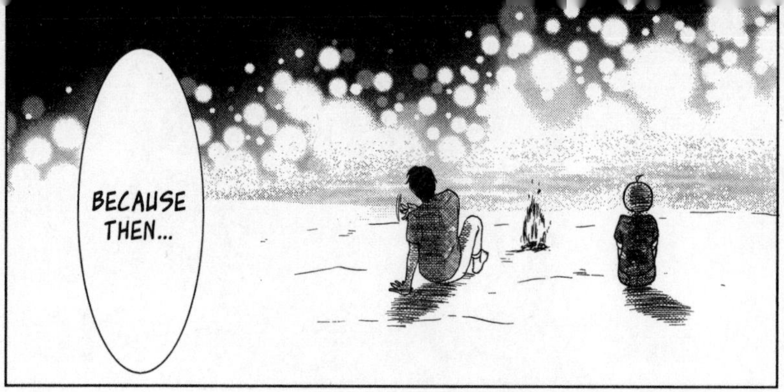
BECAUSE THEN...
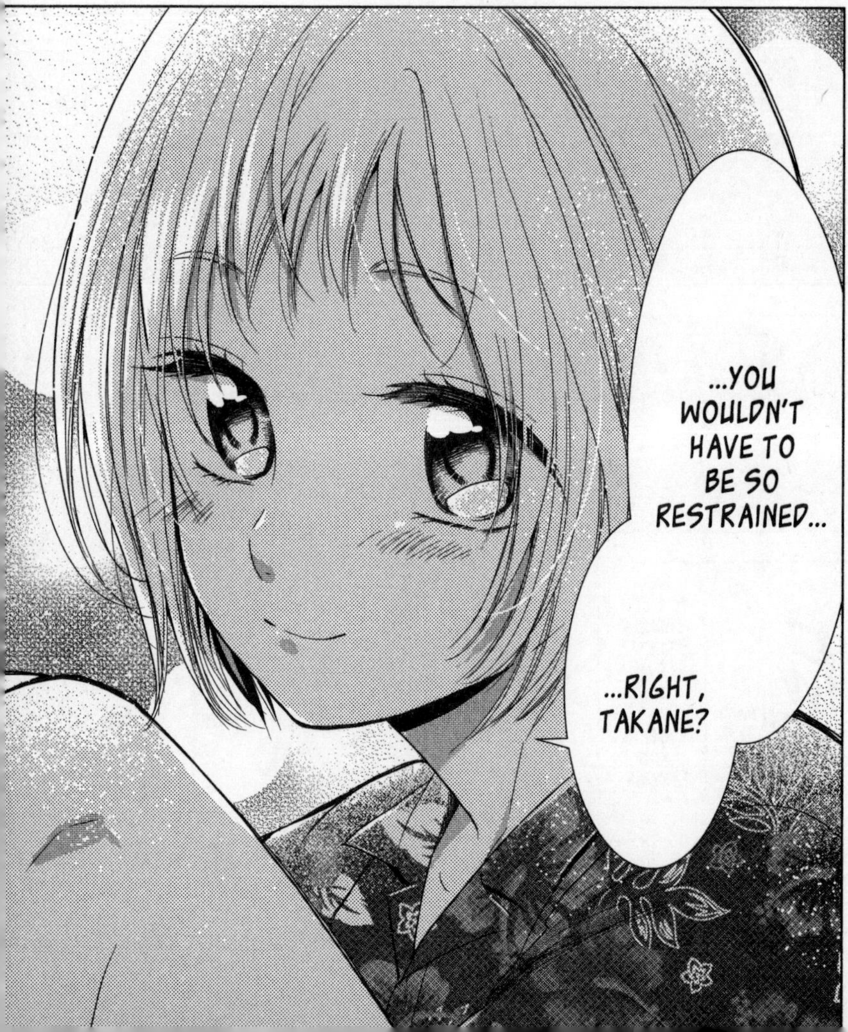
...YOU WOULDN'T HAVE TO BE SO RESTRAINED...
...RIGHT, TAKANE?

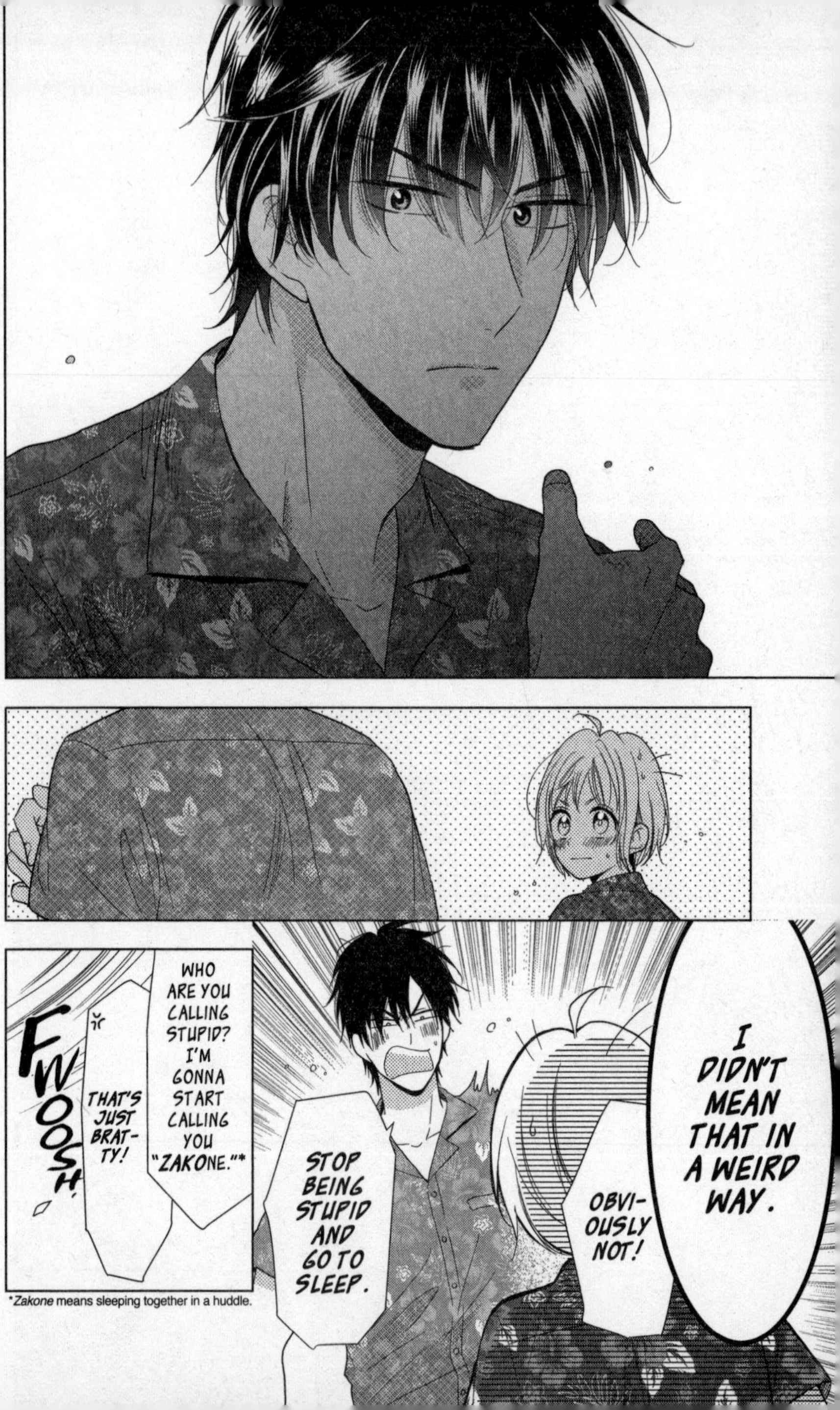
I DIDN'T MEAN THAT IN A WEIRD WAY.
OBVIOUSLY NOT!
STOP BEING STUPID AND GO TO SLEEP.
WHO ARE YOU CALLING STUPID? I'M GONNA START CALLING YOU "ZAKONE."*
THAT'S JUST BRATTY!
FWOOSH!

*Zakone means sleeping together in a huddle.

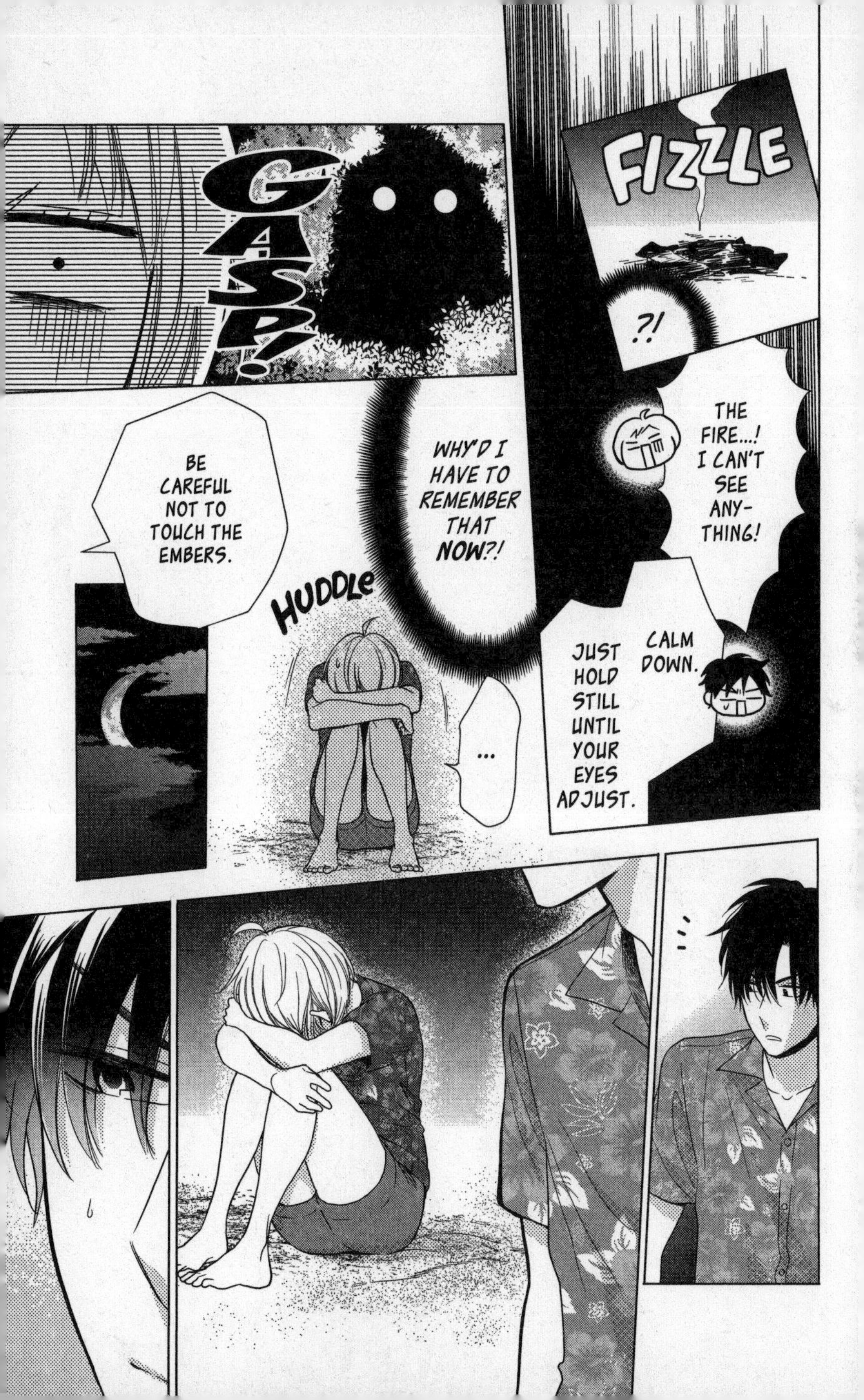
FIZZLE
?!
GASP!
THE FIRE...! I CAN'T SEE ANY-THING!
CALM DOWN.
JUST HOLD STILL UNTIL YOUR EYES ADJUST.
WHY'D I HAVE TO REMEMBER THAT NOW?!
HUDDLE
...
BE CAREFUL NOT TO TOUCH THE EMBERS.

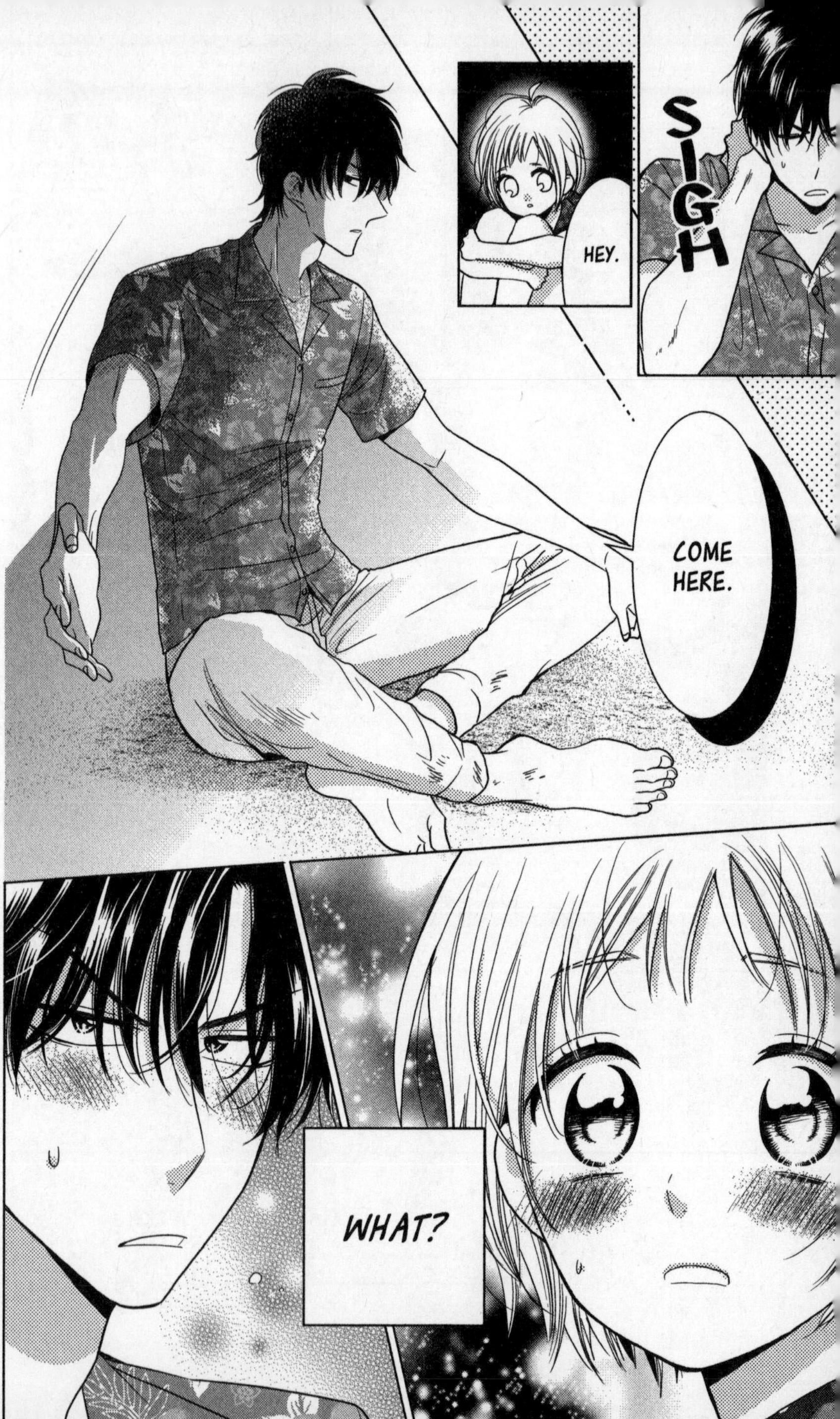
SIGH
HEY.
COME HERE.
WHAT?

I DON'T MEAN IT IN A WEIRD WAY.

THE NIGHT WIND'S CHILLY, SO I'M TELLING YOU TO BE MY HEAT PACK.

EITHER COME OVER OR DON'T. YOUR CALL.

I KNOW THAT.

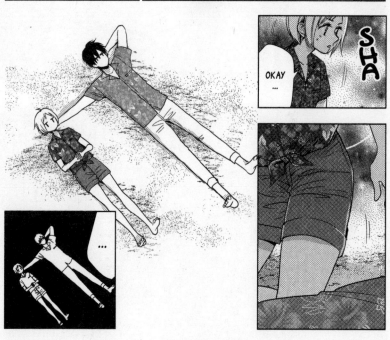

OKAY...

SHA

...

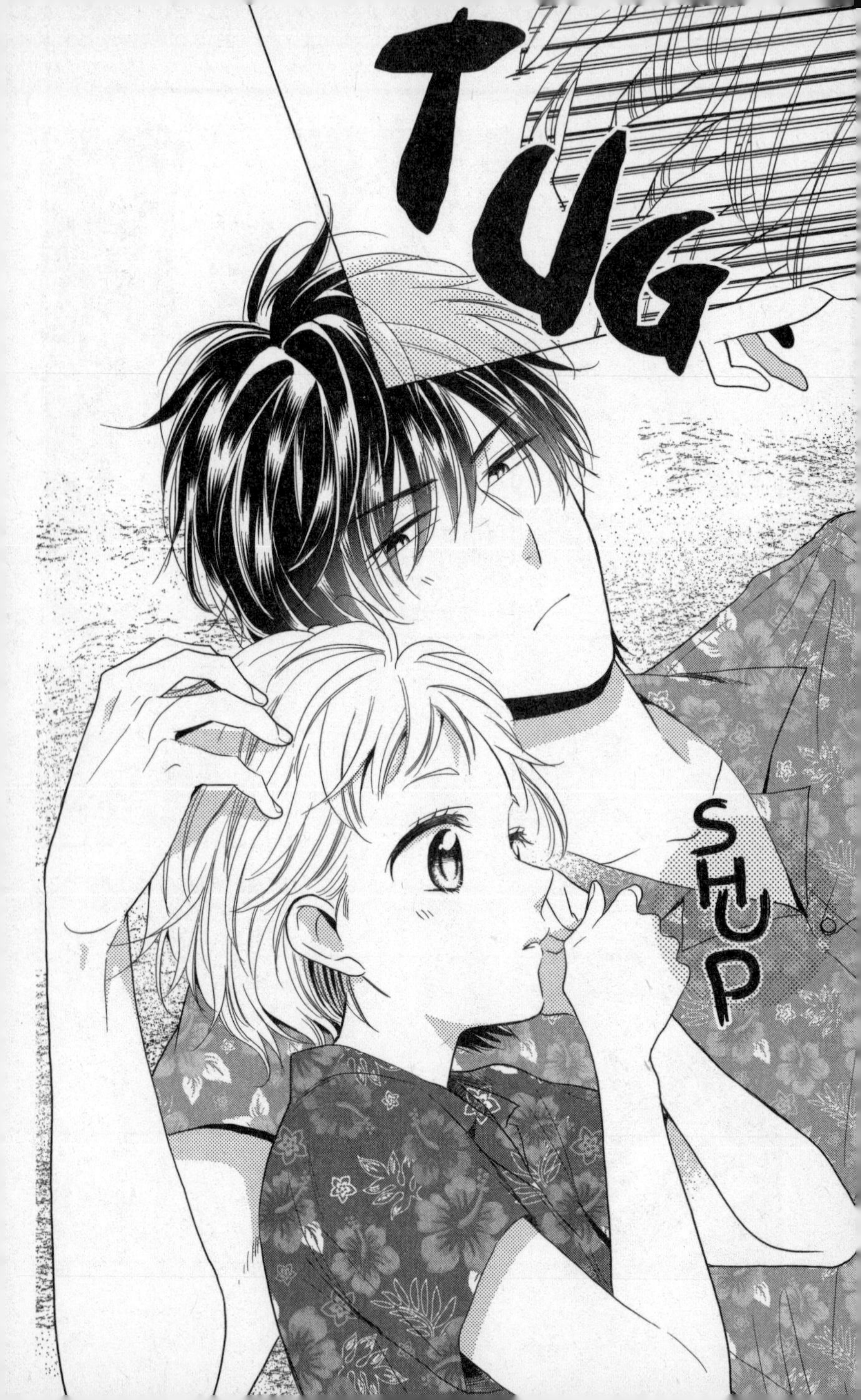
TUG
SHUP

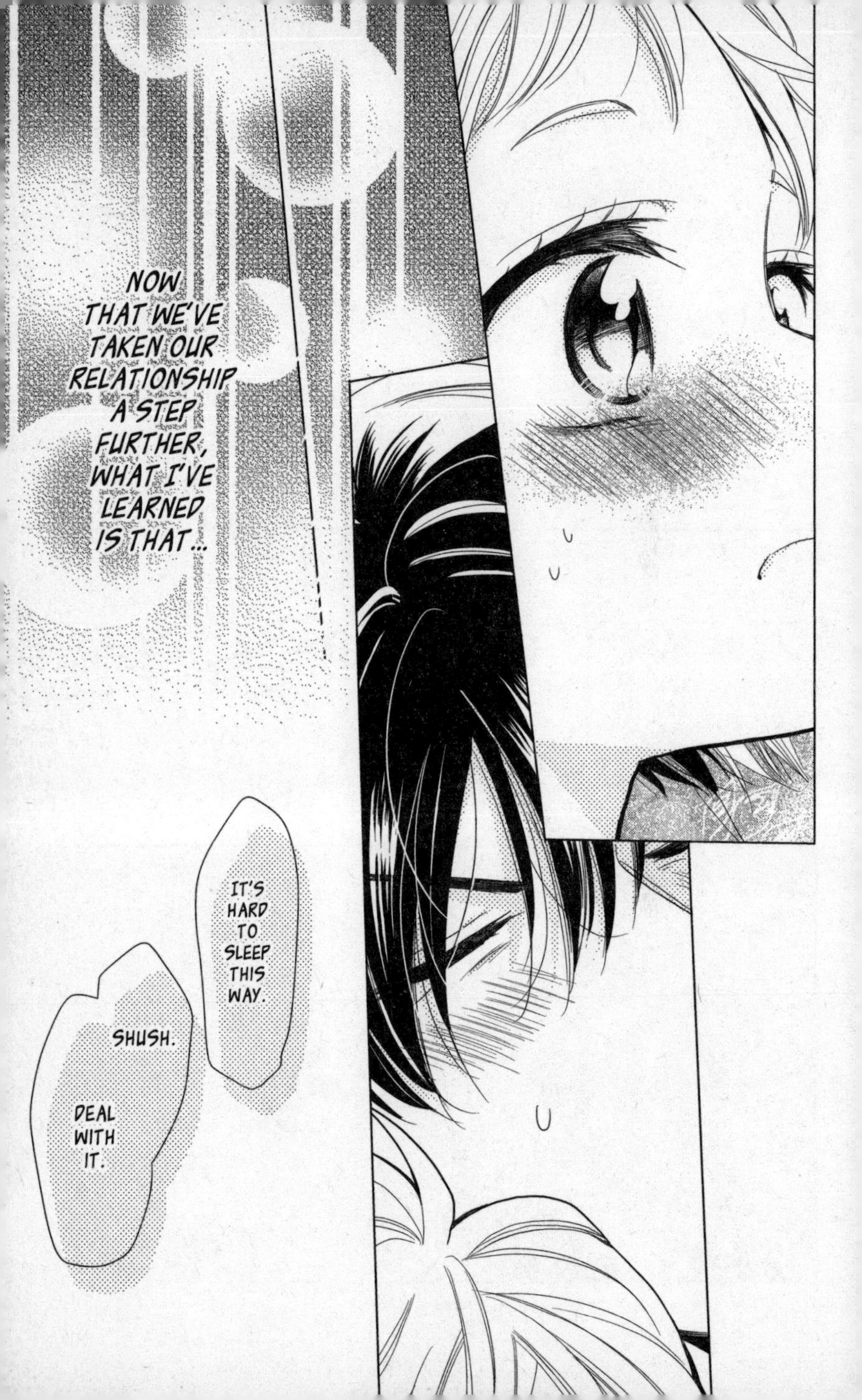
NOW THAT WE'VE TAKEN OUR RELATIONSHIP A STEP FURTHER, WHAT I'VE LEARNED IS THAT...
IT'S HARD TO SLEEP THIS WAY.
SHUSH.
DEAL WITH IT.

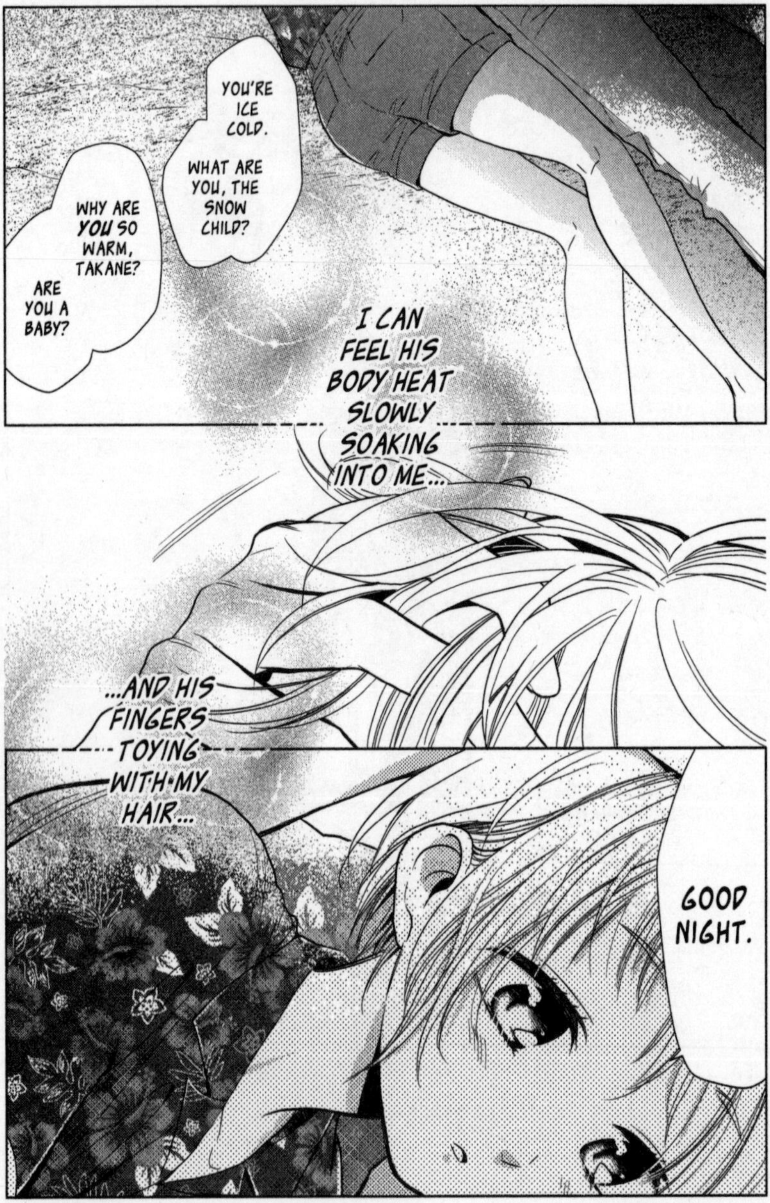
YOU'RE ICE COLD.
WHAT ARE YOU, THE SNOW CHILD?
WHY ARE *YOU* SO WARM, TAKANE?
ARE YOU A BABY?
I CAN FEEL HIS BODY HEAT SLOWLY SOAKING INTO ME...
...AND HIS FINGERS TOYING WITH MY HAIR...
GOOD NIGHT.

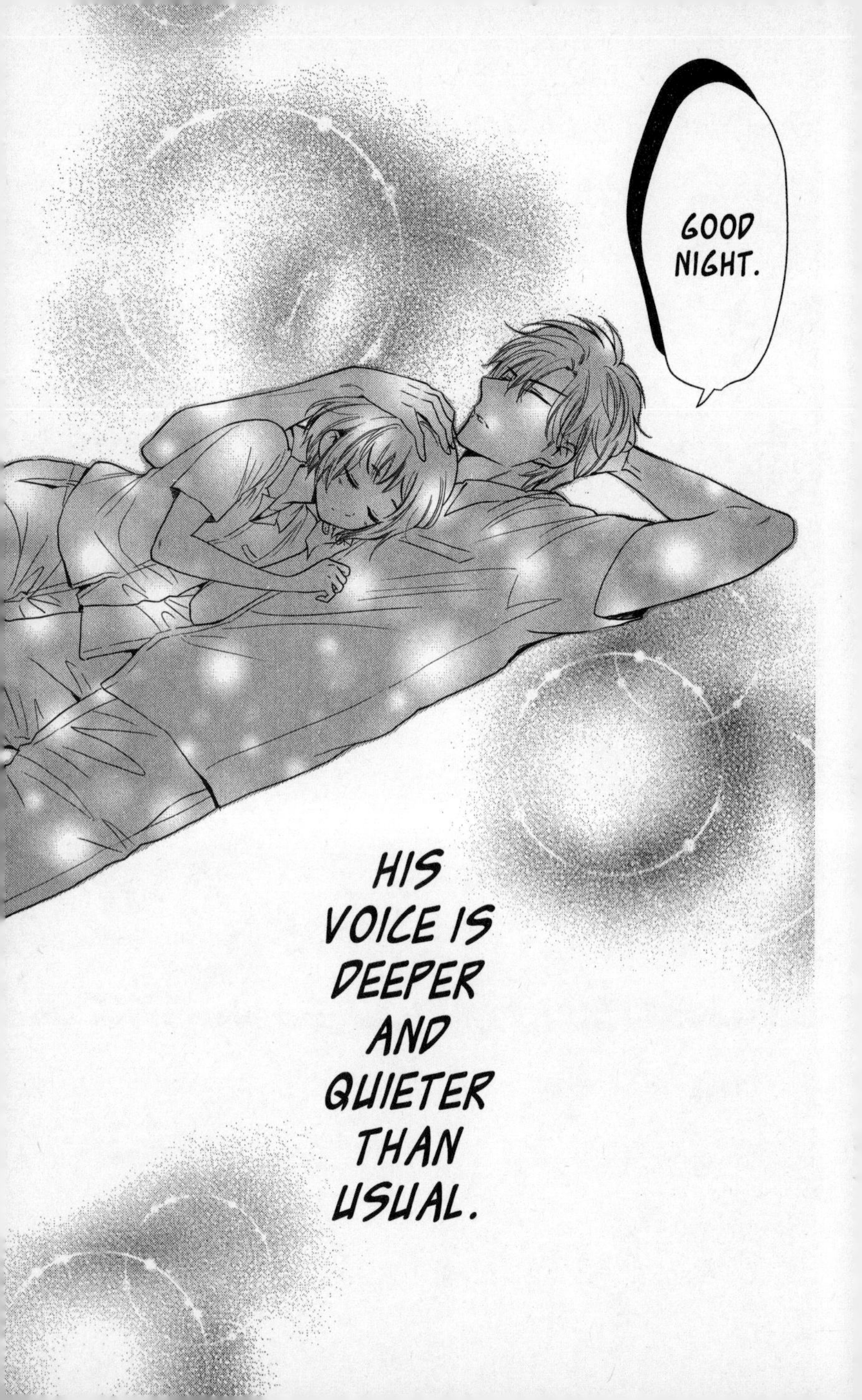
GOOD NIGHT.
HIS VOICE IS DEEPER AND QUIETER THAN USUAL.

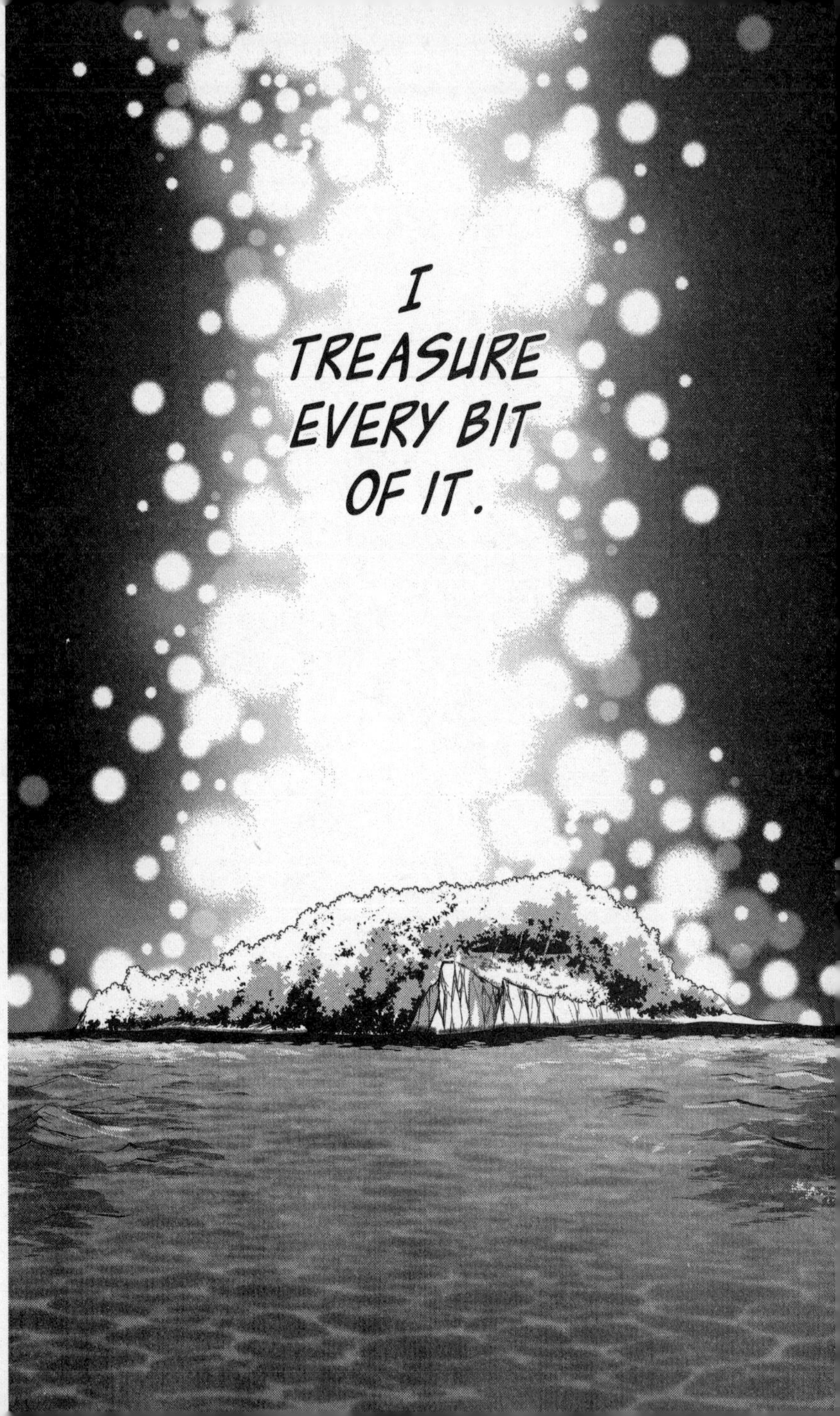
I TREASURE EVERY BIT OF IT.

Three Hours of Despair

ZSSSH
LET'S PLAY SHIRITORI!*
HMM?
"RI"... RE...
"RE-NEW."
A NICE POSITIVE WORD.
NEW... "NUDIE."
D... DIE...
DIE...

*A game where your opponent comes up with a word that begins with the final syllable of the word you say

Restless Sleep

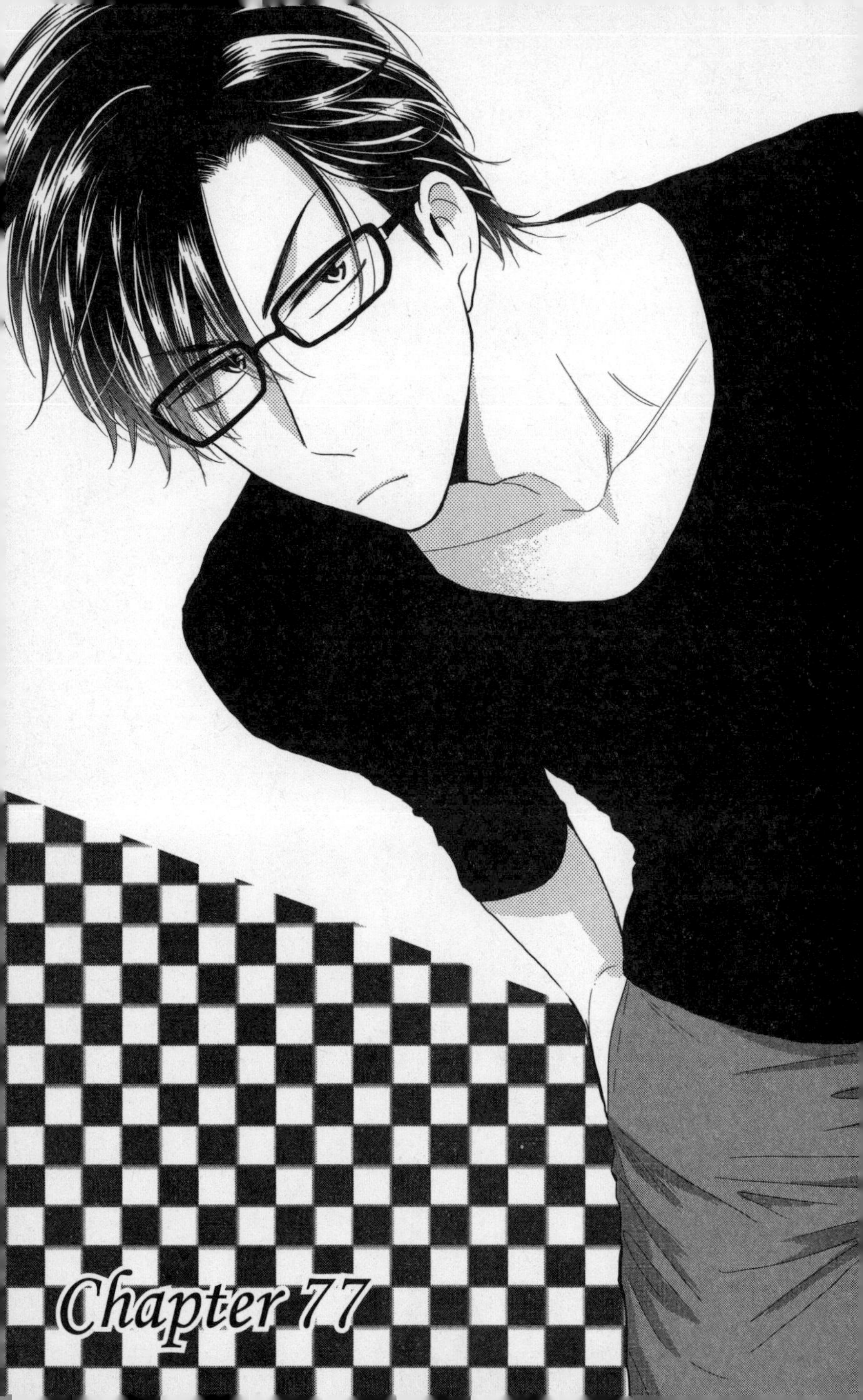
Chapter 77

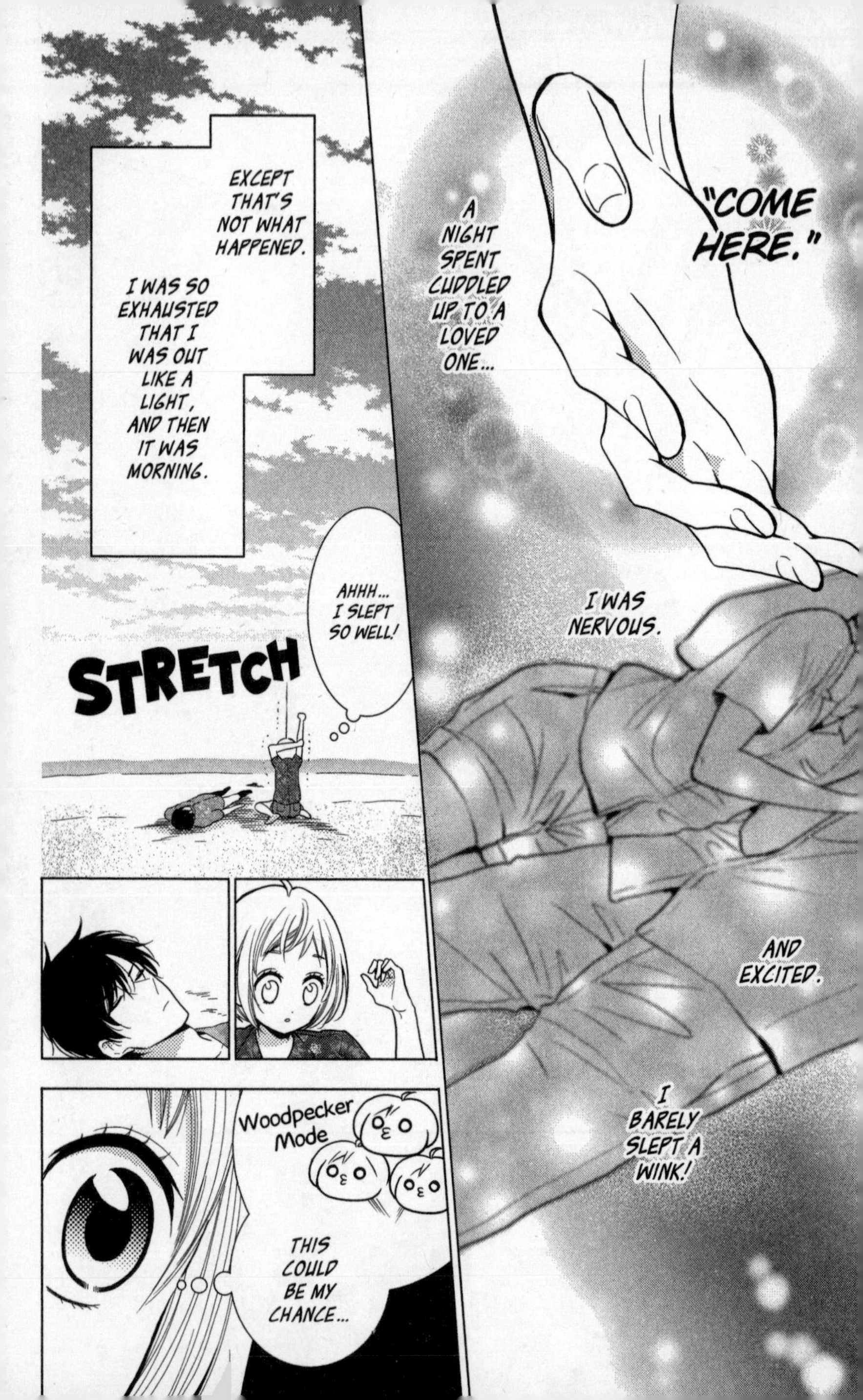
"COME HERE."
A NIGHT SPENT CUDDLED UP TO A LOVED ONE...
I WAS NERVOUS.
AND EXCITED.
I BARELY SLEPT A WINK!
EXCEPT THAT'S NOT WHAT HAPPENED.
I WAS SO EXHAUSTED THAT I WAS OUT LIKE A LIGHT, AND THEN IT WAS MORNING.
AHHH... I SLEPT SO WELL!
STRETCH
Woodpecker Mode
THIS COULD BE MY CHANCE...

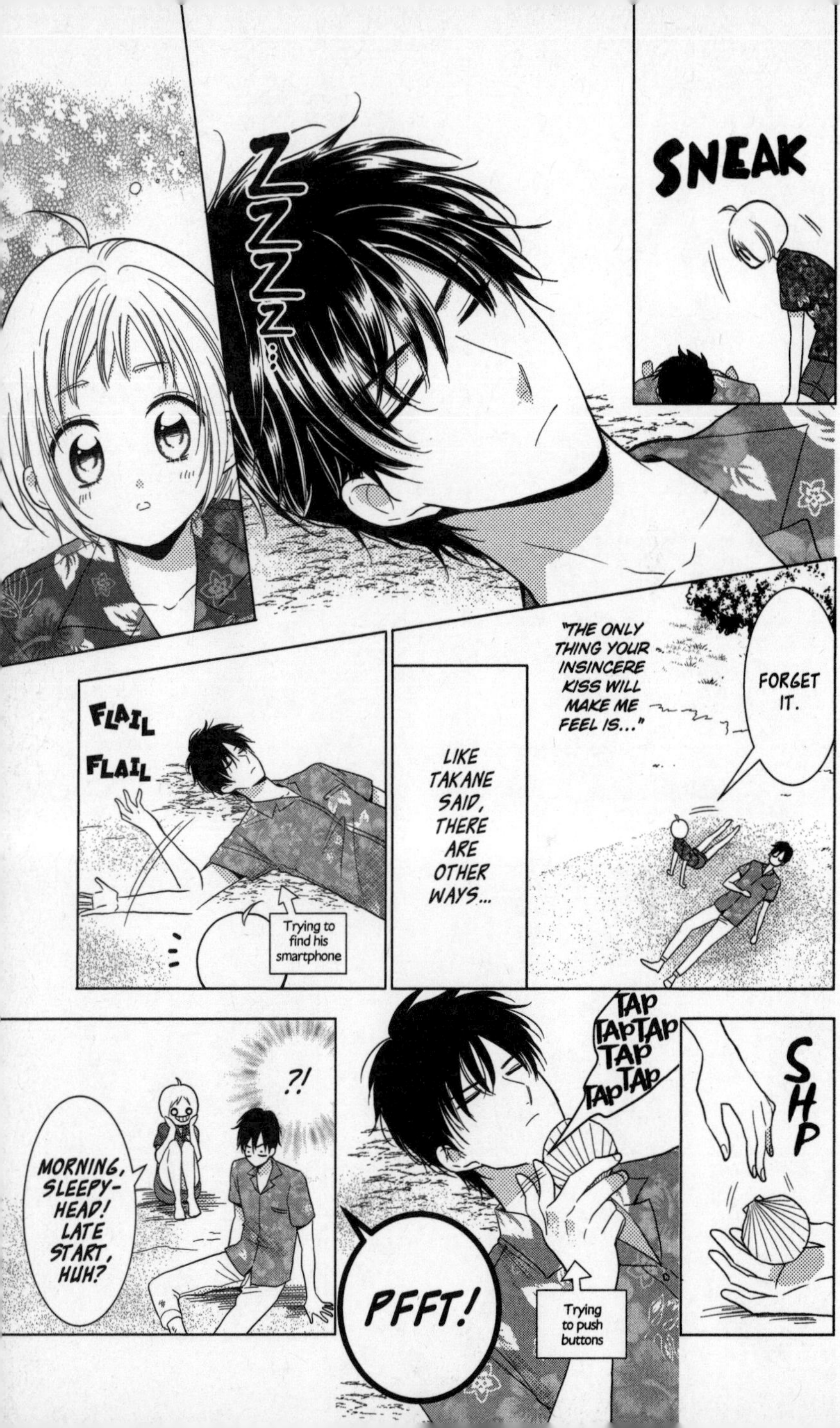
SNEAK
ZZZZ...
FORGET IT.
"THE ONLY THING YOUR INSINCERE KISS WILL MAKE ME FEEL IS..."
LIKE TAKANE SAID, THERE ARE OTHER WAYS...
FLAIL FLAIL
Trying to find his smartphone
SHP
TAP TAP TAP TAP TAP TAP
PFFT!
Trying to push buttons
?!
MORNING, SLEEPY-HEAD! LATE START, HUH?

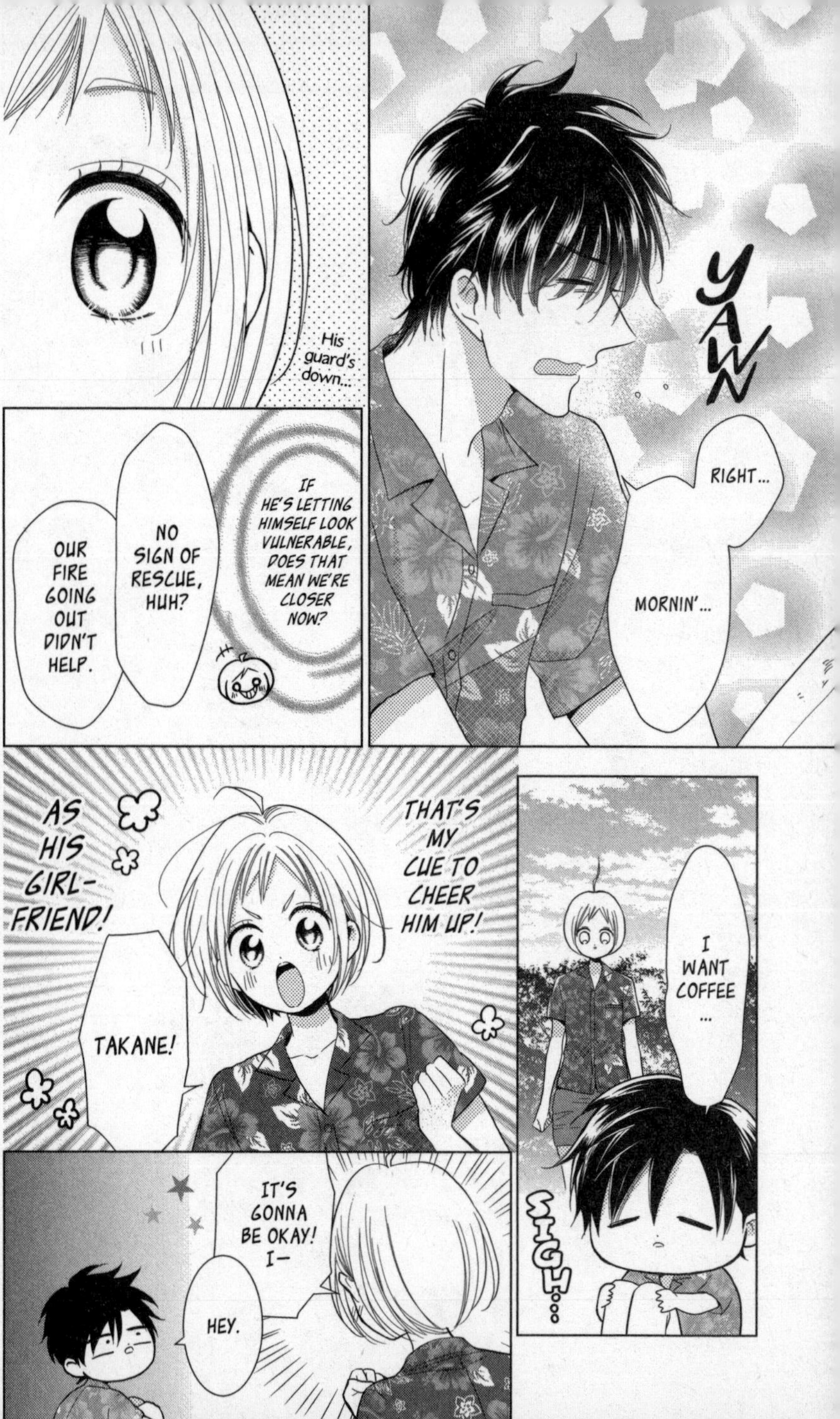
YAWN
RIGHT...
MORNIN'...
His guard's down...
IF HE'S LETTING HIMSELF LOOK VULNERABLE, DOES THAT MEAN WE'RE CLOSER NOW?
NO SIGN OF RESCUE, HUH?
OUR FIRE GOING OUT DIDN'T HELP.
I WANT COFFEE ...
SIGH...
THAT'S MY CUE TO CHEER HIM UP!
AS HIS GIRLFRIEND!
TAKANE!
IT'S GONNA BE OKAY! I—
HEY.

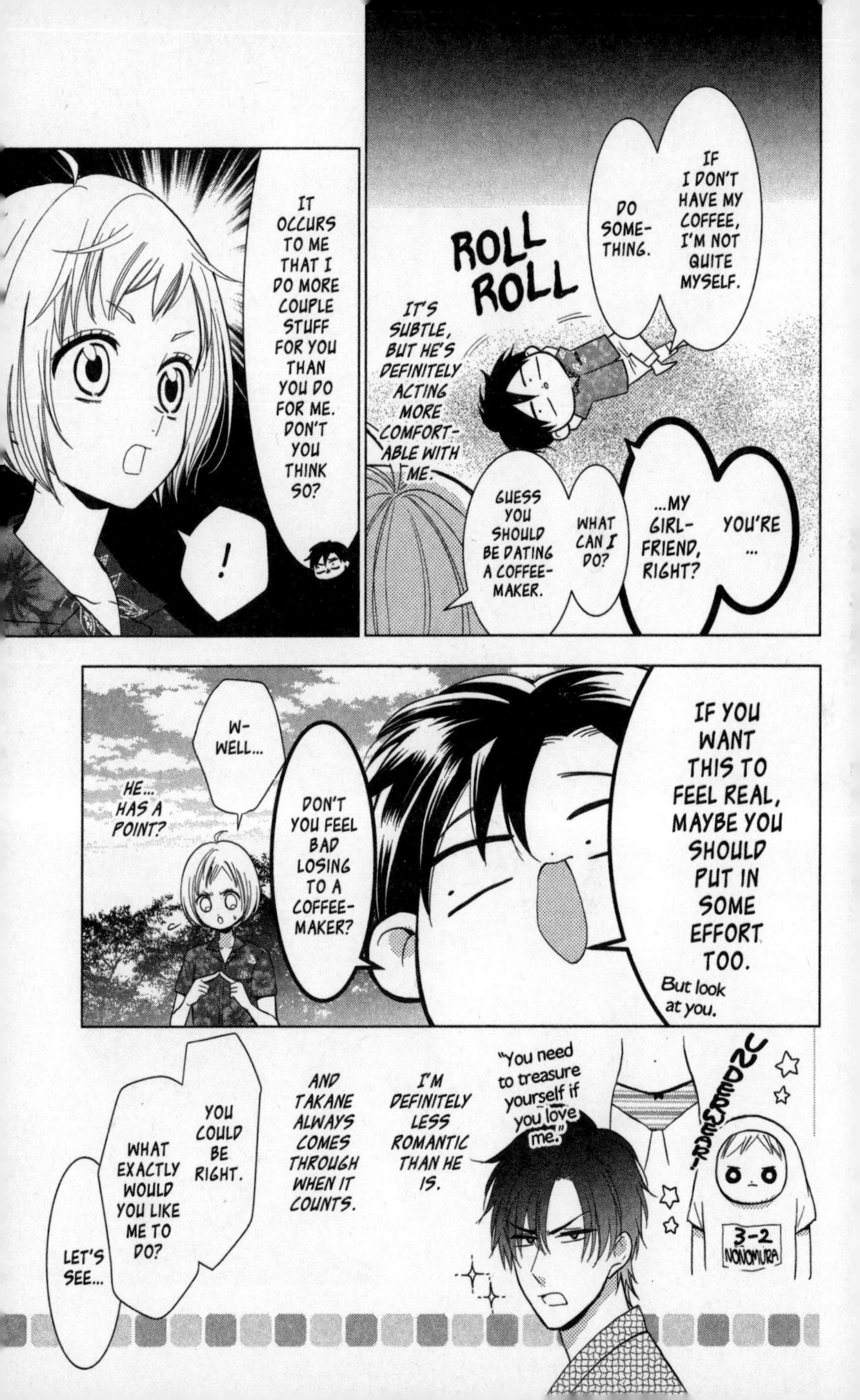
IF I DON'T HAVE MY COFFEE, I'M NOT QUITE MYSELF.
DO SOME-THING.
ROLL ROLL
IT'S SUBTLE, BUT HE'S DEFINITELY ACTING MORE COMFORT-ABLE WITH ME.
YOU'RE ...
...MY GIRL-FRIEND, RIGHT?
WHAT CAN I DO?
GUESS YOU SHOULD BE DATING A COFFEE-MAKER.
IT OCCURS TO ME THAT I DO MORE COUPLE STUFF FOR YOU THAN YOU DO FOR ME. DON'T YOU THINK SO?
!
IF YOU WANT THIS TO FEEL REAL, MAYBE YOU SHOULD PUT IN SOME EFFORT TOO.
But look at you.
DON'T YOU FEEL BAD LOSING TO A COFFEE-MAKER?
W-WELL...
HE... HAS A POINT?
UNDERWEAR!
3-2 NONOMURA
"You need to treasure yourself if you love me."
I'M DEFINITELY LESS ROMANTIC THAN HE IS.
AND TAKANE ALWAYS COMES THROUGH WHEN IT COUNTS.
YOU COULD BE RIGHT.
WHAT EXACTLY WOULD YOU LIKE ME TO DO?
LET'S SEE...

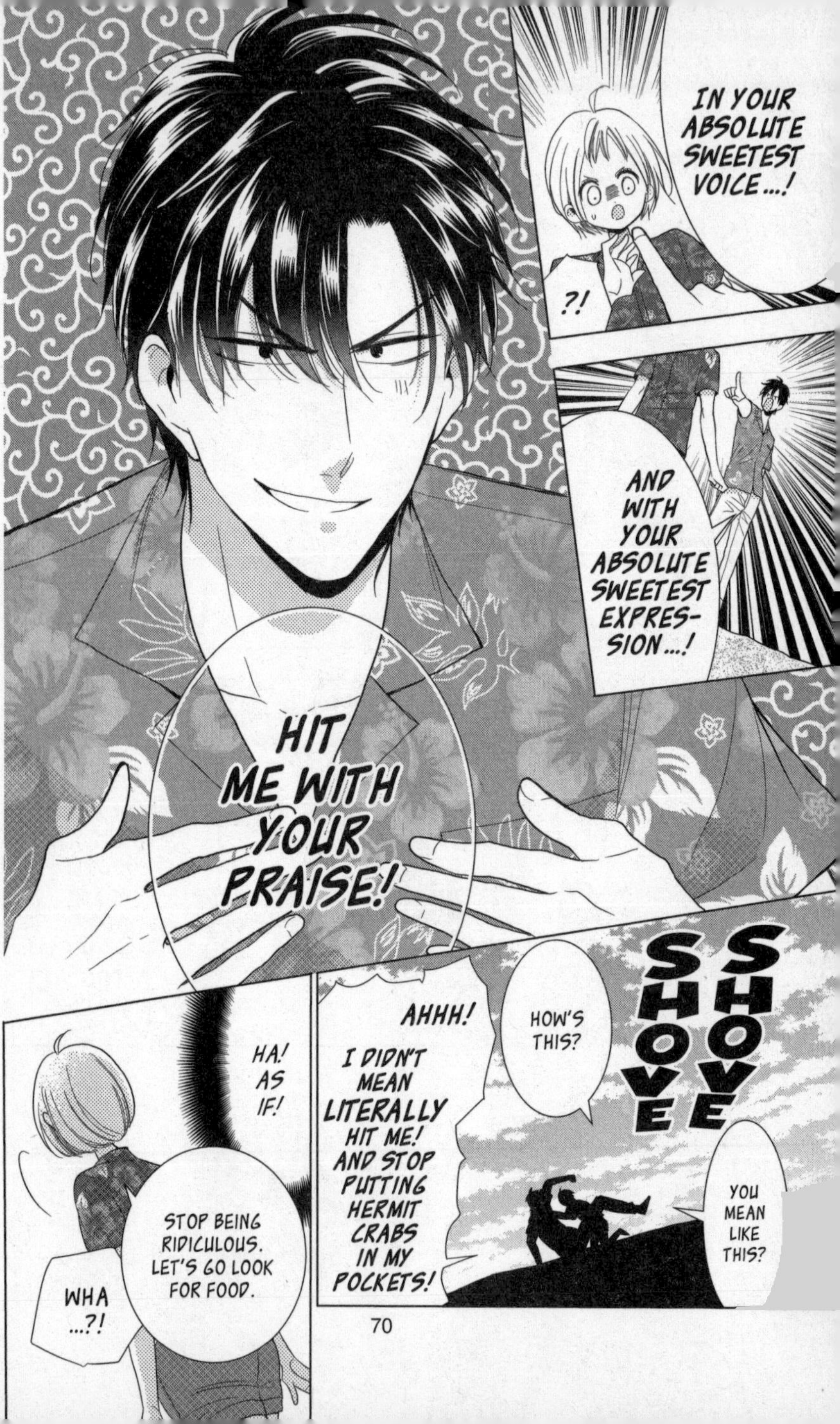
IN YOUR ABSOLUTE SWEETEST VOICE...!
?!
AND WITH YOUR ABSOLUTE SWEETEST EXPRES-SION...!
HIT ME WITH YOUR PRAISE!
SHOVE SHOVE
HOW'S THIS?
YOU MEAN LIKE THIS?
AHHH!
I DIDN'T MEAN LITERALLY HIT ME! AND STOP PUTTING HERMIT CRABS IN MY POCKETS!
HA! AS IF!
STOP BEING RIDICULOUS. LET'S GO LOOK FOR FOOD.
WHA ...?!

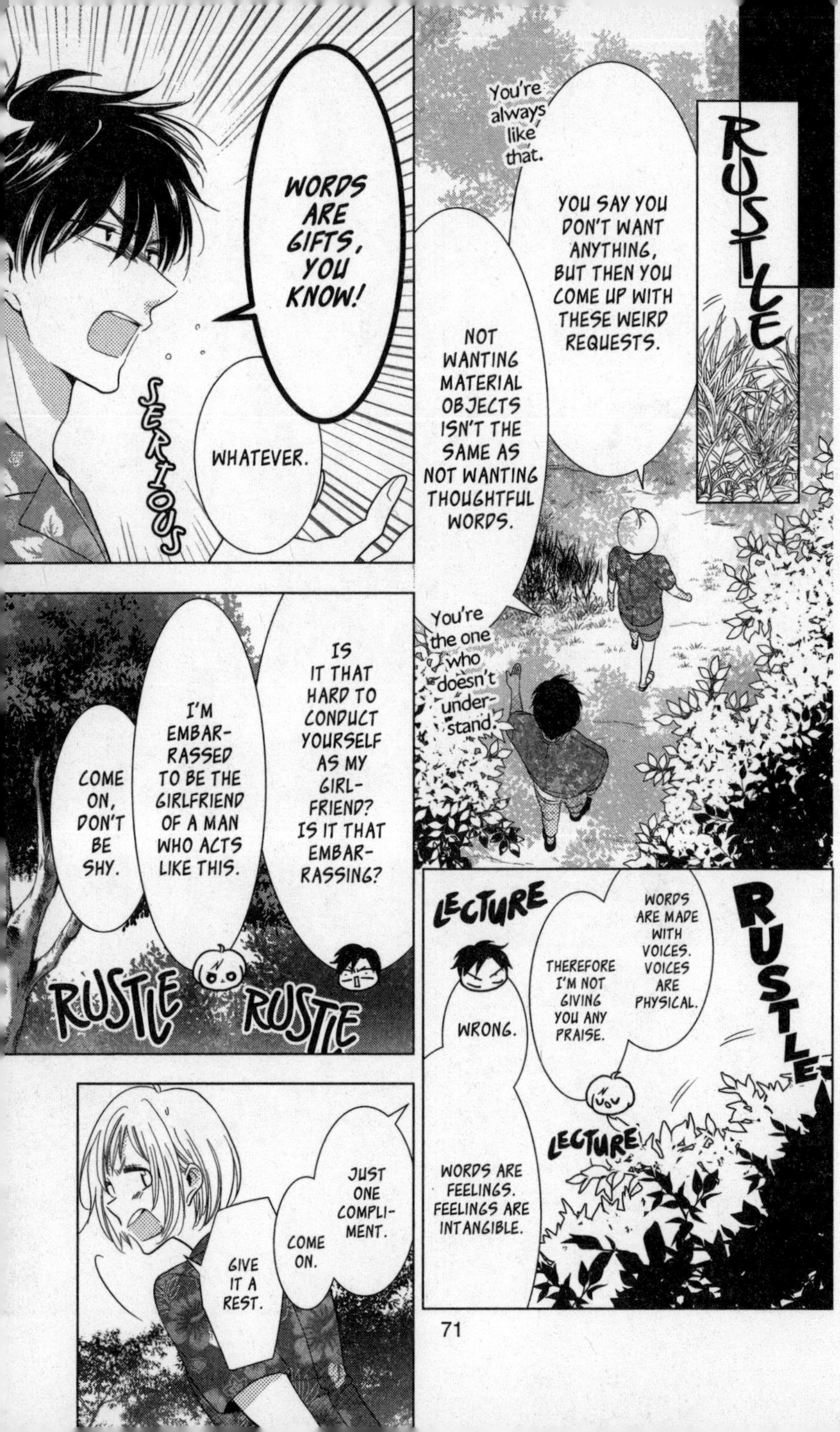
RUSTLE
You're always like that.
YOU SAY YOU DON'T WANT ANYTHING, BUT THEN YOU COME UP WITH THESE WEIRD REQUESTS.
NOT WANTING MATERIAL OBJECTS ISN'T THE SAME AS NOT WANTING THOUGHTFUL WORDS.
You're the one who doesn't understand.
WORDS ARE GIFTS, YOU KNOW!
WHATEVER.
SERIOUS
IS IT THAT HARD TO CONDUCT YOURSELF AS MY GIRLFRIEND? IS IT THAT EMBARRASSING?
I'M EMBARRASSED TO BE THE GIRLFRIEND OF A MAN WHO ACTS LIKE THIS.
COME ON, DON'T BE SHY.
RUSTLE
RUSTLE
RUSTLE
LECTURE
WORDS ARE MADE WITH VOICES. VOICES ARE PHYSICAL.
THEREFORE I'M NOT GIVING YOU ANY PRAISE.
WRONG.
WORDS ARE FEELINGS. FEELINGS ARE INTANGIBLE.
LECTURE
JUST ONE COMPLIMENT.
COME ON.
GIVE IT A REST.

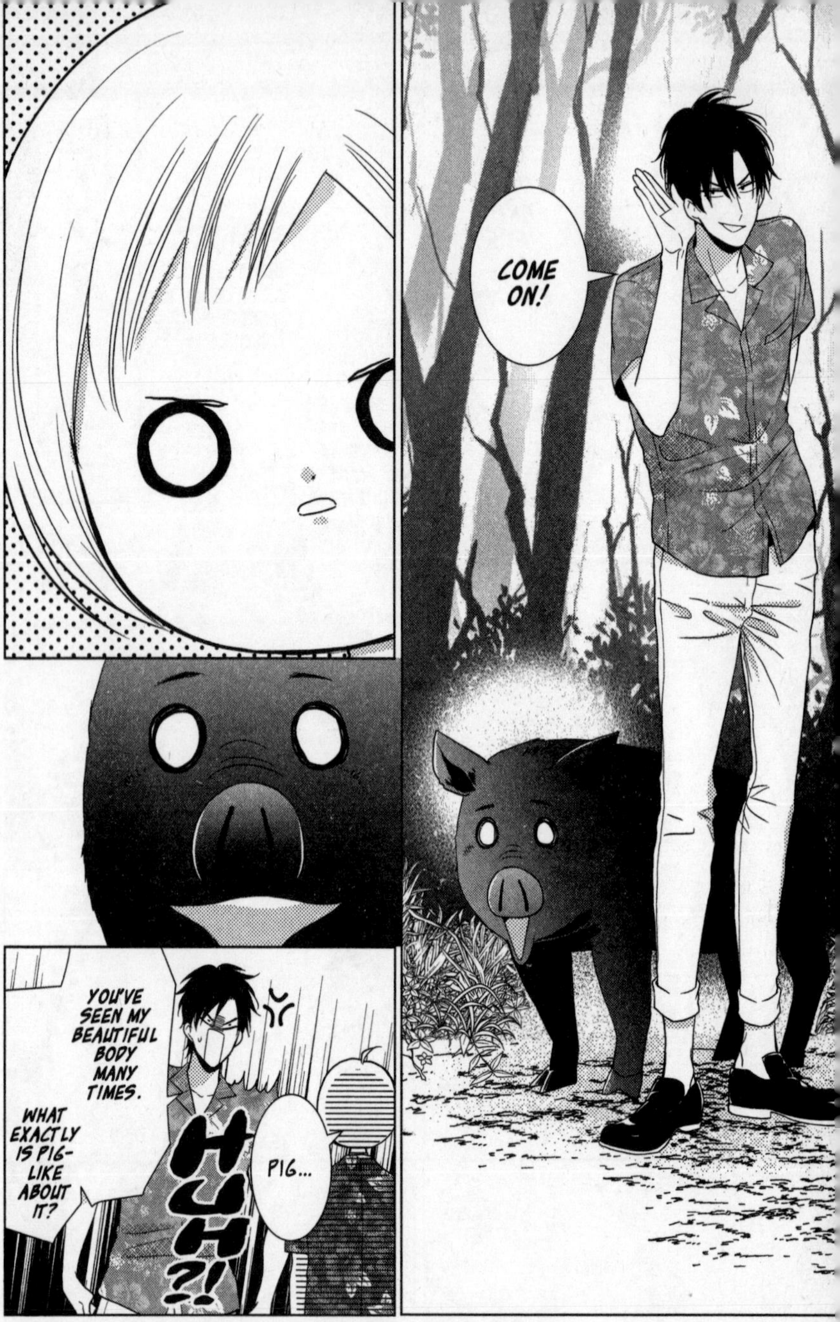
COME ON!
YOU'VE SEEN MY BEAUTIFUL BODY MANY TIMES.
WHAT EXACTLY IS PIG-LIKE ABOUT IT?
HUH?!
PIG...

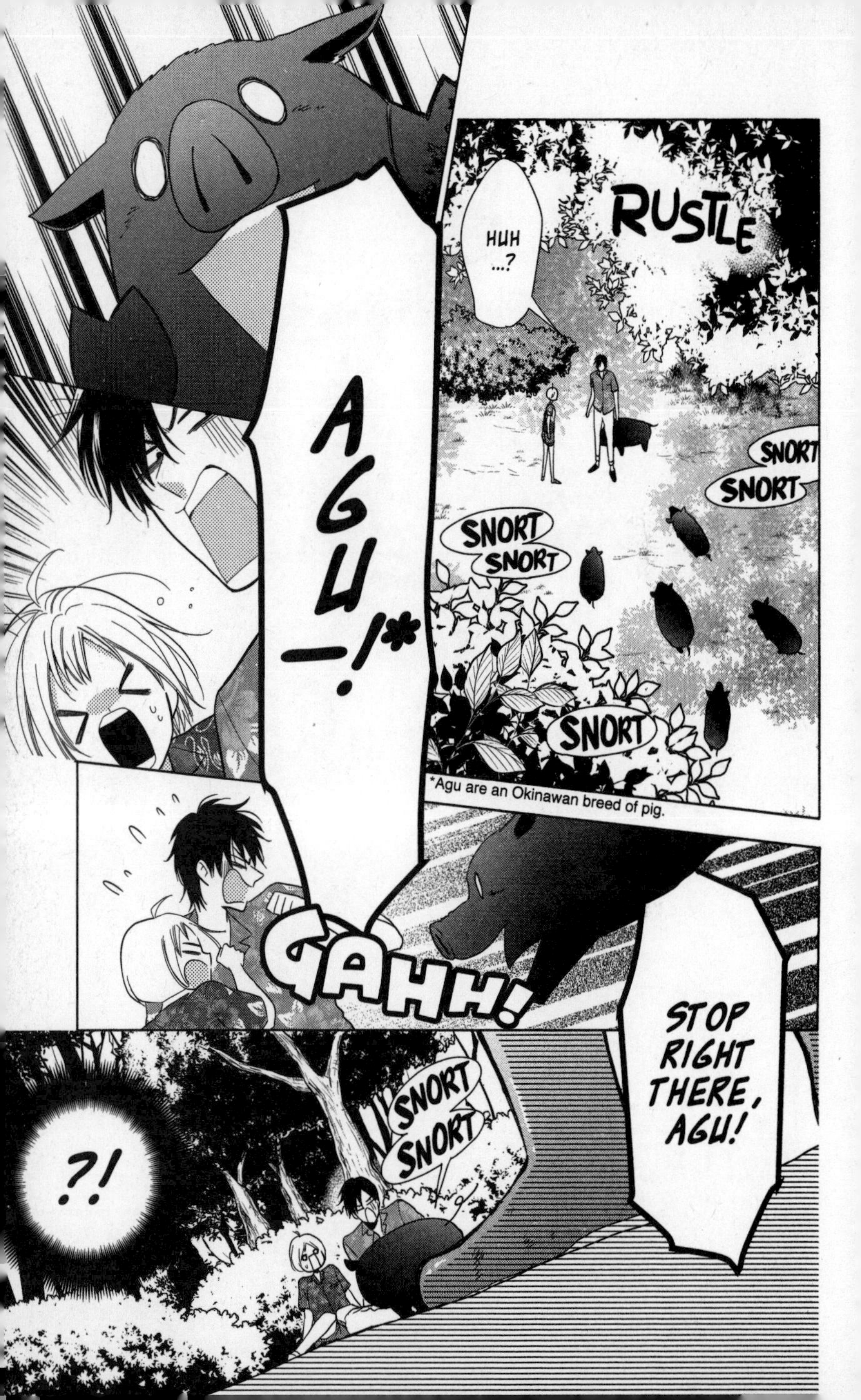
RUSTLE
HUH ...?
SNORT SNORT
SNORT SNORT
SNORT
AGU—!*
STOP RIGHT THERE, AGU!
GAHH!
SNORT SNORT
?!
*Agu are an Okinawan breed of pig.

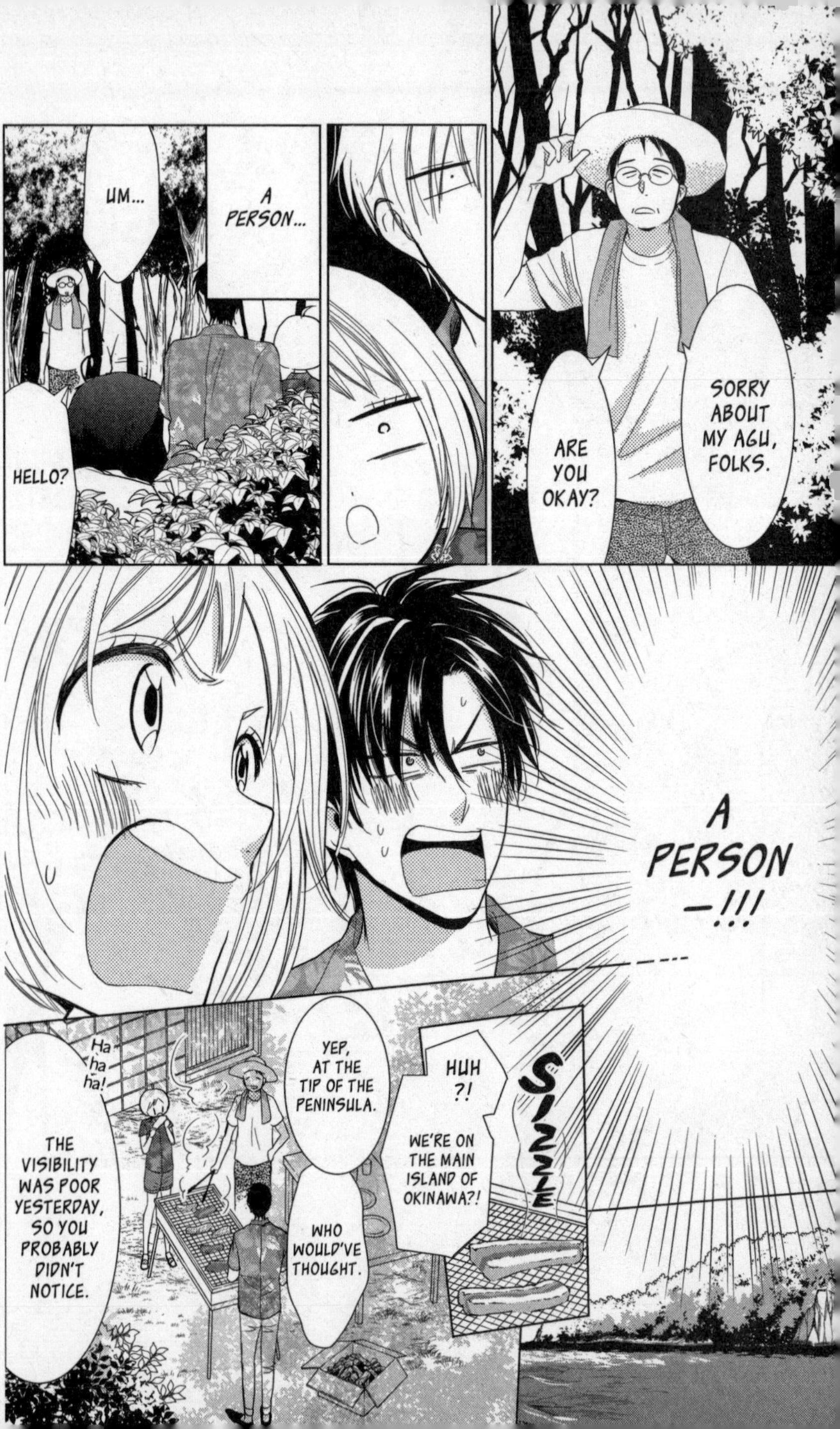

SORRY ABOUT MY AGU, FOLKS.
ARE YOU OKAY?
A PERSON...
UM...
HELLO?
A PERSON—!!!
SIZZLE
HUH?!
WE'RE ON THE MAIN ISLAND OF OKINAWA?!
YEP, AT THE TIP OF THE PENINSULA.
WHO WOULD'VE THOUGHT.
Ha ha ha!
THE VISIBILITY WAS POOR YESTERDAY, SO YOU PROBABLY DIDN'T NOTICE.

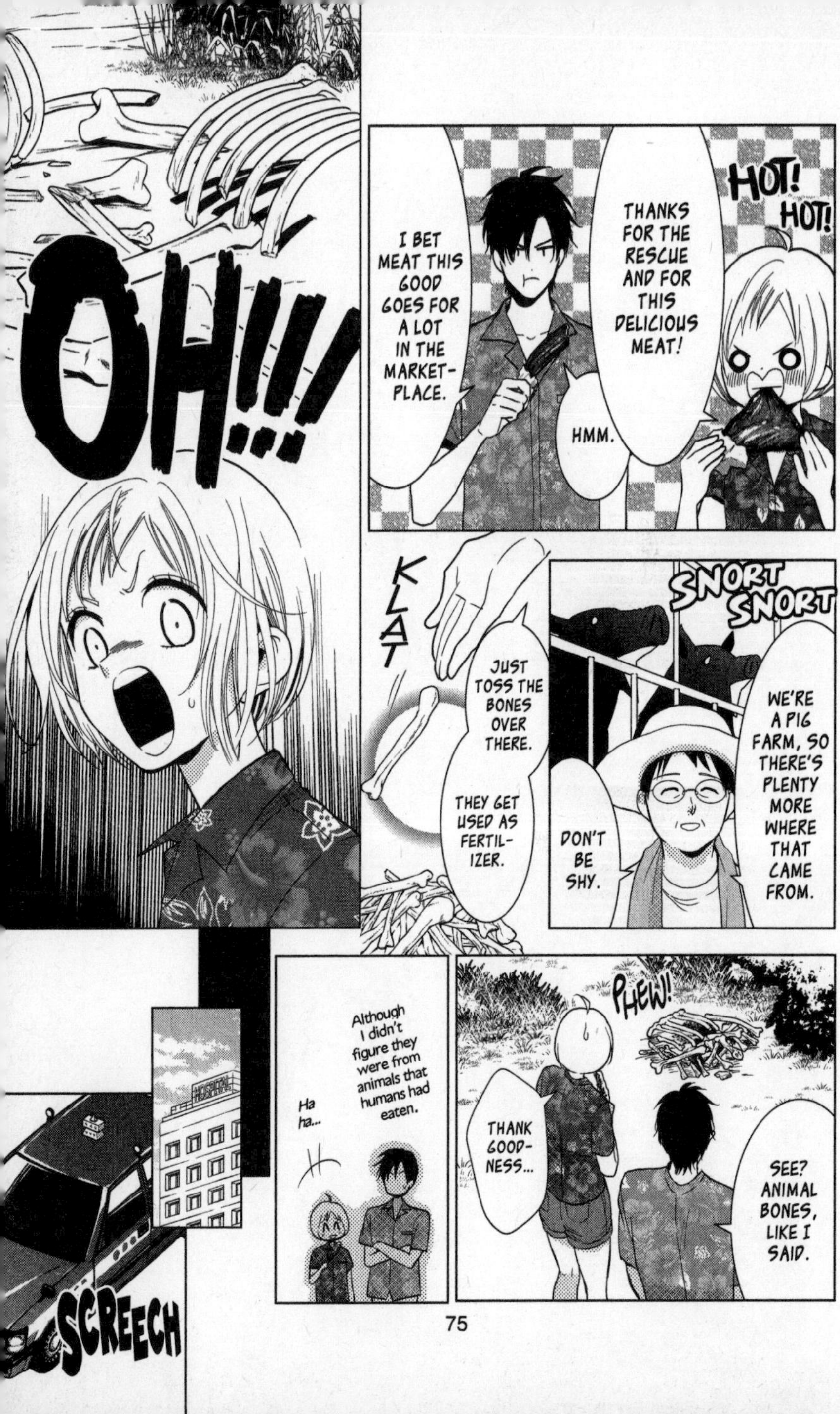

HOT! HOT!
THANKS FOR THE RESCUE AND FOR THIS DELICIOUS MEAT!
HMM.
I BET MEAT THIS GOOD GOES FOR A LOT IN THE MARKET-PLACE.
SNORT SNORT
WE'RE A PIG FARM, SO THERE'S PLENTY MORE WHERE THAT CAME FROM.
DON'T BE SHY.
JUST TOSS THE BONES OVER THERE.
THEY GET USED AS FERTIL-IZER.
KLAT
OH!!!
PHEW!
SEE? ANIMAL BONES, LIKE I SAID.
THANK GOOD-NESS...
Although I didn't figure they were from animals that humans had eaten.
Ha ha...
HOSPITAL
SCREECH

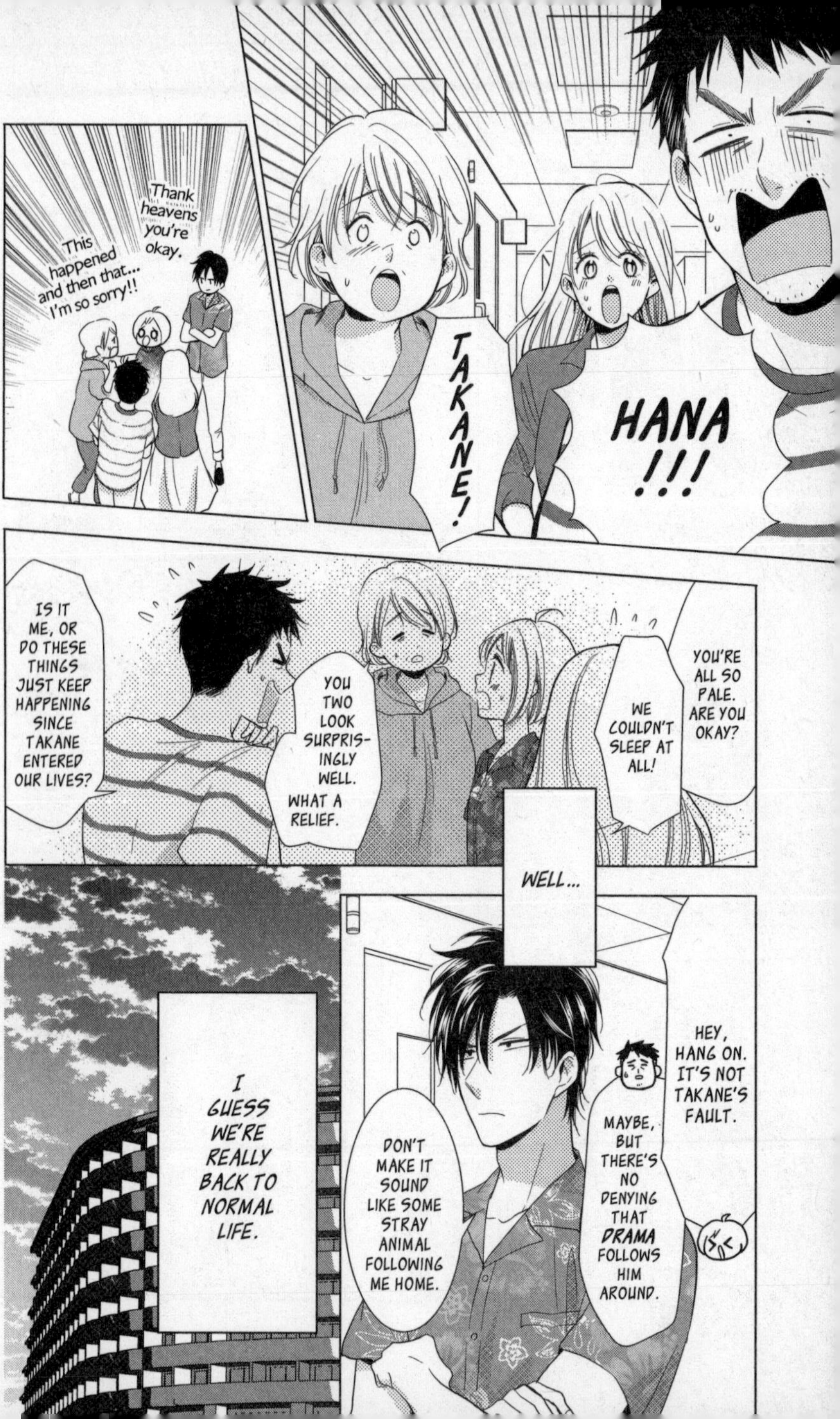
HANA !!!
TAKANE!
Thank heavens you're okay.
This happened and then that... I'm so sorry!!
YOU'RE ALL SO PALE. ARE YOU OKAY?
WE COULDN'T SLEEP AT ALL!
YOU TWO LOOK SURPRISINGLY WELL.
WHAT A RELIEF.
IS IT ME, OR DO THESE THINGS JUST KEEP HAPPENING SINCE TAKANE ENTERED OUR LIVES?
WELL...
HEY, HANG ON. IT'S NOT TAKANE'S FAULT.
MAYBE, BUT THERE'S NO DENYING THAT DRAMA FOLLOWS HIM AROUND.
DON'T MAKE IT SOUND LIKE SOME STRAY ANIMAL FOLLOWING ME HOME.
I GUESS WE'RE REALLY BACK TO NORMAL LIFE.

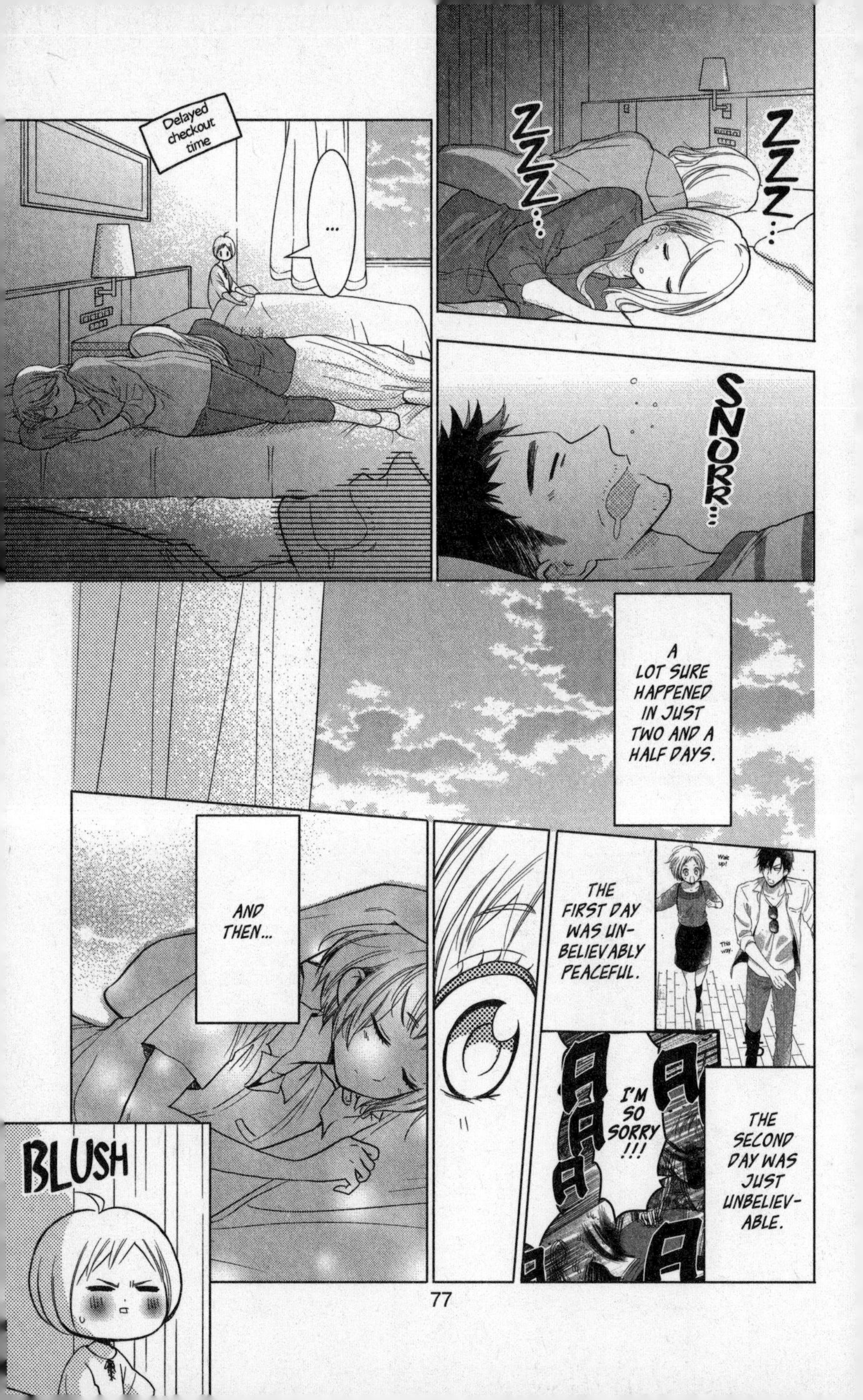
ZZZ...
ZZZ...
SNORR...
Delayed checkout time
...
A LOT SURE HAPPENED IN JUST TWO AND A HALF DAYS.
Wake up!
This way.
THE FIRST DAY WAS UNBELIEVABLY PEACEFUL.
THE SECOND DAY WAS JUST UNBELIEVABLE.
I'M SO SORRY!!!
AAAA
AND THEN...
BLUSH

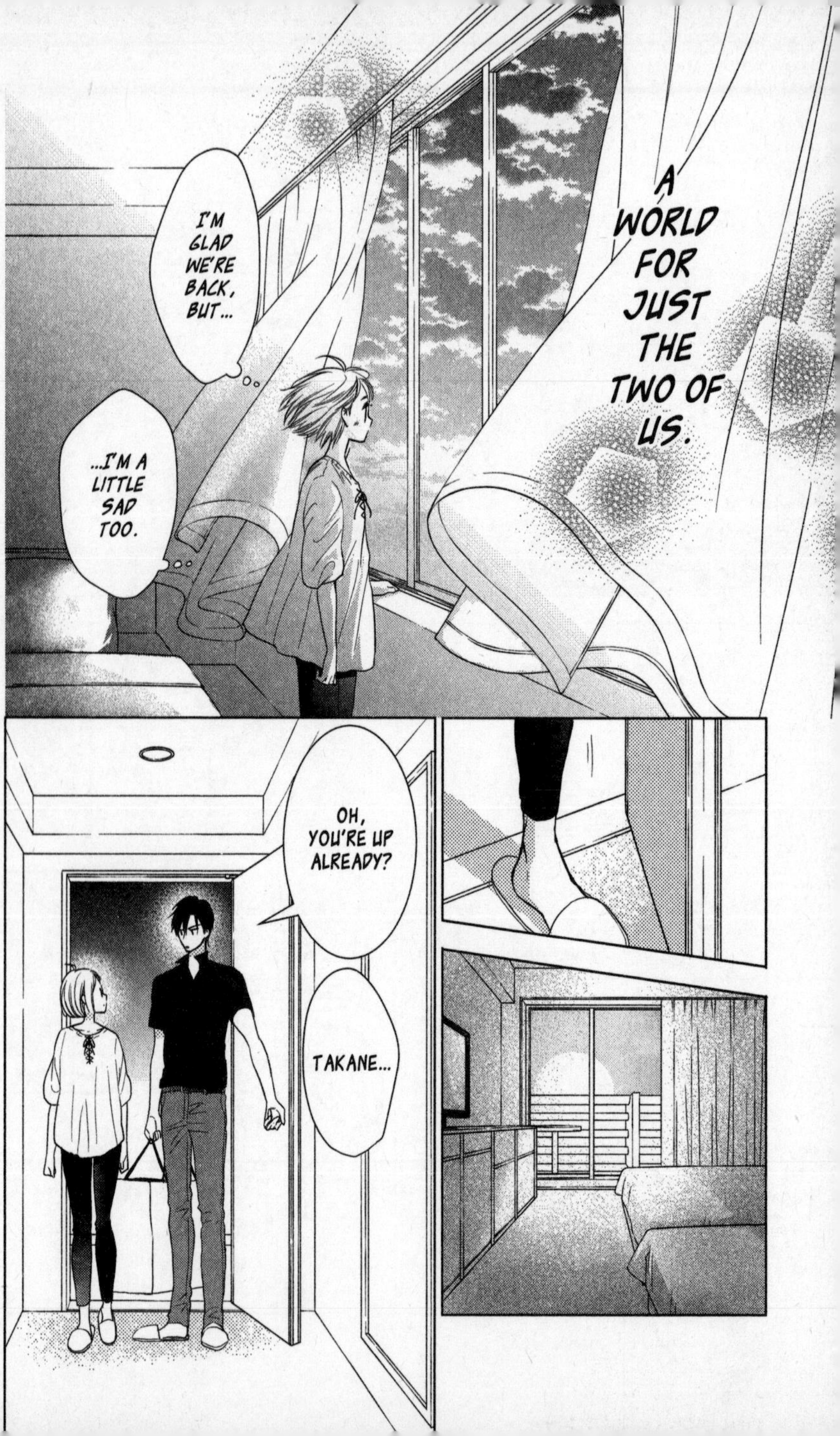
A WORLD FOR JUST THE TWO OF US.
I'M GLAD WE'RE BACK, BUT...
...I'M A LITTLE SAD TOO.
OH, YOU'RE UP ALREADY?
TAKANE...

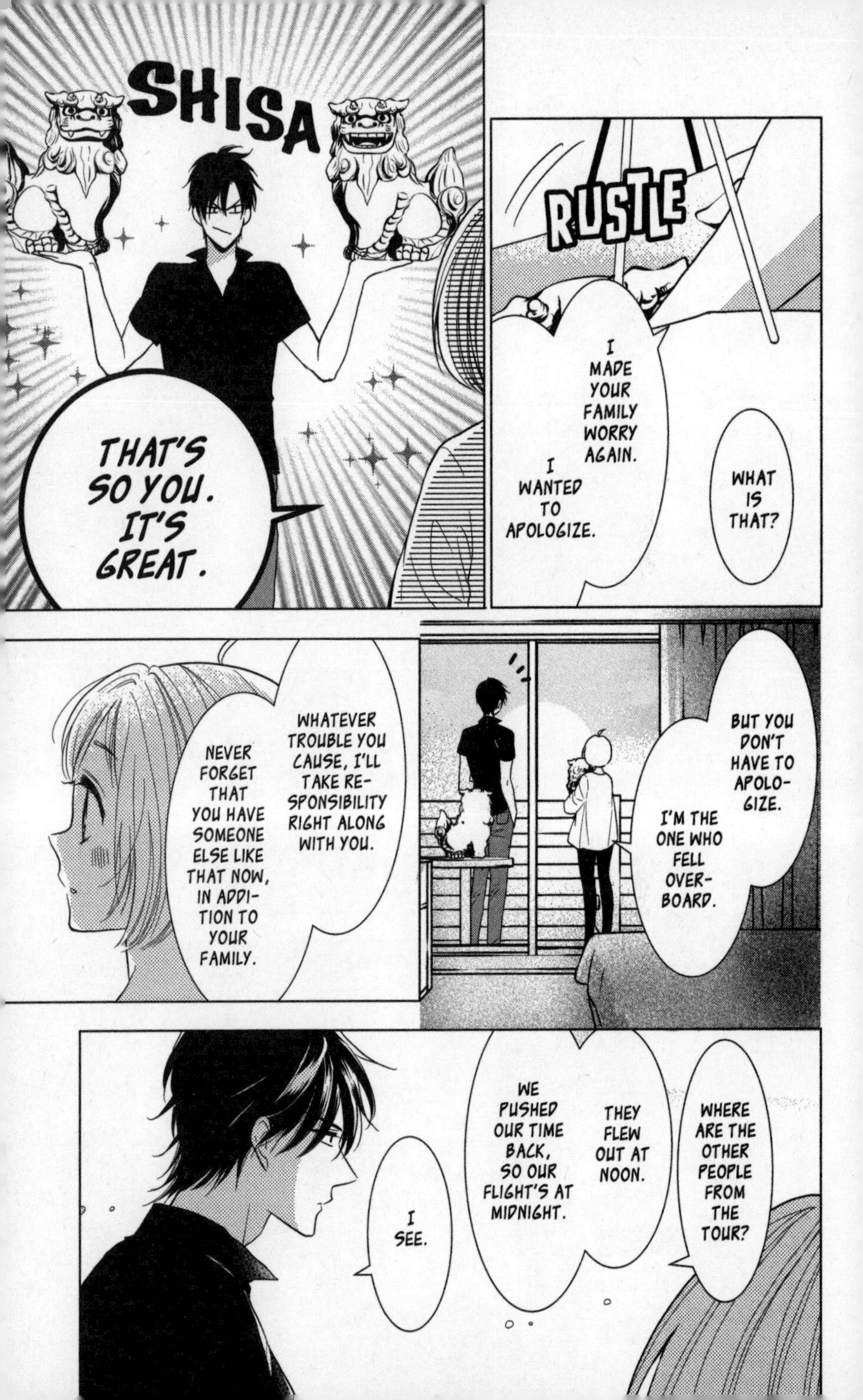
RUSTLE
WHAT IS THAT?
I MADE YOUR FAMILY WORRY AGAIN.
I WANTED TO APOLOGIZE.
SHISA
THAT'S SO YOU. IT'S GREAT.
BUT YOU DON'T HAVE TO APOLO-GIZE.
I'M THE ONE WHO FELL OVER-BOARD.
WHATEVER TROUBLE YOU CAUSE, I'LL TAKE RE-SPONSIBILITY RIGHT ALONG WITH YOU.
NEVER FORGET THAT YOU HAVE SOMEONE ELSE LIKE THAT NOW, IN ADDI-TION TO YOUR FAMILY.
WHERE ARE THE OTHER PEOPLE FROM THE TOUR?
THEY FLEW OUT AT NOON.
WE PUSHED OUR TIME BACK, SO OUR FLIGHT'S AT MIDNIGHT.
I SEE.

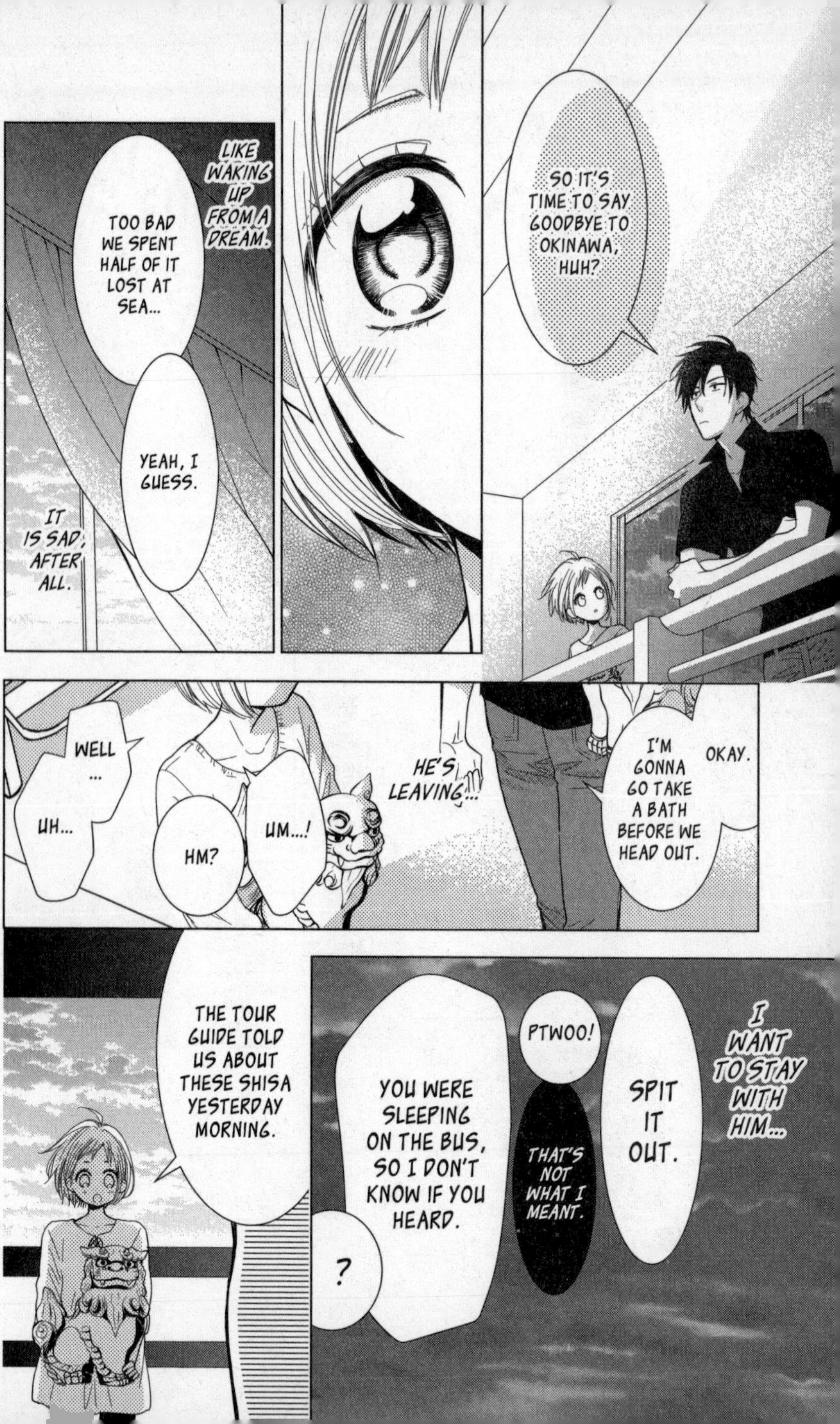
SO IT'S TIME TO SAY GOODBYE TO OKINAWA, HUH?
LIKE WAKING UP FROM A DREAM.
TOO BAD WE SPENT HALF OF IT LOST AT SEA...
YEAH, I GUESS.
IT IS SAD, AFTER ALL.
OKAY.
I'M GONNA GO TAKE A BATH BEFORE WE HEAD OUT.
HE'S LEAVING...
UM...!
HM?
WELL ...
UH...
I WANT TO STAY WITH HIM...
SPIT IT OUT.
PTWOO!
THAT'S NOT WHAT I MEANT.
THE TOUR GUIDE TOLD US ABOUT THESE SHISA YESTERDAY MORNING.
YOU WERE SLEEPING ON THE BUS, SO I DON'T KNOW IF YOU HEARD.
?

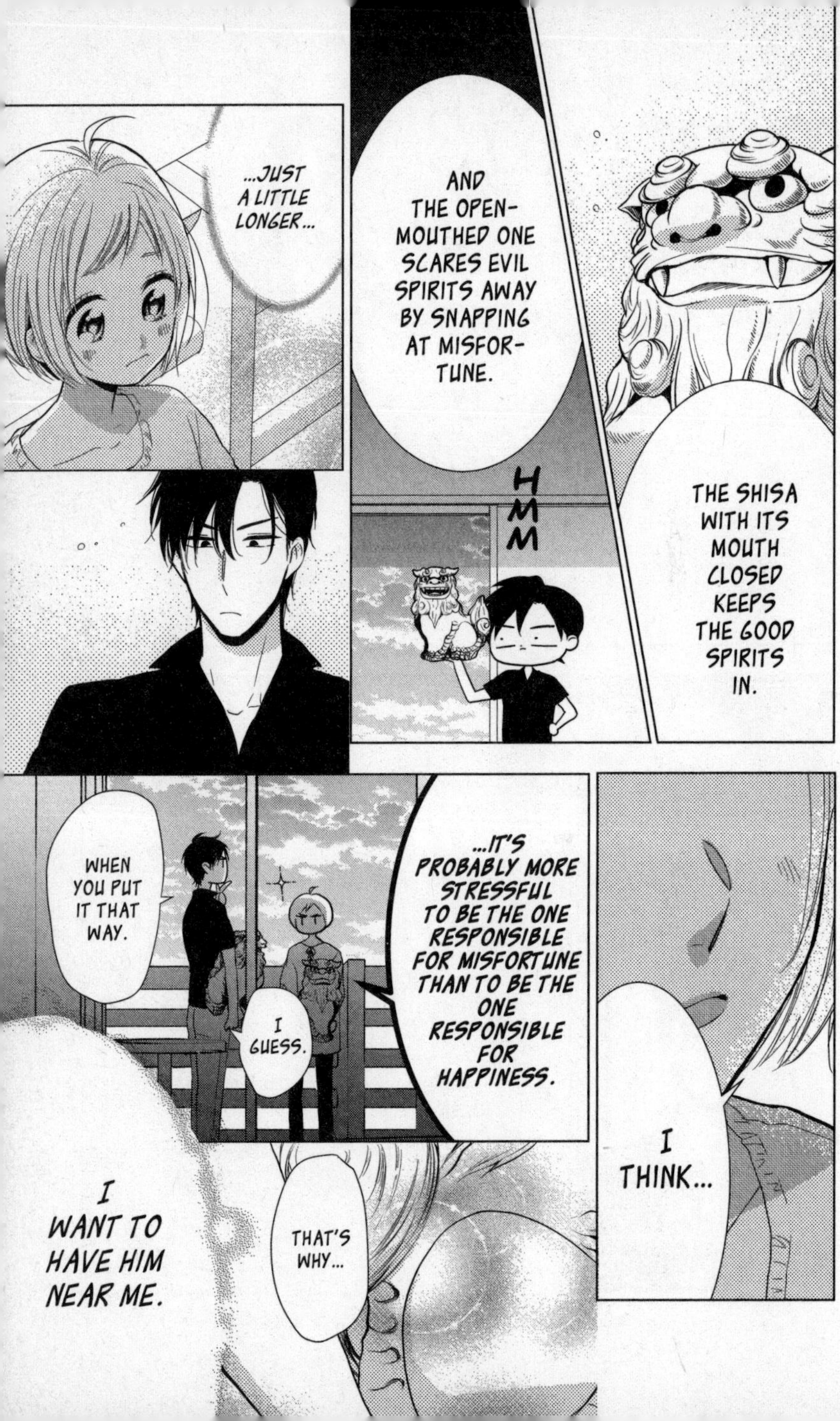
THE SHISA WITH ITS MOUTH CLOSED KEEPS THE GOOD SPIRITS IN.
AND THE OPEN-MOUTHED ONE SCARES EVIL SPIRITS AWAY BY SNAPPING AT MISFORTUNE.
HMM
...JUST A LITTLE LONGER...
I THINK...
...IT'S PROBABLY MORE STRESSFUL TO BE THE ONE RESPONSIBLE FOR MISFORTUNE THAN TO BE THE ONE RESPONSIBLE FOR HAPPINESS.
WHEN YOU PUT IT THAT WAY.
I GUESS.
THAT'S WHY...
I WANT TO HAVE HIM NEAR ME.

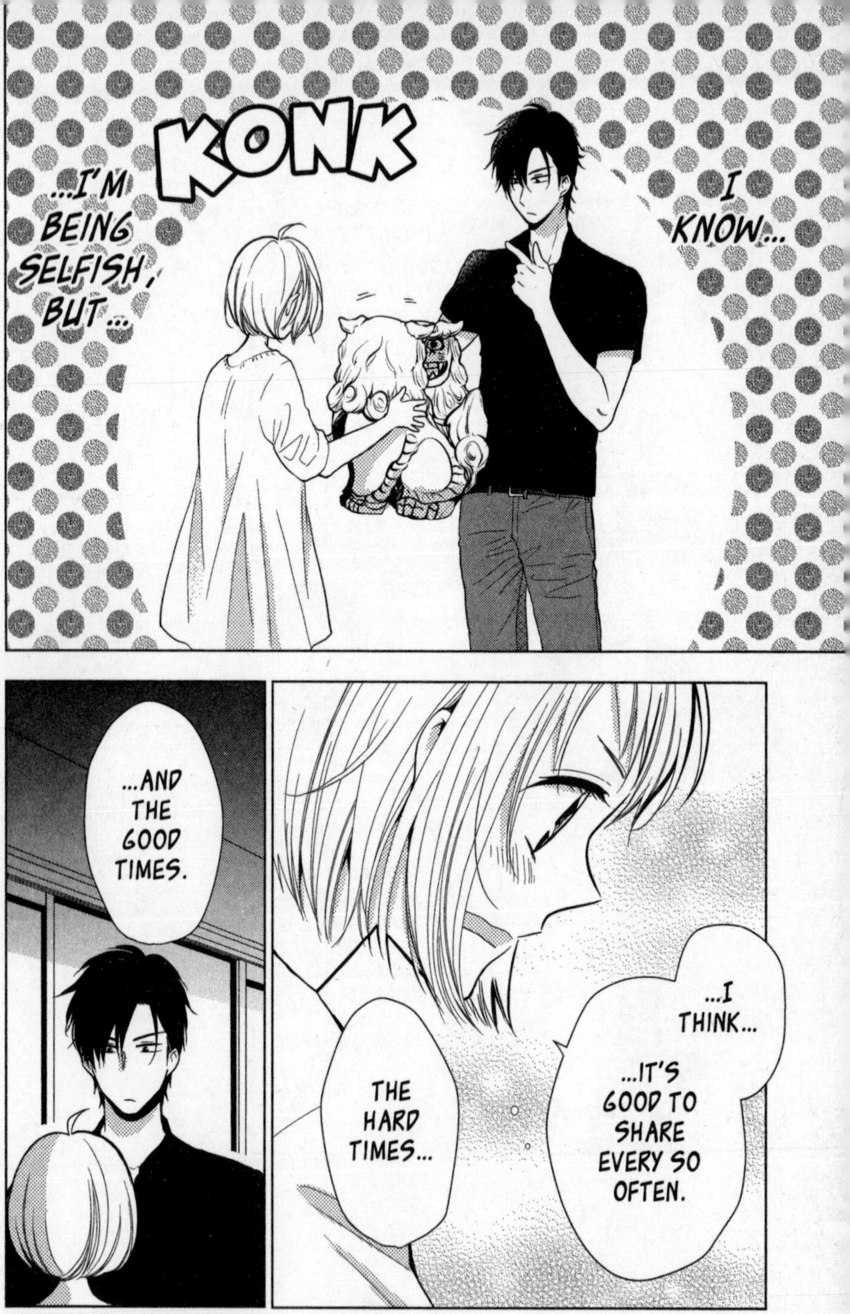
I KNOW...
KONK
...I'M BEING SELFISH, BUT...
...I THINK...
...IT'S GOOD TO SHARE EVERY SO OFTEN.
THE HARD TIMES...
...AND THE GOOD TIMES.

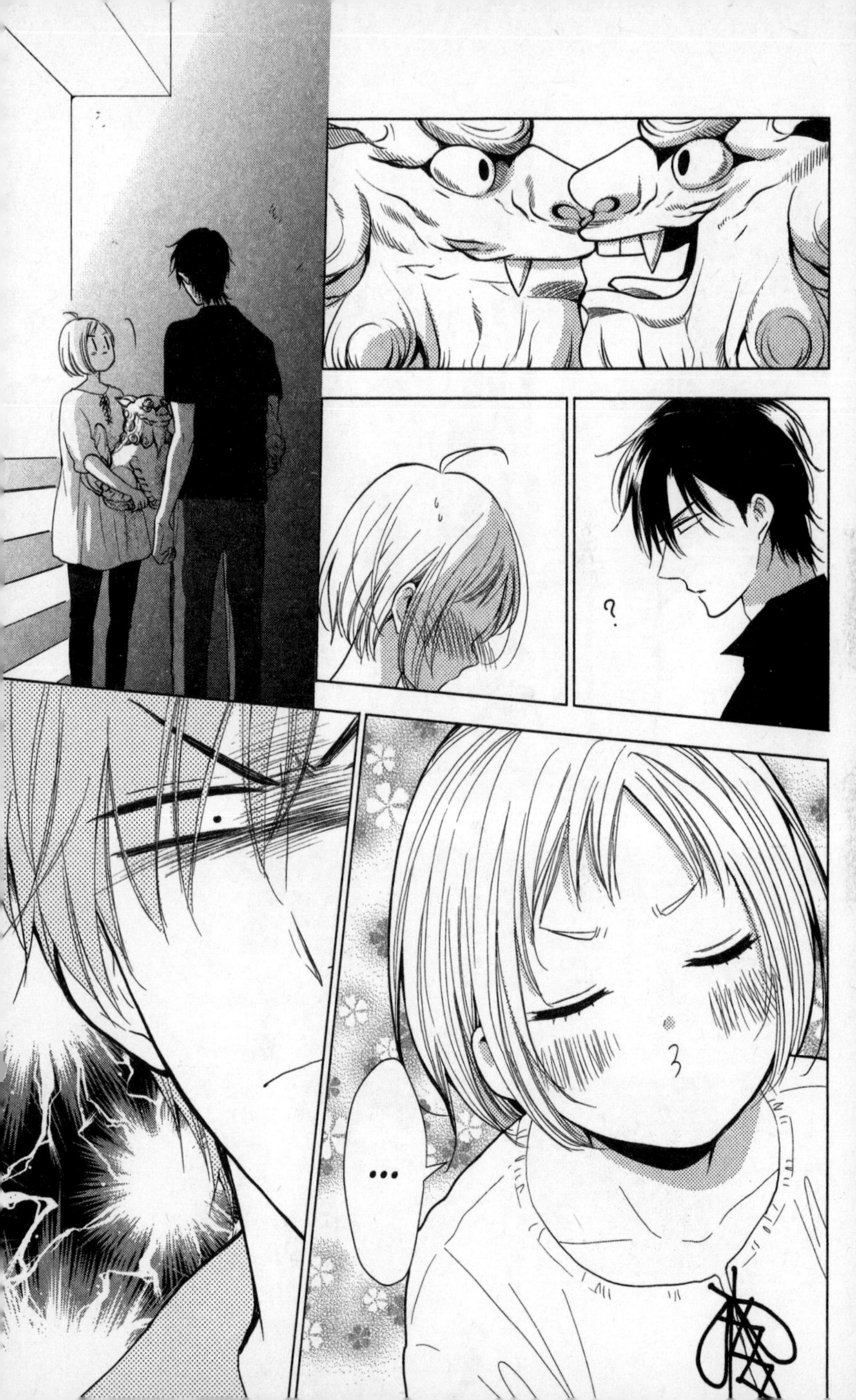
?
...

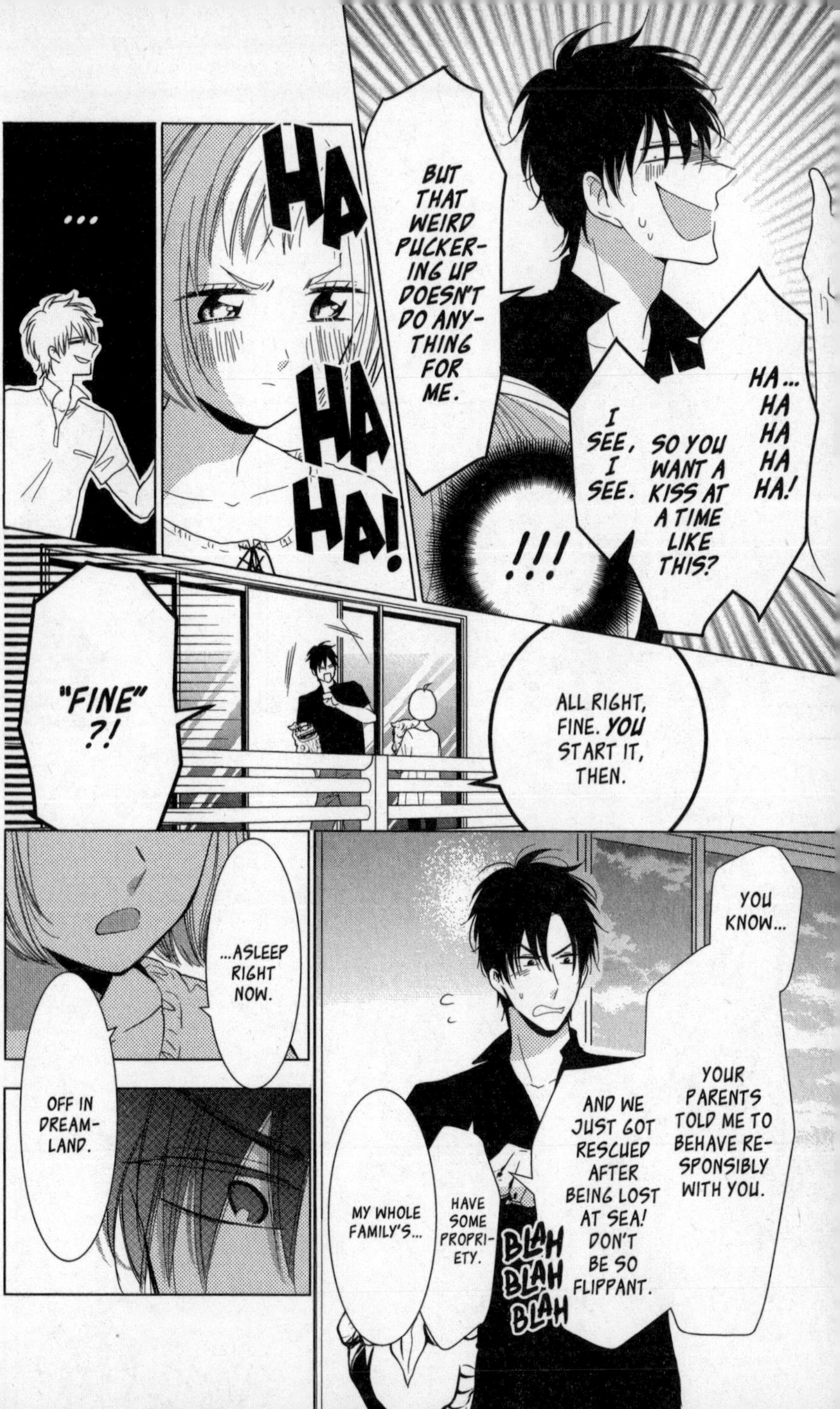
HA... HA HA HA HA!
I SEE, I SEE.
SO YOU WANT A KISS AT A TIME LIKE THIS?
BUT THAT WEIRD PUCKERING UP DOESN'T DO ANYTHING FOR ME.
!!!
HA HA HA!
...
ALL RIGHT, FINE. YOU START IT, THEN.
"FINE" ?!
YOU KNOW...
YOUR PARENTS TOLD ME TO BEHAVE RESPONSIBLY WITH YOU.
AND WE JUST GOT RESCUED AFTER BEING LOST AT SEA! DON'T BE SO FLIPPANT.
BLAH BLAH BLAH
HAVE SOME PROPRIETY.
MY WHOLE FAMILY'S...
...ASLEEP RIGHT NOW.
OFF IN DREAMLAND.

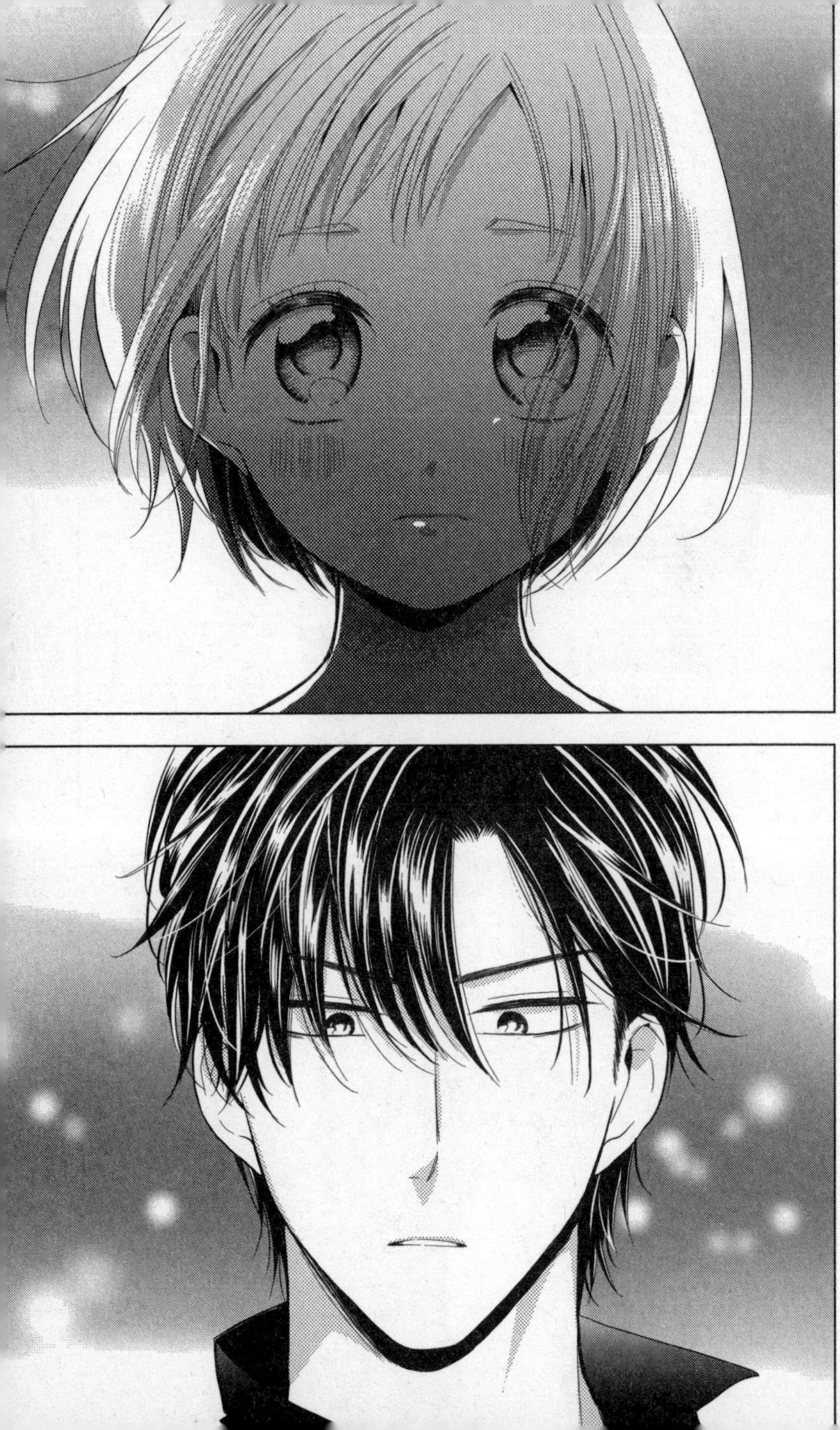

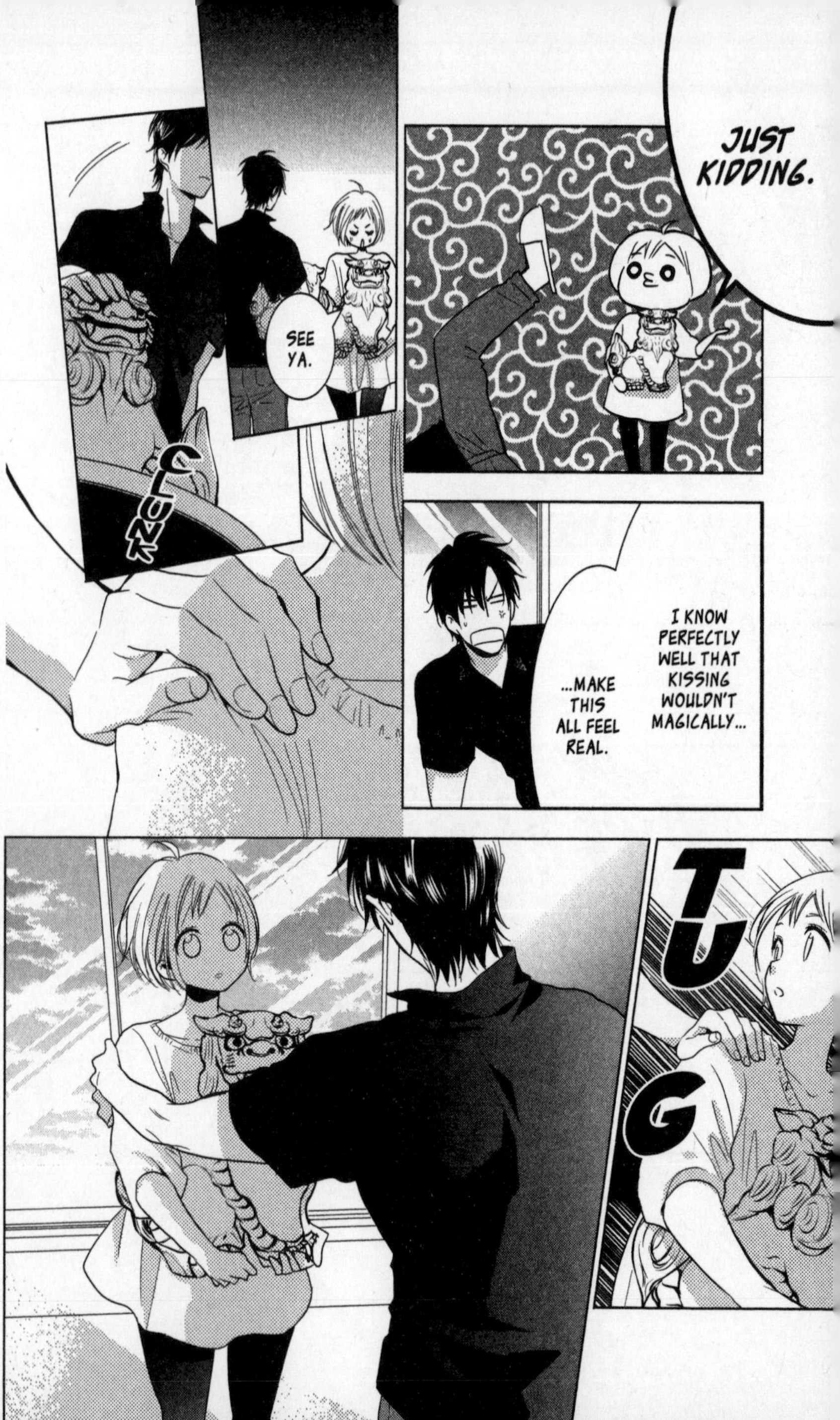
JUST KIDDING.
SEE YA.
CLUNK
I KNOW PERFECTLY WELL THAT KISSING WOULDN'T MAGICALLY...
...MAKE THIS ALL FEEL REAL.
TUG

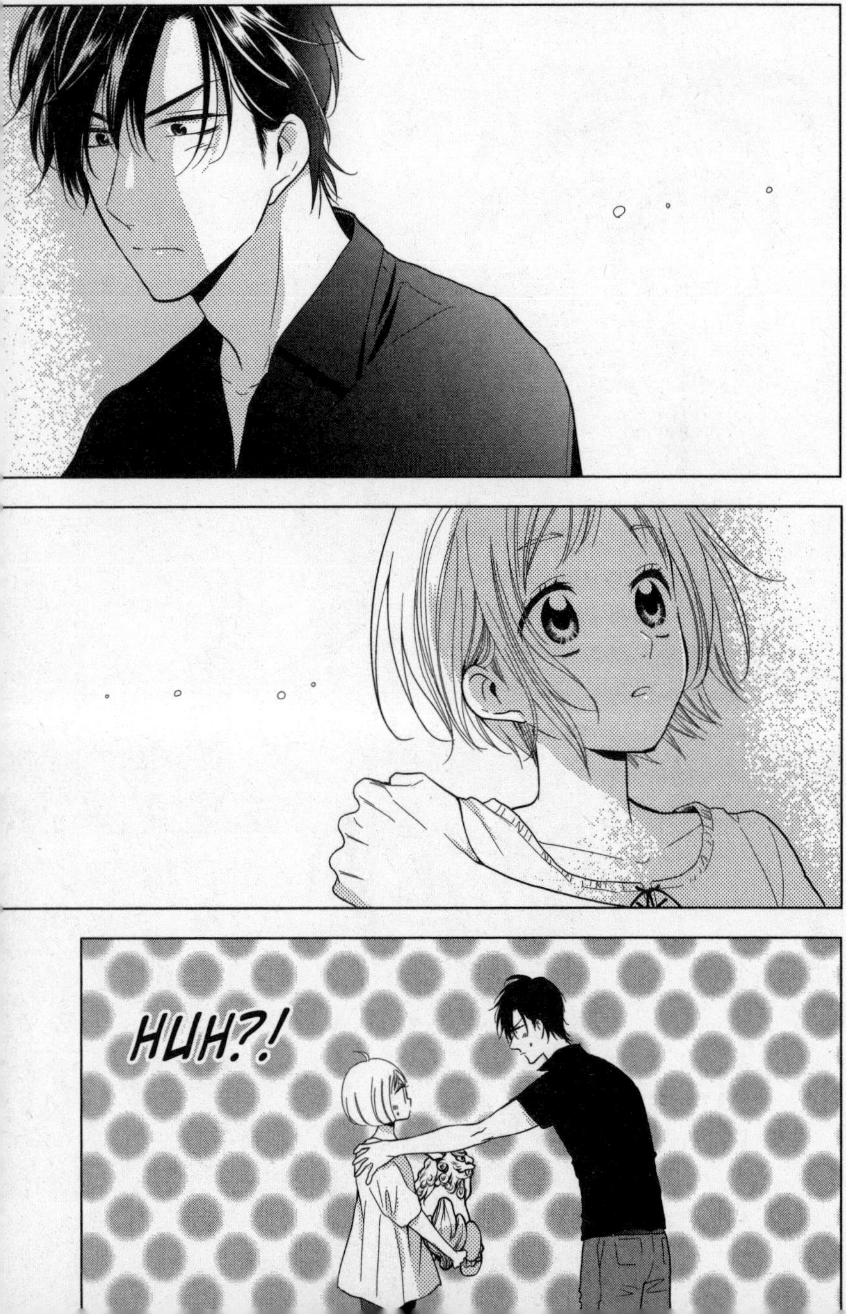
HUH?!

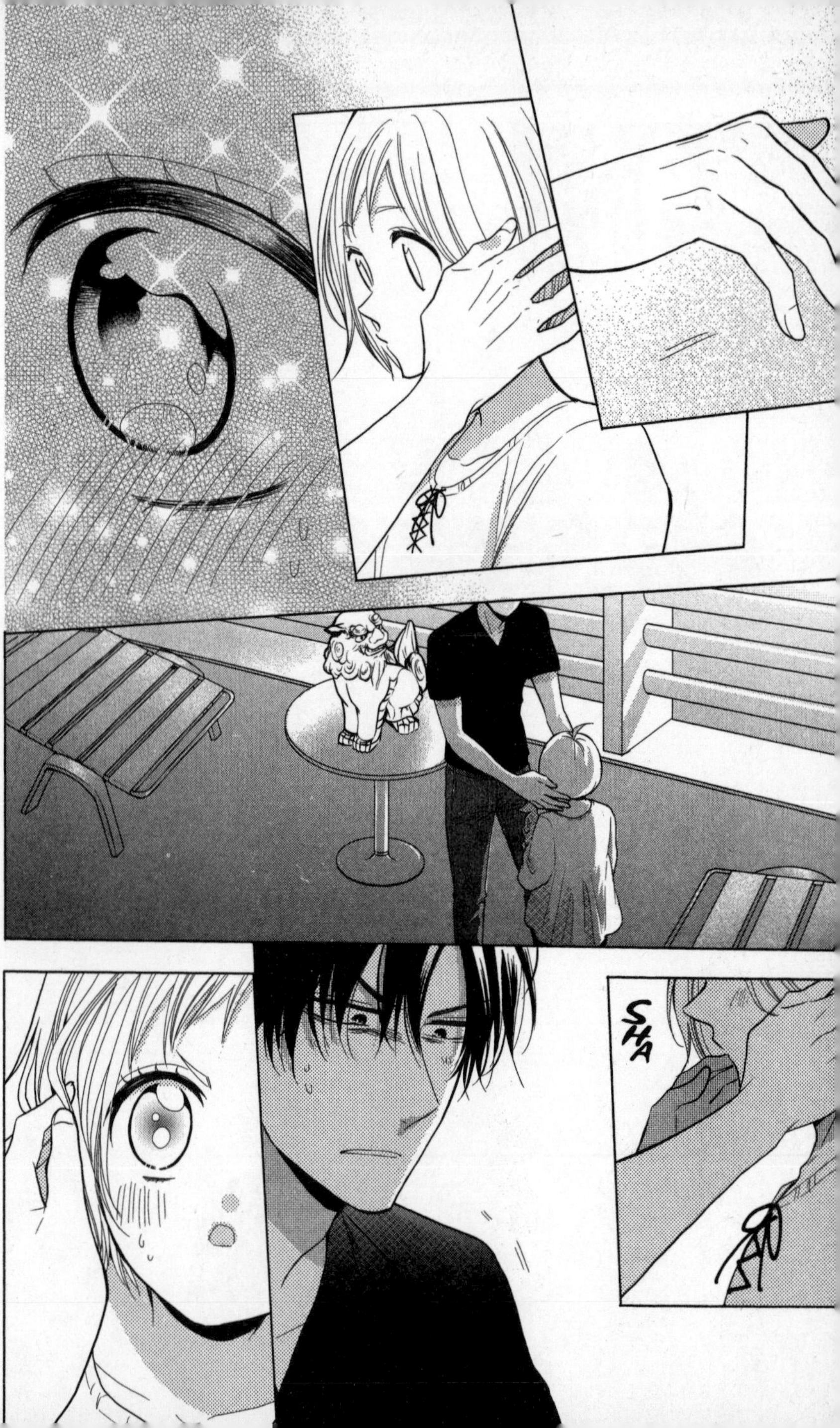
SHA

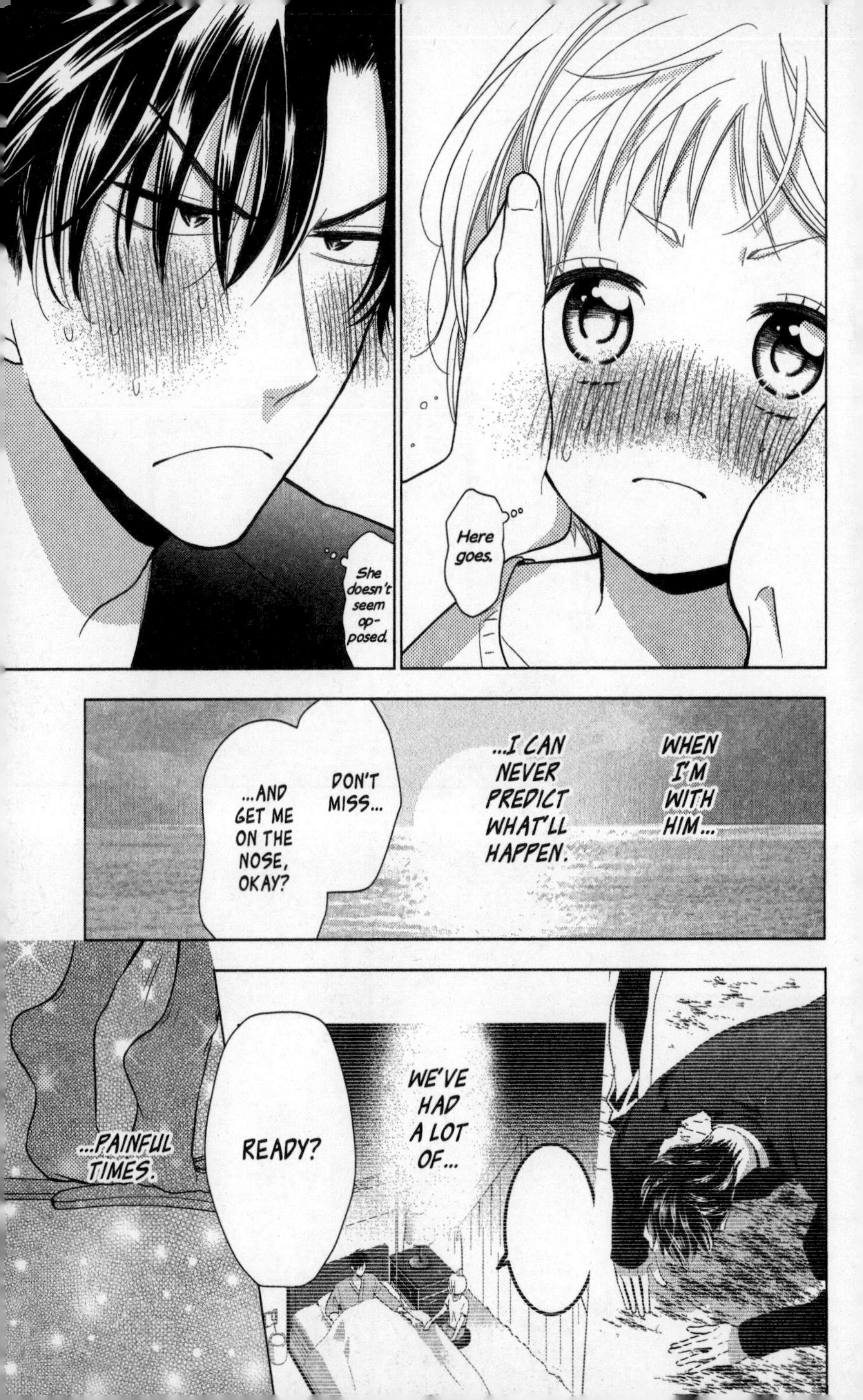
Here goes.
She doesn't seem op-posed.
WHEN I'M WITH HIM...
...I CAN NEVER PREDICT WHAT'LL HAPPEN.
DON'T MISS...
...AND GET ME ON THE NOSE, OKAY?
WE'VE HAD A LOT OF...
READY?
...PAINFUL TIMES.

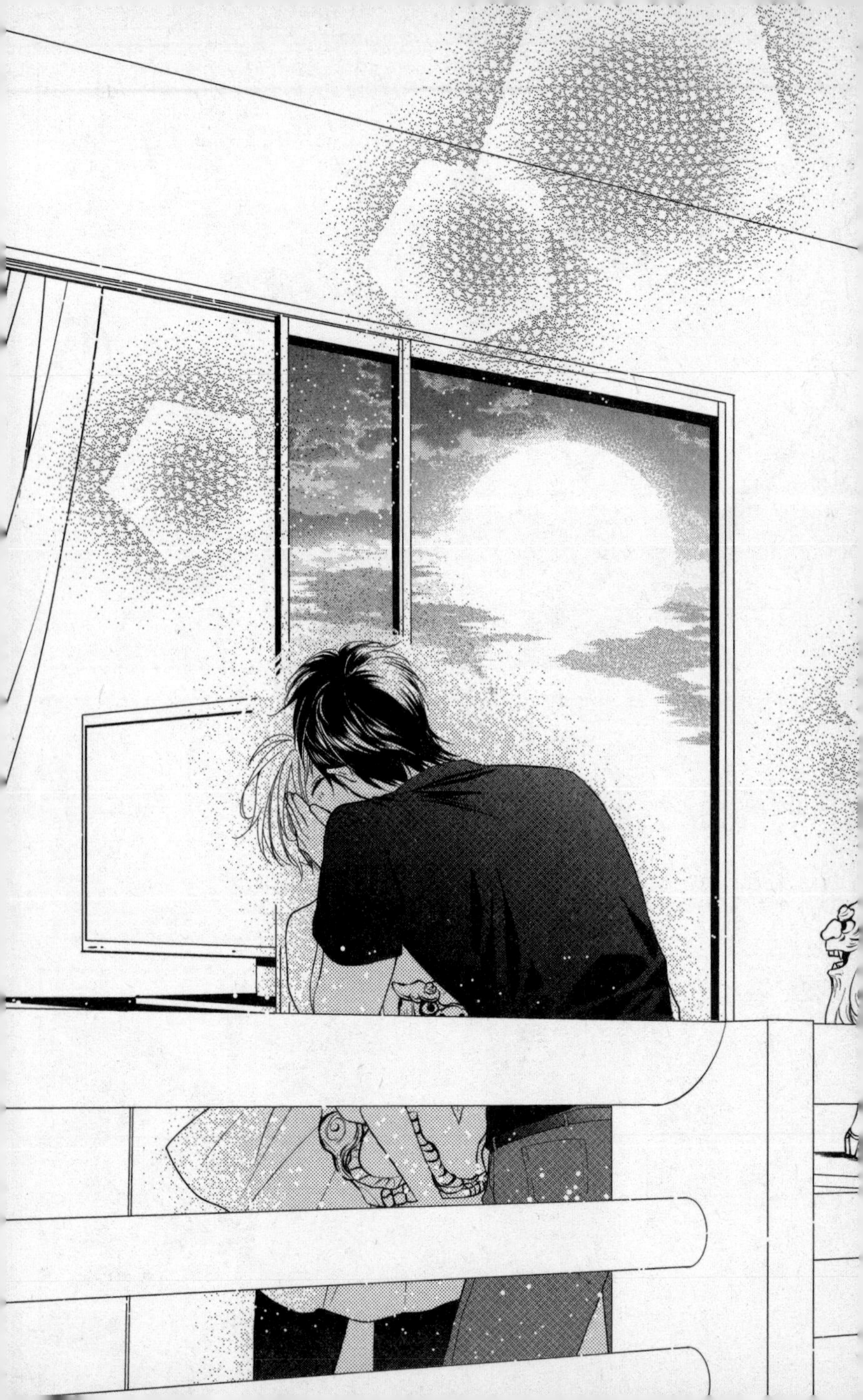

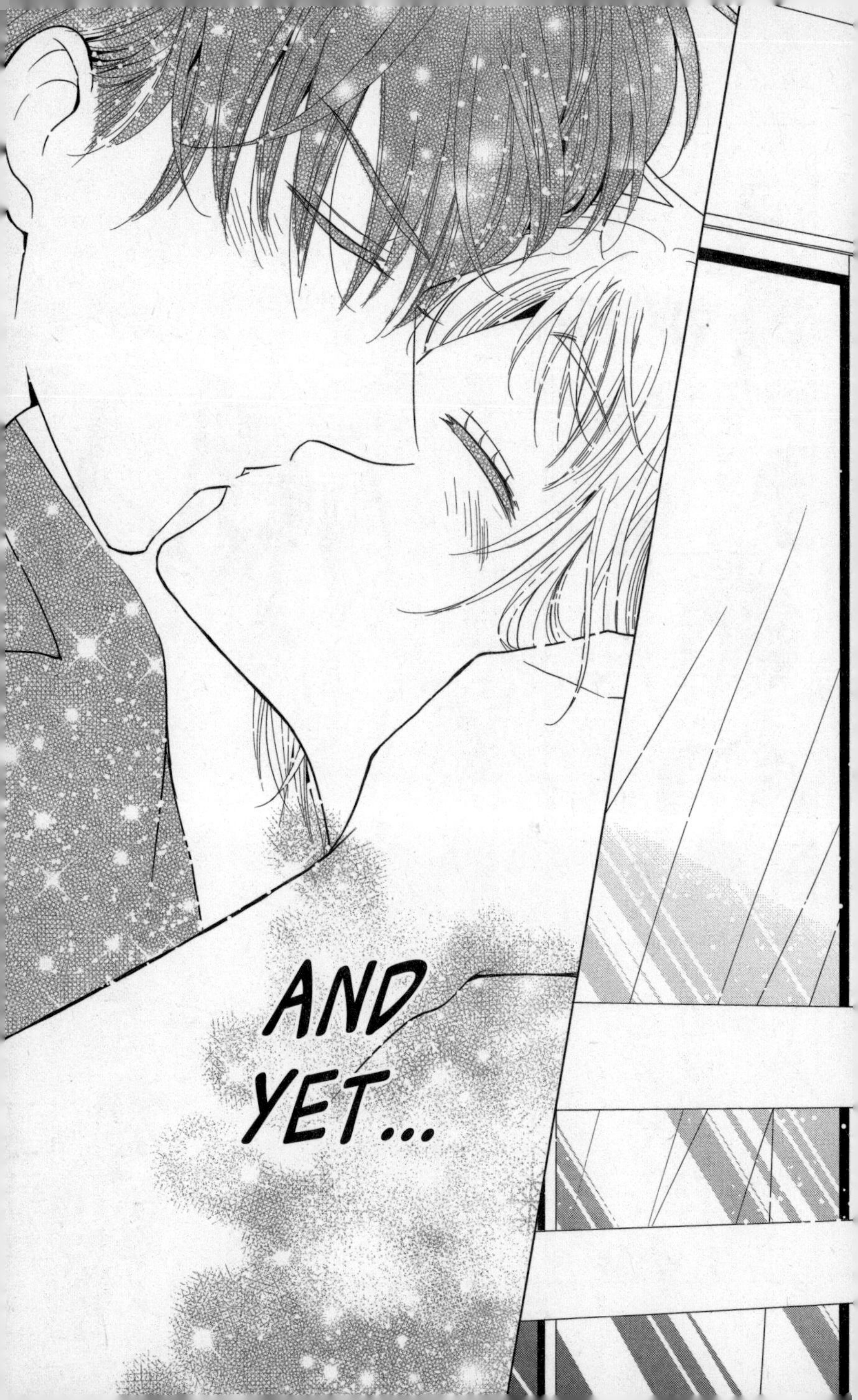
AND YET...

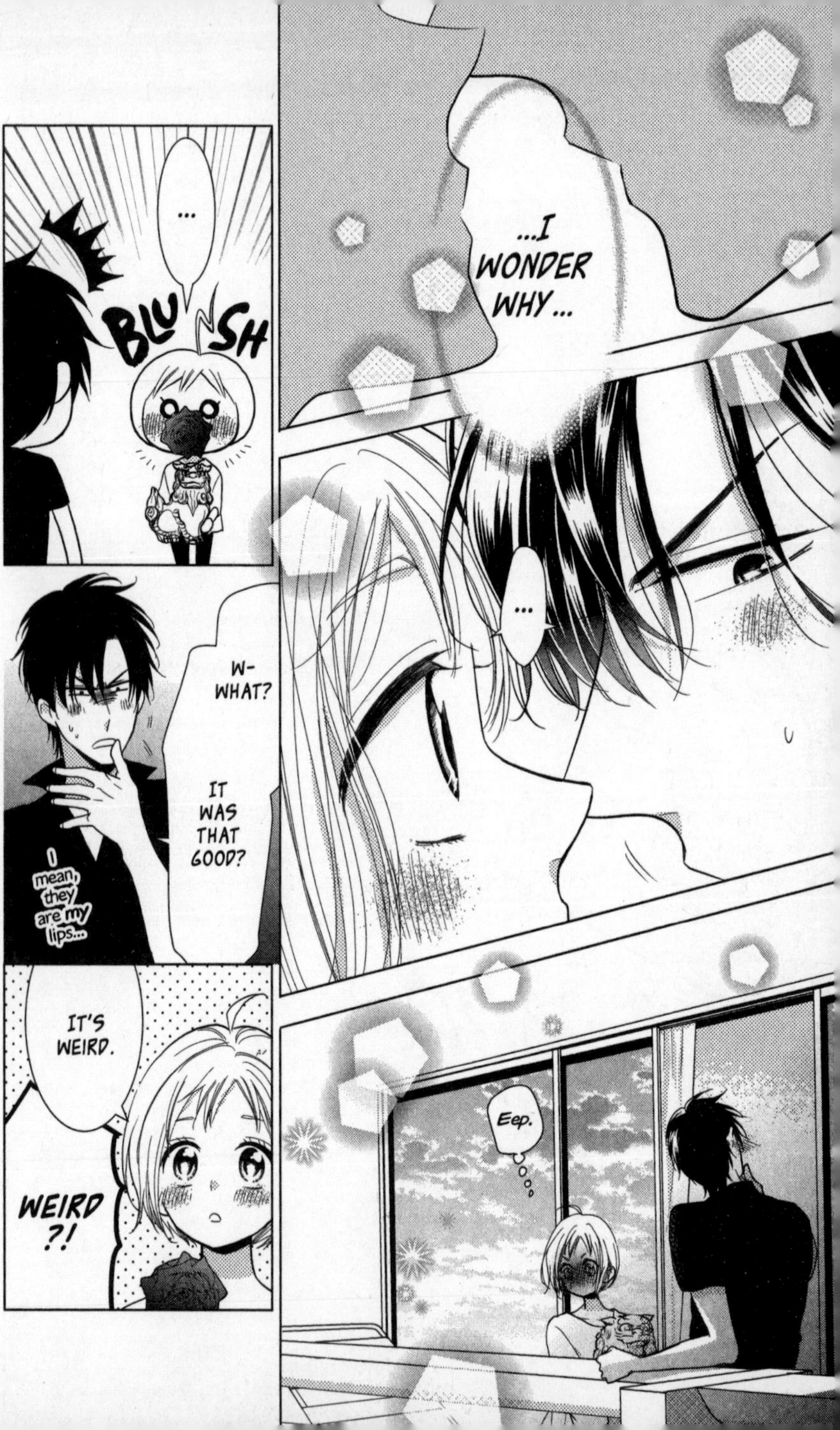
...I WONDER WHY...
...
Eep.
...
BLUSH
W- WHAT?
IT WAS THAT GOOD?
I mean, they are my lips...
IT'S WEIRD.
WEIRD ?!

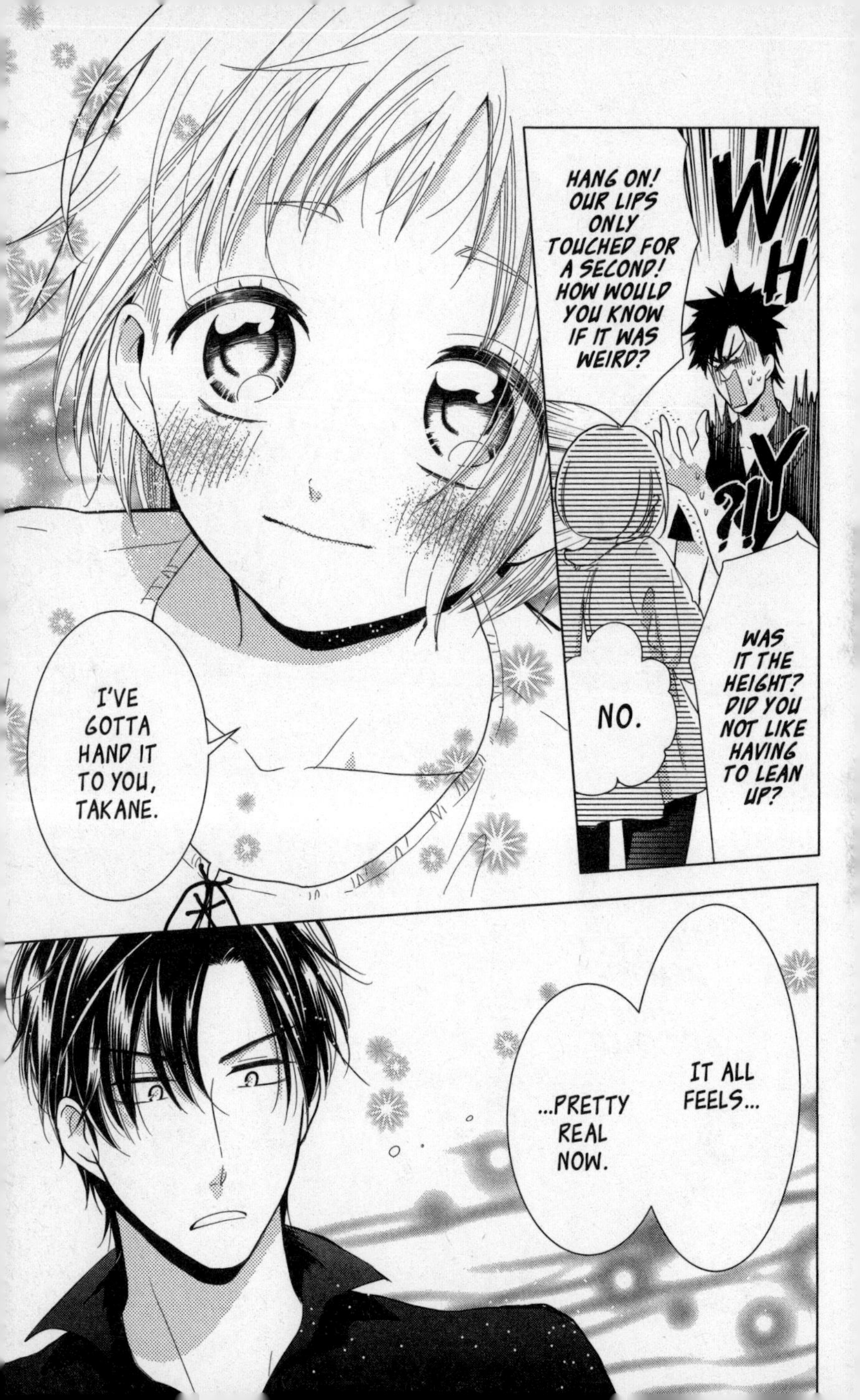
WHY?!
HANG ON! OUR LIPS ONLY TOUCHED FOR A SECOND! HOW WOULD YOU KNOW IF IT WAS WEIRD?
WAS IT THE HEIGHT? DID YOU NOT LIKE HAVING TO LEAN UP?
NO.
I'VE GOTTA HAND IT TO YOU, TAKANE.
IT ALL FEELS...
...PRETTY REAL NOW.

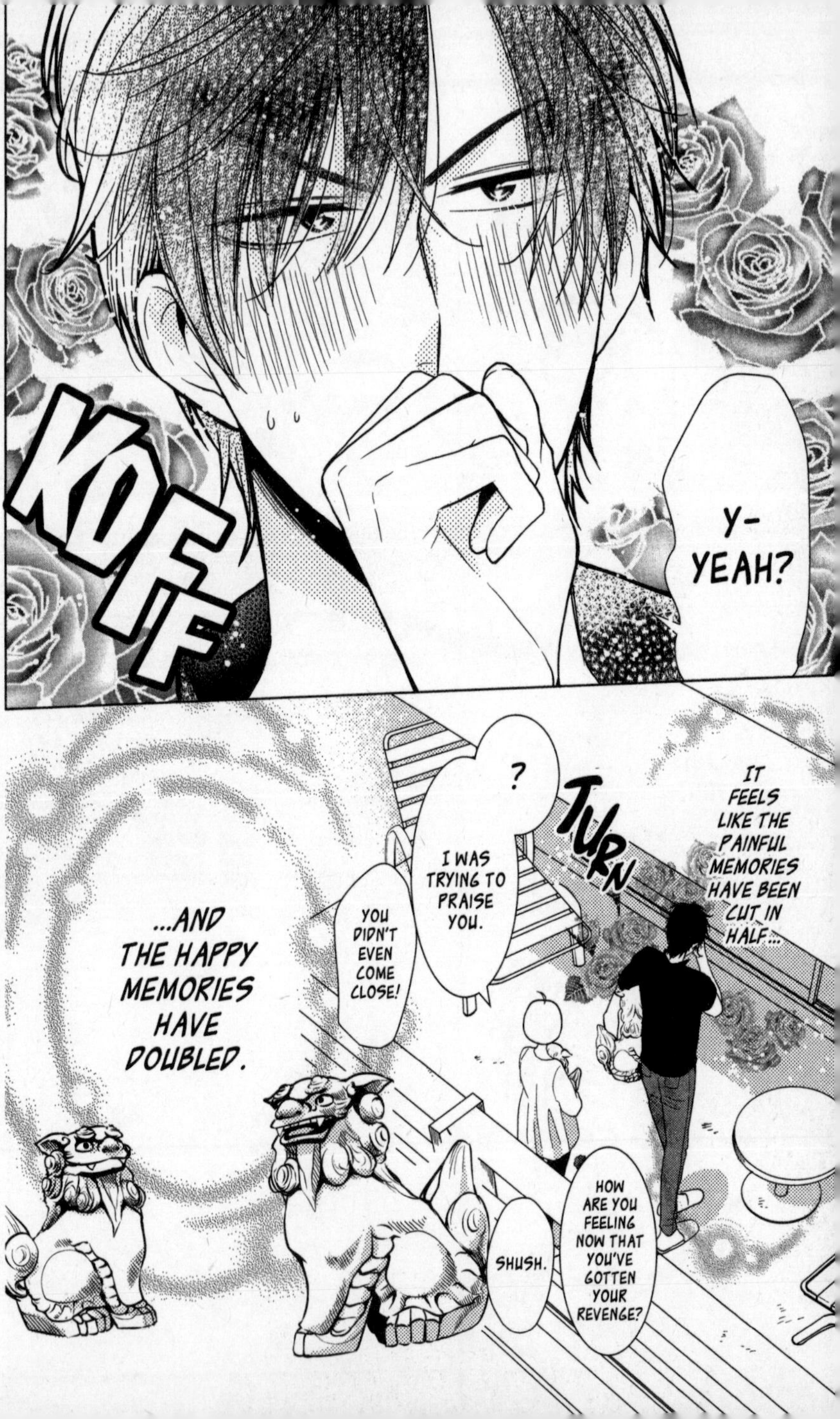
Y-
YEAH?
KOFF
IT FEELS LIKE THE PAINFUL MEMORIES HAVE BEEN CUT IN HALF...
TURN
?
I WAS TRYING TO PRAISE YOU.
YOU DIDN'T EVEN COME CLOSE!
...AND THE HAPPY MEMORIES HAVE DOUBLED.
HOW ARE YOU FEELING NOW THAT YOU'VE GOTTEN YOUR REVENGE?
SHUSH.

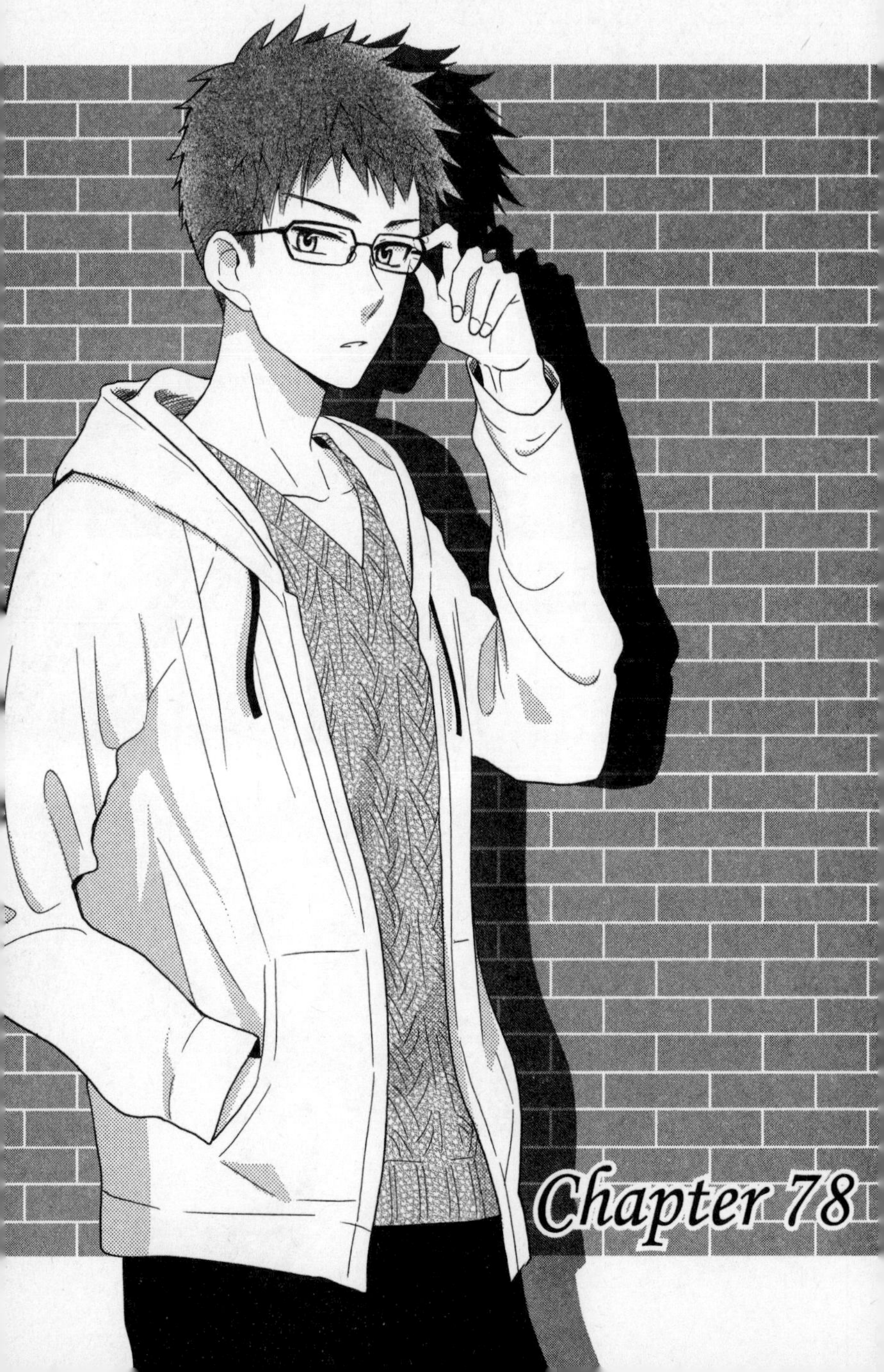
Chapter 78

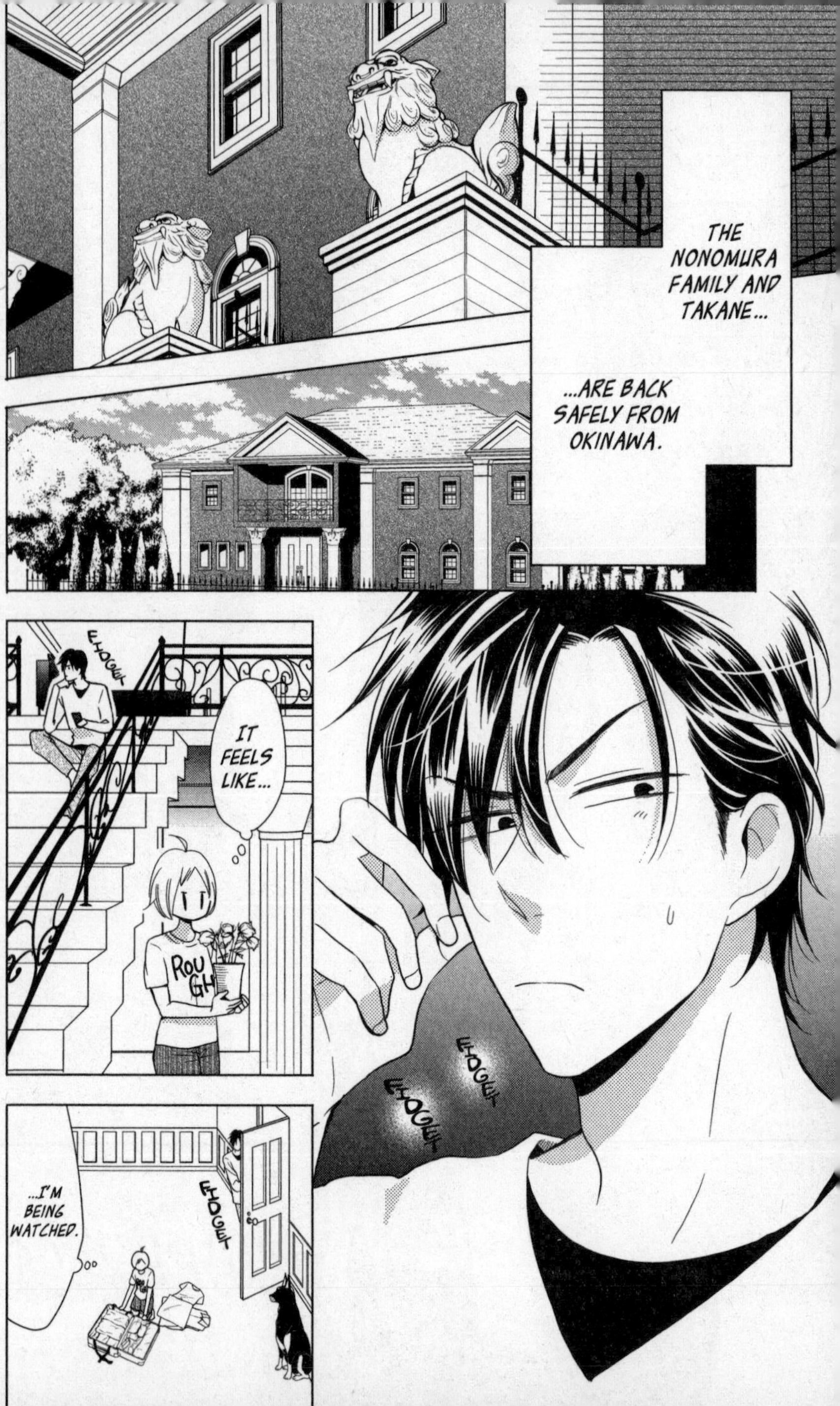
THE NONOMURA FAMILY AND TAKANE...
...ARE BACK SAFELY FROM OKINAWA.
FIDGET
FIDGET
FIDGET
IT FEELS LIKE...
ROUGH
FIDGET
...I'M BEING WATCHED.

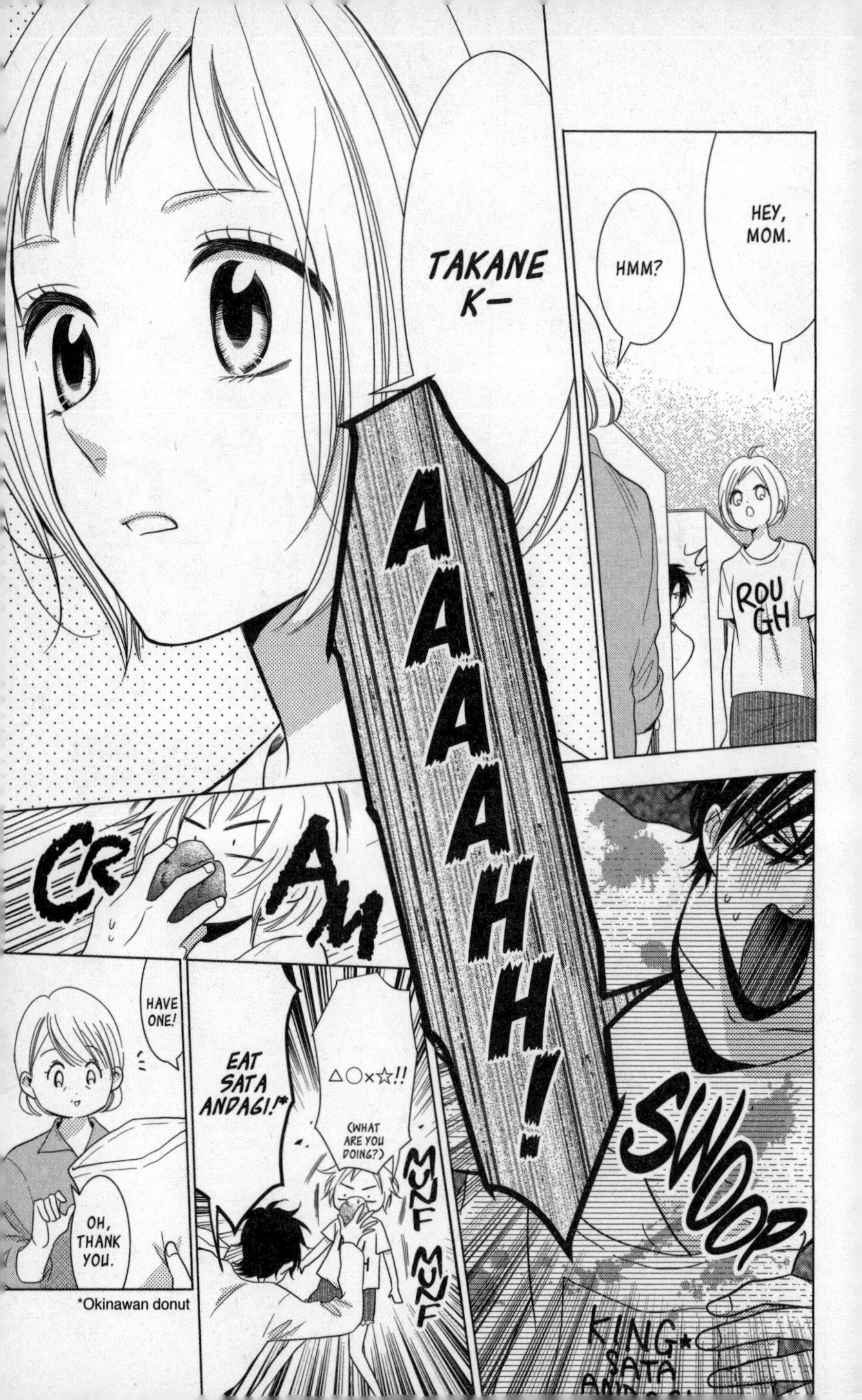
HEY, MOM.
HMM?
ROU GH
TAKANE K—
AAAAHH!
SWOOP
CRAM
KING★ SATA
EAT SATA ANDAGI!*
△○×☆!!
(WHAT ARE YOU DOING?)
MUNF MUNF
HAVE ONE!
OH, THANK YOU.
*Okinawan donut

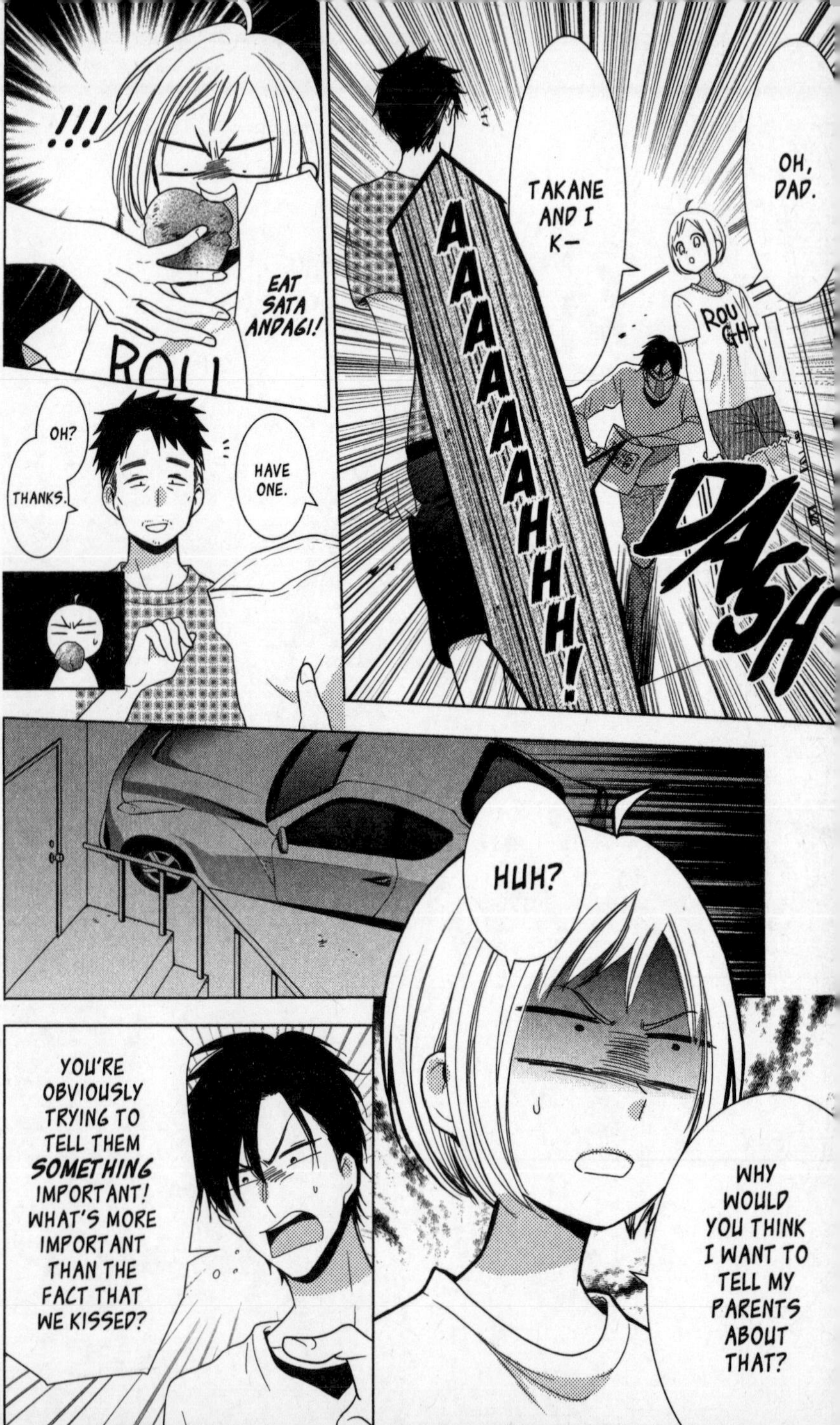
OH, DAD.
TAKANE AND I K—
AAAAAAHHHH!
DASH
!!!
EAT SATA ANDAGI!
ROU
ROU GH
HAVE ONE.
OH?
THANKS.
HUH?
WHY WOULD YOU THINK I WANT TO TELL MY PARENTS ABOUT THAT?
YOU'RE OBVIOUSLY TRYING TO TELL THEM *SOMETHING* IMPORTANT! WHAT'S MORE IMPORTANT THAN THE FACT THAT WE KISSED?

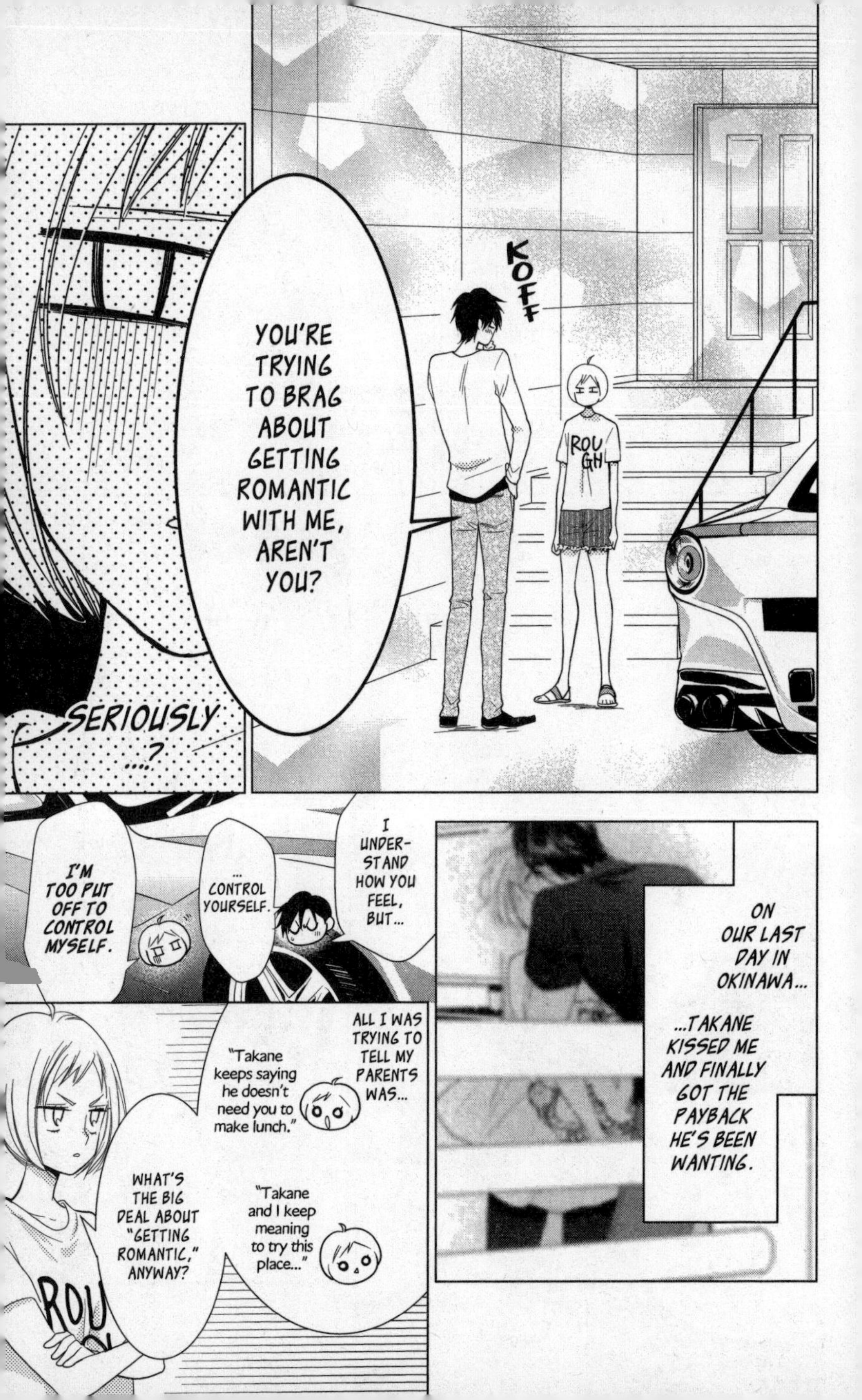
KOFF
YOU'RE TRYING TO BRAG ABOUT GETTING ROMANTIC WITH ME, AREN'T YOU?
SERIOUSLY ...?
ON OUR LAST DAY IN OKINAWA...
...TAKANE KISSED ME AND FINALLY GOT THE PAYBACK HE'S BEEN WANTING.
I UNDERSTAND HOW YOU FEEL, BUT...
...CONTROL YOURSELF.
I'M TOO PUT OFF TO CONTROL MYSELF.
ALL I WAS TRYING TO TELL MY PARENTS WAS...
"Takane keeps saying he doesn't need you to make lunch."
"Takane and I keep meaning to try this place..."
WHAT'S THE BIG DEAL ABOUT "GETTING ROMANTIC," ANYWAY?

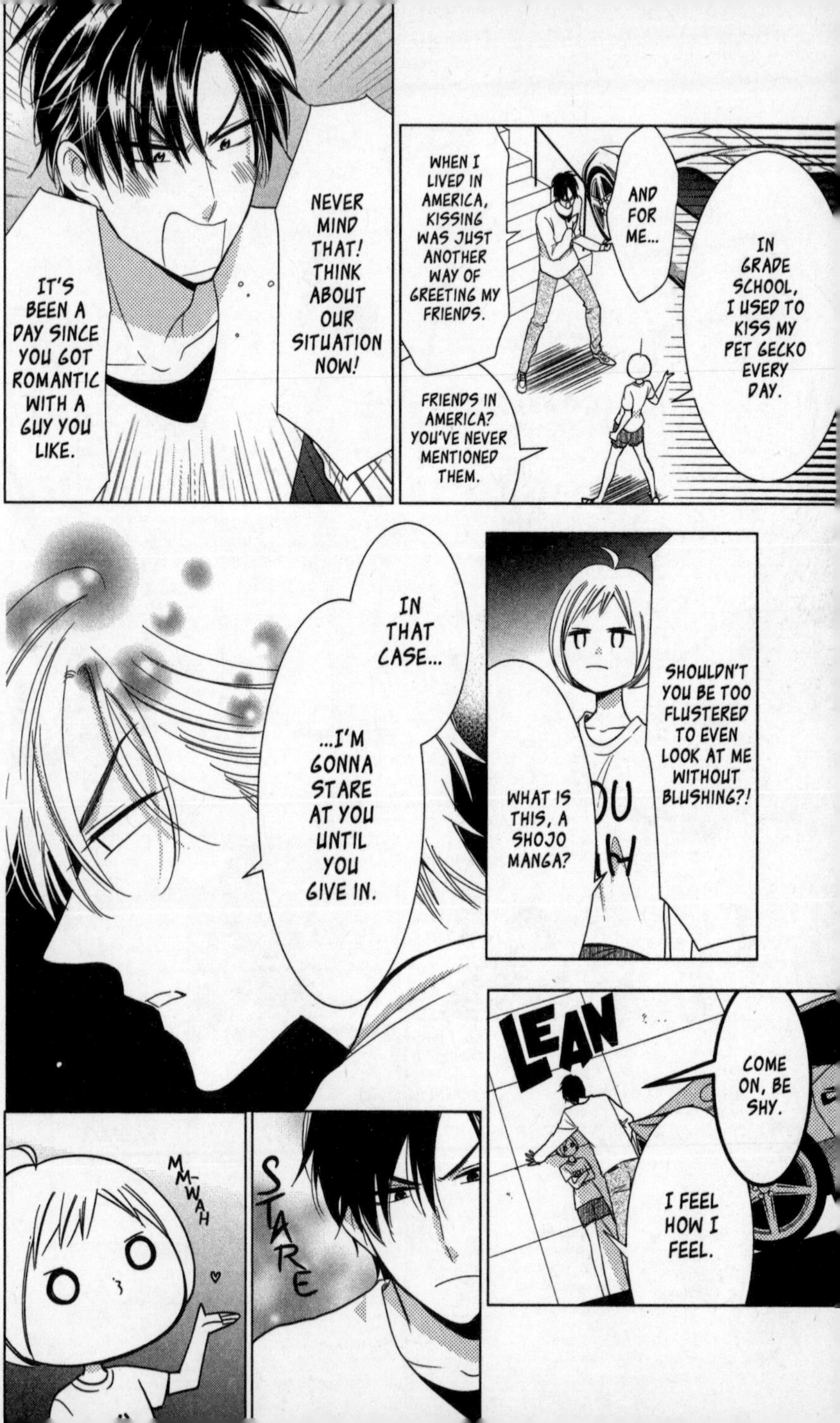
AND FOR ME...
IN GRADE SCHOOL, I USED TO KISS MY PET GECKO EVERY DAY.
WHEN I LIVED IN AMERICA, KISSING WAS JUST ANOTHER WAY OF GREETING MY FRIENDS.
FRIENDS IN AMERICA? YOU'VE NEVER MENTIONED THEM.
NEVER MIND THAT! THINK ABOUT OUR SITUATION NOW!
IT'S BEEN A DAY SINCE YOU GOT ROMANTIC WITH A GUY YOU LIKE.
SHOULDN'T YOU BE TOO FLUSTERED TO EVEN LOOK AT ME WITHOUT BLUSHING?!
WHAT IS THIS, A SHOJO MANGA?
LEAN
COME ON, BE SHY.
I FEEL HOW I FEEL.
IN THAT CASE...
...I'M GONNA STARE AT YOU UNTIL YOU GIVE IN.
STARE
MM-WAH

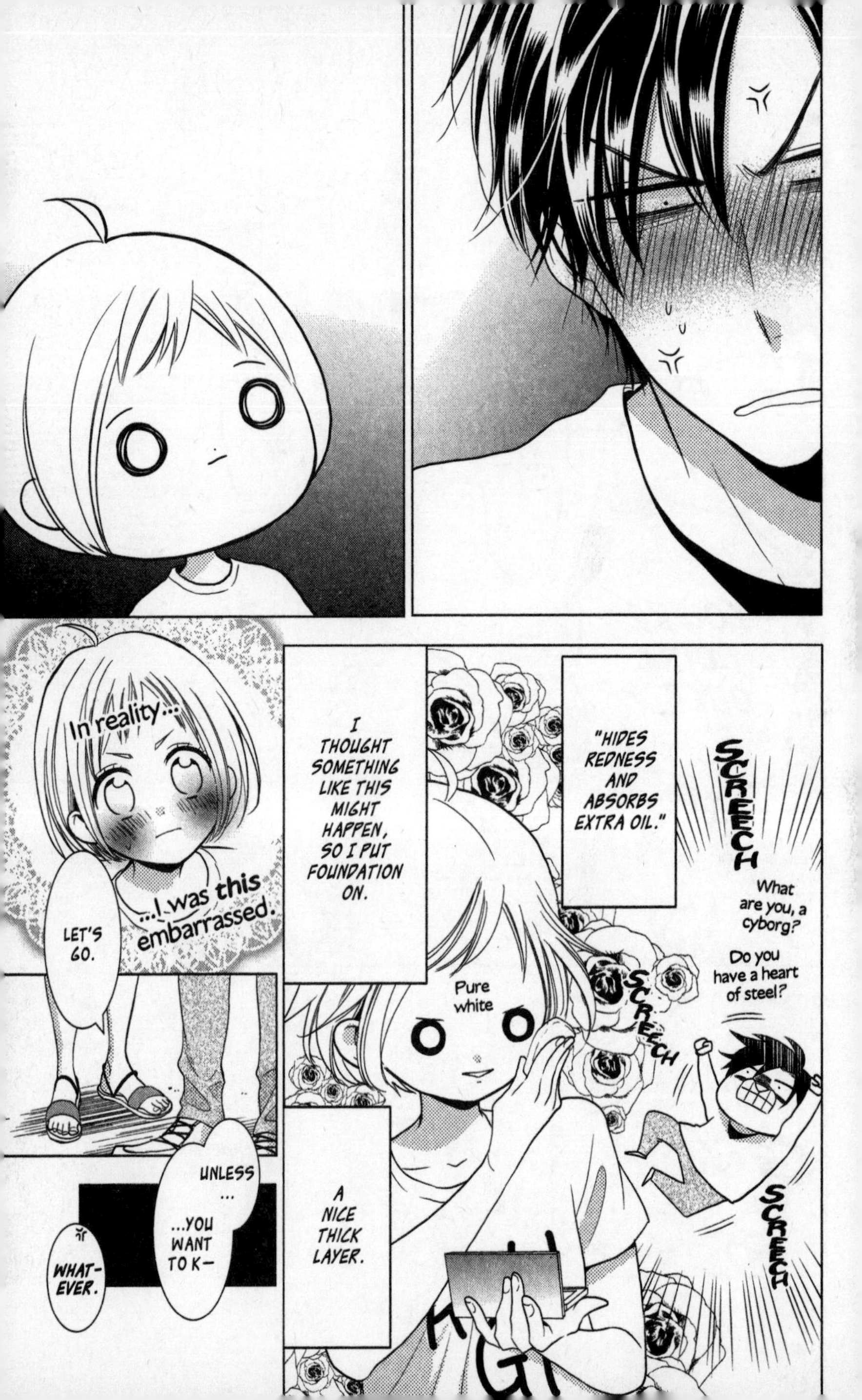
SCREECH
"HIDES REDNESS AND ABSORBS EXTRA OIL."
What are you, a cyborg?
Do you have a heart of steel?
SCREECH
Pure white
I THOUGHT SOMETHING LIKE THIS MIGHT HAPPEN, SO I PUT FOUNDATION ON.
SCREECH
A NICE THICK LAYER.
In reality...
...I was this embarrassed.
LET'S GO.
UNLESS ...
...YOU WANT TO K—
WHAT-EVER.

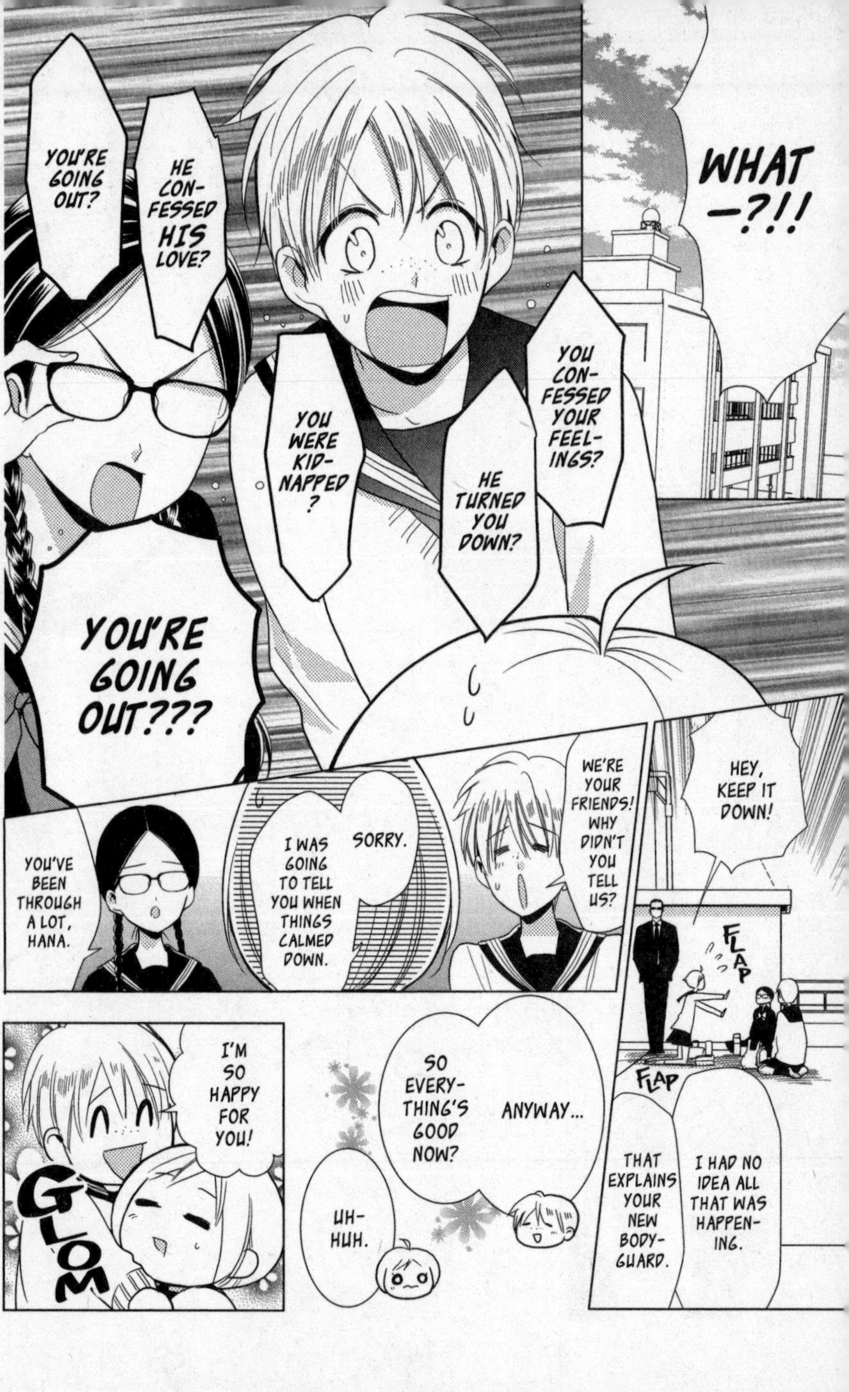
WHAT—?!!
YOU CONFESSED YOUR FEELINGS?
HE TURNED YOU DOWN?
YOU WERE KIDNAPPED?
HE CONFESSED HIS LOVE?
YOU'RE GOING OUT?
YOU'RE GOING OUT???
HEY, KEEP IT DOWN!
FLAP
FLAP
WE'RE YOUR FRIENDS! WHY DIDN'T YOU TELL US?
SORRY.
I WAS GOING TO TELL YOU WHEN THINGS CALMED DOWN.
YOU'VE BEEN THROUGH A LOT, HANA.
I HAD NO IDEA ALL THAT WAS HAPPENING.
THAT EXPLAINS YOUR NEW BODYGUARD.
ANYWAY...
SO EVERYTHING'S GOOD NOW?
UH-HUH.
I'M SO HAPPY FOR YOU!
GLOM

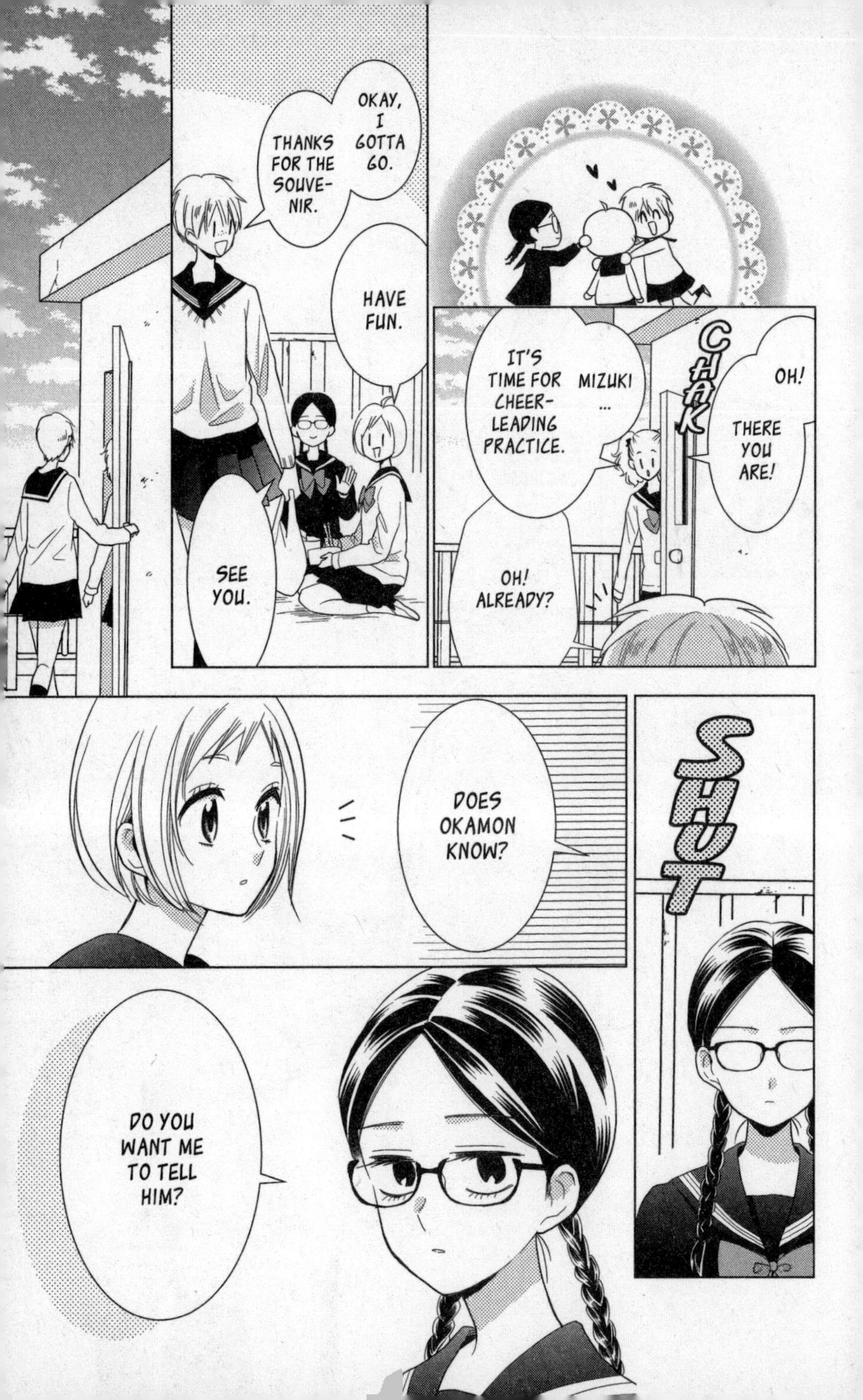
CHAK
OH! THERE YOU ARE!
MIZUKI...
IT'S TIME FOR CHEERLEADING PRACTICE.
OH! ALREADY?
OKAY, I GOTTA GO.
THANKS FOR THE SOUVENIR.
HAVE FUN.
SEE YOU.
SHUT
DOES OKAMON KNOW?
DO YOU WANT ME TO TELL HIM?

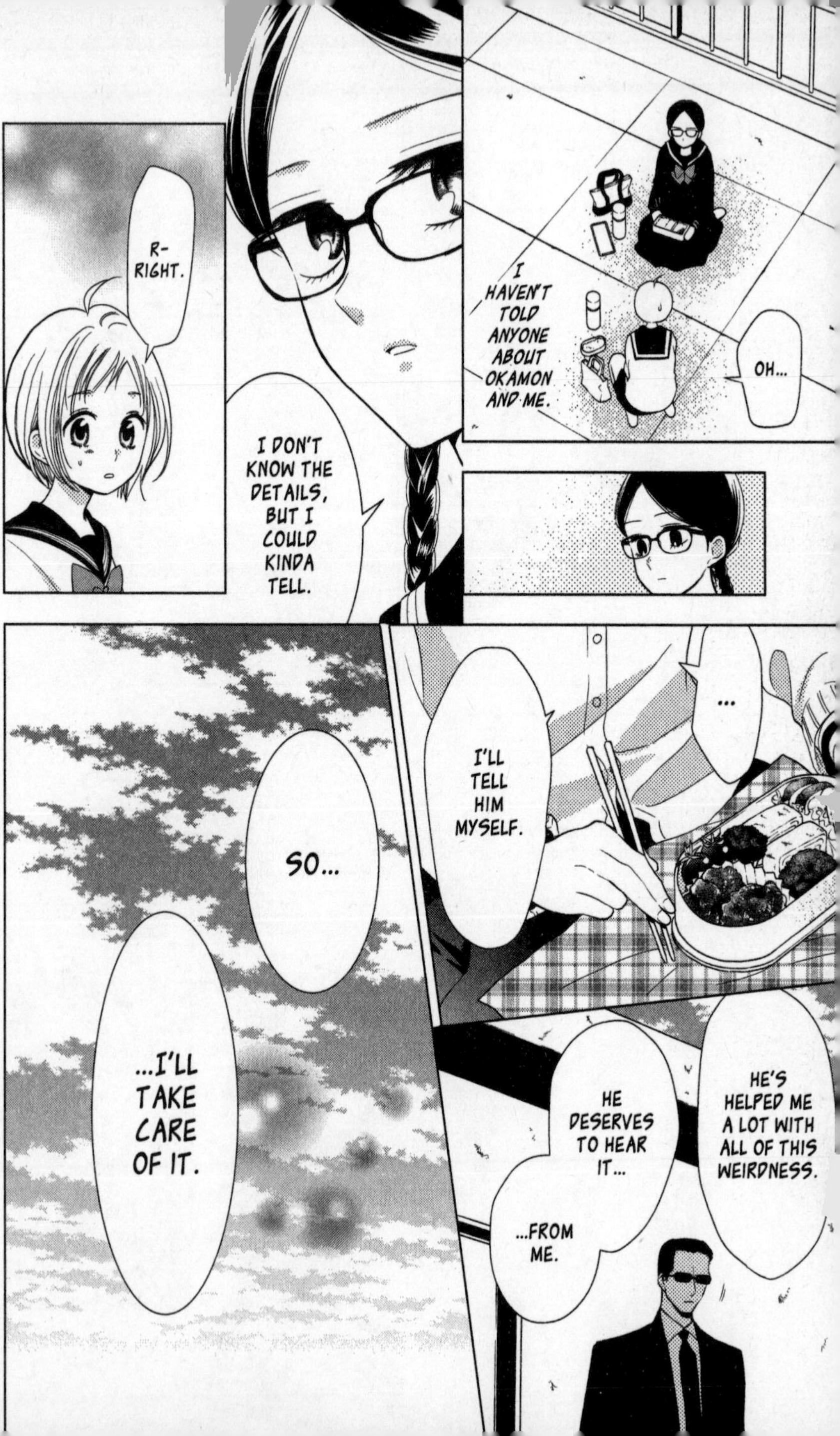
I HAVEN'T TOLD ANYONE ABOUT OKAMON AND ME.
OH...
I DON'T KNOW THE DETAILS, BUT I COULD KINDA TELL.
R-RIGHT.
...
I'LL TELL HIM MYSELF.
HE'S HELPED ME A LOT WITH ALL OF THIS WEIRDNESS.
HE DESERVES TO HEAR IT...
...FROM ME.
SO...
...I'LL TAKE CARE OF IT.

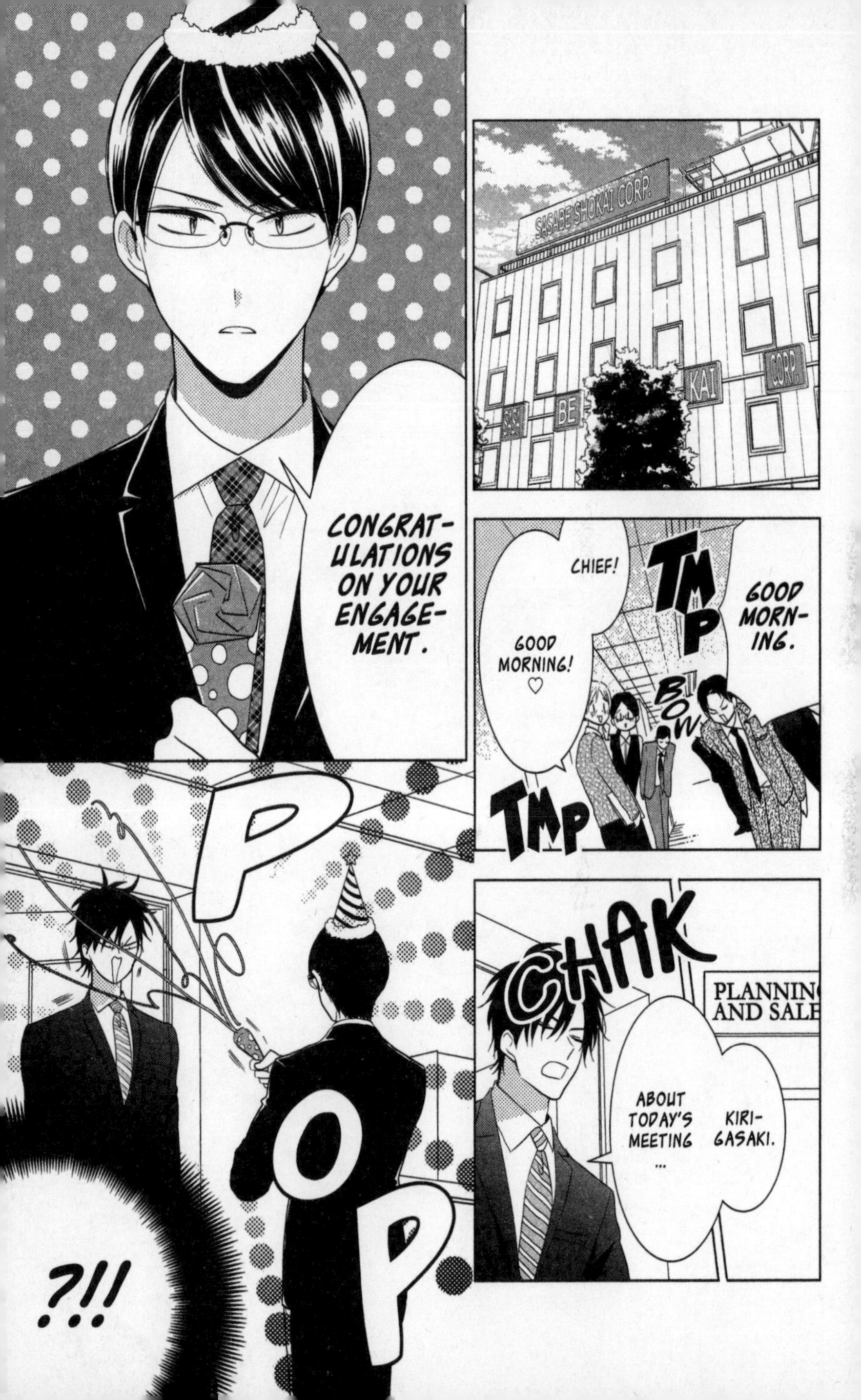
SASABE SHOKAI CORP.
SASA BE KAI CORP.
GOOD MORNING.
TMP
CHIEF!
GOOD MORNING! ♡
BOW
TMP
CHAK
PLANNING AND SALE
KIRIGASAKI.
ABOUT TODAY'S MEETING ...
CONGRATULATIONS ON YOUR ENGAGEMENT.
POP
?!!

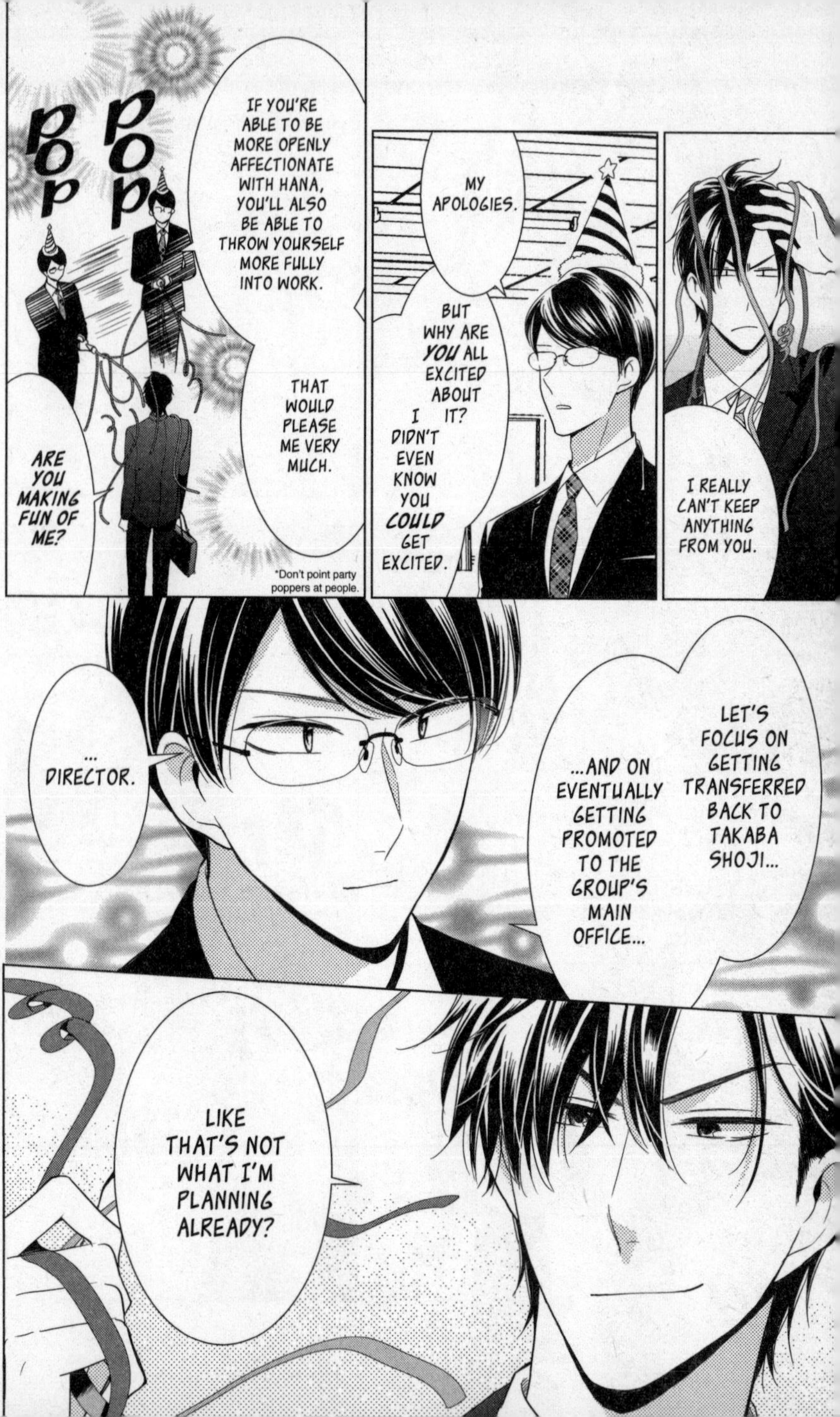

I REALLY CAN'T KEEP ANYTHING FROM YOU.
MY APOLOGIES.
BUT WHY ARE YOU ALL EXCITED ABOUT IT?
I DIDN'T EVEN KNOW YOU COULD GET EXCITED.
POP POP
IF YOU'RE ABLE TO BE MORE OPENLY AFFECTIONATE WITH HANA, YOU'LL ALSO BE ABLE TO THROW YOURSELF MORE FULLY INTO WORK.
THAT WOULD PLEASE ME VERY MUCH.
ARE YOU MAKING FUN OF ME?
*Don't point party poppers at people.
LET'S FOCUS ON GETTING TRANSFERRED BACK TO TAKABA SHOJI...
...AND ON EVENTUALLY GETTING PROMOTED TO THE GROUP'S MAIN OFFICE...
...DIRECTOR.
LIKE THAT'S NOT WHAT I'M PLANNING ALREADY?

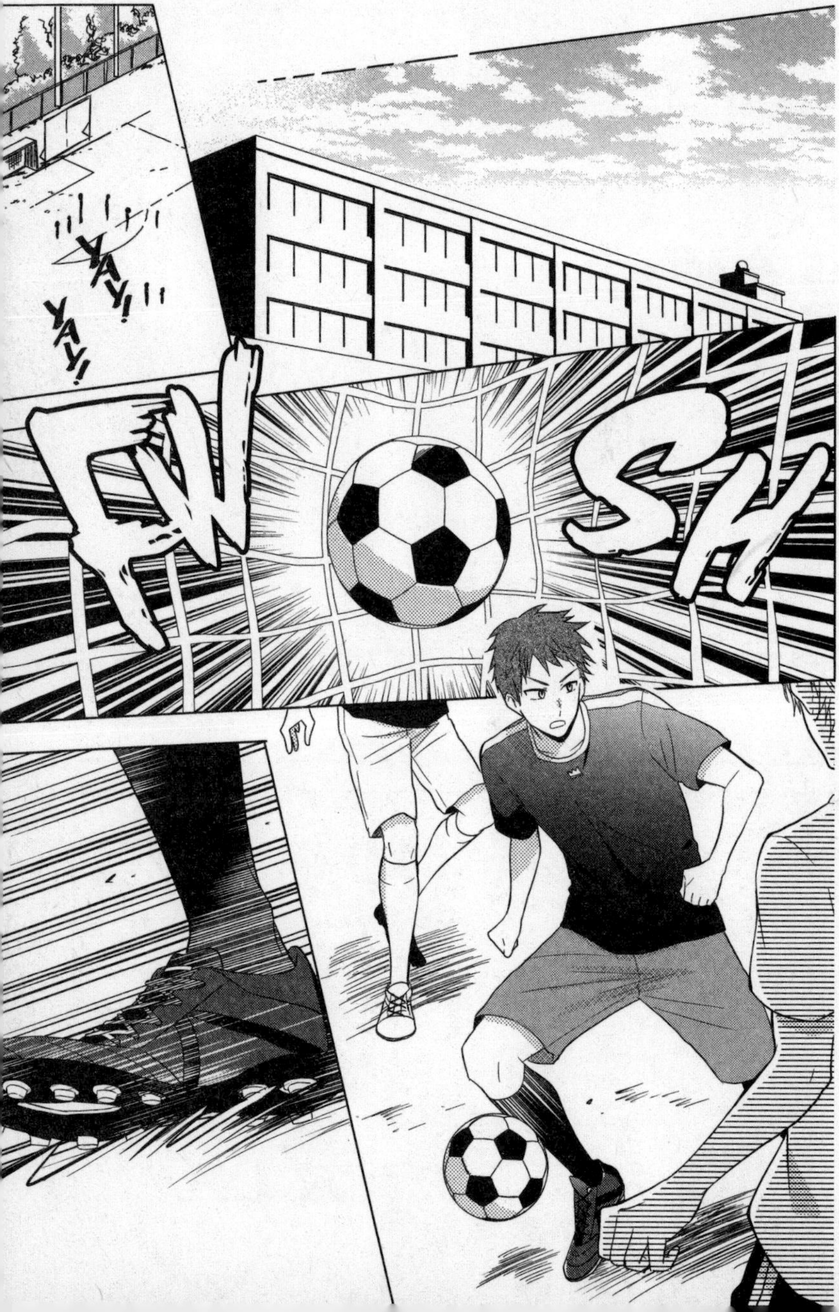
YAY!
YAY!
FWOSH

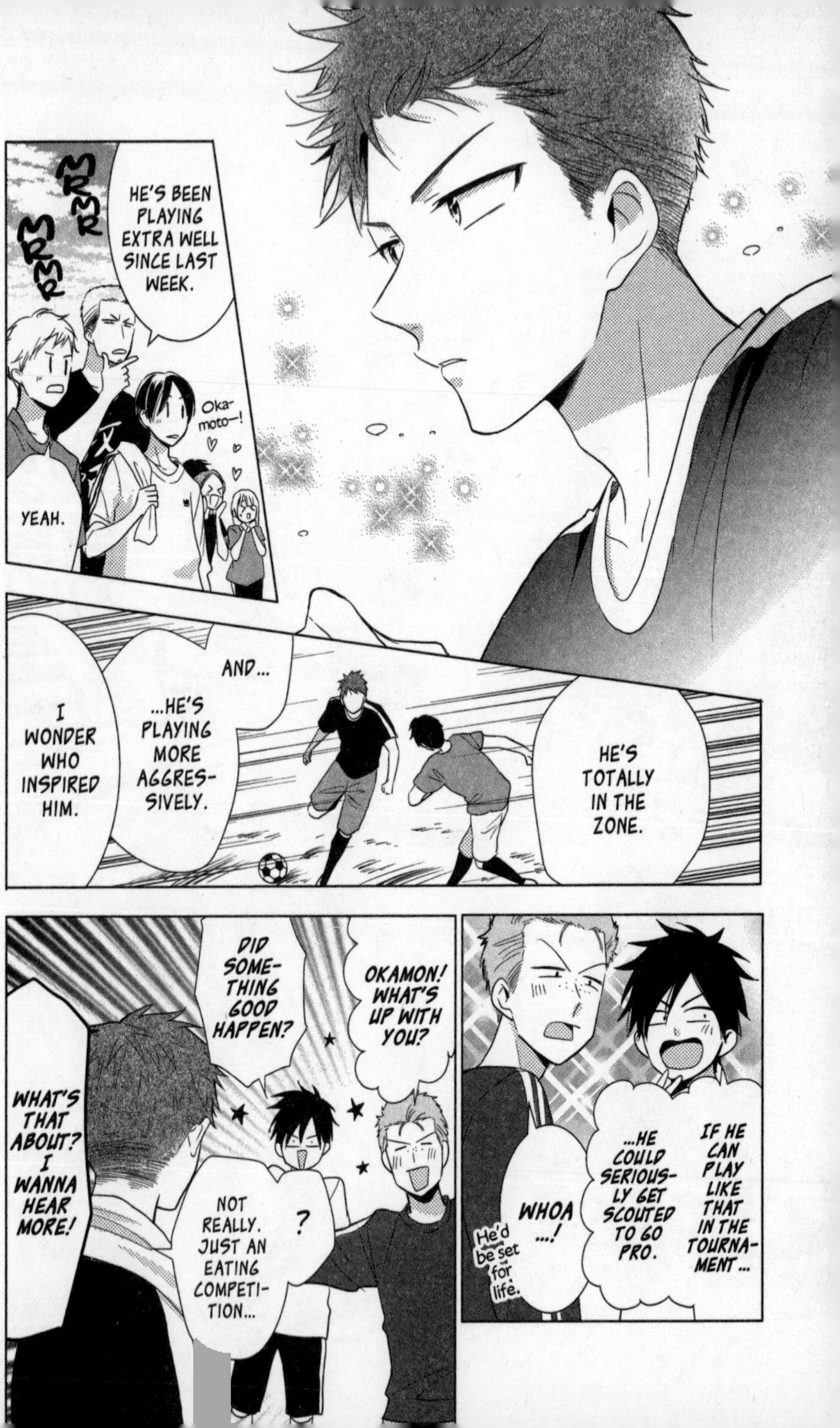
HE'S BEEN PLAYING EXTRA WELL SINCE LAST WEEK.
MRMR
MRMR
Oka-moto—!
YEAH.
HE'S TOTALLY IN THE ZONE.
AND...
...HE'S PLAYING MORE AGGRES-SIVELY.
I WONDER WHO INSPIRED HIM.
IF HE CAN PLAY LIKE THAT IN THE TOURNA-MENT...
...HE COULD SERIOUS-LY GET SCOUTED TO GO PRO.
WHOA ...!
He'd be set for life.
OKAMON! WHAT'S UP WITH YOU?
DID SOME-THING GOOD HAPPEN?
?
NOT REALLY. JUST AN EATING COMPETI-TION...
WHAT'S THAT ABOUT? I WANNA HEAR MORE!

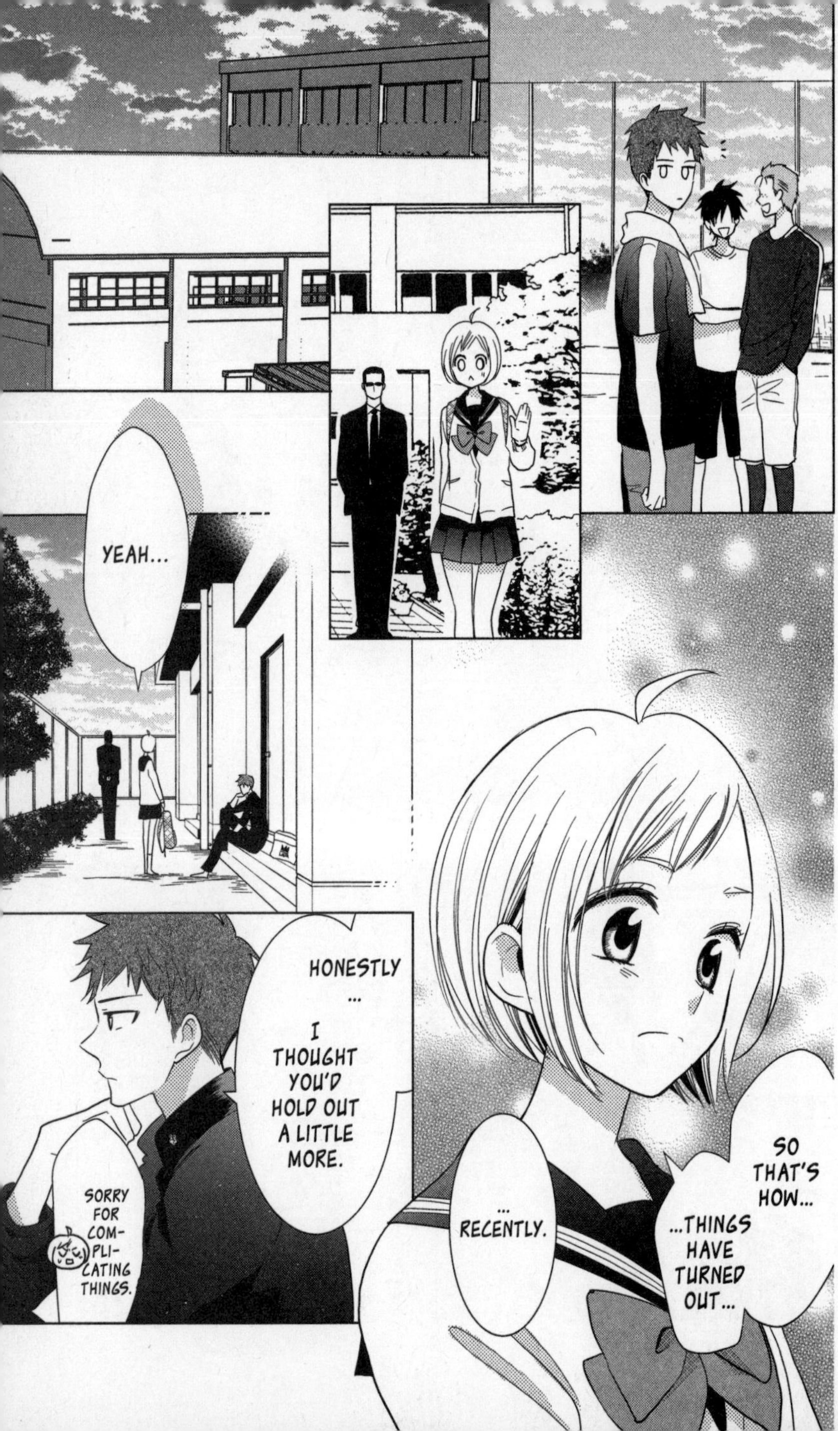
YEAH...
SO THAT'S HOW...
...THINGS HAVE TURNED OUT...
... RECENTLY.
HONESTLY ...
I THOUGHT YOU'D HOLD OUT A LITTLE MORE.
SORRY FOR COMPLICATING THINGS.

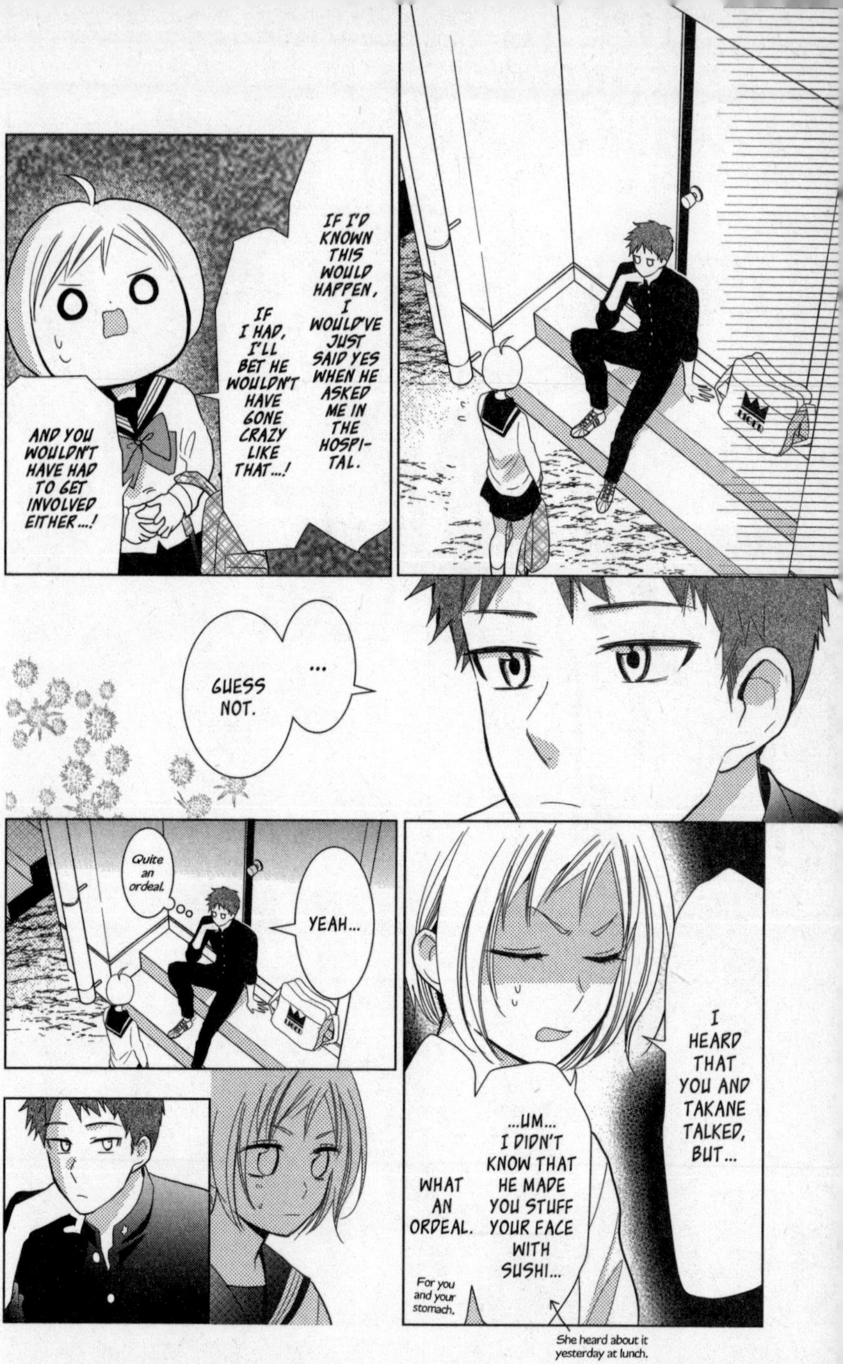
IF I'D KNOWN THIS WOULD HAPPEN, I WOULD'VE JUST SAID YES WHEN HE ASKED ME IN THE HOSPITAL.
IF I HAD, I'LL BET HE WOULDN'T HAVE GONE CRAZY LIKE THAT...!
AND YOU WOULDN'T HAVE HAD TO GET INVOLVED EITHER...!
... GUESS NOT.
I HEARD THAT YOU AND TAKANE TALKED, BUT...
...UM... I DIDN'T KNOW THAT HE MADE YOU STUFF YOUR FACE WITH SUSHI...
She heard about it yesterday at lunch.
WHAT AN ORDEAL.
For you and your stomach.
YEAH...
Quite an ordeal.

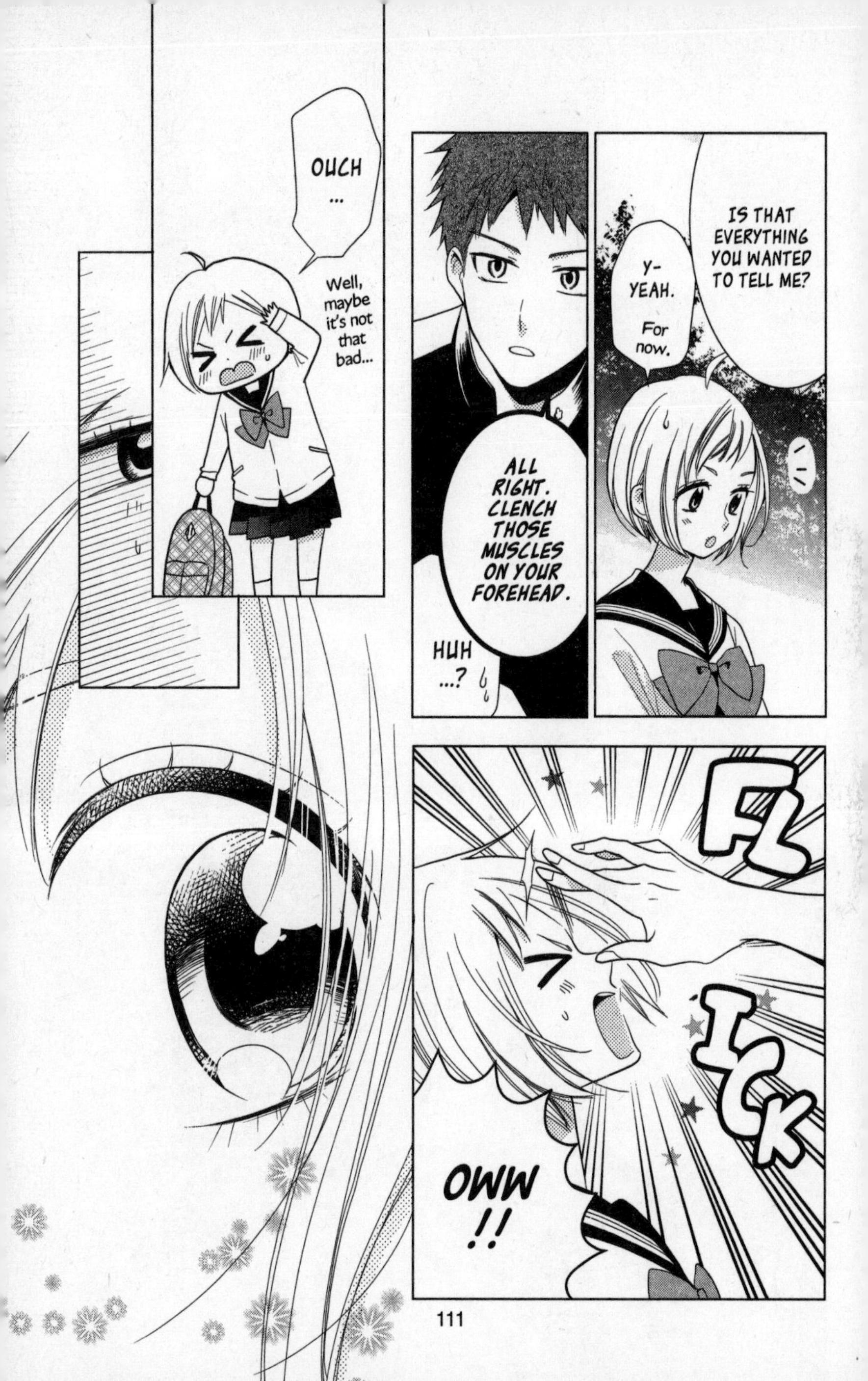
IS THAT EVERYTHING YOU WANTED TO TELL ME?
Y-YEAH.
For now.
...
ALL RIGHT. CLENCH THOSE MUSCLES ON YOUR FOREHEAD.
HUH ...?
FLICK
OWW !!
OUCH ...
Well, maybe it's not that bad...

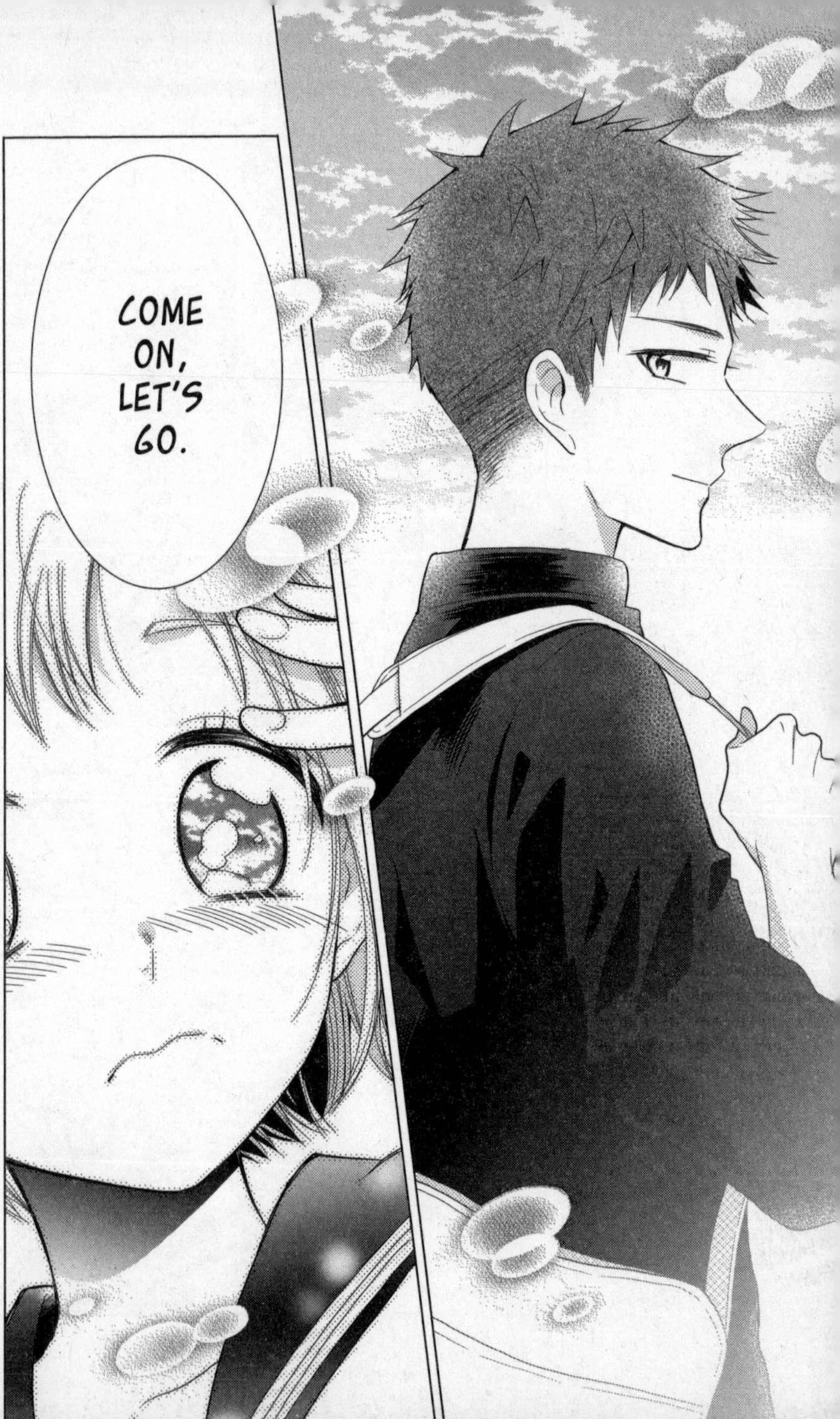
COME ON, LET'S GO.

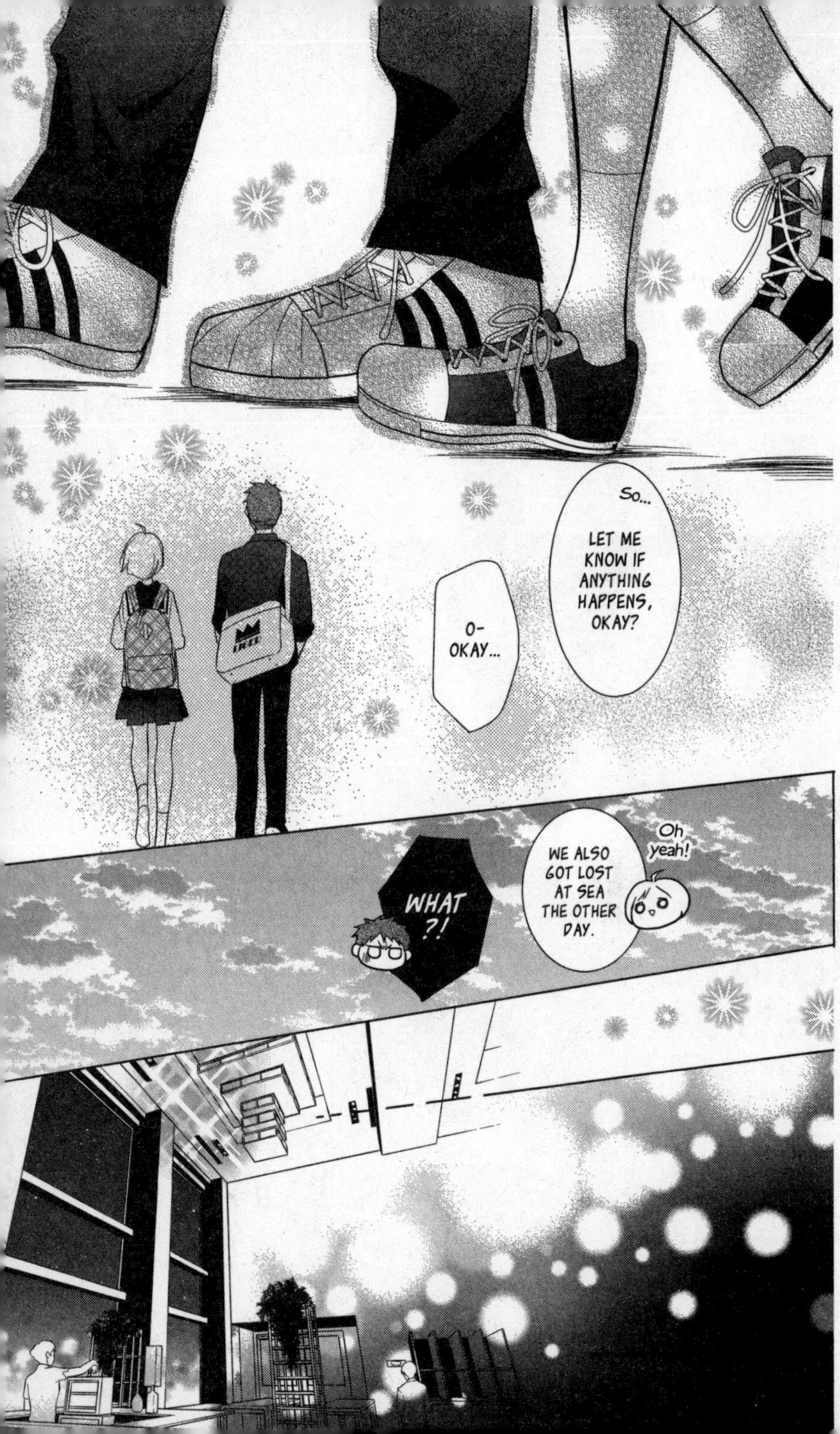
So...
LET ME KNOW IF ANYTHING HAPPENS, OKAY?
O-OKAY...
Oh yeah!
WE ALSO GOT LOST AT SEA THE OTHER DAY.
WHAT?!

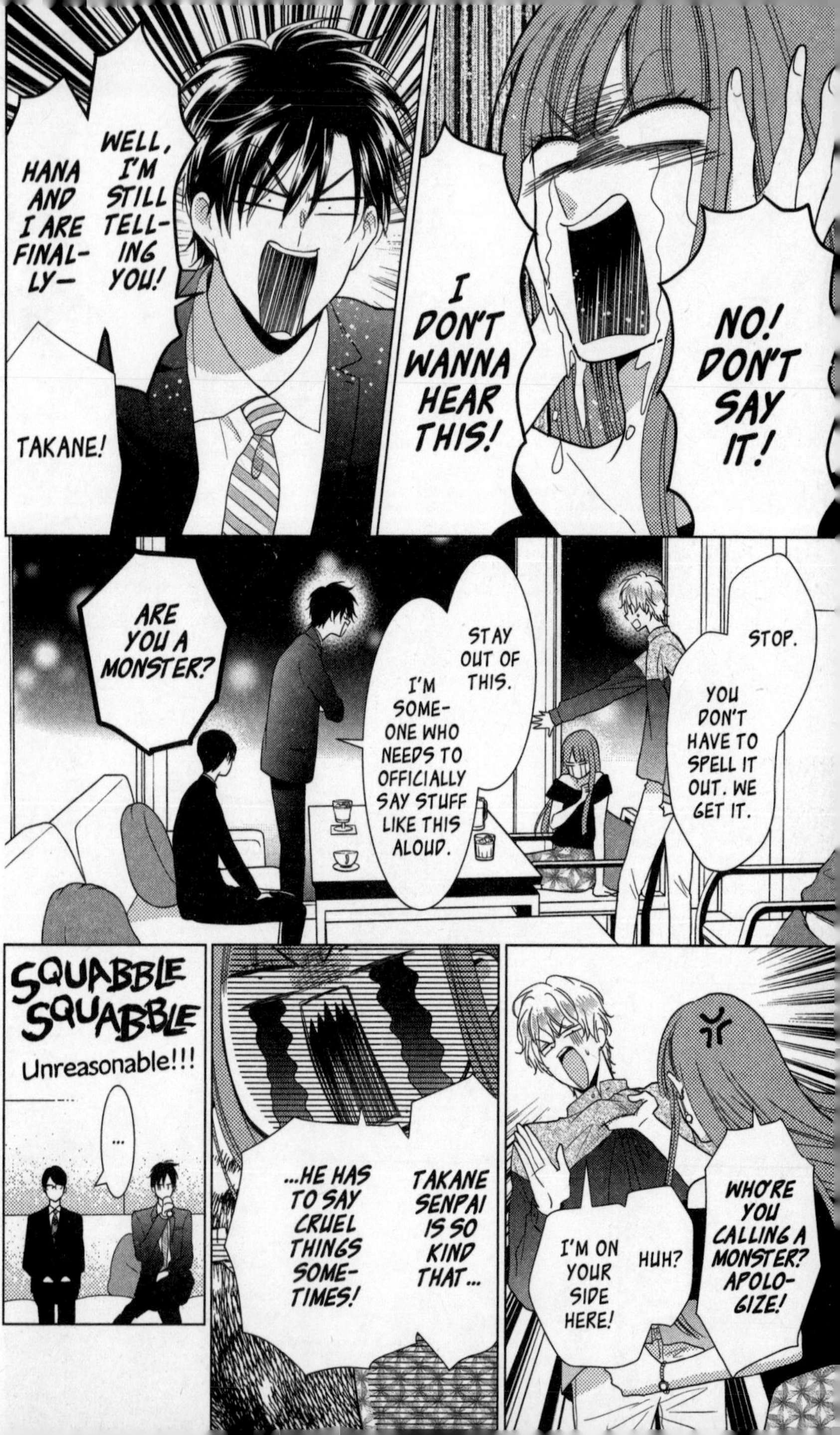
NO! DON'T SAY IT!
I DON'T WANNA HEAR THIS!
WELL, I'M STILL TELLING YOU!
HANA AND I ARE FINALLY—
TAKANE!
STOP.
YOU DON'T HAVE TO SPELL IT OUT. WE GET IT.
STAY OUT OF THIS.
I'M SOMEONE WHO NEEDS TO OFFICIALLY SAY STUFF LIKE THIS ALOUD.
ARE YOU A MONSTER?
WHO'RE YOU CALLING A MONSTER? APOLOGIZE!
HUH?
I'M ON YOUR SIDE HERE!
TAKANE SENPAI IS SO KIND THAT...
...HE HAS TO SAY CRUEL THINGS SOMETIMES!
SQUABBLE SQUABBLE
Unreasonable!!!
...

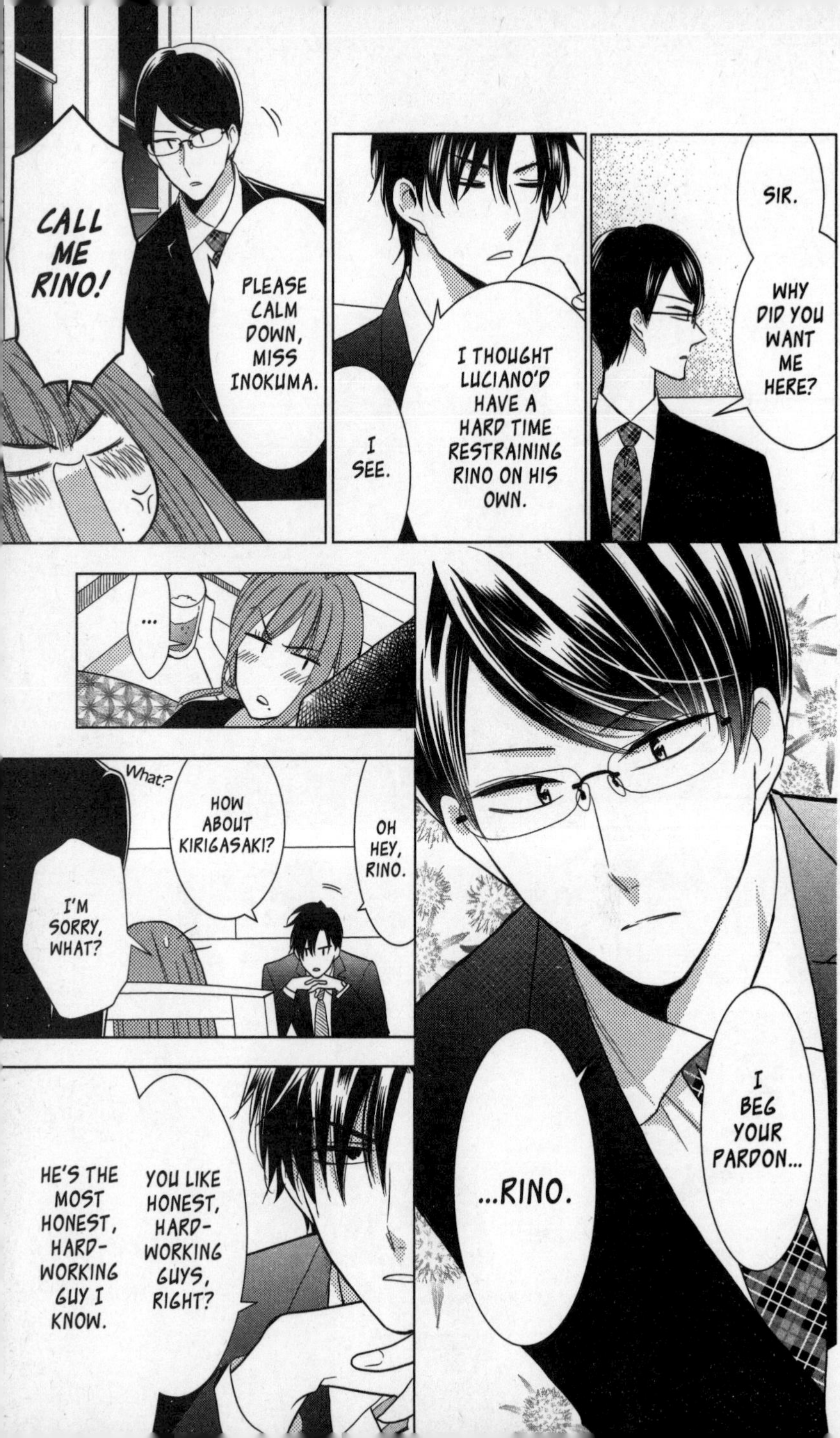
SIR.
WHY DID YOU WANT ME HERE?
I THOUGHT LUCIANO'D HAVE A HARD TIME RESTRAINING RINO ON HIS OWN.
I SEE.
PLEASE CALM DOWN, MISS INOKUMA.
CALL ME RINO!
I BEG YOUR PARDON...
...RINO.
...
OH HEY, RINO.
HOW ABOUT KIRIGASAKI?
What?
I'M SORRY, WHAT?
YOU LIKE HONEST, HARD-WORKING GUYS, RIGHT?
HE'S THE MOST HONEST, HARD-WORKING GUY I KNOW.

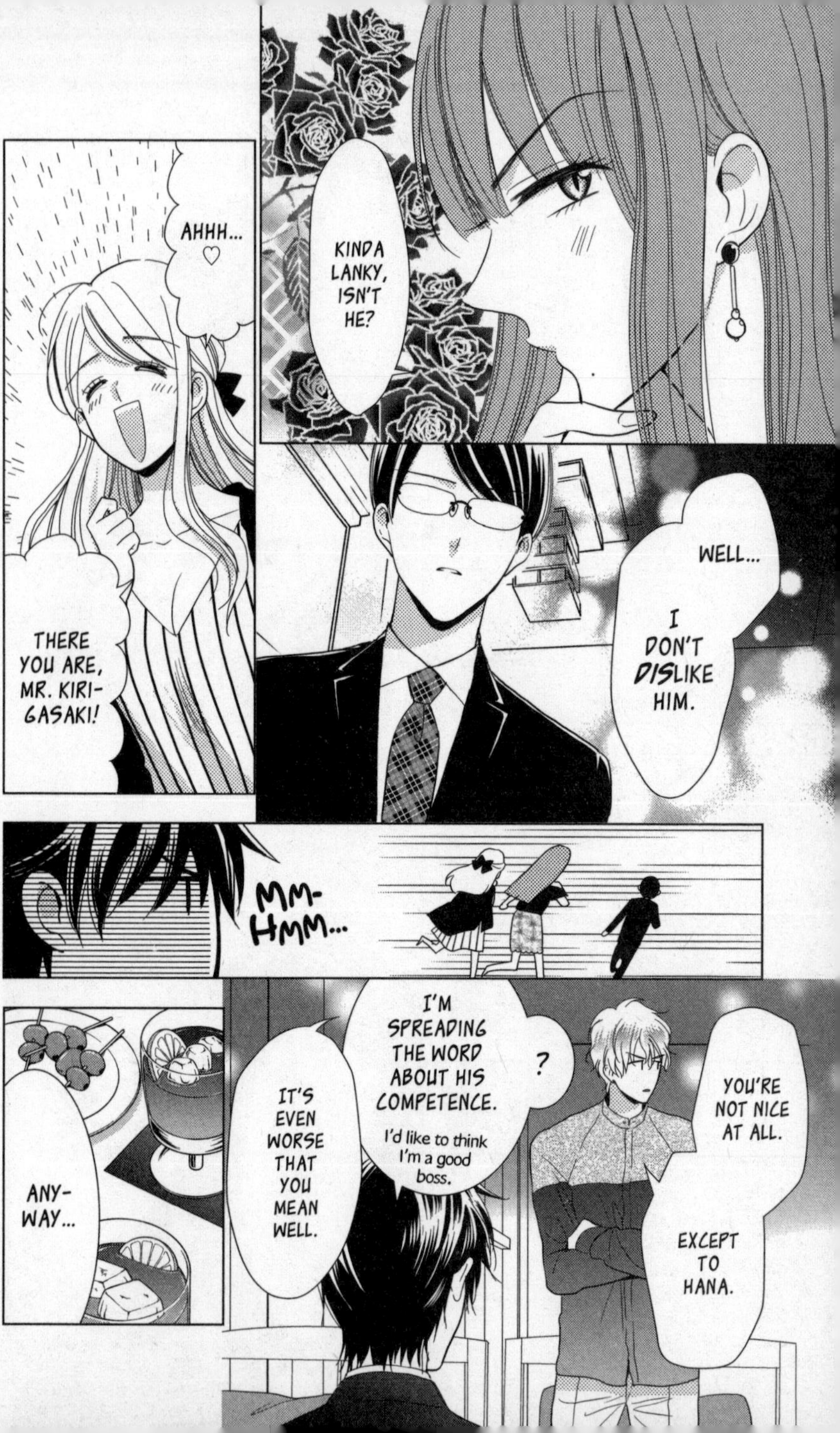
KINDA LANKY, ISN'T HE?
WELL...
I DON'T DISLIKE HIM.
AHHH... ♡
THERE YOU ARE, MR. KIRI-GASAKI!
MM-HMM...
YOU'RE NOT NICE AT ALL.
EXCEPT TO HANA.
?
I'M SPREADING THE WORD ABOUT HIS COMPETENCE.
I'd like to think I'm a good boss.
IT'S EVEN WORSE THAT YOU MEAN WELL.
ANY-WAY...

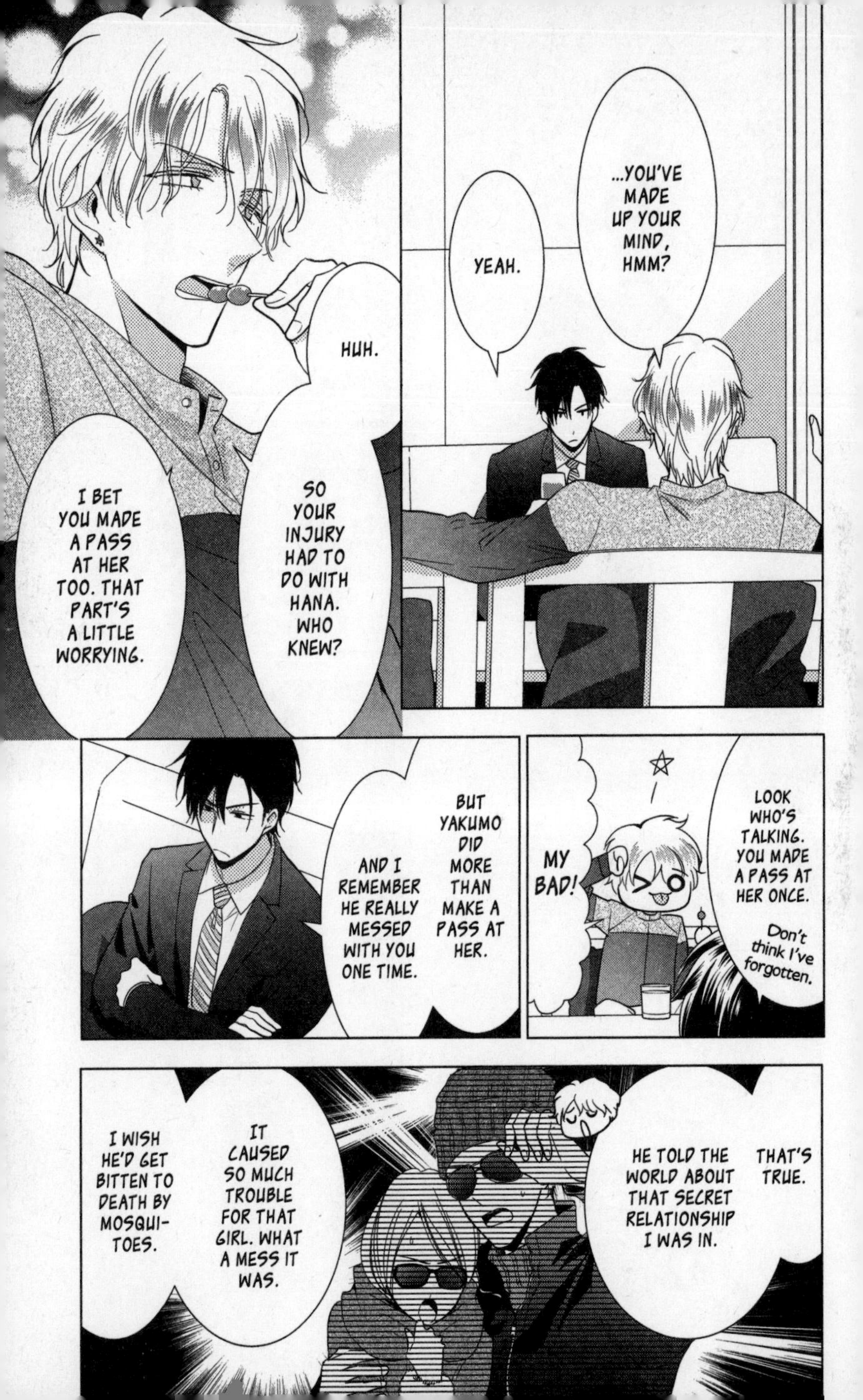
...YOU'VE MADE UP YOUR MIND, HMM?
YEAH.
HUH.
SO YOUR INJURY HAD TO DO WITH HANA. WHO KNEW?
I BET YOU MADE A PASS AT HER TOO. THAT PART'S A LITTLE WORRYING.
LOOK WHO'S TALKING. YOU MADE A PASS AT HER ONCE.
Don't think I've forgotten.
MY BAD!
BUT YAKUMO DID MORE THAN MAKE A PASS AT HER.
AND I REMEMBER HE REALLY MESSED WITH YOU ONE TIME.
THAT'S TRUE.
HE TOLD THE WORLD ABOUT THAT SECRET RELATIONSHIP I WAS IN.
IT CAUSED SO MUCH TROUBLE FOR THAT GIRL. WHAT A MESS IT WAS.
I WISH HE'D GET BITTEN TO DEATH BY MOSQUI-TOES.

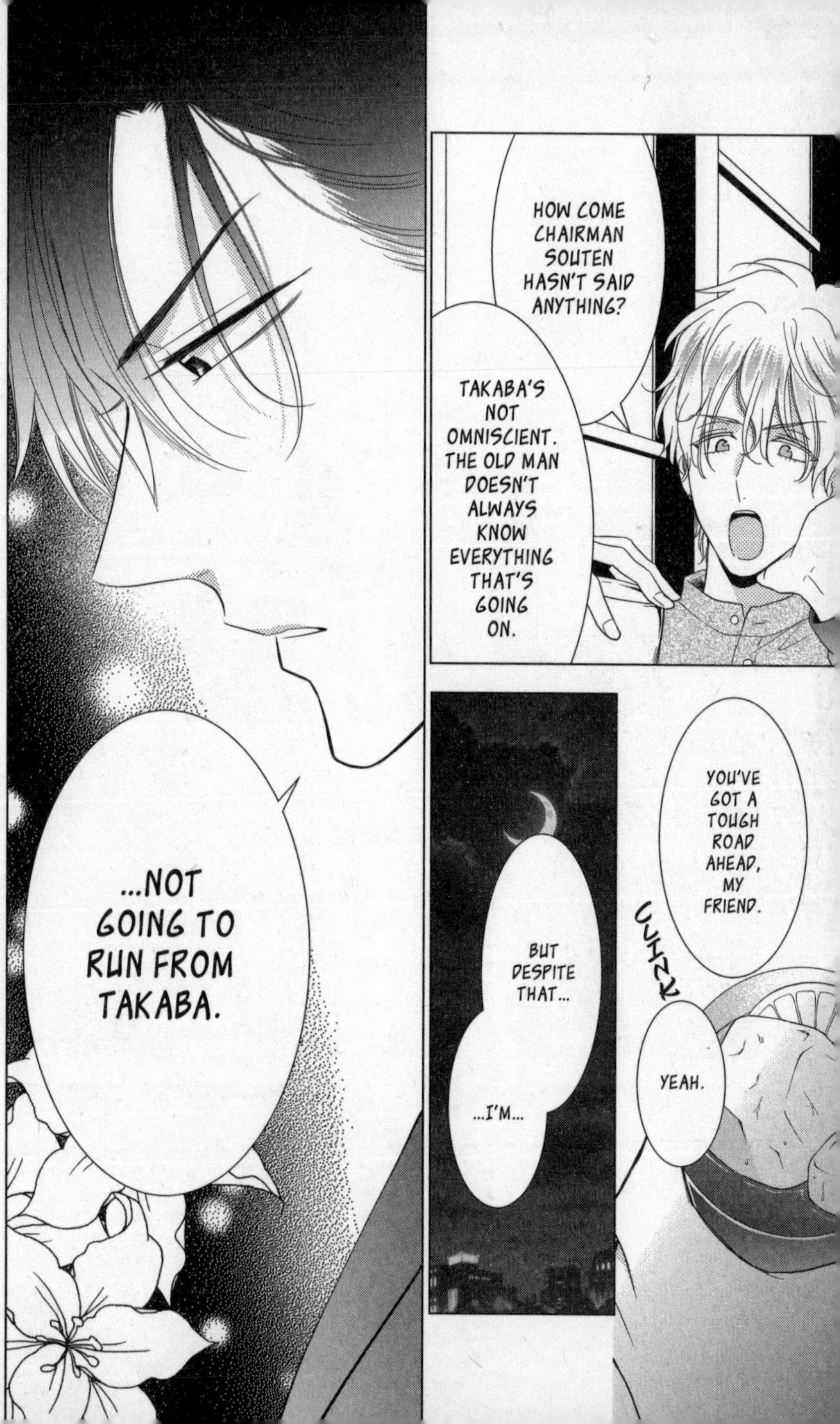
HOW COME CHAIRMAN SOUTEN HASN'T SAID ANYTHING?
TAKABA'S NOT OMNISCIENT. THE OLD MAN DOESN'T ALWAYS KNOW EVERYTHING THAT'S GOING ON.
YOU'VE GOT A TOUGH ROAD AHEAD, MY FRIEND.
CLINK
YEAH.
BUT DESPITE THAT...
...I'M...
...NOT GOING TO RUN FROM TAKABA.

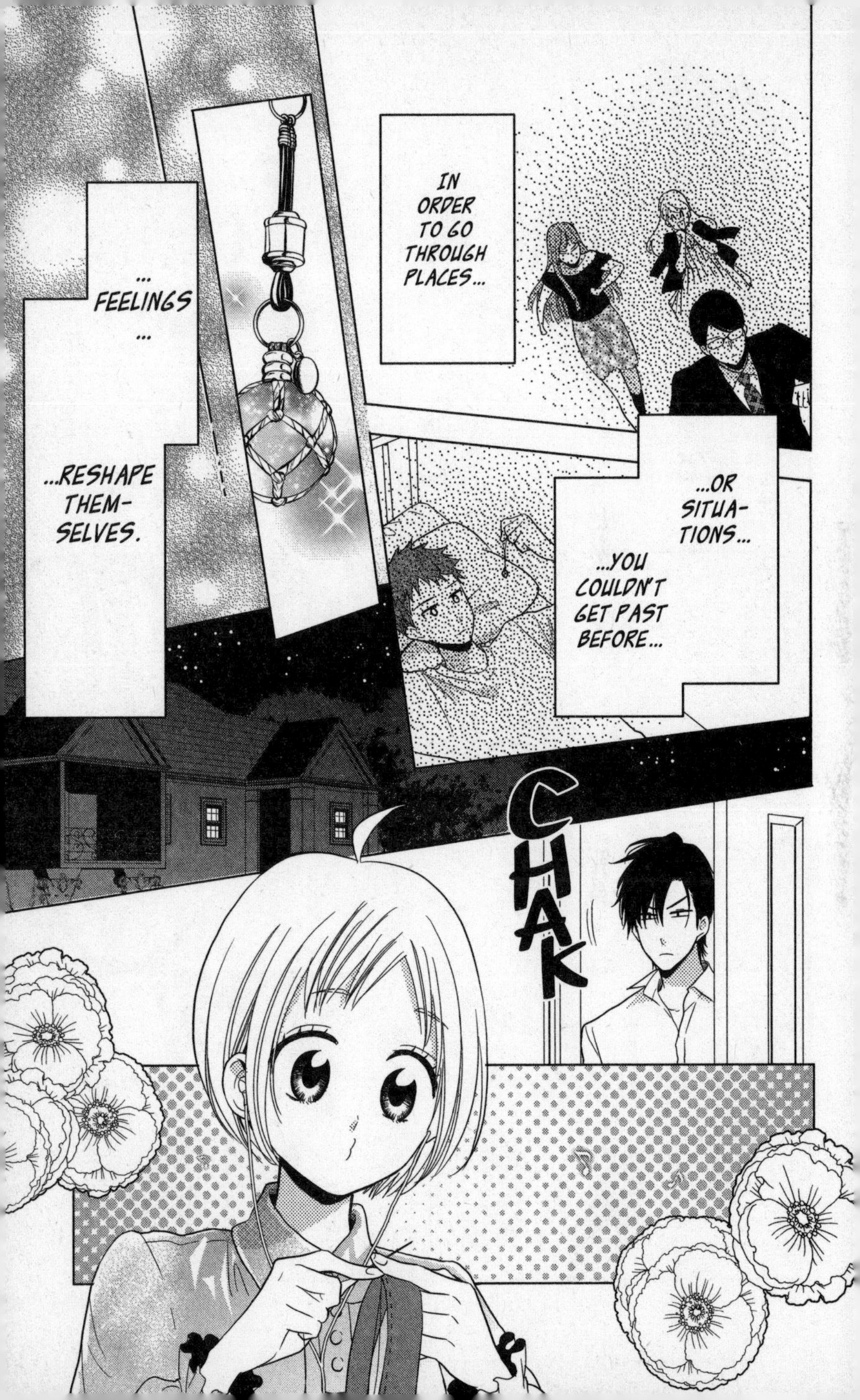

IN ORDER TO GO THROUGH PLACES...
...OR SITUATIONS...
...YOU COULDN'T GET PAST BEFORE...
... FEELINGS ...
...RESHAPE THEMSELVES.
CHAK

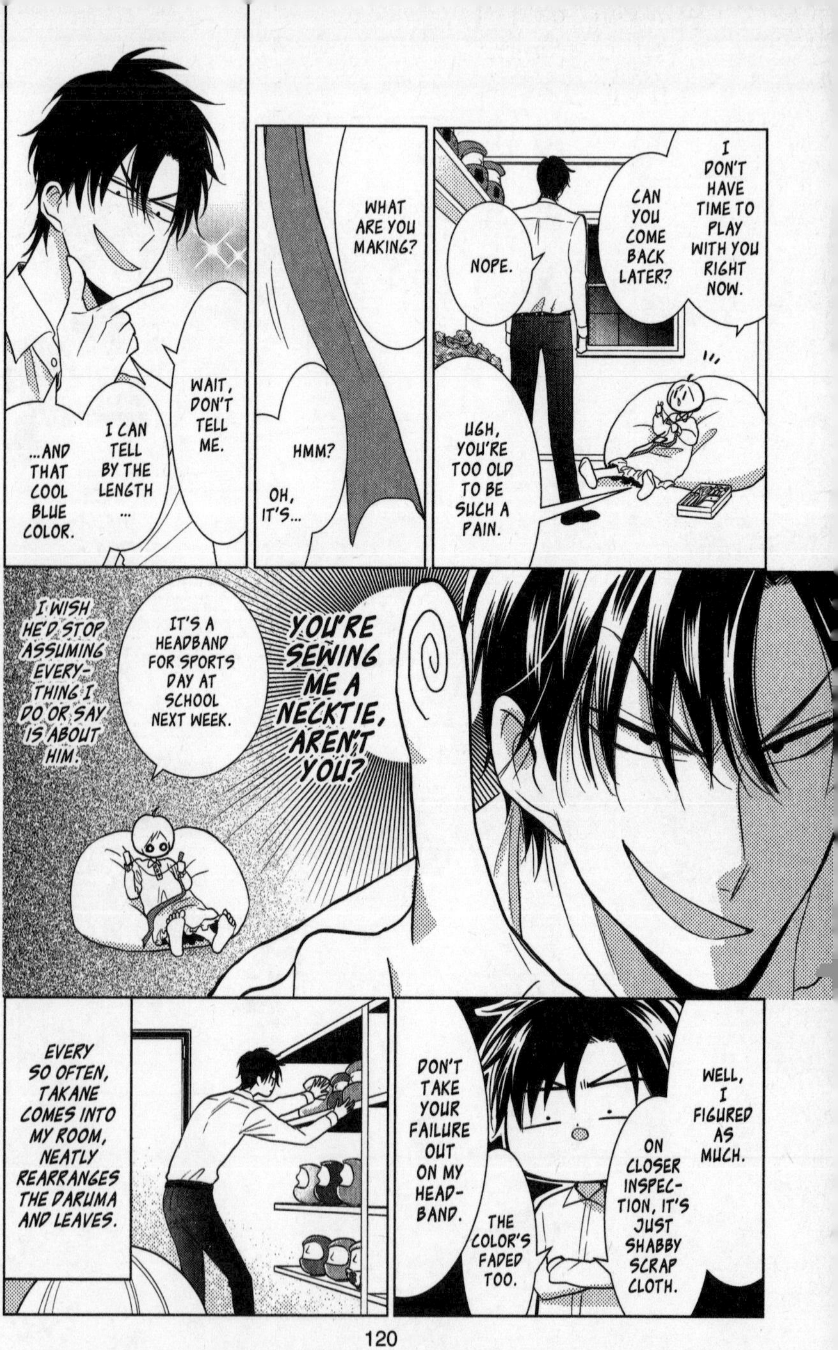
I DON'T HAVE TIME TO PLAY WITH YOU RIGHT NOW.
CAN YOU COME BACK LATER?
NOPE.
UGH, YOU'RE TOO OLD TO BE SUCH A PAIN.
WHAT ARE YOU MAKING?
HMM?
OH, IT'S...
WAIT, DON'T TELL ME.
I CAN TELL BY THE LENGTH...
...AND THAT COOL BLUE COLOR.
YOU'RE SEWING ME A NECKTIE, AREN'T YOU?
IT'S A HEADBAND FOR SPORTS DAY AT SCHOOL NEXT WEEK.
I WISH HE'D STOP ASSUMING EVERYTHING I DO OR SAY IS ABOUT HIM.
WELL, I FIGURED AS MUCH.
ON CLOSER INSPECTION, IT'S JUST SHABBY SCRAP CLOTH.
THE COLOR'S FADED TOO.
DON'T TAKE YOUR FAILURE OUT ON MY HEADBAND.
EVERY SO OFTEN, TAKANE COMES INTO MY ROOM, NEATLY REARRANGES THE DARUMA AND LEAVES.

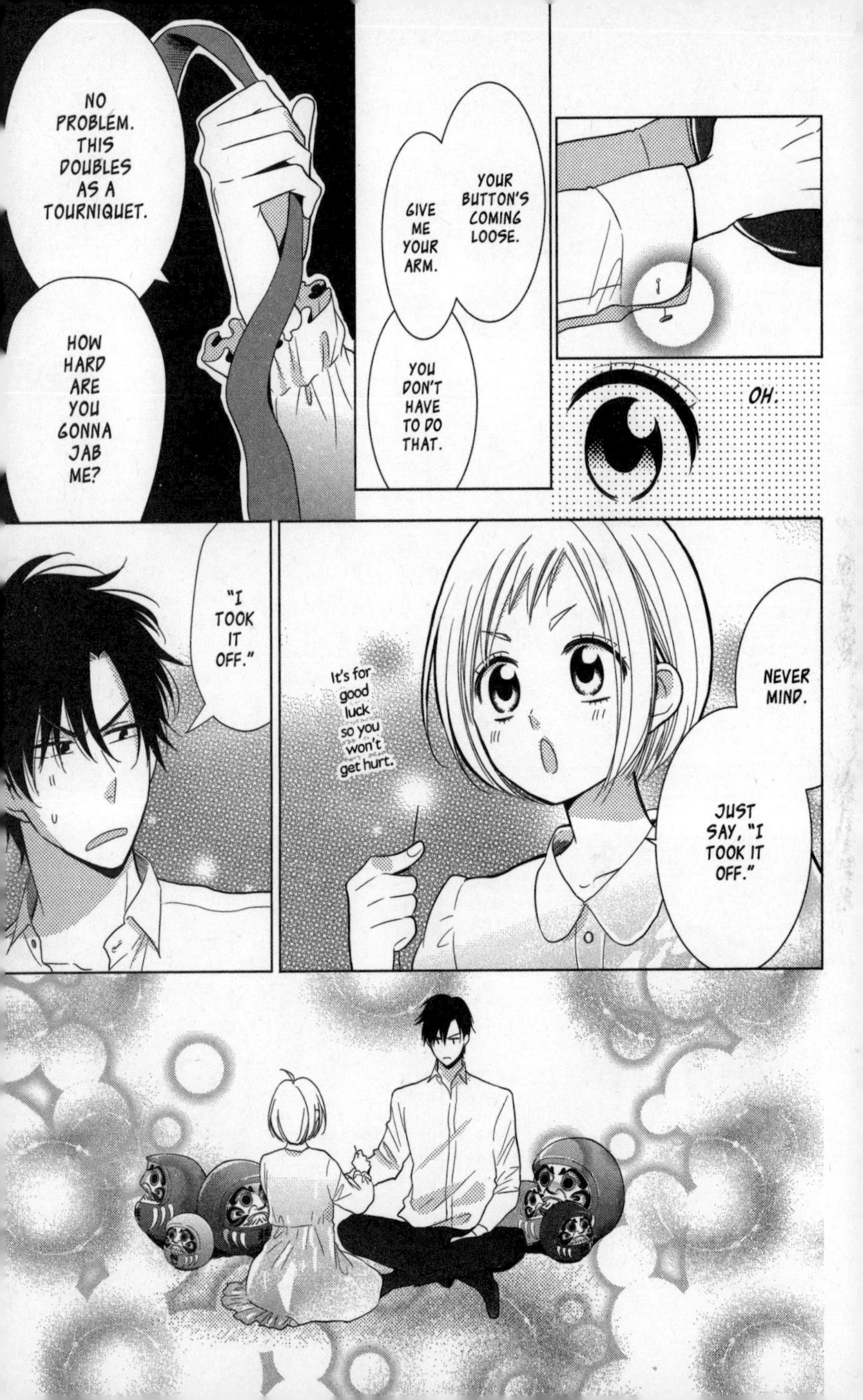
OH.
YOUR BUTTON'S COMING LOOSE.
GIVE ME YOUR ARM.
YOU DON'T HAVE TO DO THAT.
NO PROBLEM. THIS DOUBLES AS A TOURNIQUET.
HOW HARD ARE YOU GONNA JAB ME?
NEVER MIND.
JUST SAY, "I TOOK IT OFF."
It's for good luck so you won't get hurt.
"I TOOK IT OFF."

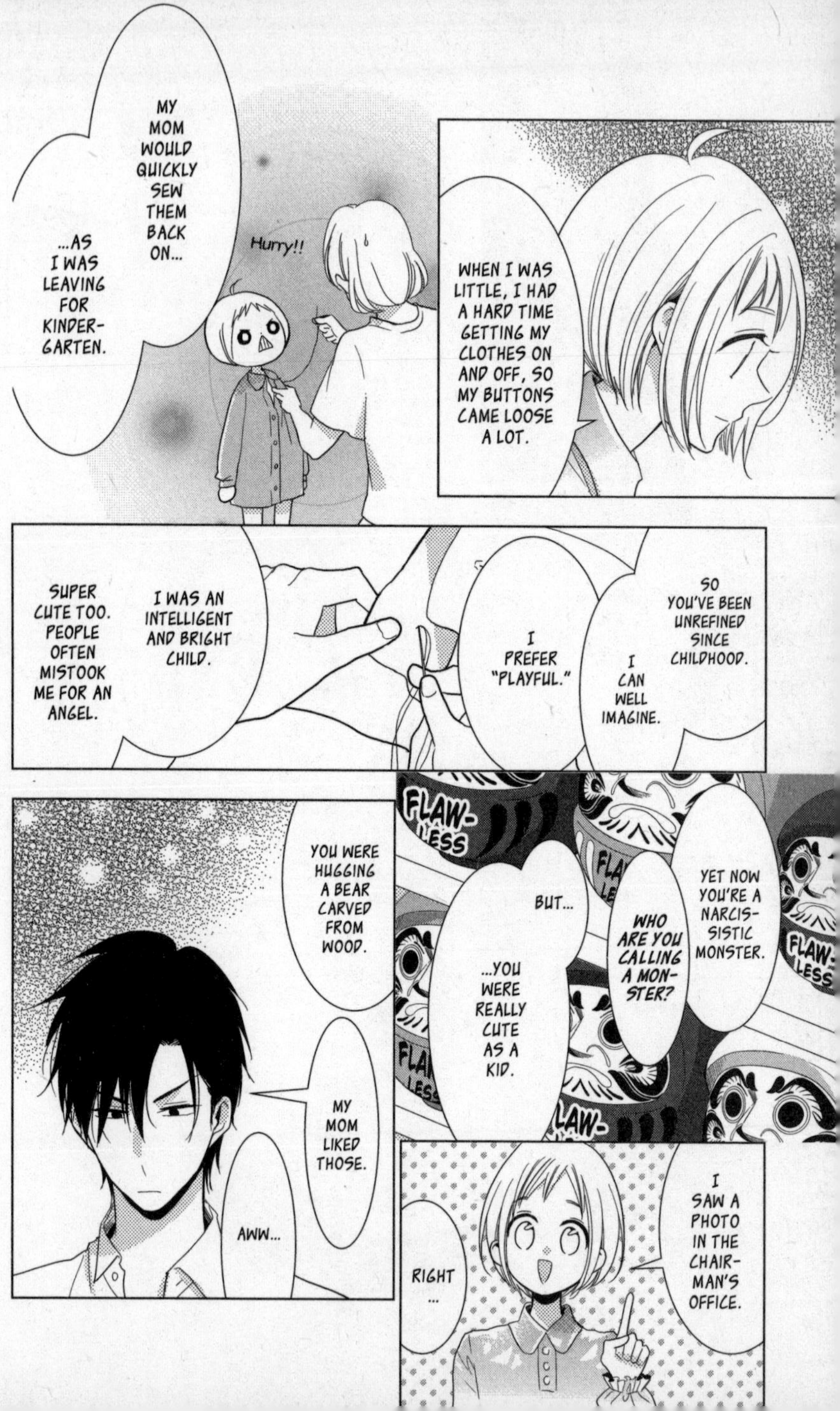
WHEN I WAS LITTLE, I HAD A HARD TIME GETTING MY CLOTHES ON AND OFF, SO MY BUTTONS CAME LOOSE A LOT.
MY MOM WOULD QUICKLY SEW THEM BACK ON...
Hurry!!
...AS I WAS LEAVING FOR KINDERGARTEN.
SO YOU'VE BEEN UNREFINED SINCE CHILDHOOD.
I CAN WELL IMAGINE.
I PREFER "PLAYFUL."
I WAS AN INTELLIGENT AND BRIGHT CHILD.
SUPER CUTE TOO. PEOPLE OFTEN MISTOOK ME FOR AN ANGEL.
YET NOW YOU'RE A NARCISSISTIC MONSTER.
WHO ARE YOU CALLING A MONSTER?
FLAWLESS
BUT...
...YOU WERE REALLY CUTE AS A KID.
I SAW A PHOTO IN THE CHAIRMAN'S OFFICE.
RIGHT...
YOU WERE HUGGING A BEAR CARVED FROM WOOD.
MY MOM LIKED THOSE.
AWW...

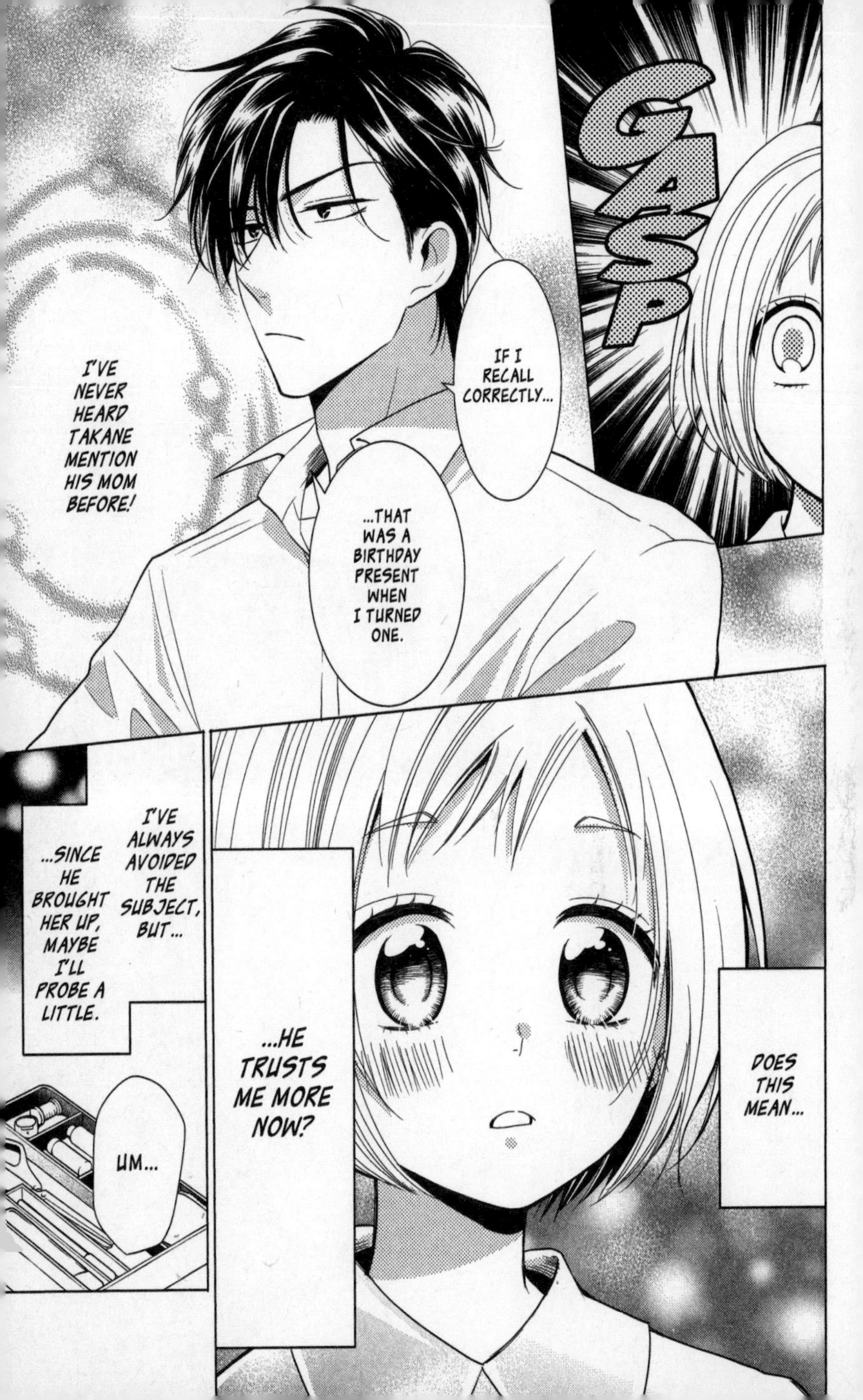
GASP
IF I RECALL CORRECTLY...
...THAT WAS A BIRTHDAY PRESENT WHEN I TURNED ONE.
I'VE NEVER HEARD TAKANE MENTION HIS MOM BEFORE!
DOES THIS MEAN...
...HE TRUSTS ME MORE NOW?
I'VE ALWAYS AVOIDED THE SUBJECT, BUT...
...SINCE HE BROUGHT HER UP, MAYBE I'LL PROBE A LITTLE.
UM...

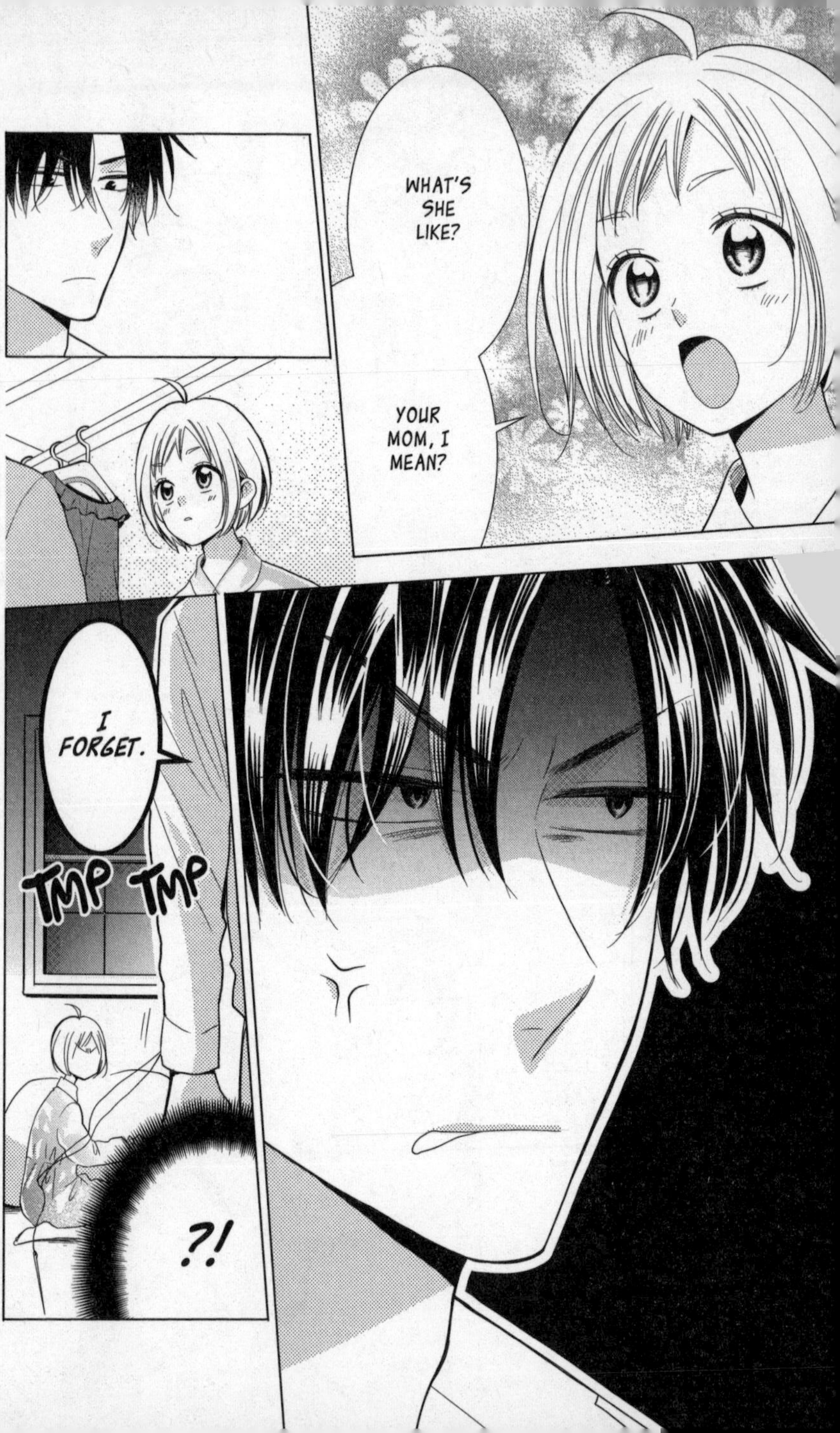
WHAT'S SHE LIKE?
YOUR MOM, I MEAN?
I FORGET.
TMP TMP
?!

After Chapter 77

HOW DO YOU FEEL NOW THAT WE'RE FINALLY EVEN?
SHUSH.
TMP
TMP
FREEZE
TUG
HAS NO GOOD COMEBACK, SO HE REPLIES WITH A GESTURE IMPLYING IT WAS ALL A DREAM.

After Chapter 78

TMP
TMP
TURN
?!
SHUP
!!

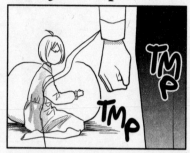

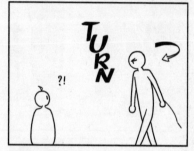

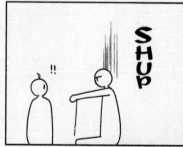

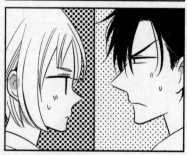

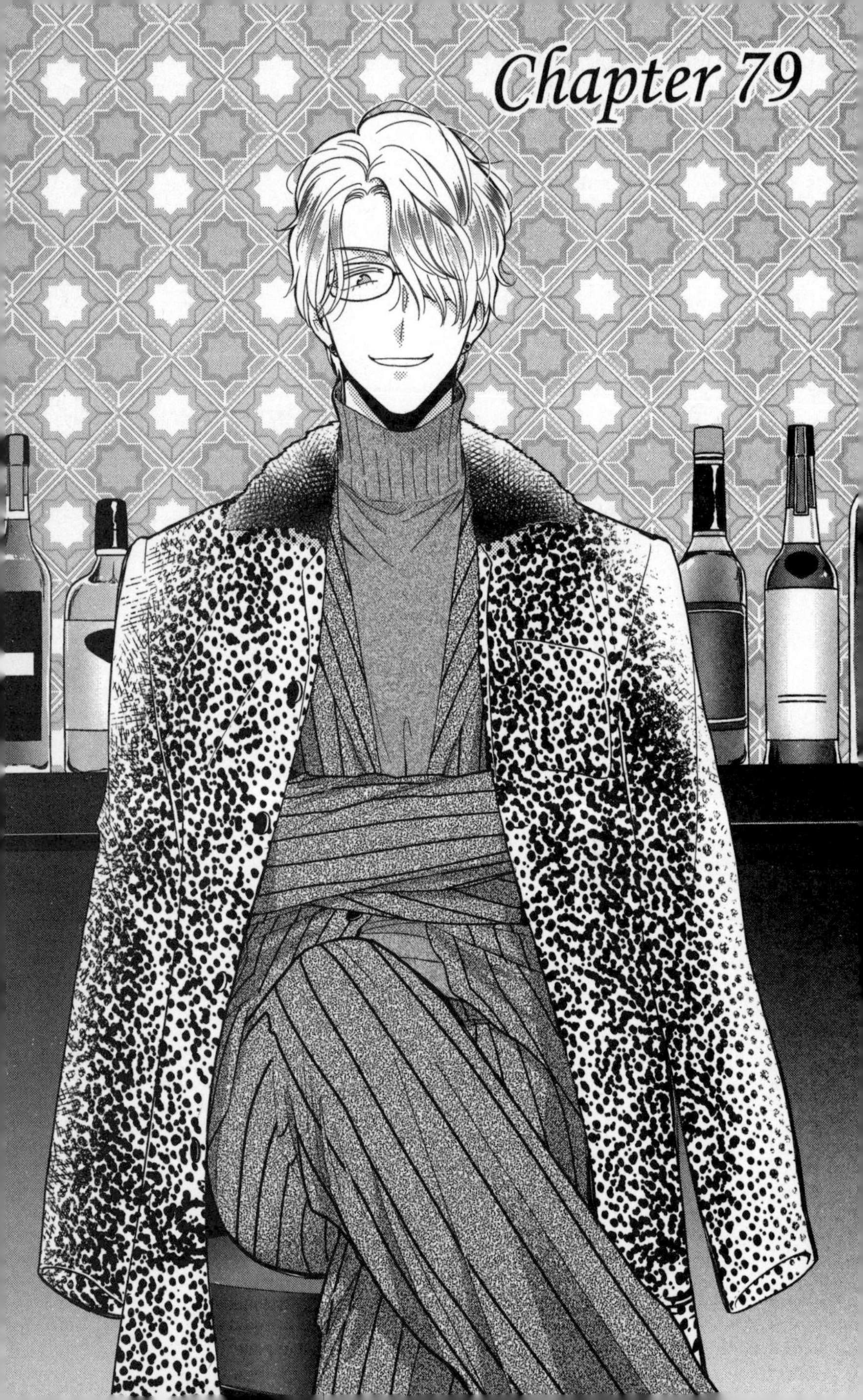
Chapter 79

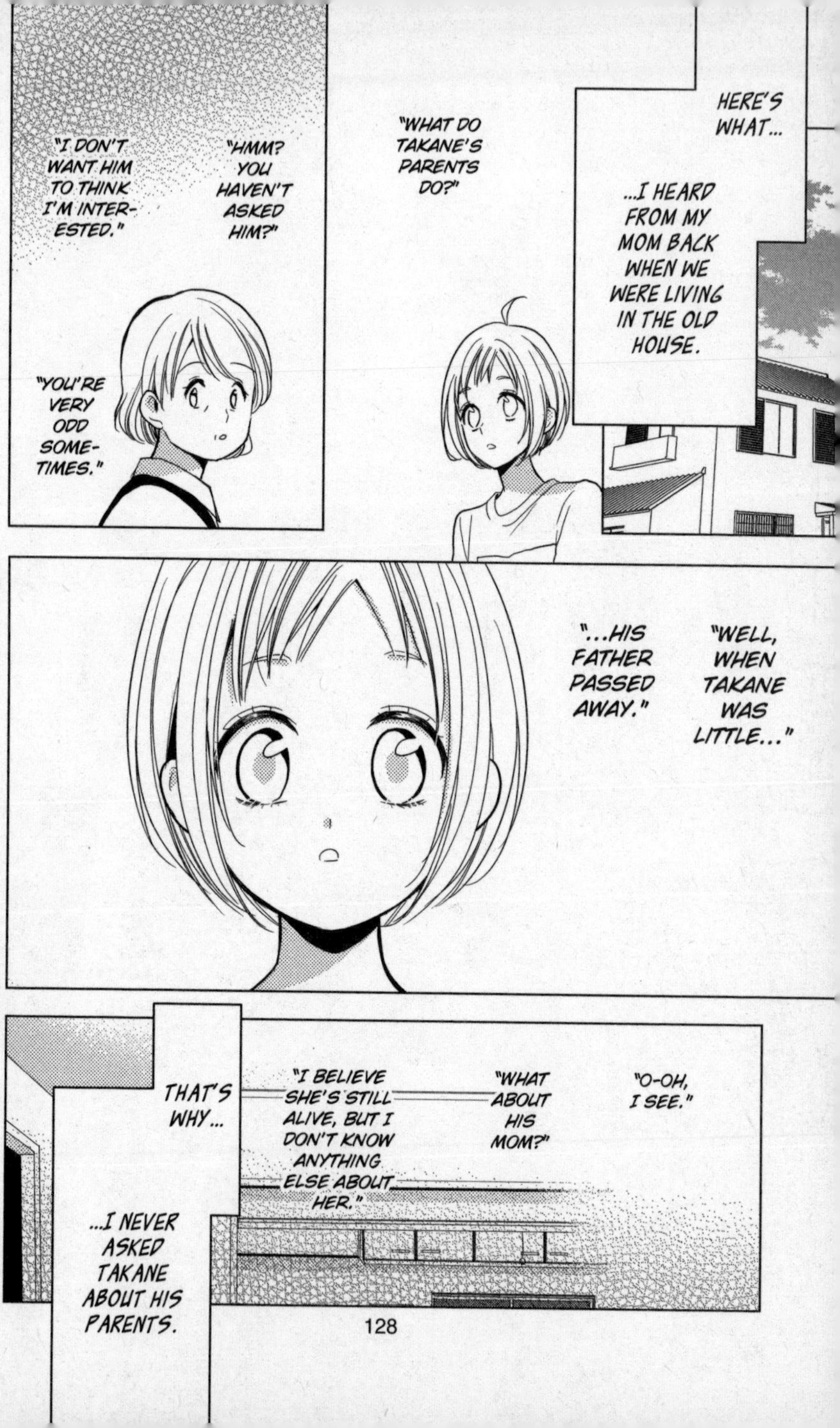
HERE'S WHAT...
...I HEARD FROM MY MOM BACK WHEN WE WERE LIVING IN THE OLD HOUSE.
"WHAT DO TAKANE'S PARENTS DO?"
"HMM? YOU HAVEN'T ASKED HIM?"
"I DON'T WANT HIM TO THINK I'M INTER-ESTED."
"YOU'RE VERY ODD SOME-TIMES."
"WELL, WHEN TAKANE WAS LITTLE..."
"...HIS FATHER PASSED AWAY."
"O-OH, I SEE."
"WHAT ABOUT HIS MOM?"
"I BELIEVE SHE'S STILL ALIVE, BUT I DON'T KNOW ANYTHING ELSE ABOUT HER."
THAT'S WHY...
...I NEVER ASKED TAKANE ABOUT HIS PARENTS.

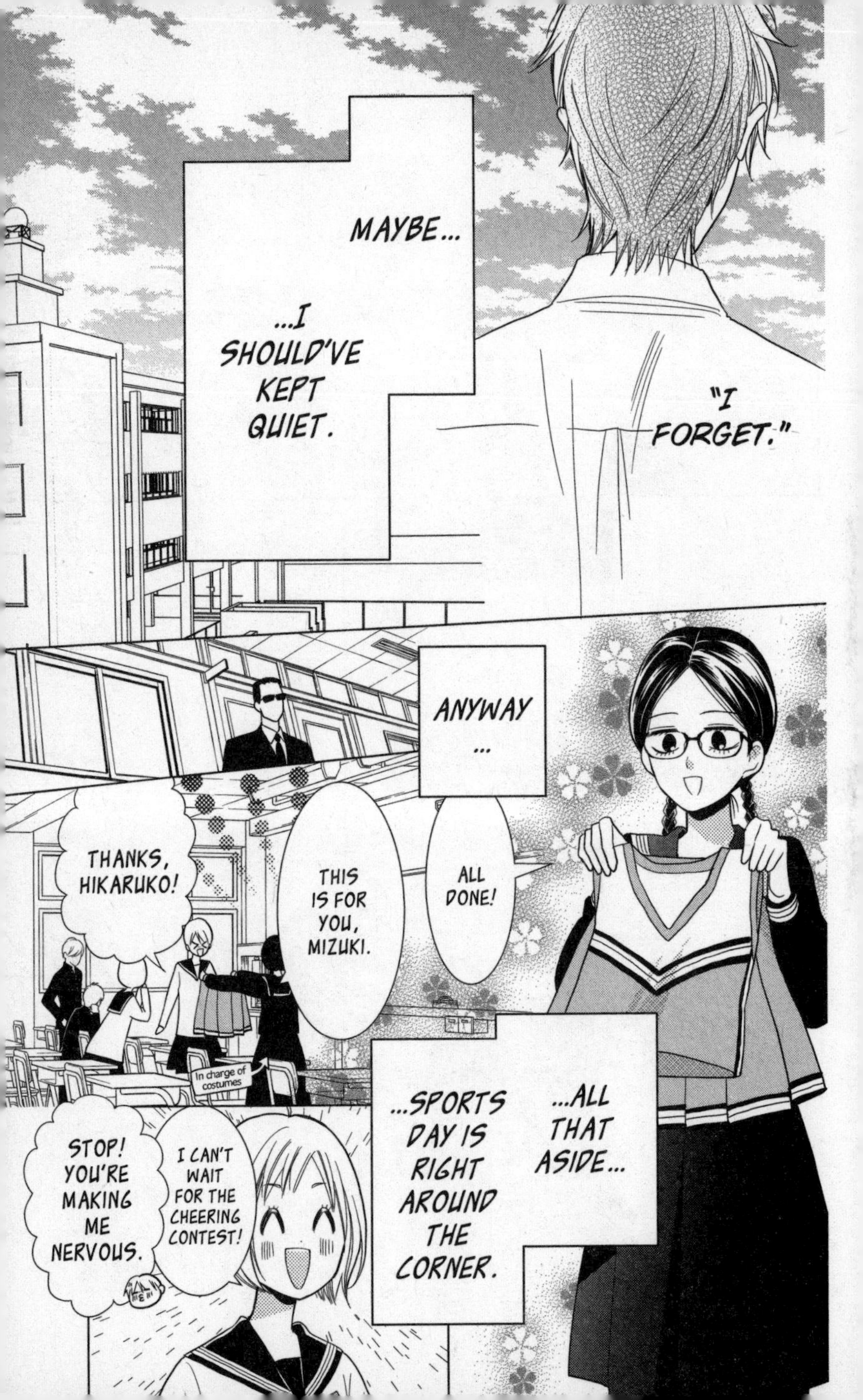
"I FORGET."
MAYBE...
...I SHOULD'VE KEPT QUIET.
ANYWAY...
ALL DONE!
THIS IS FOR YOU, MIZUKI.
THANKS, HIKARUKO!
In charge of costumes
...ALL THAT ASIDE...
...SPORTS DAY IS RIGHT AROUND THE CORNER.
I CAN'T WAIT FOR THE CHEERING CONTEST!
STOP! YOU'RE MAKING ME NERVOUS.

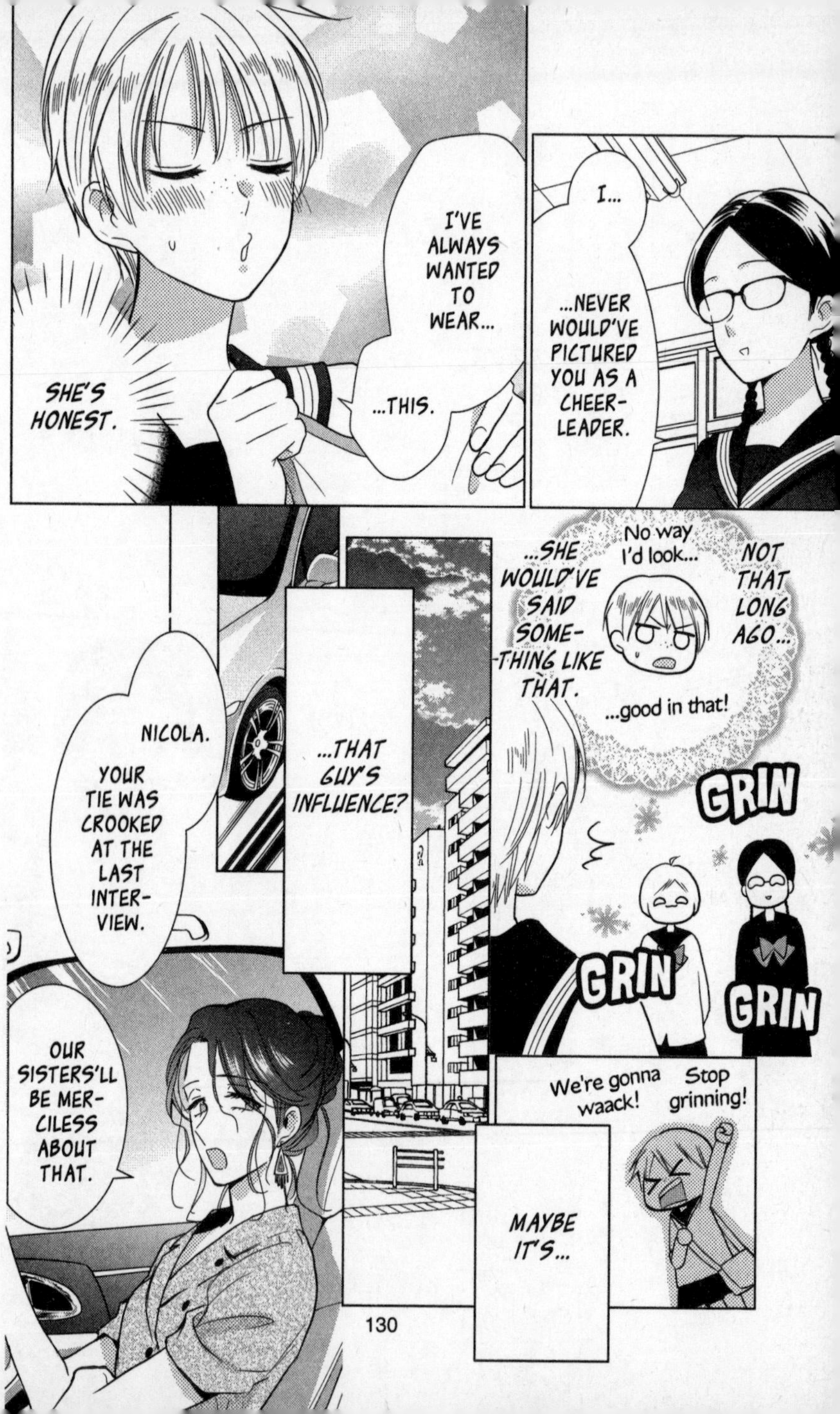
I...
...NEVER WOULD'VE PICTURED YOU AS A CHEERLEADER.
I'VE ALWAYS WANTED TO WEAR...
...THIS.
SHE'S HONEST.
NOT THAT LONG AGO...
No way I'd look...
...SHE WOULD'VE SAID SOMETHING LIKE THAT.
...good in that!
GRIN
GRIN
GRIN
Stop grinning!
We're gonna waack!
MAYBE IT'S...
...THAT GUY'S INFLUENCE?
NICOLA.
YOUR TIE WAS CROOKED AT THE LAST INTERVIEW.
OUR SISTERS'LL BE MERCILESS ABOUT THAT.

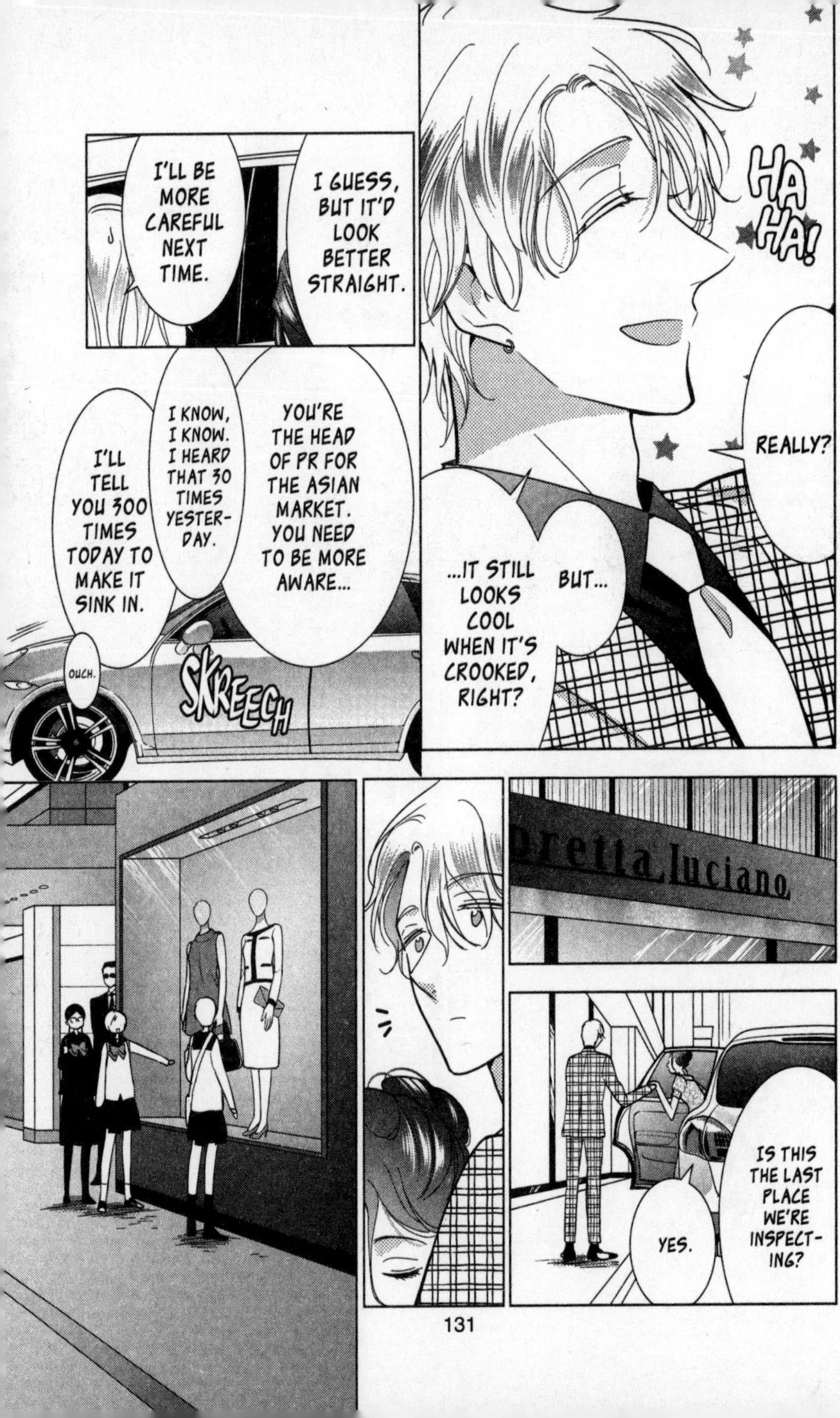
HA HA!
REALLY?
BUT...
...IT STILL LOOKS COOL WHEN IT'S CROOKED, RIGHT?
I GUESS, BUT IT'D LOOK BETTER STRAIGHT.
I'LL BE MORE CAREFUL NEXT TIME.
YOU'RE THE HEAD OF PR FOR THE ASIAN MARKET. YOU NEED TO BE MORE AWARE...
I KNOW, I KNOW. I HEARD THAT 30 TIMES YESTER-DAY.
I'LL TELL YOU 300 TIMES TODAY TO MAKE IT SINK IN.
SKREECH
OUCH.
oretta luciano
IS THIS THE LAST PLACE WE'RE INSPECT-ING?
YES.

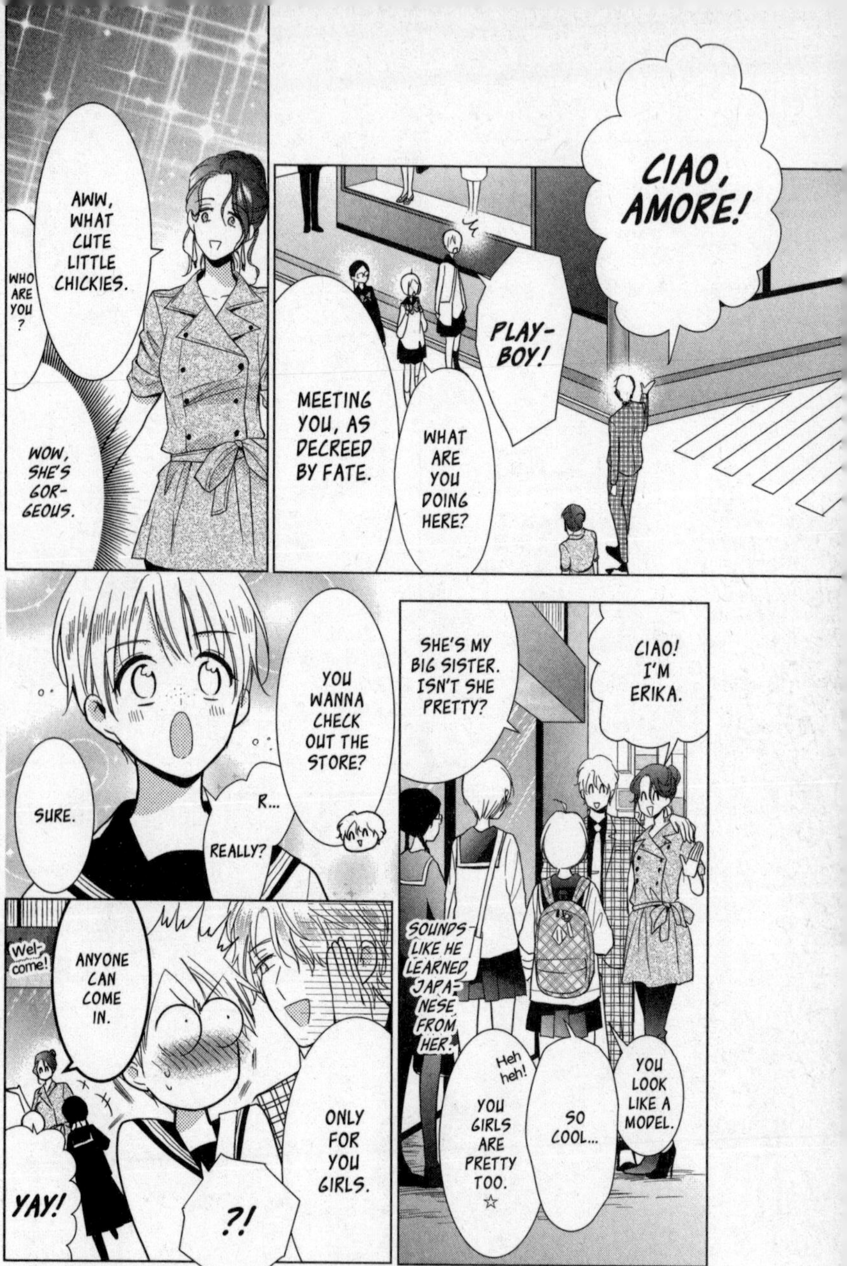
CIAO, AMORE!
PLAY-BOY!
WHAT ARE YOU DOING HERE?
MEETING YOU, AS DECREED BY FATE.
AWW, WHAT CUTE LITTLE CHICKIES.
WHO ARE YOU?
WOW, SHE'S GORGEOUS.
CIAO! I'M ERIKA.
SHE'S MY BIG SISTER. ISN'T SHE PRETTY?
YOU LOOK LIKE A MODEL.
SO COOL...
Heh heh!
YOU GIRLS ARE PRETTY TOO. ☆
SOUNDS LIKE HE LEARNED JAPANESE FROM HER.
YOU WANNA CHECK OUT THE STORE?
R...
REALLY?
SURE.
ONLY FOR YOU GIRLS.
?!
ANYONE CAN COME IN.
Wel-come!
YAY!

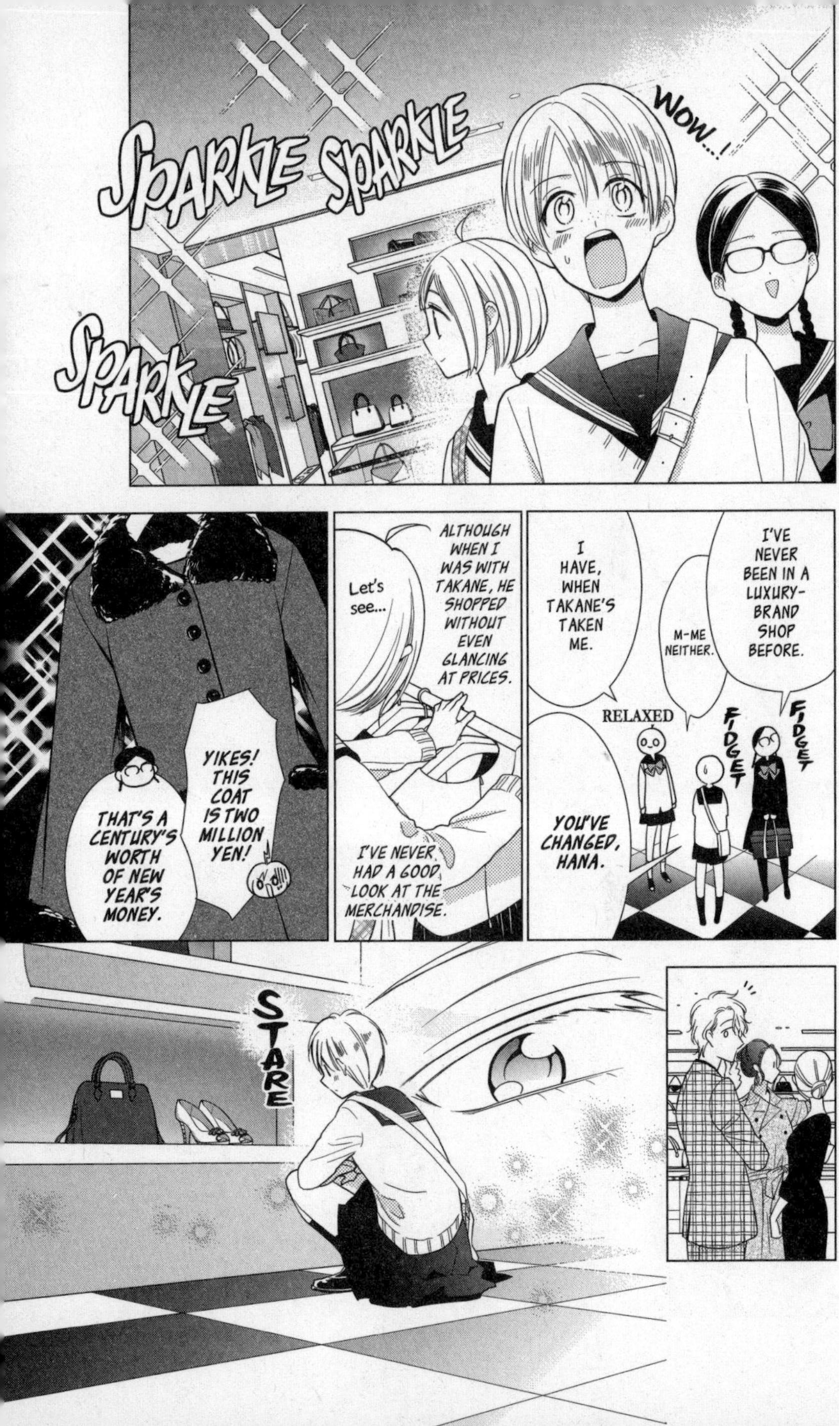
WOW...!
SPARKLE SPARKLE
SPARKLE
I'VE NEVER BEEN IN A LUXURY-BRAND SHOP BEFORE.
FIDGET
FIDGET
M-ME NEITHER.
I HAVE, WHEN TAKANE'S TAKEN ME.
RELAXED
YOU'VE CHANGED, HANA.
ALTHOUGH WHEN I WAS WITH TAKANE, HE SHOPPED WITHOUT EVEN GLANCING AT PRICES.
Let's see...
I'VE NEVER HAD A GOOD LOOK AT THE MERCHANDISE.
YIKES! THIS COAT IS TWO MILLION YEN!
THAT'S A CENTURY'S WORTH OF NEW YEAR'S MONEY.
STARE

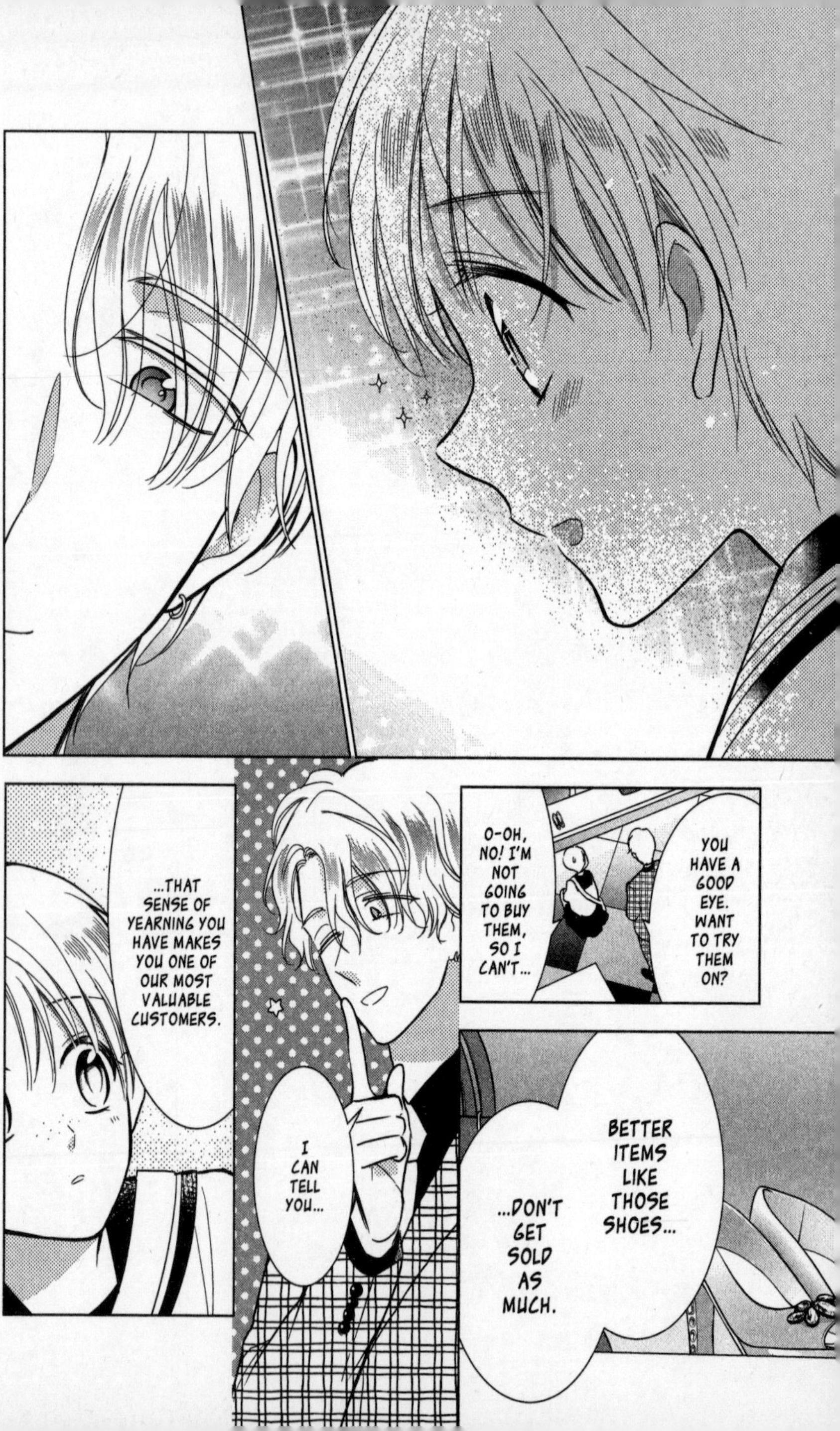
YOU HAVE A GOOD EYE. WANT TO TRY THEM ON?
O-OH, NO! I'M NOT GOING TO BUY THEM, SO I CAN'T...
BETTER ITEMS LIKE THOSE SHOES...
...DON'T GET SOLD AS MUCH.
I CAN TELL YOU...
...THAT SENSE OF YEARNING YOU HAVE MAKES YOU ONE OF OUR MOST VALUABLE CUSTOMERS.

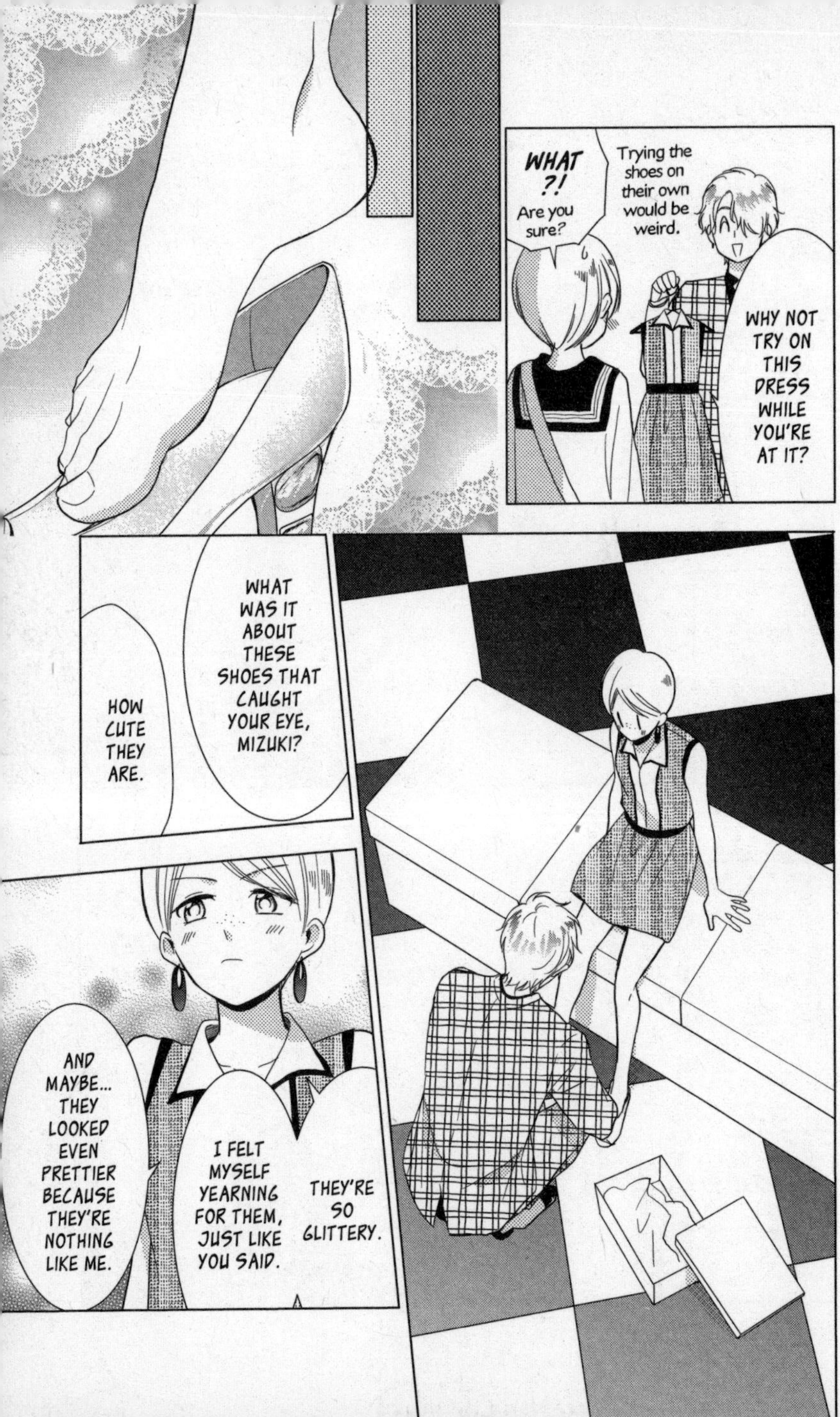

WHY NOT TRY ON THIS DRESS WHILE YOU'RE AT IT?
Trying the shoes on their own would be weird.
WHAT?! Are you sure?
WHAT WAS IT ABOUT THESE SHOES THAT CAUGHT YOUR EYE, MIZUKI?
HOW CUTE THEY ARE.
THEY'RE SO GLITTERY.
I FELT MYSELF YEARNING FOR THEM, JUST LIKE YOU SAID.
AND MAYBE... THEY LOOKED EVEN PRETTIER BECAUSE THEY'RE NOTHING LIKE ME.

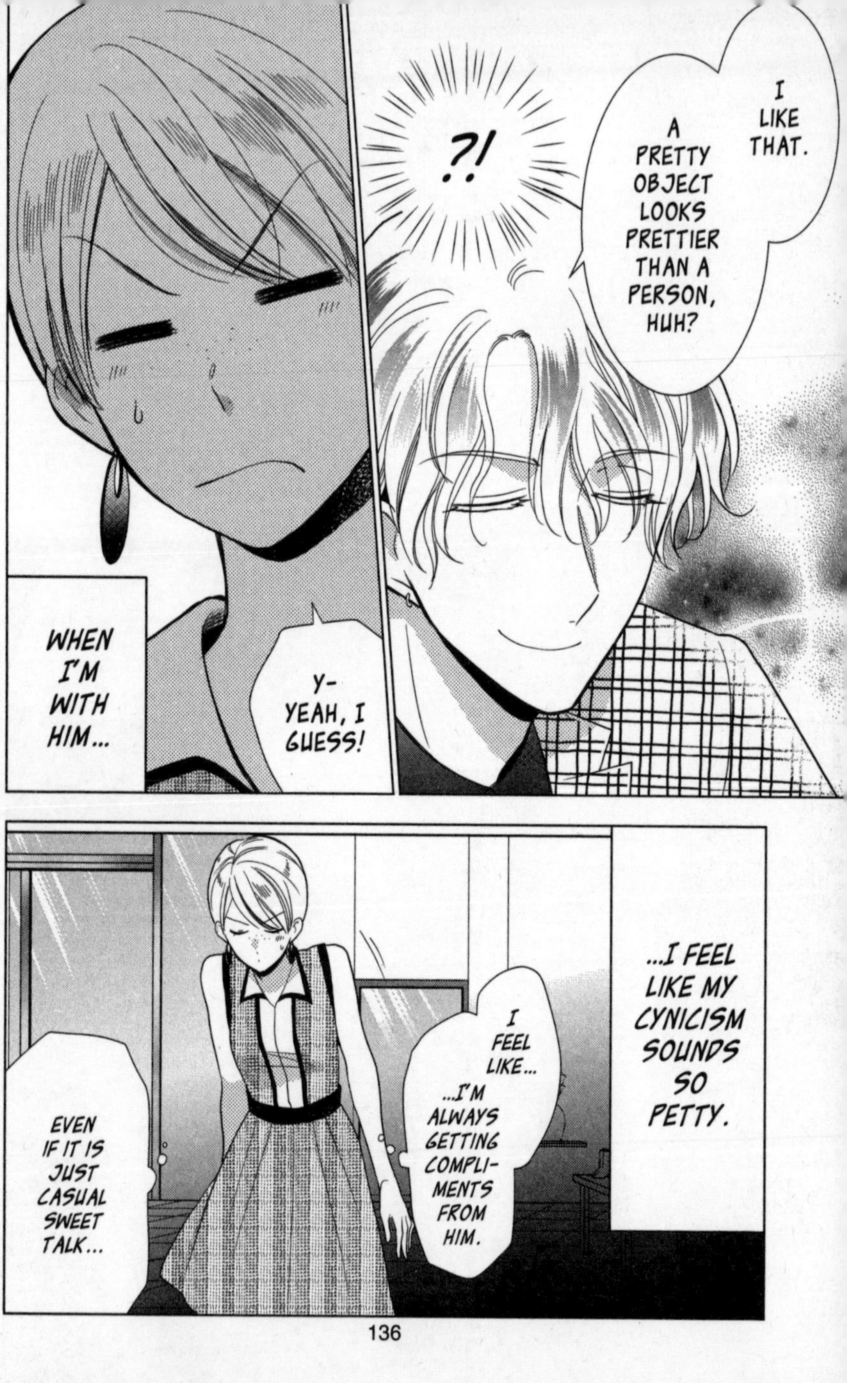
A PRETTY OBJECT LOOKS PRETTIER THAN A PERSON, HUH? I LIKE THAT.
?!
Y-YEAH, I GUESS!
WHEN I'M WITH HIM...
...I FEEL LIKE MY CYNICISM SOUNDS SO PETTY.
I FEEL LIKE... ...I'M ALWAYS GETTING COMPLI-MENTS FROM HIM.
EVEN IF IT IS JUST CASUAL SWEET TALK...

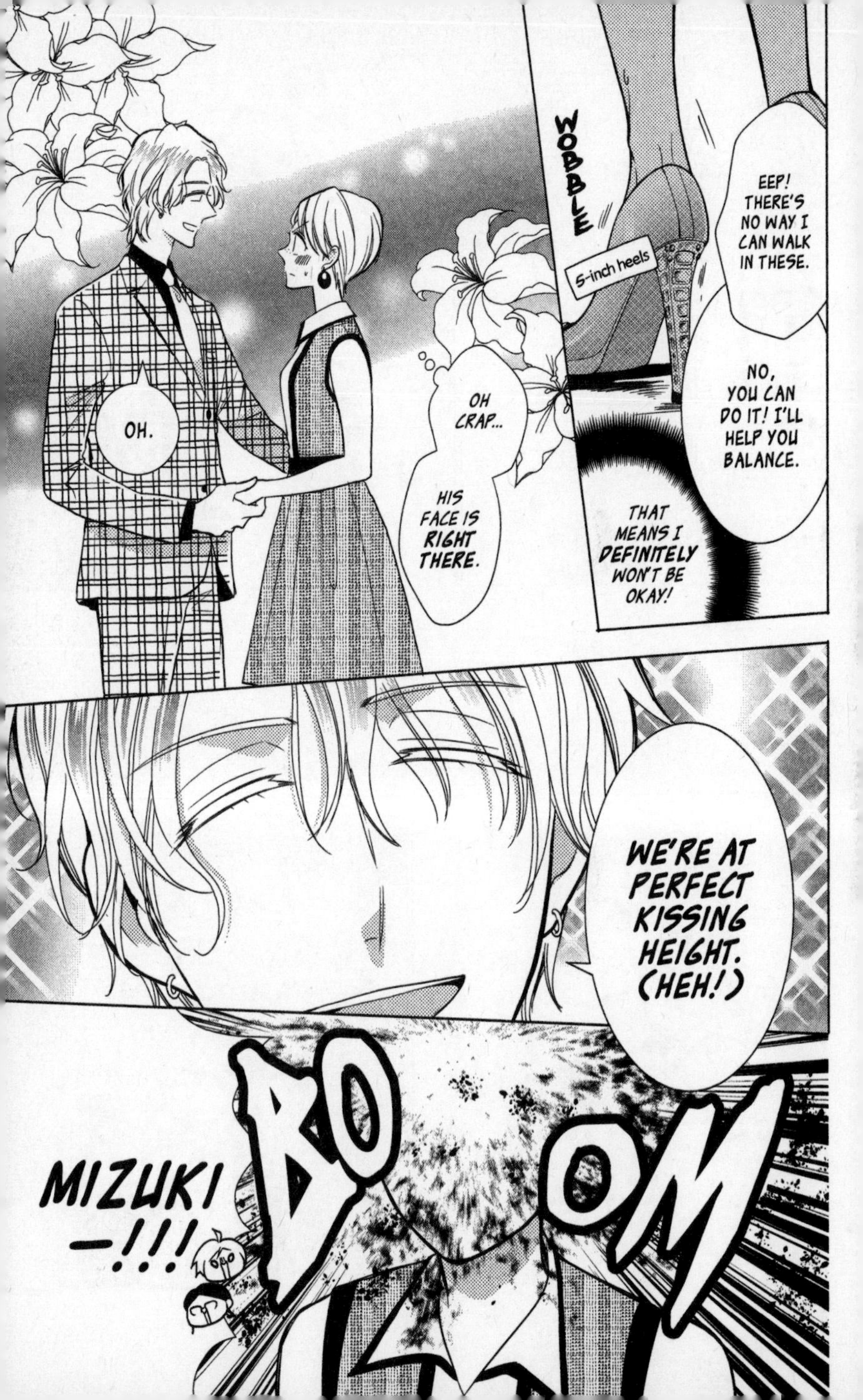

WOBBLE
EEP! THERE'S NO WAY I CAN WALK IN THESE.
5-inch heels
NO, YOU CAN DO IT! I'LL HELP YOU BALANCE.
THAT MEANS I DEFINITELY WON'T BE OKAY!
OH CRAP... HIS FACE IS RIGHT THERE.
OH.
WE'RE AT PERFECT KISSING HEIGHT. (HEH!)
BOOM
MIZUKI—!!!

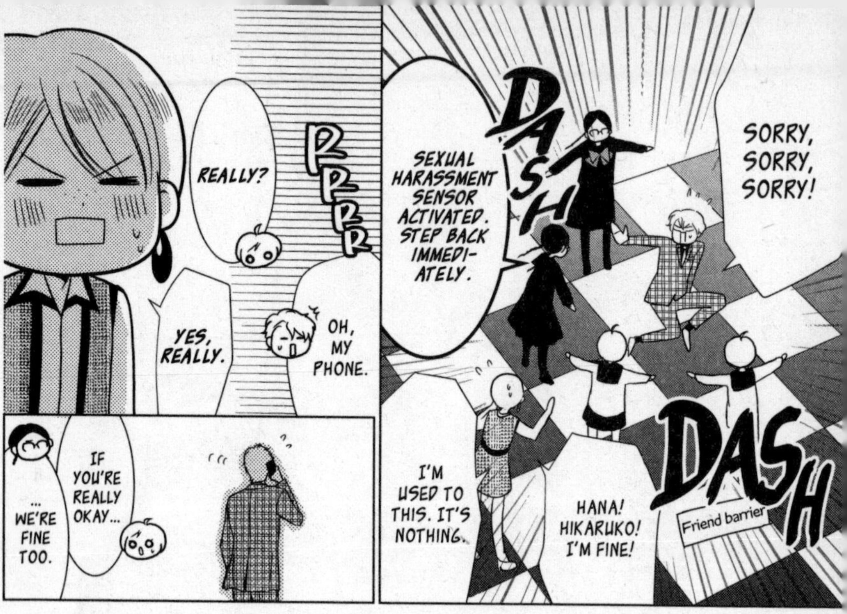
SORRY, SORRY, SORRY!
DASH
SEXUAL HARASSMENT SENSOR ACTIVATED. STEP BACK IMMEDIATELY.
DASH
Friend barrier
HANA! HIKARUKO! I'M FINE!
I'M USED TO THIS. IT'S NOTHING.
RRRR
OH, MY PHONE.
REALLY?
YES, REALLY.
IF YOU'RE REALLY OKAY...
...WE'RE FINE TOO.

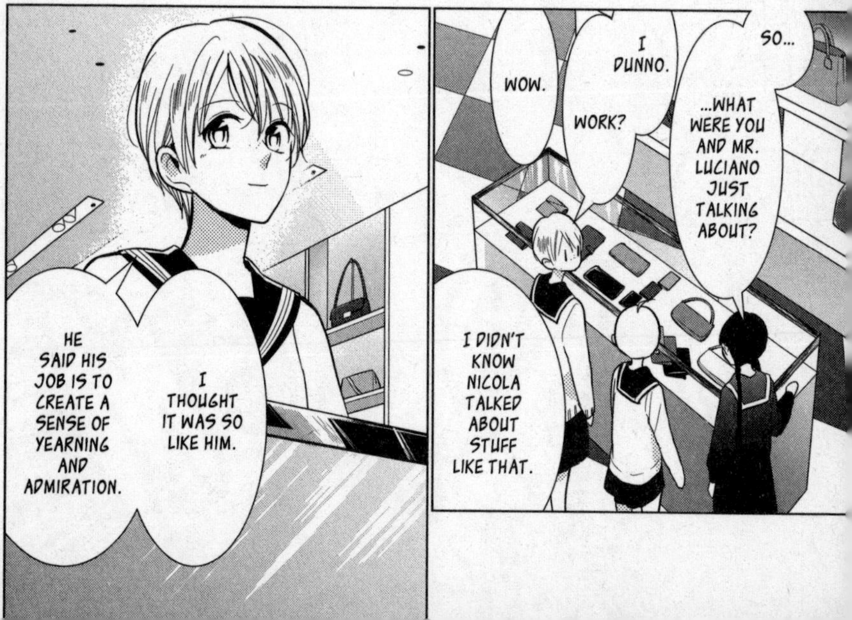
SO...
...WHAT WERE YOU AND MR. LUCIANO JUST TALKING ABOUT?
I DUNNO.
WORK?
WOW.
I DIDN'T KNOW NICOLA TALKED ABOUT STUFF LIKE THAT.
HE SAID HIS JOB IS TO CREATE A SENSE OF YEARNING AND ADMIRATION.
I THOUGHT IT WAS SO LIKE HIM.

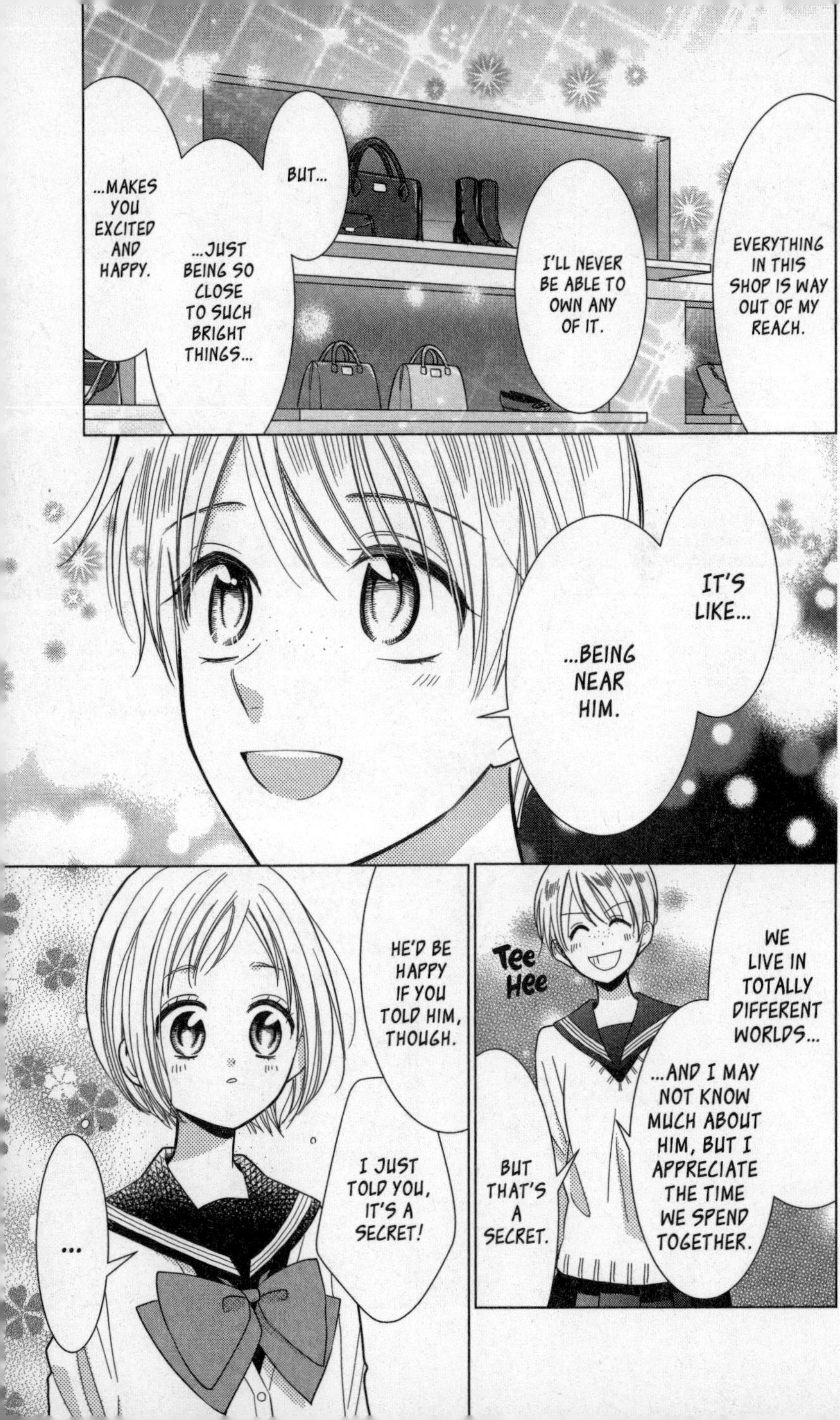
EVERYTHING IN THIS SHOP IS WAY OUT OF MY REACH.
I'LL NEVER BE ABLE TO OWN ANY OF IT.
BUT...
...JUST BEING SO CLOSE TO SUCH BRIGHT THINGS...
...MAKES YOU EXCITED AND HAPPY.
IT'S LIKE...
...BEING NEAR HIM.
WE LIVE IN TOTALLY DIFFERENT WORLDS...
...AND I MAY NOT KNOW MUCH ABOUT HIM, BUT I APPRECIATE THE TIME WE SPEND TOGETHER.
Tee Hee
BUT THAT'S A SECRET.
HE'D BE HAPPY IF YOU TOLD HIM, THOUGH.
I JUST TOLD YOU, IT'S A SECRET!
...

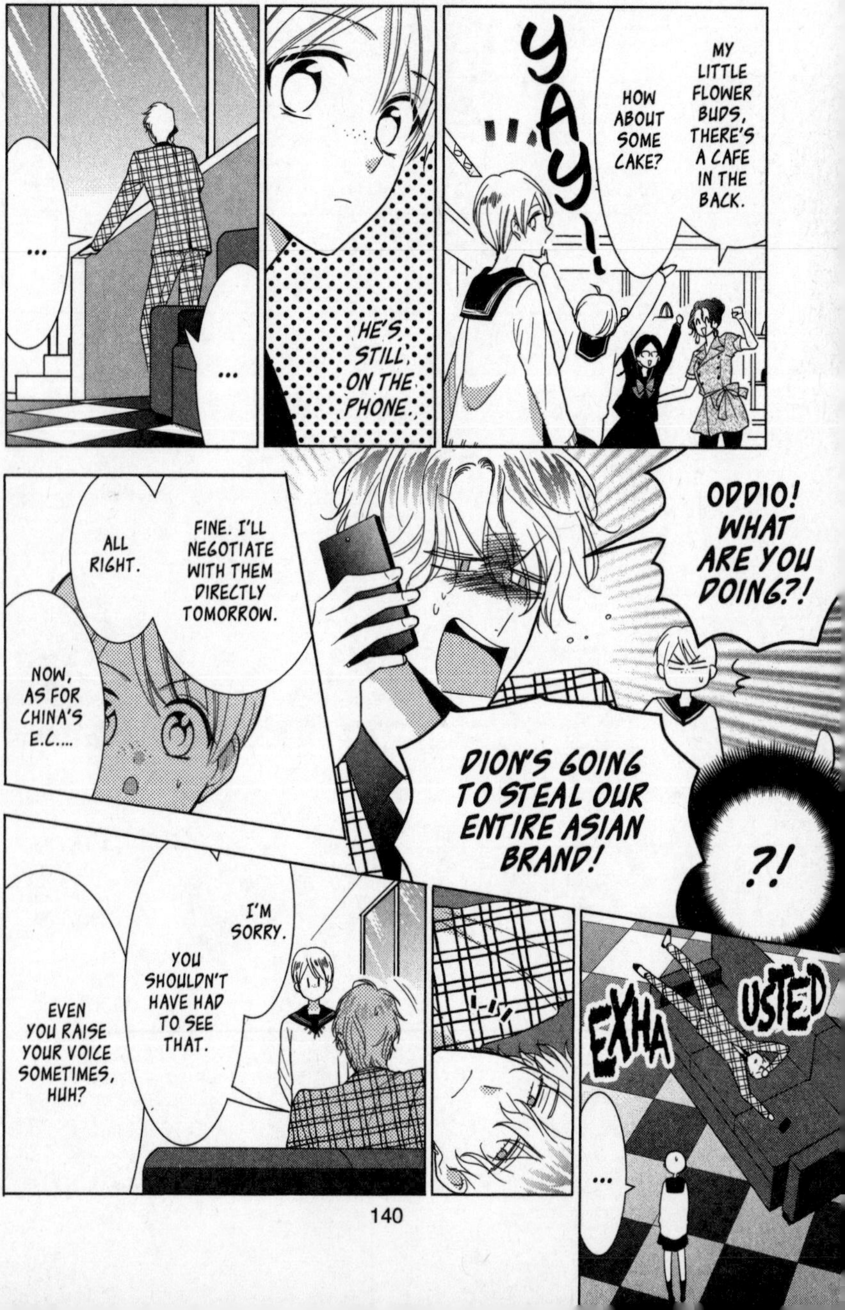
MY LITTLE FLOWER BUDS, THERE'S A CAFE IN THE BACK.
HOW ABOUT SOME CAKE?
YAY!!
HE'S STILL ON THE PHONE.
...
...
ODDIO! WHAT ARE YOU DOING?!
FINE. I'LL NEGOTIATE WITH THEM DIRECTLY TOMORROW.
ALL RIGHT.
NOW, AS FOR CHINA'S E.C....
DION'S GOING TO STEAL OUR ENTIRE ASIAN BRAND!
?!
EXHAUSTED
...
I'M SORRY.
YOU SHOULDN'T HAVE HAD TO SEE THAT.
EVEN YOU RAISE YOUR VOICE SOMETIMES, HUH?

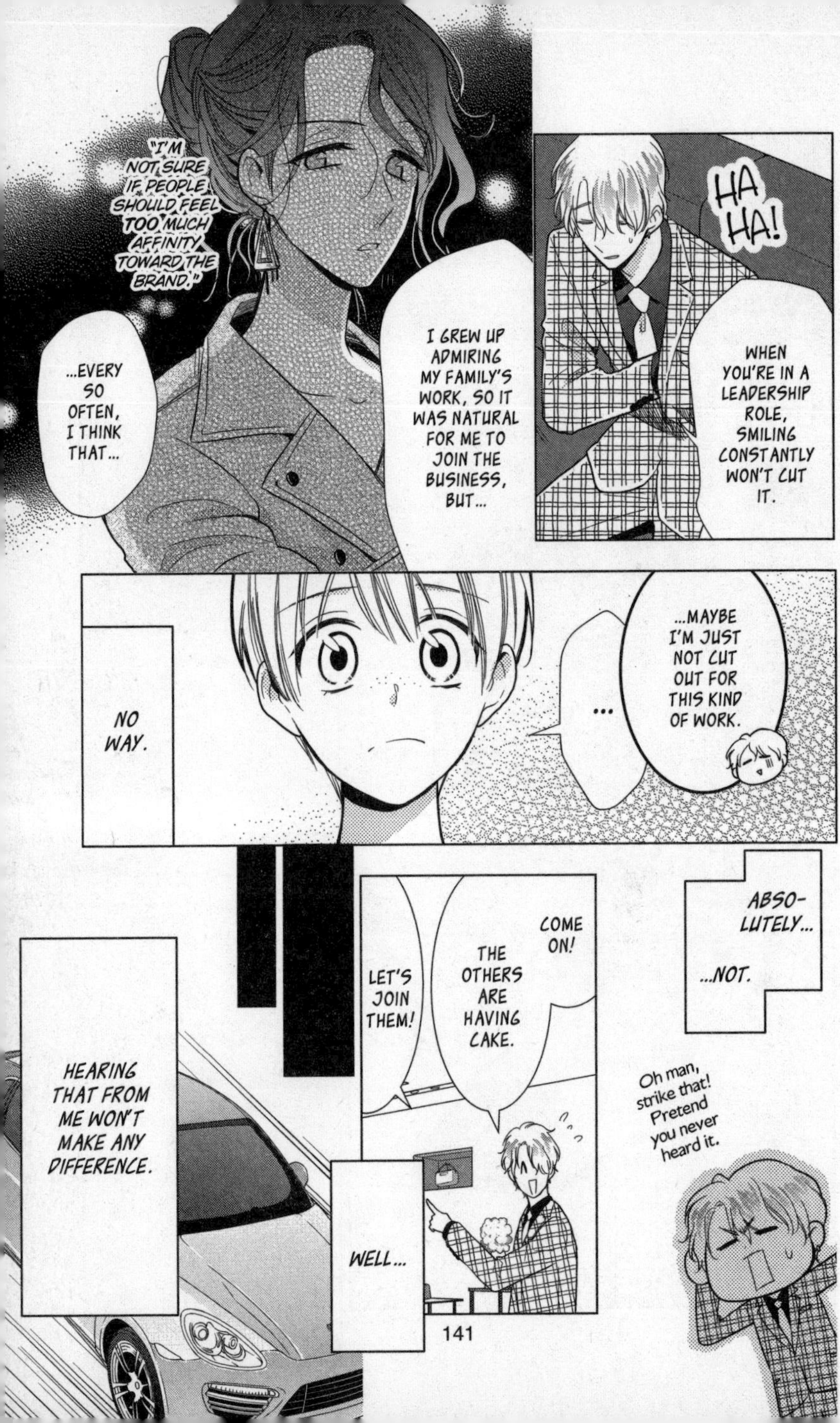
HA HA!
WHEN YOU'RE IN A LEADERSHIP ROLE, SMILING CONSTANTLY WON'T CUT IT.
I GREW UP ADMIRING MY FAMILY'S WORK, SO IT WAS NATURAL FOR ME TO JOIN THE BUSINESS, BUT...
...EVERY SO OFTEN, I THINK THAT...
"I'M NOT SURE IF PEOPLE SHOULD FEEL TOO MUCH AFFINITY TOWARD THE BRAND."
...MAYBE I'M JUST NOT CUT OUT FOR THIS KIND OF WORK.
...
NO WAY.
ABSO-LUTELY...
...NOT.
Oh man, strike that! Pretend you never heard it.
COME ON!
THE OTHERS ARE HAVING CAKE.
LET'S JOIN THEM!
WELL...
HEARING THAT FROM ME WON'T MAKE ANY DIFFERENCE.

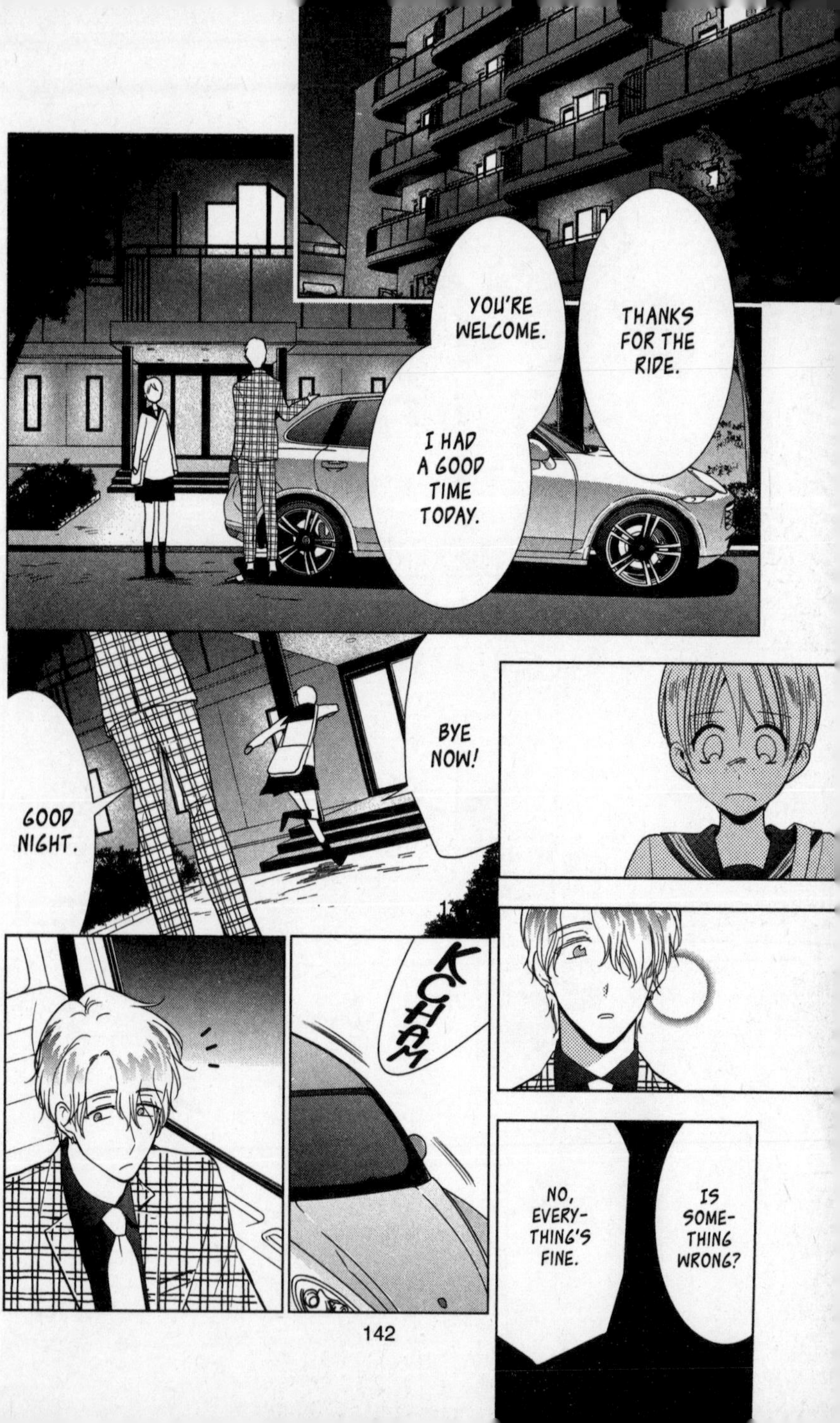
THANKS FOR THE RIDE.
YOU'RE WELCOME.
I HAD A GOOD TIME TODAY.
BYE NOW!
GOOD NIGHT.
KCHAM
IS SOMETHING WRONG?
NO, EVERYTHING'S FINE.

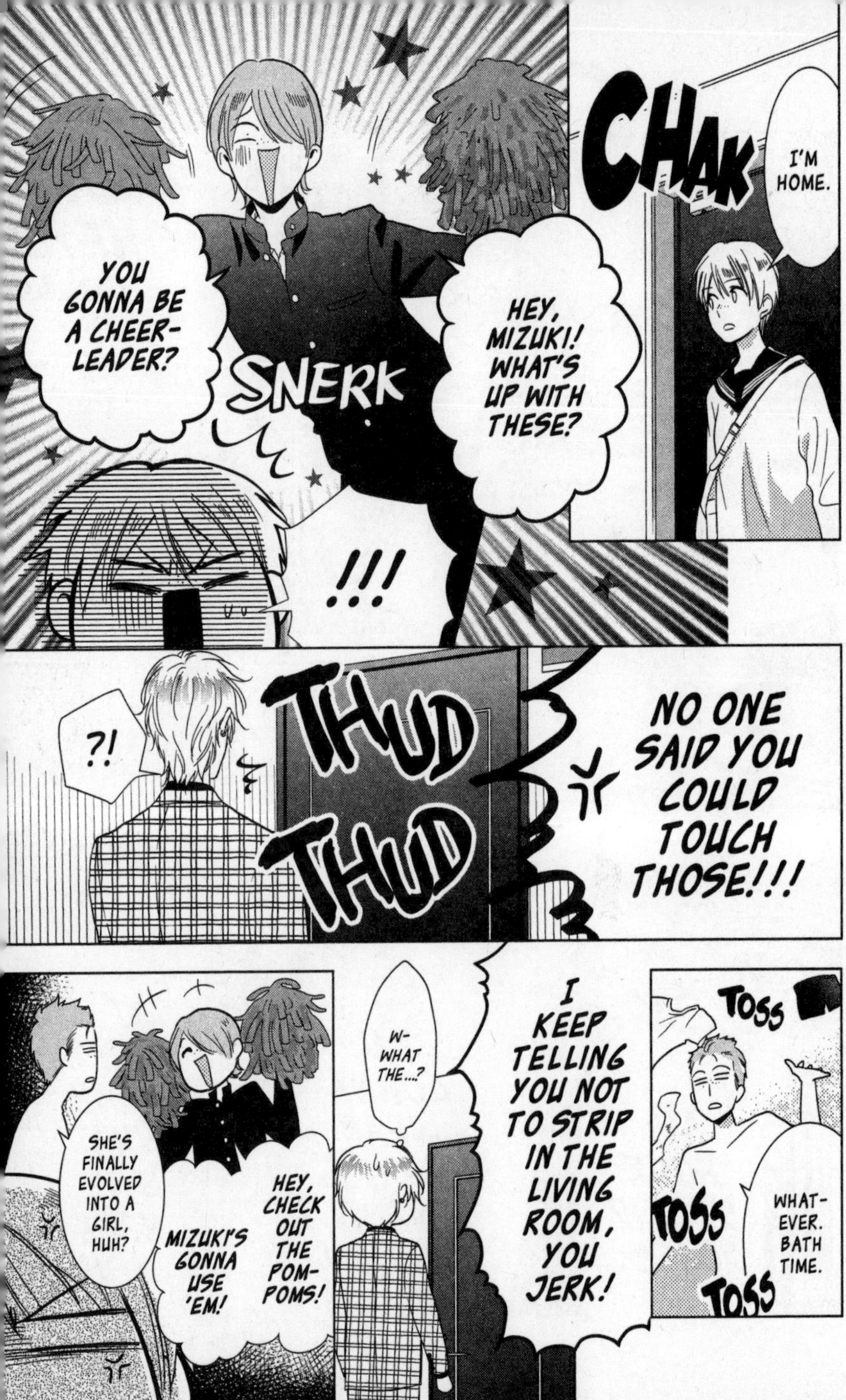
CHAK
I'M HOME.
HEY, MIZUKI! WHAT'S UP WITH THESE?
SNERK
YOU GONNA BE A CHEER-LEADER?
!!!
NO ONE SAID YOU COULD TOUCH THOSE!!!
THUD THUD
?!
TOSS
WHAT-EVER. BATH TIME.
TOSS
TOSS
I KEEP TELLING YOU NOT TO STRIP IN THE LIVING ROOM, YOU JERK!
W-WHAT THE...?
HEY, CHECK OUT THE POM-POMS!
MIZUKI'S GONNA USE 'EM!
SHE'S FINALLY EVOLVED INTO A GIRL, HUH?

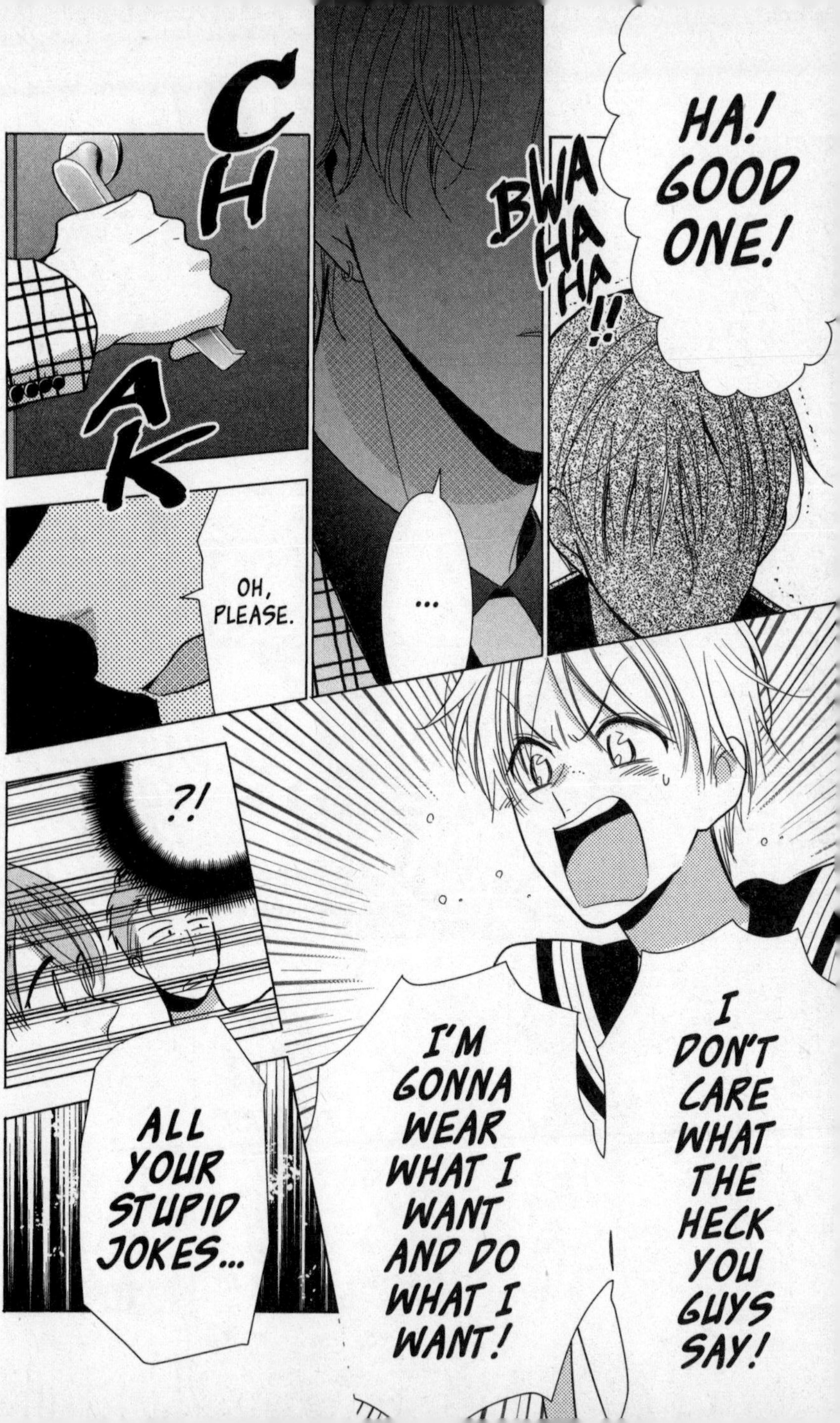
HA! GOOD ONE!
BWA HA HA HA!!
...
CHAK
OH, PLEASE.
I DON'T CARE WHAT THE HECK YOU GUYS SAY!
I'M GONNA WEAR WHAT I WANT AND DO WHAT I WANT!
?!
ALL YOUR STUPID JOKES...

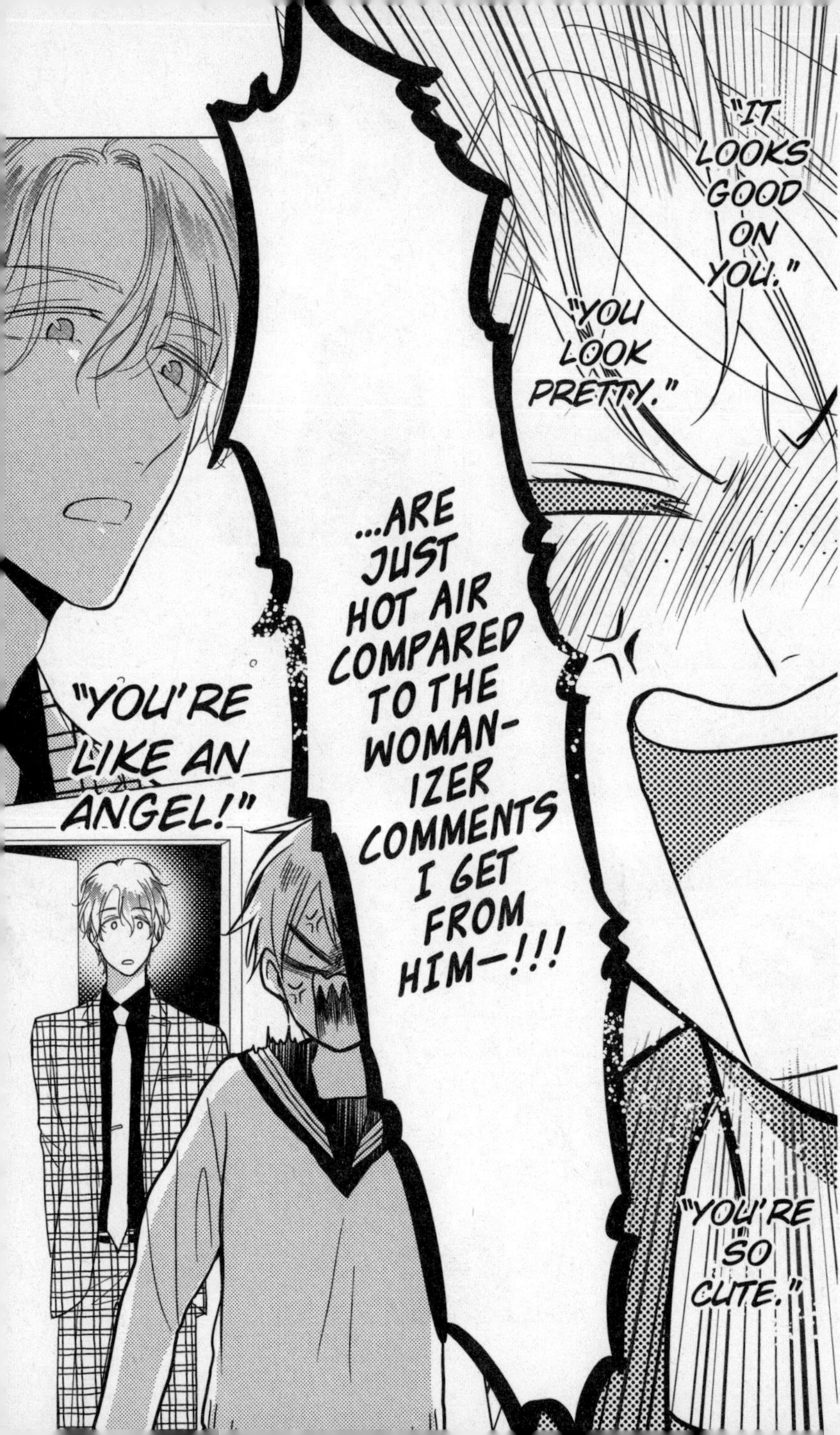
"IT LOOKS GOOD ON YOU."
"YOU LOOK PRETTY."
"YOU'RE SO CUTE."
"YOU'RE LIKE AN ANGEL!"
...ARE JUST HOT AIR COMPARED TO THE WOMAN-IZER COMMENTS I GET FROM HIM—!!!

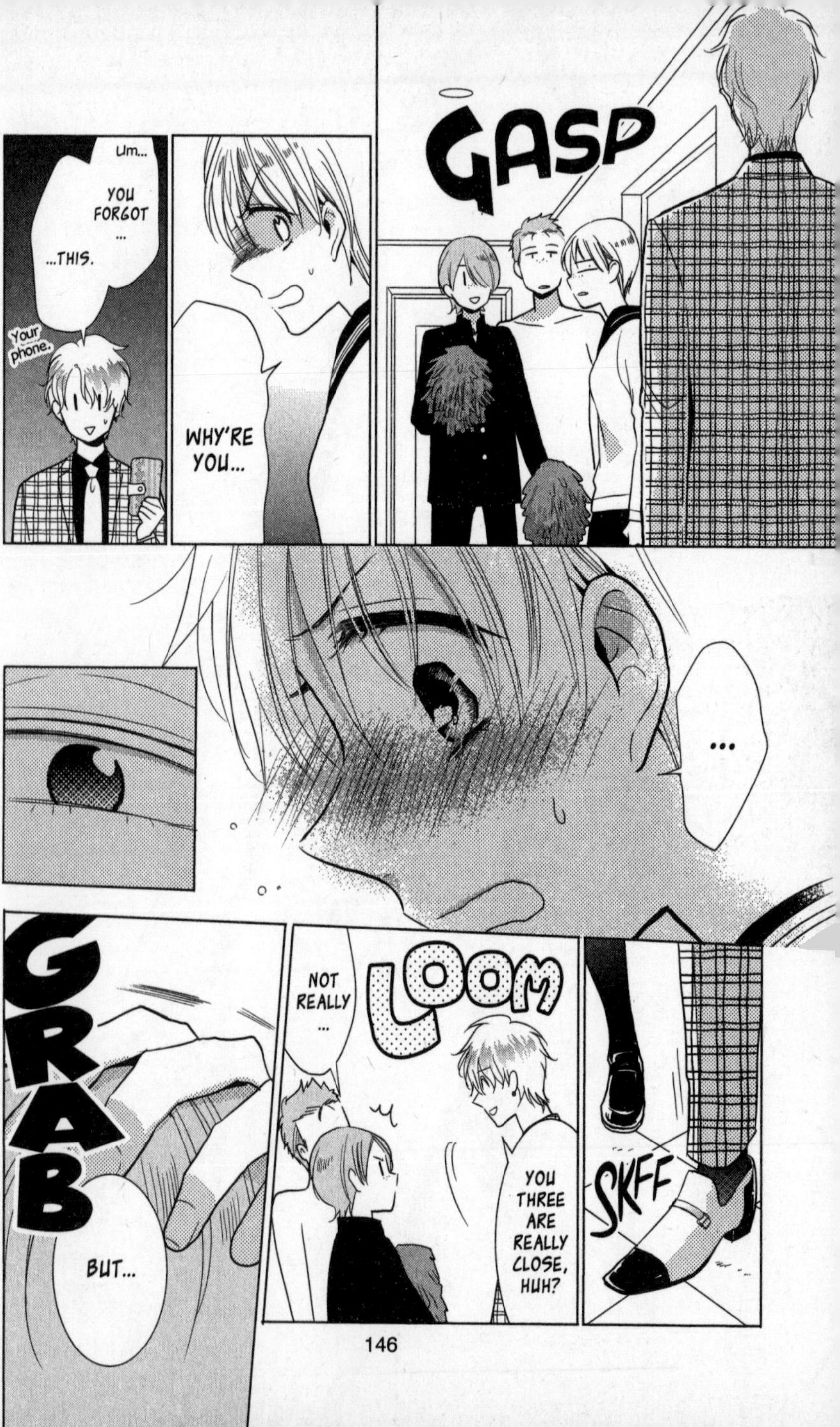
GASP
WHY'RE YOU...
Um... YOU FORGOT ... ...THIS.
Your phone.
...
SKFF
LOOM
NOT REALLY ...
YOU THREE ARE REALLY CLOSE, HUH?
GRAB
BUT...

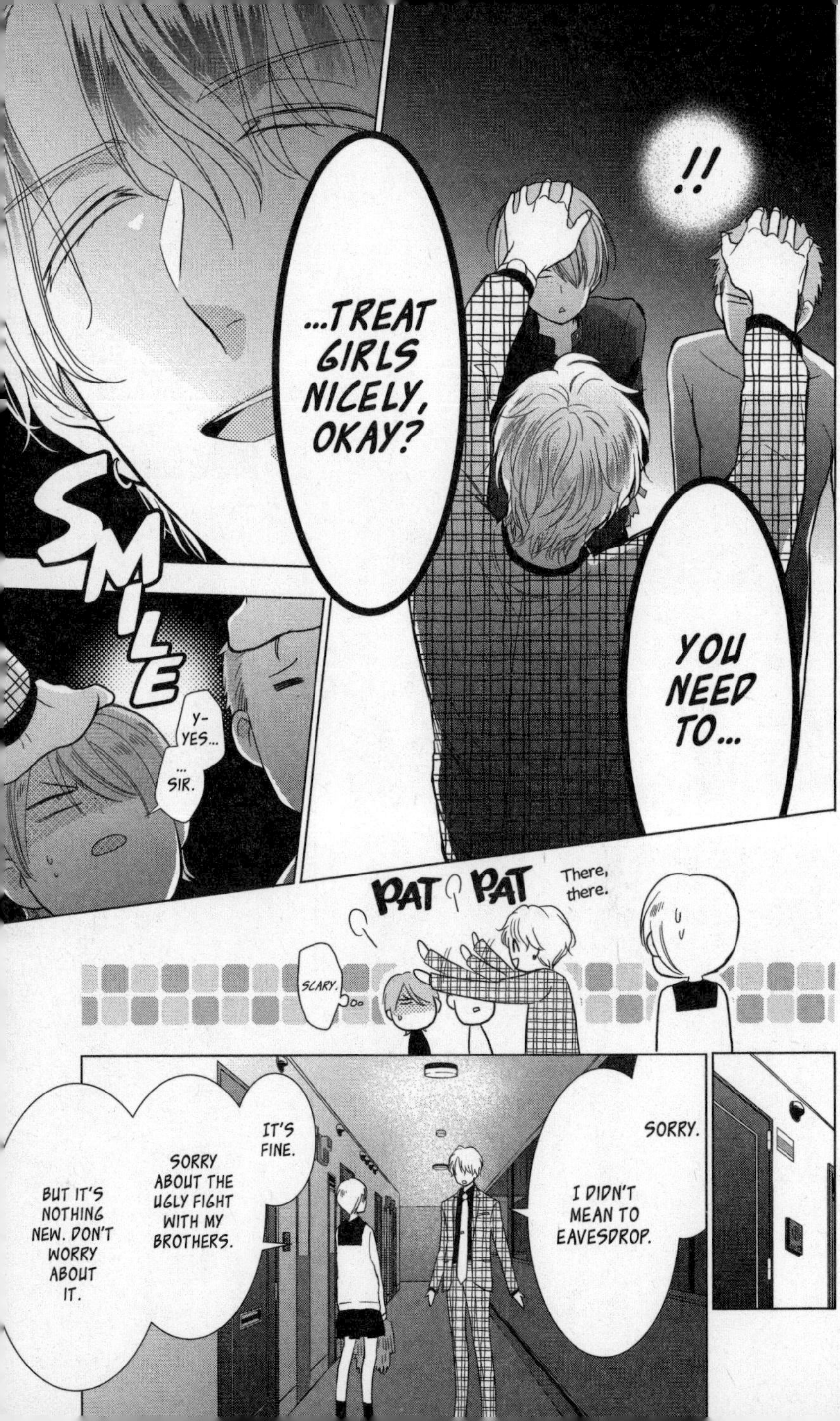
!!
YOU NEED TO...
...TREAT GIRLS NICELY, OKAY?
SMILE
Y-YES...
...SIR.
PAT PAT
There, there.
SCARY.
SORRY.
I DIDN'T MEAN TO EAVESDROP.
IT'S FINE.
SORRY ABOUT THE UGLY FIGHT WITH MY BROTHERS.
BUT IT'S NOTHING NEW. DON'T WORRY ABOUT IT.

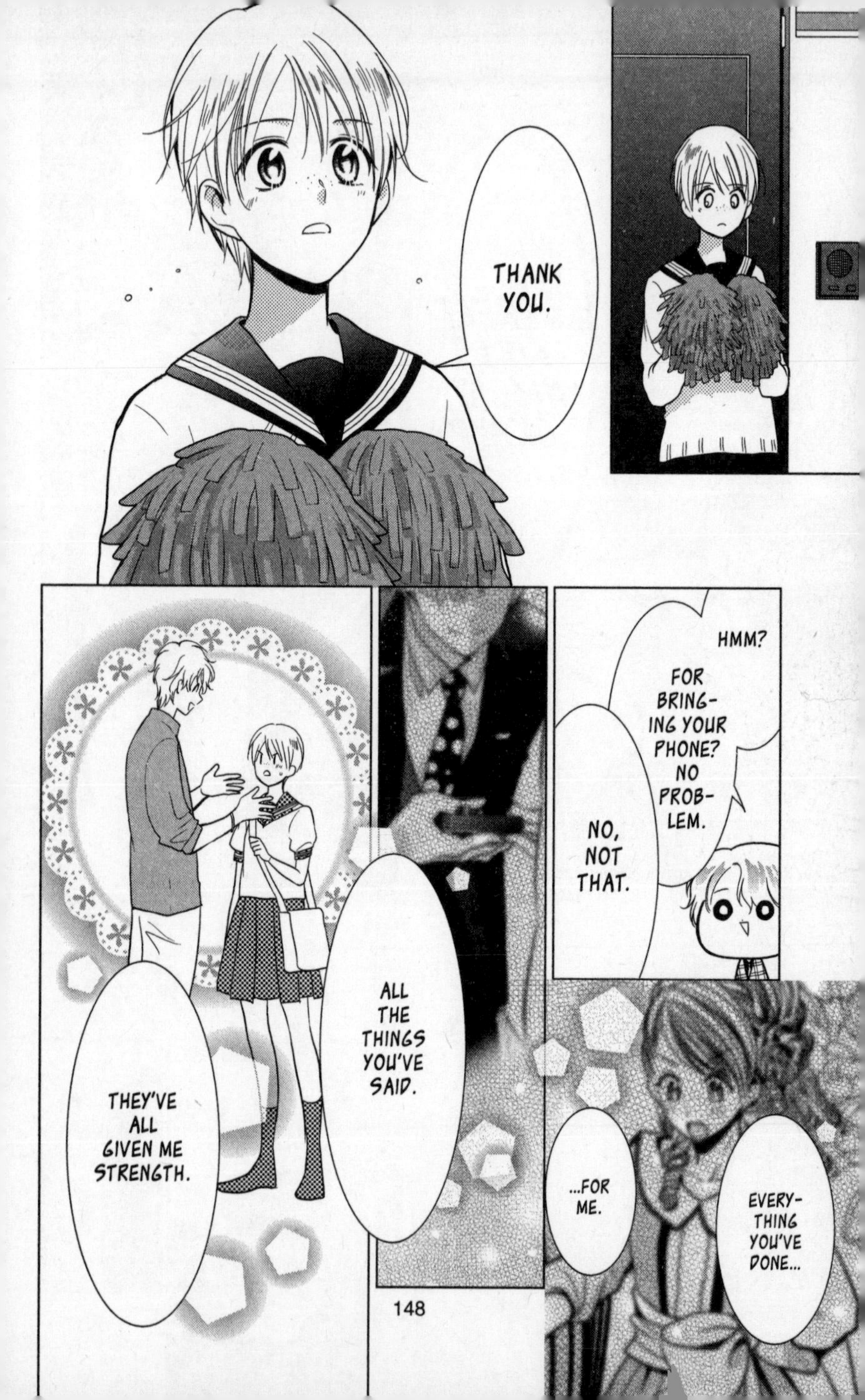
THANK YOU.
HMM?
FOR BRINGING YOUR PHONE? NO PROBLEM.
NO, NOT THAT.
EVERYTHING YOU'VE DONE...
...FOR ME.
ALL THE THINGS YOU'VE SAID.
THEY'VE ALL GIVEN ME STRENGTH.

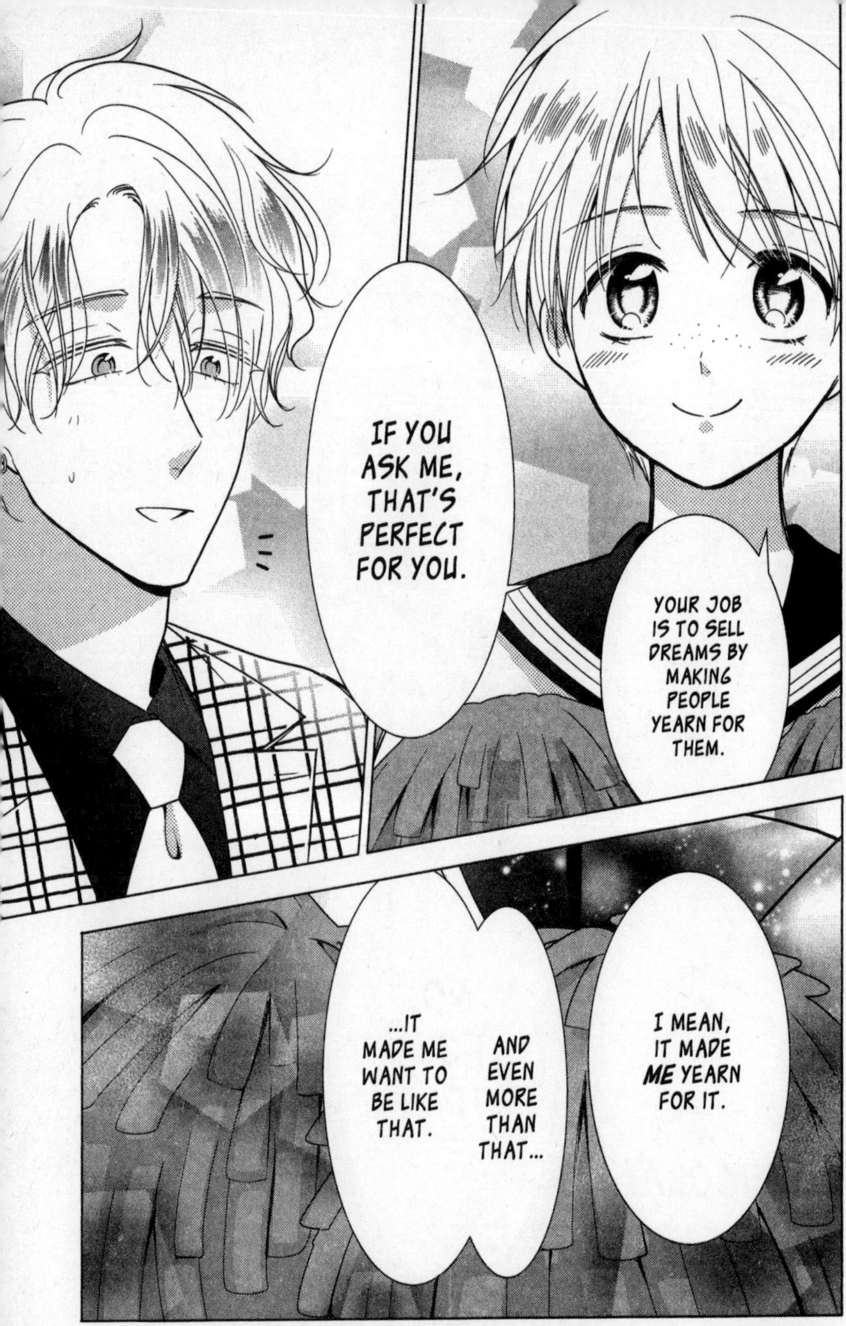
YOUR JOB IS TO SELL DREAMS BY MAKING PEOPLE YEARN FOR THEM.
IF YOU ASK ME, THAT'S PERFECT FOR YOU.
I MEAN, IT MADE **ME** YEARN FOR IT.
AND EVEN MORE THAN THAT...
...IT MADE ME WANT TO BE LIKE THAT.

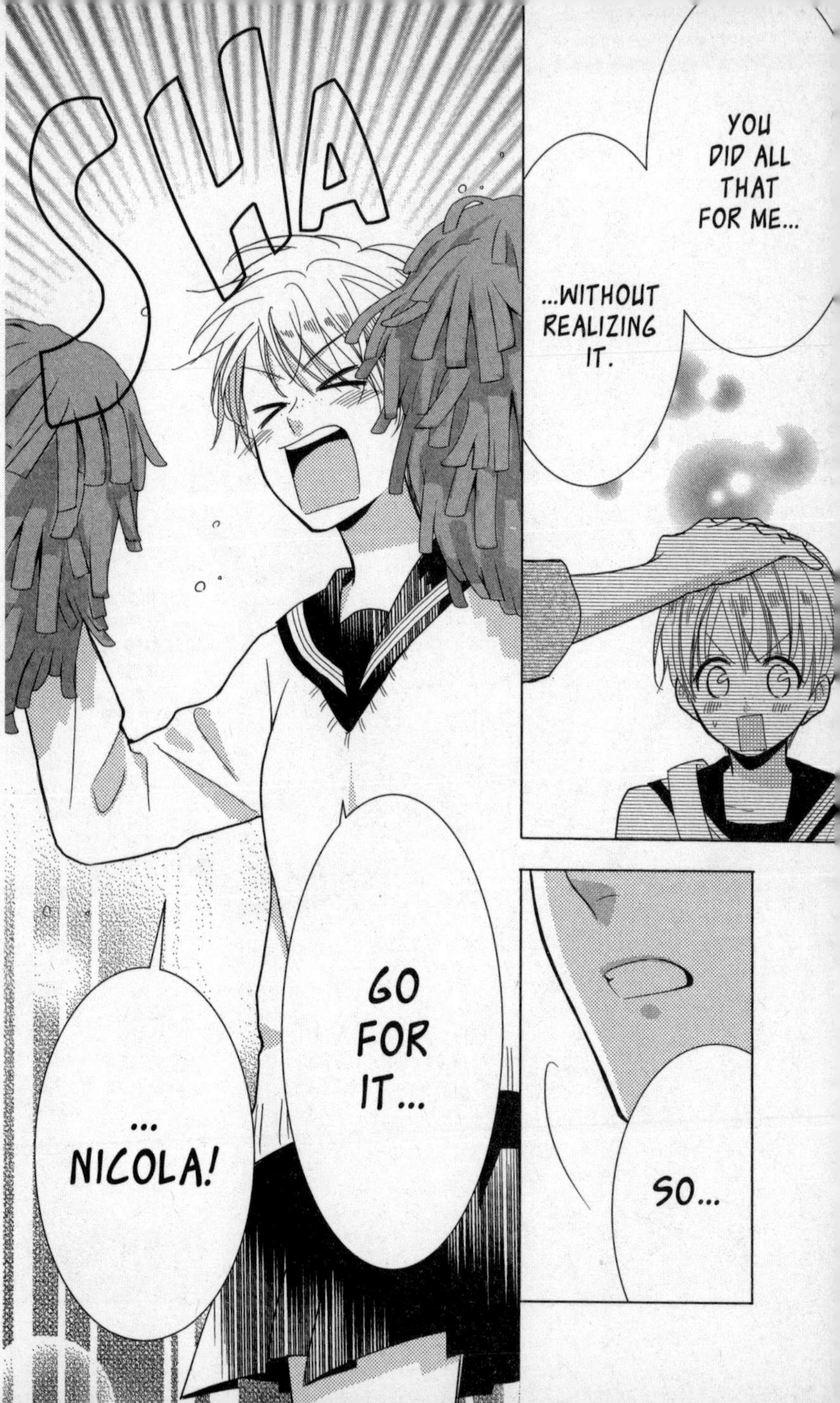
YOU DID ALL THAT FOR ME...
...WITHOUT REALIZING IT.
SO...
SHA
GO FOR IT...
... NICOLA!

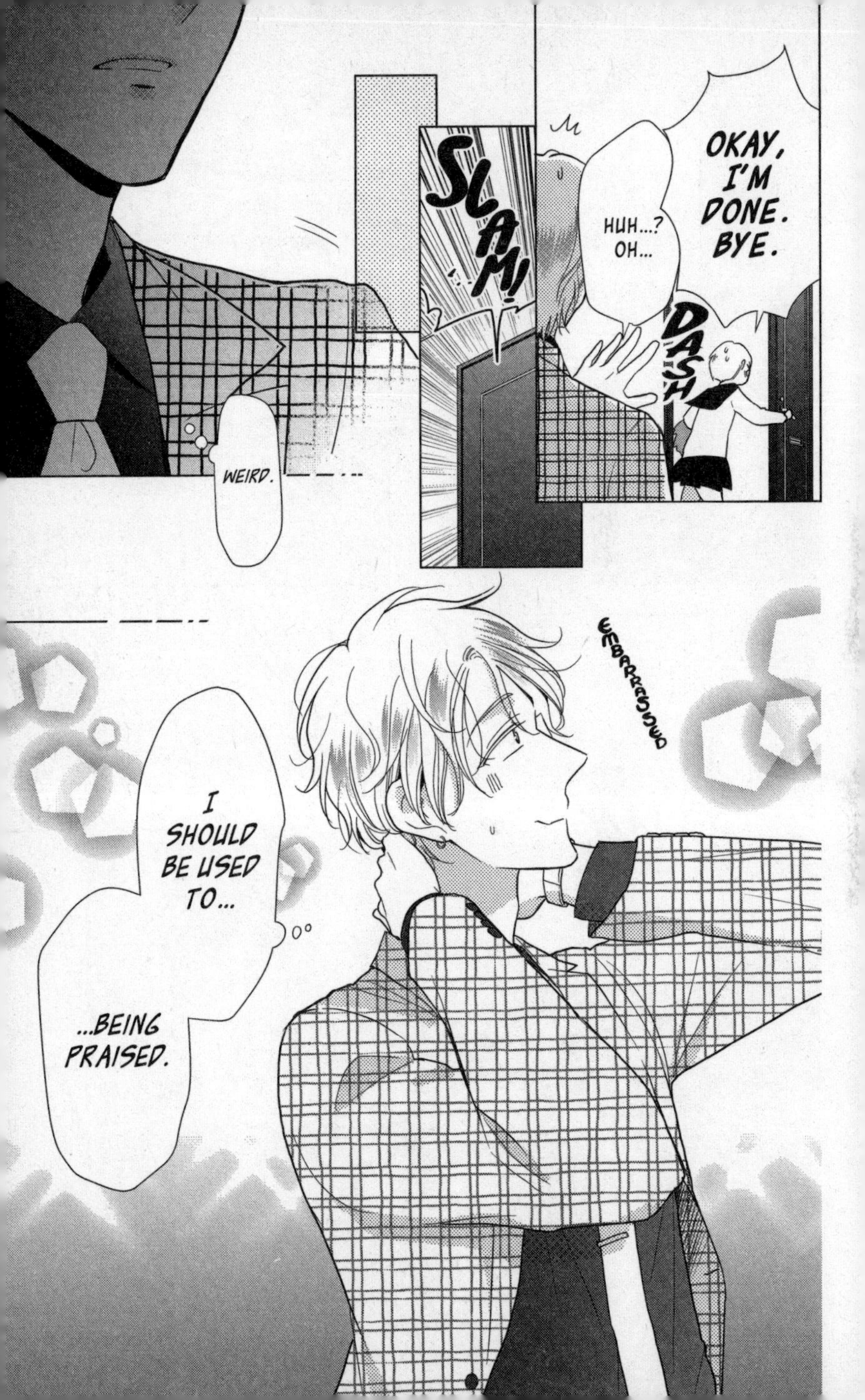
OKAY, I'M DONE. BYE.
HUH...? OH...
DASH
SLAM!
WEIRD.
EMBARRASSED
I SHOULD BE USED TO...
...BEING PRAISED.

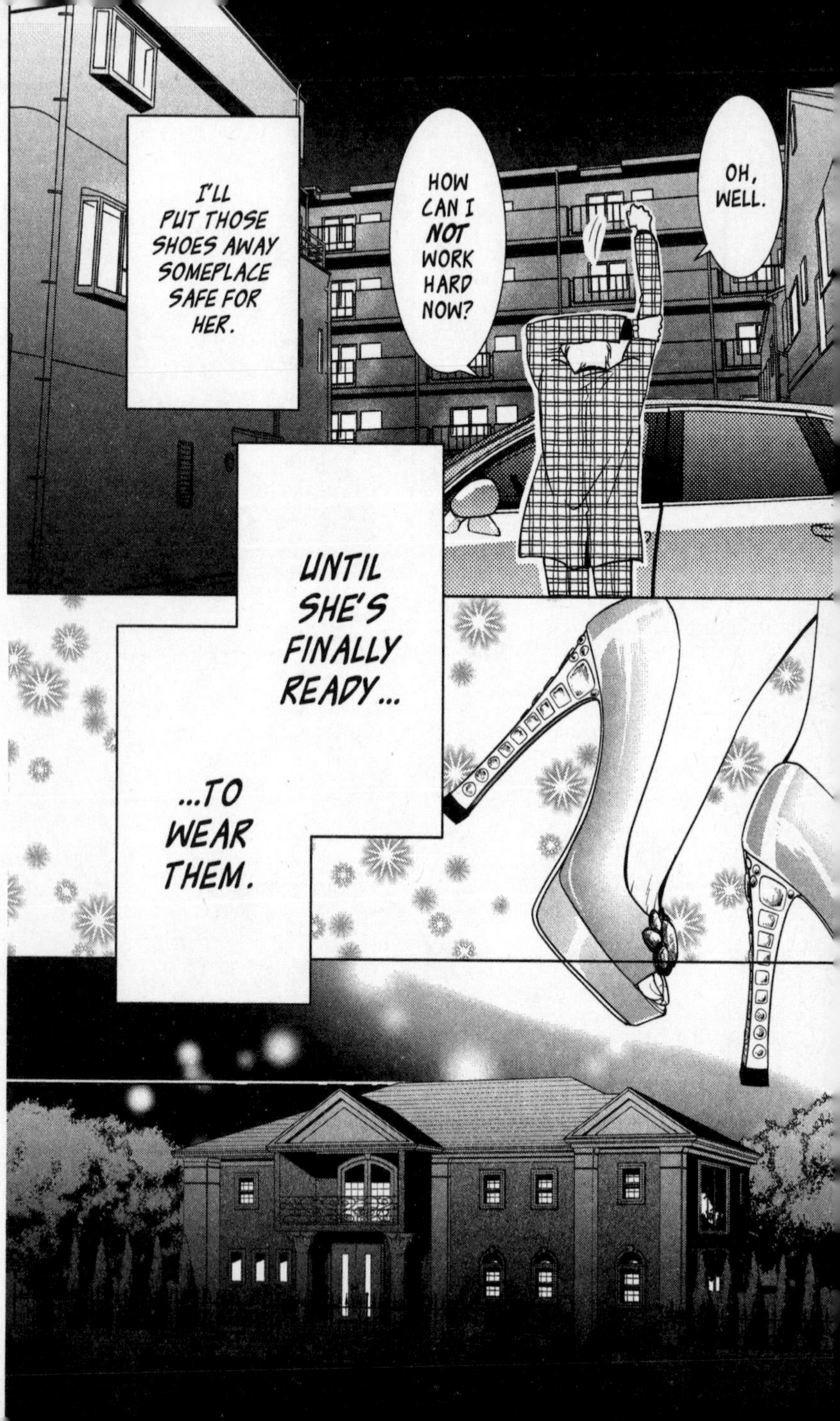
OH, WELL.
HOW CAN I NOT WORK HARD NOW?
I'LL PUT THOSE SHOES AWAY SOMEPLACE SAFE FOR HER.
UNTIL SHE'S FINALLY READY...
...TO WEAR THEM.

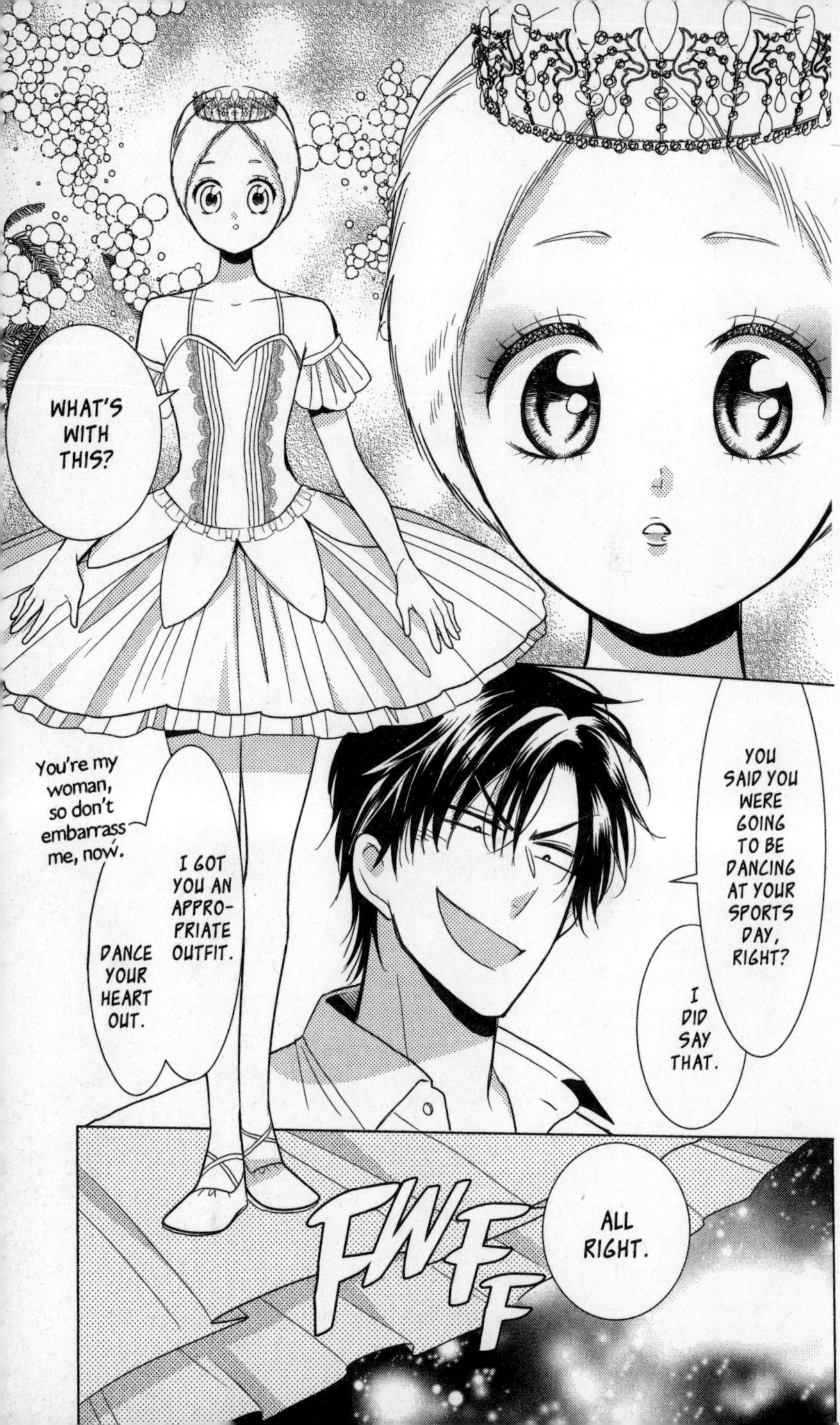
YOU SAID YOU WERE GOING TO BE DANCING AT YOUR SPORTS DAY, RIGHT?
I DID SAY THAT.
FWFF
ALL RIGHT.
WHAT'S WITH THIS?
I GOT YOU AN APPRO-PRIATE OUTFIT.
DANCE YOUR HEART OUT.
You're my woman, so don't embarrass me, now.

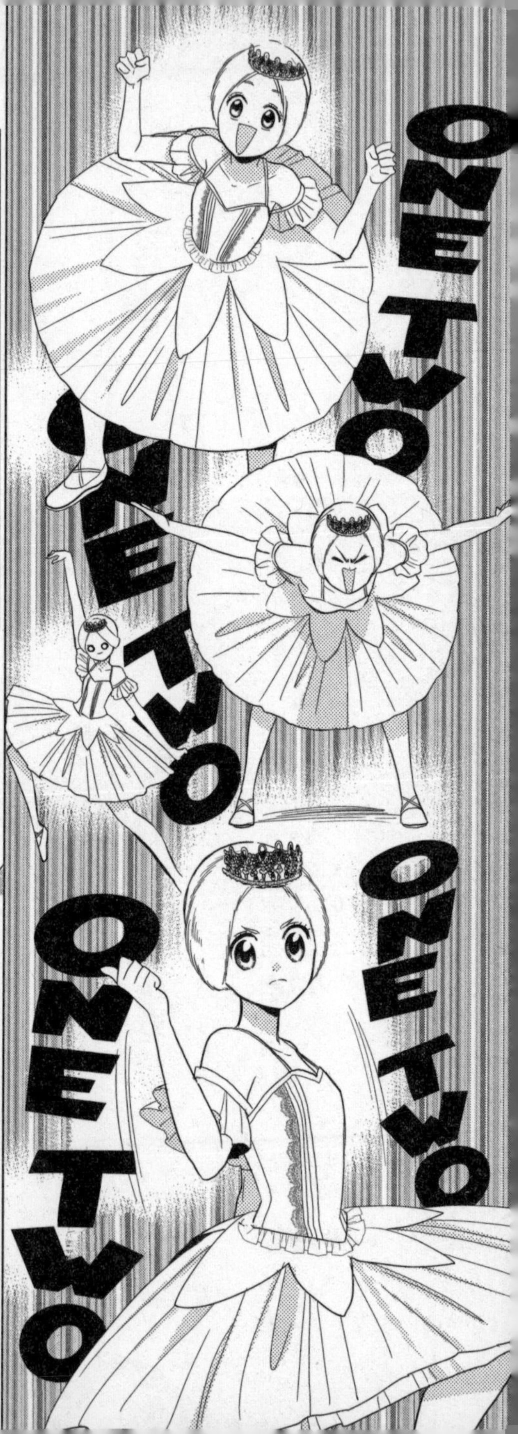
ONE TWO
ONE TWO
ONE TWO
ONE TWO

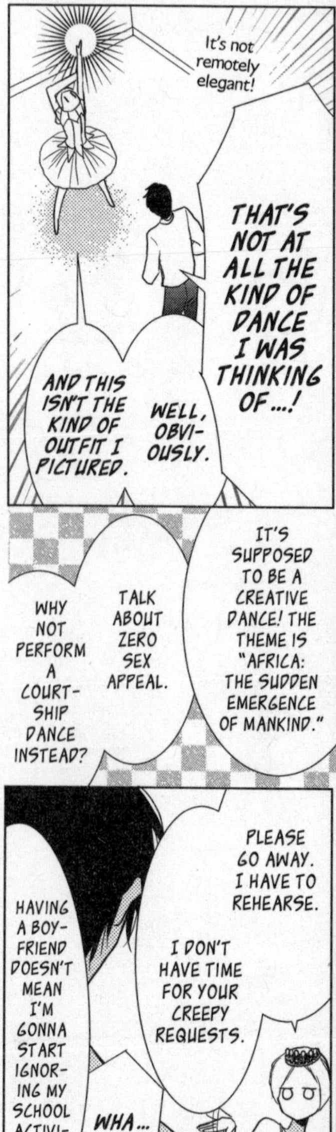
It's not remotely elegant!
THAT'S NOT AT ALL THE KIND OF DANCE I WAS THINKING OF...!
WELL, OBVIOUSLY.
AND THIS ISN'T THE KIND OF OUTFIT I PICTURED.
IT'S SUPPOSED TO BE A CREATIVE DANCE! THE THEME IS "AFRICA: THE SUDDEN EMERGENCE OF MANKIND."
TALK ABOUT ZERO SEX APPEAL.
WHY NOT PERFORM A COURTSHIP DANCE INSTEAD?
PLEASE GO AWAY. I HAVE TO REHEARSE.
I DON'T HAVE TIME FOR YOUR CREEPY REQUESTS.
HAVING A BOYFRIEND DOESN'T MEAN I'M GONNA START IGNORING MY SCHOOL ACTIVITIES.
WHA...

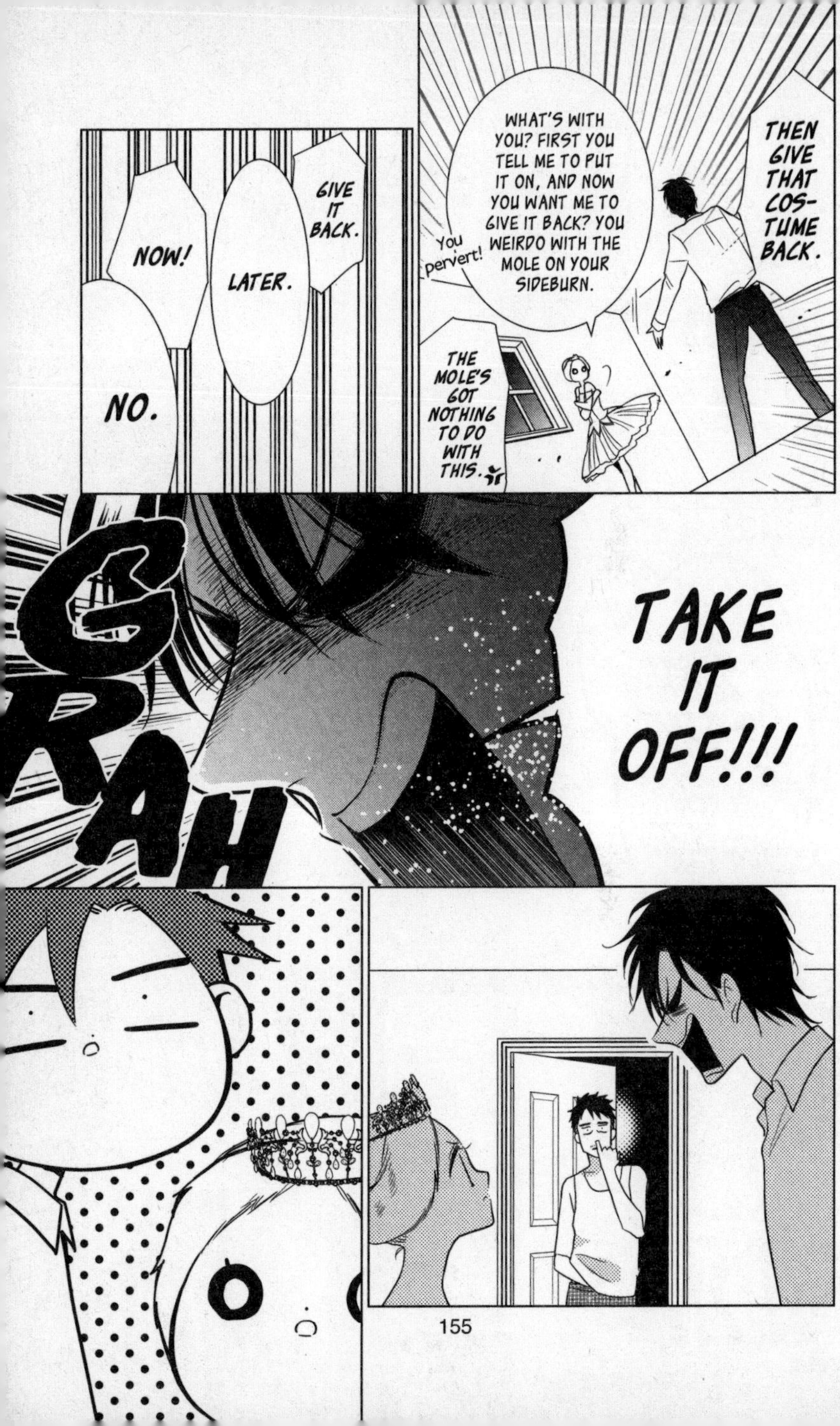
THEN GIVE THAT COS-TUME BACK.
WHAT'S WITH YOU? FIRST YOU TELL ME TO PUT IT ON, AND NOW YOU WANT ME TO GIVE IT BACK? YOU WEIRDO WITH THE MOLE ON YOUR SIDEBURN.
You pervert!
THE MOLE'S GOT NOTHING TO DO WITH THIS.
GIVE IT BACK.
LATER.
NOW!
NO.
TAKE IT OFF!!!
GRAH

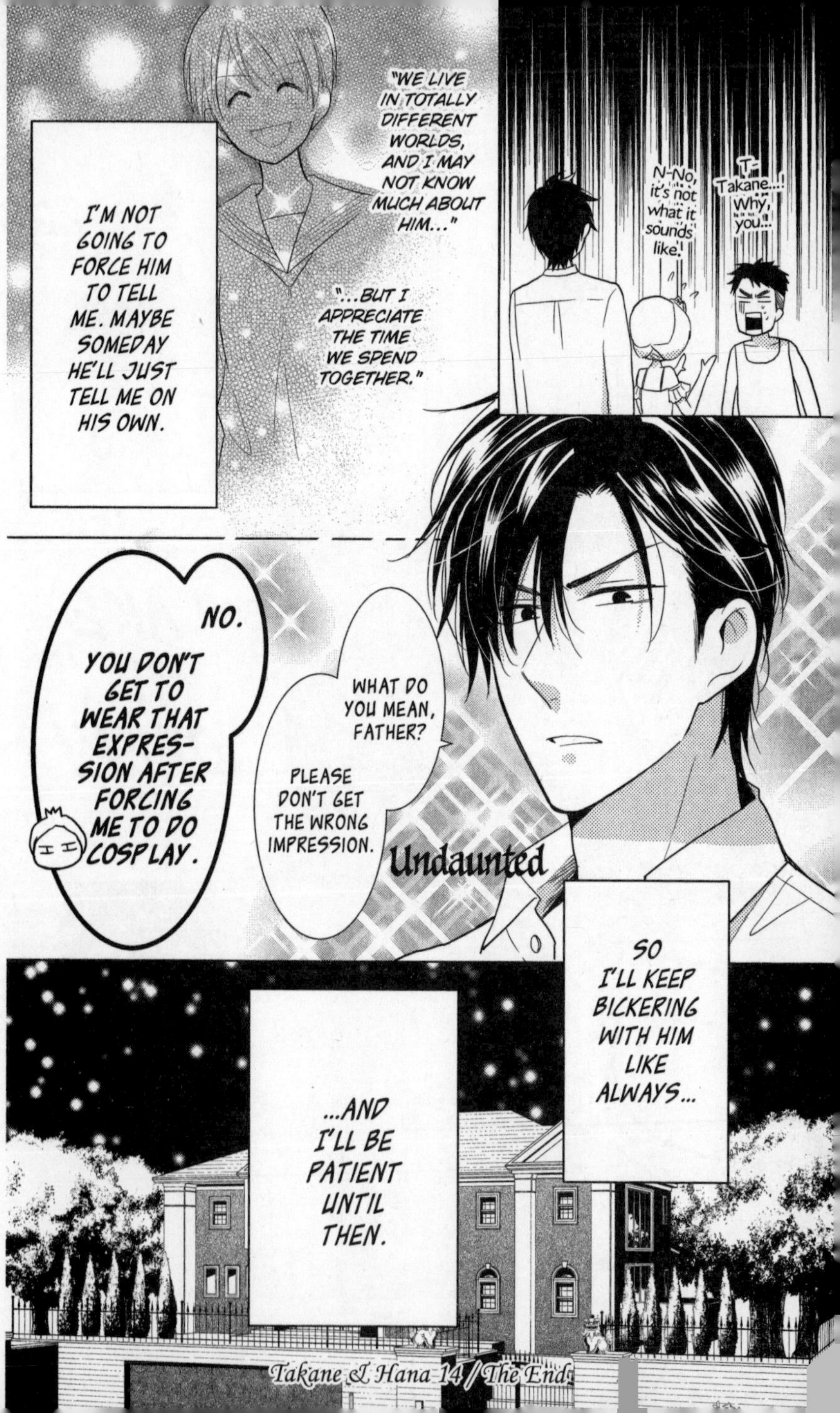
T-Takane...! Why, you...!
N-No, it's not what it sounds like!
"WE LIVE IN TOTALLY DIFFERENT WORLDS, AND I MAY NOT KNOW MUCH ABOUT HIM..."
"...BUT I APPRECIATE THE TIME WE SPEND TOGETHER."
I'M NOT GOING TO FORCE HIM TO TELL ME. MAYBE SOMEDAY HE'LL JUST TELL ME ON HIS OWN.
WHAT DO YOU MEAN, FATHER?
PLEASE DON'T GET THE WRONG IMPRESSION.
NO.
YOU DON'T GET TO WEAR THAT EXPRESSION AFTER FORCING ME TO DO COSPLAY.
Undaunted
SO I'LL KEEP BICKERING WITH HIM LIKE ALWAYS...
...AND I'LL BE PATIENT UNTIL THEN.
Takane & Hana 14 / The End

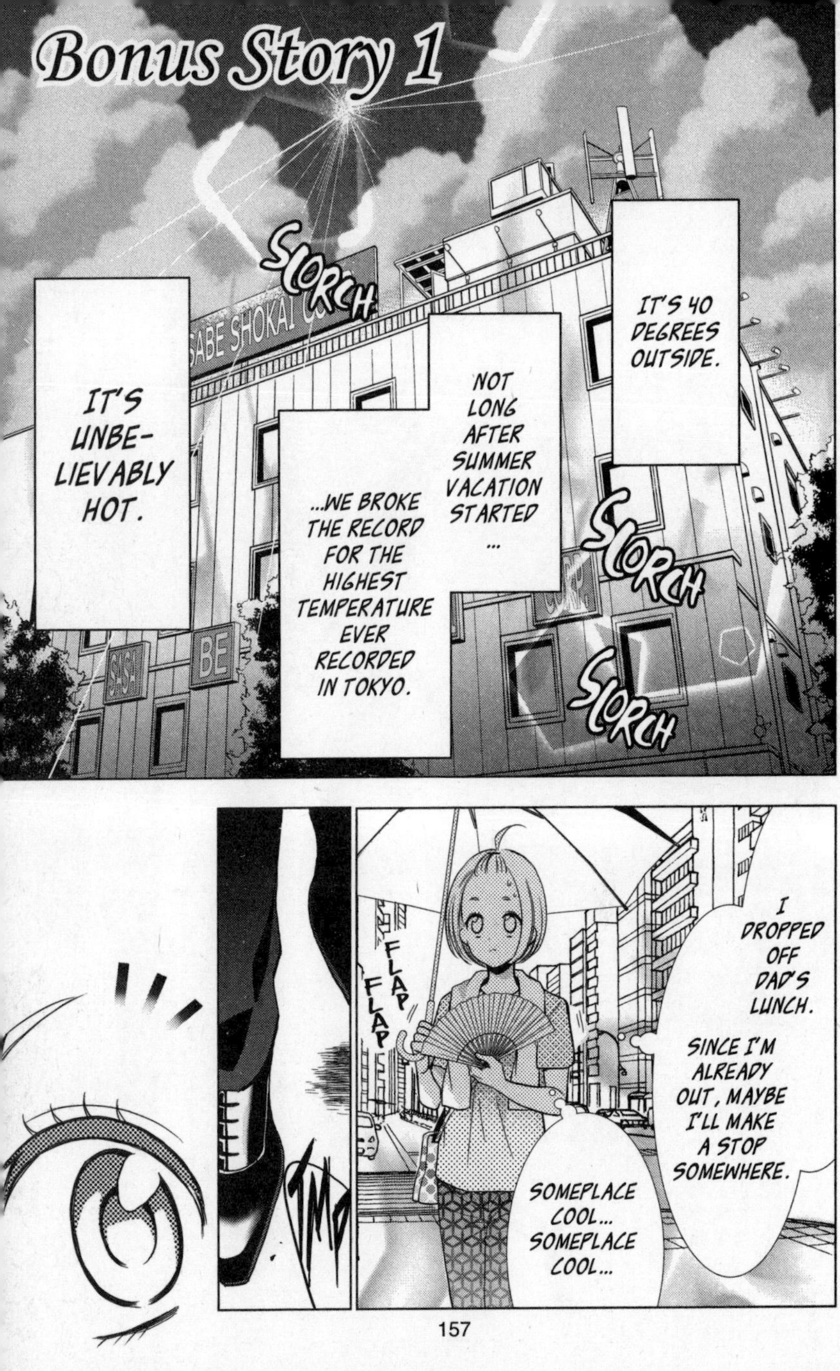
Bonus Story 1
IT'S 40 DEGREES OUTSIDE.
NOT LONG AFTER SUMMER VACATION STARTED...
...WE BROKE THE RECORD FOR THE HIGHEST TEMPERATURE EVER RECORDED IN TOKYO.
IT'S UNBE-LIEVABLY HOT.
SCORCH
SCORCH
SCORCH
I DROPPED OFF DAD'S LUNCH.
SINCE I'M ALREADY OUT, MAYBE I'LL MAKE A STOP SOMEWHERE.
FLAP FLAP
SOMEPLACE COOL... SOMEPLACE COOL...

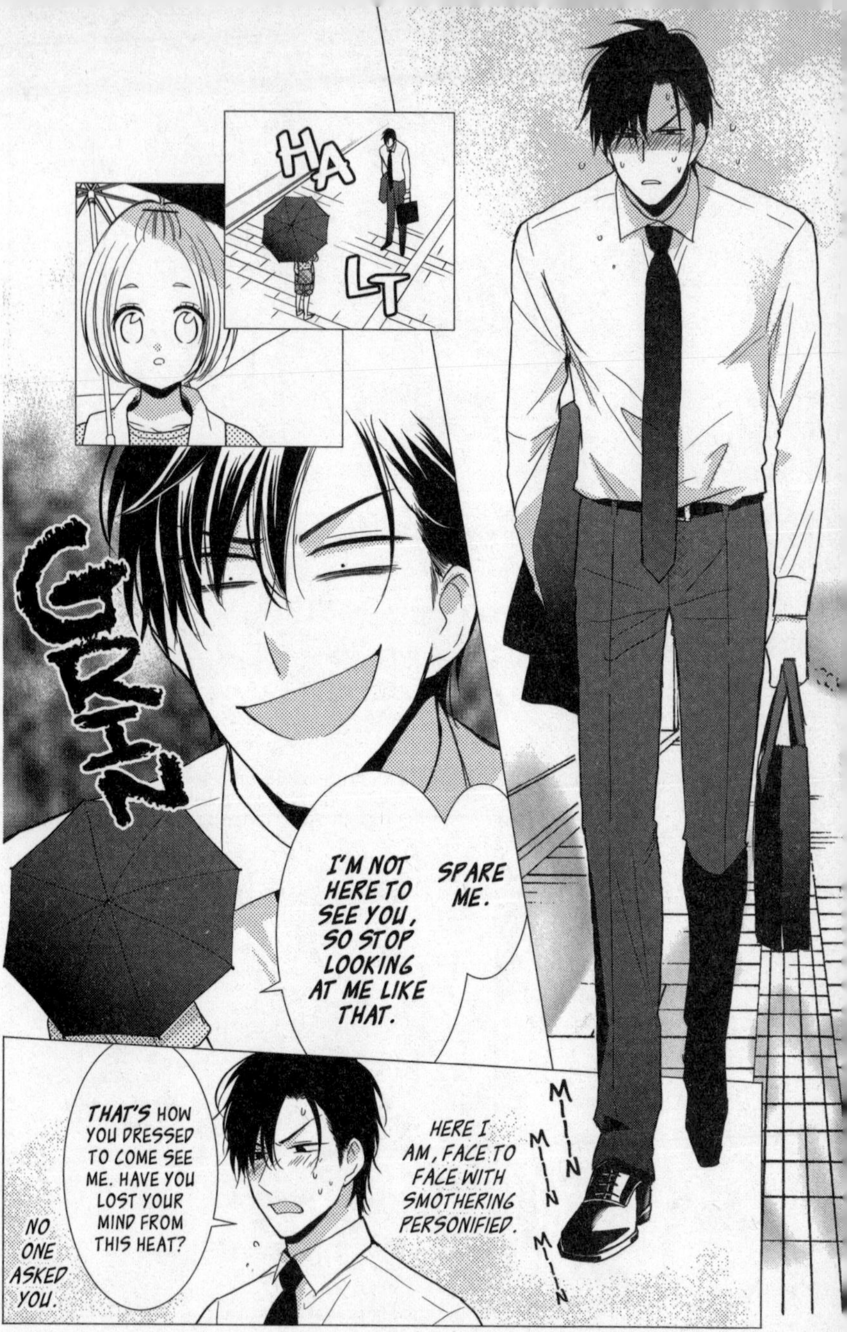
HALT
GRIN
SPARE ME.
I'M NOT HERE TO SEE YOU, SO STOP LOOKING AT ME LIKE THAT.
MIIN MIIN MIIN
HERE I AM, FACE TO FACE WITH SMOTHERING PERSONIFIED.
THAT'S HOW YOU DRESSED TO COME SEE ME. HAVE YOU LOST YOUR MIND FROM THIS HEAT?
NO ONE ASKED YOU.

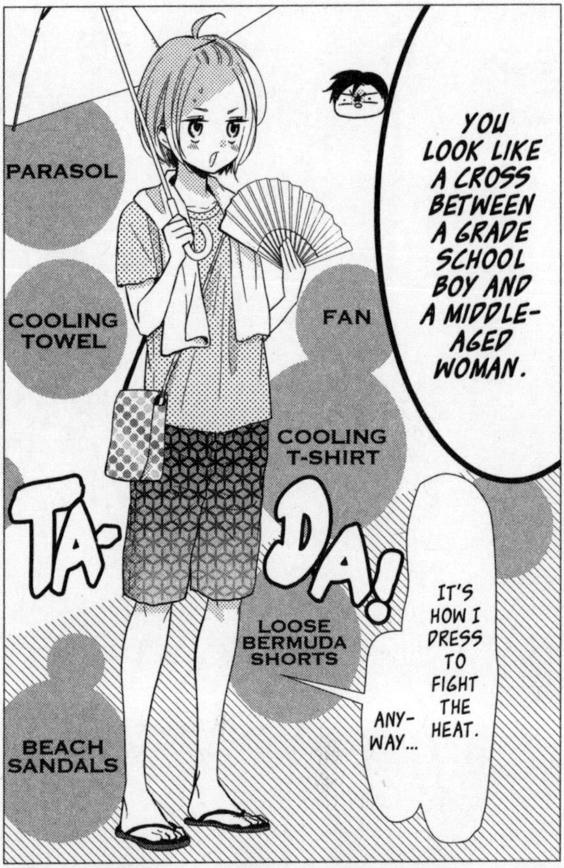
YOU LOOK LIKE A CROSS BETWEEN A GRADE SCHOOL BOY AND A MIDDLE-AGED WOMAN.
PARASOL
FAN
COOLING TOWEL
COOLING T-SHIRT
TA-DA!
IT'S HOW I DRESS TO FIGHT THE HEAT.
ANY-WAY...
LOOSE BERMUDA SHORTS
BEACH SANDALS

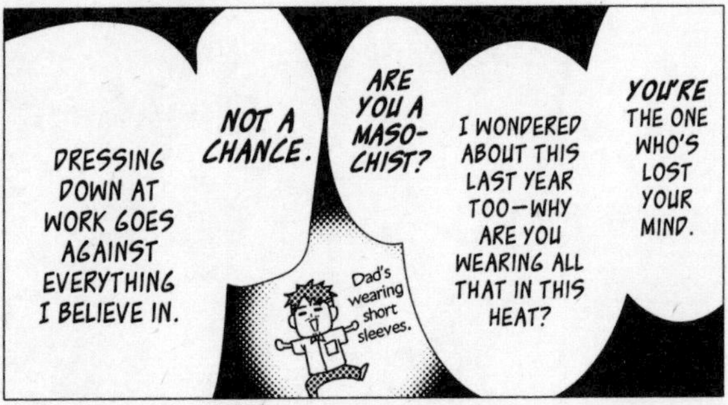
YOU'RE THE ONE WHO'S LOST YOUR MIND.
I WONDERED ABOUT THIS LAST YEAR TOO—WHY ARE YOU WEARING ALL THAT IN THIS HEAT?
ARE YOU A MASOCHIST?
NOT A CHANCE.
DRESSING DOWN AT WORK GOES AGAINST EVERYTHING I BELIEVE IN.
Dad's wearing short sleeves.

All the bonus stories in this volume were previously published in *The Hana to Yume*, but there was a theme for each one.

• Bonus Story 1 •

"Summer love (with a touch of eroticism)" was the theme for this story. I tried to incorporate that while also making sure the story conveyed what I wanted it to. I also planted "ero" in the story somewhere.

• Bonus Story 2 •

The theme for this one was "laughter." I tried to make it more humorous than usual, but I'm sure people's reactions will vary. "Bubbly Takane" was the vibe I was going for when I drew the original color illustration.

• Bonus Story 3 •

"Invincible girl" was the theme this time.

To pay tribute to the live-action drama, I decided to write a story about acting.

Takane is a super masochist so this is nothing for him.

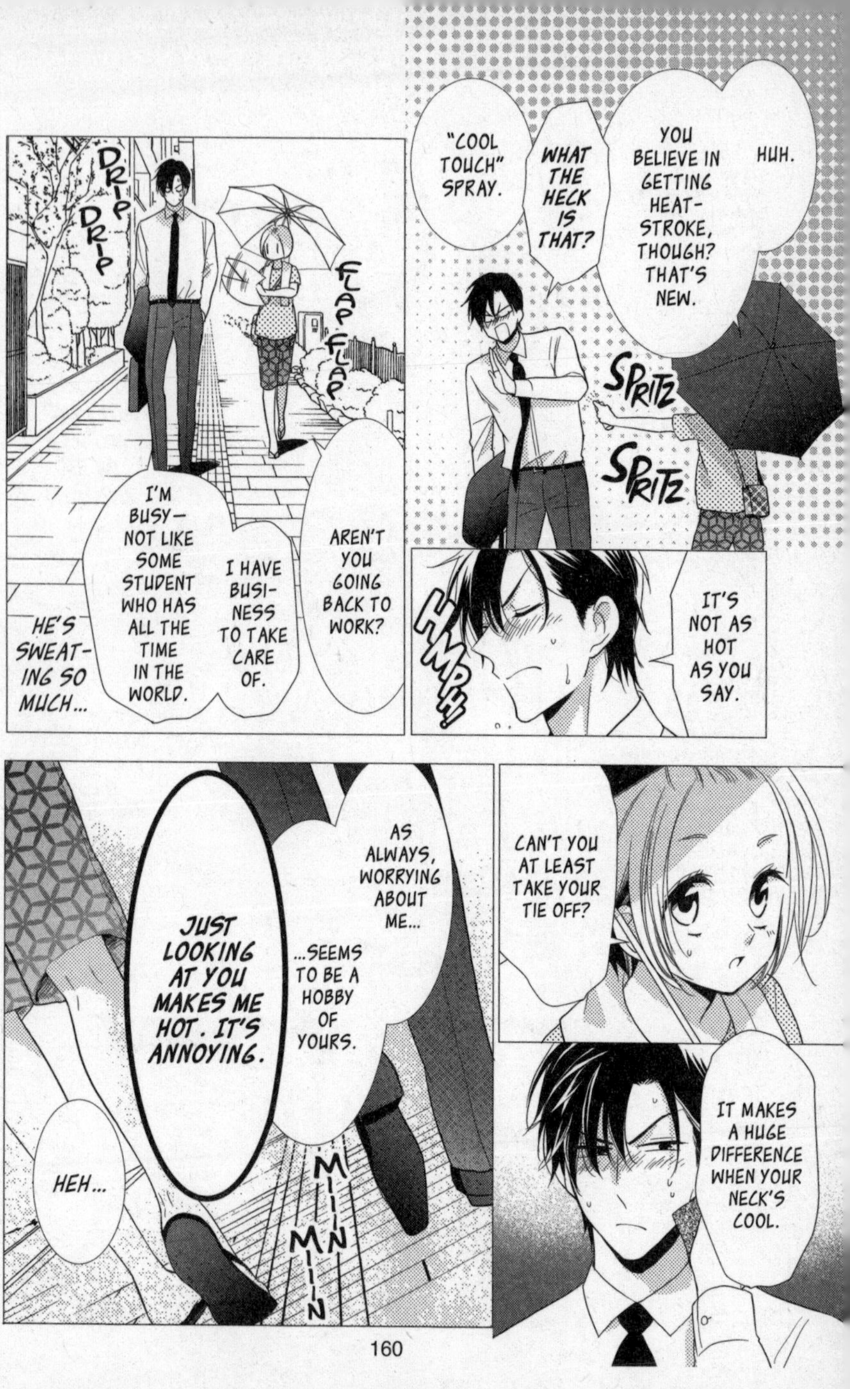
HUH.
YOU BELIEVE IN GETTING HEAT-STROKE, THOUGH? THAT'S NEW.
WHAT THE HECK IS THAT?
"COOL TOUCH" SPRAY.
SPRITZ
SPRITZ
IT'S NOT AS HOT AS YOU SAY.
HMPH!
FLAP FLAP
DRIP DRIP
AREN'T YOU GOING BACK TO WORK?
I HAVE BUSINESS TO TAKE CARE OF.
I'M BUSY—NOT LIKE SOME STUDENT WHO HAS ALL THE TIME IN THE WORLD.
HE'S SWEATING SO MUCH...
CAN'T YOU AT LEAST TAKE YOUR TIE OFF?
IT MAKES A HUGE DIFFERENCE WHEN YOUR NECK'S COOL.
AS ALWAYS, WORRYING ABOUT ME...
...SEEMS TO BE A HOBBY OF YOURS.
JUST LOOKING AT YOU MAKES ME HOT. IT'S ANNOYING.
MIIIN
MIIIN
HEH...

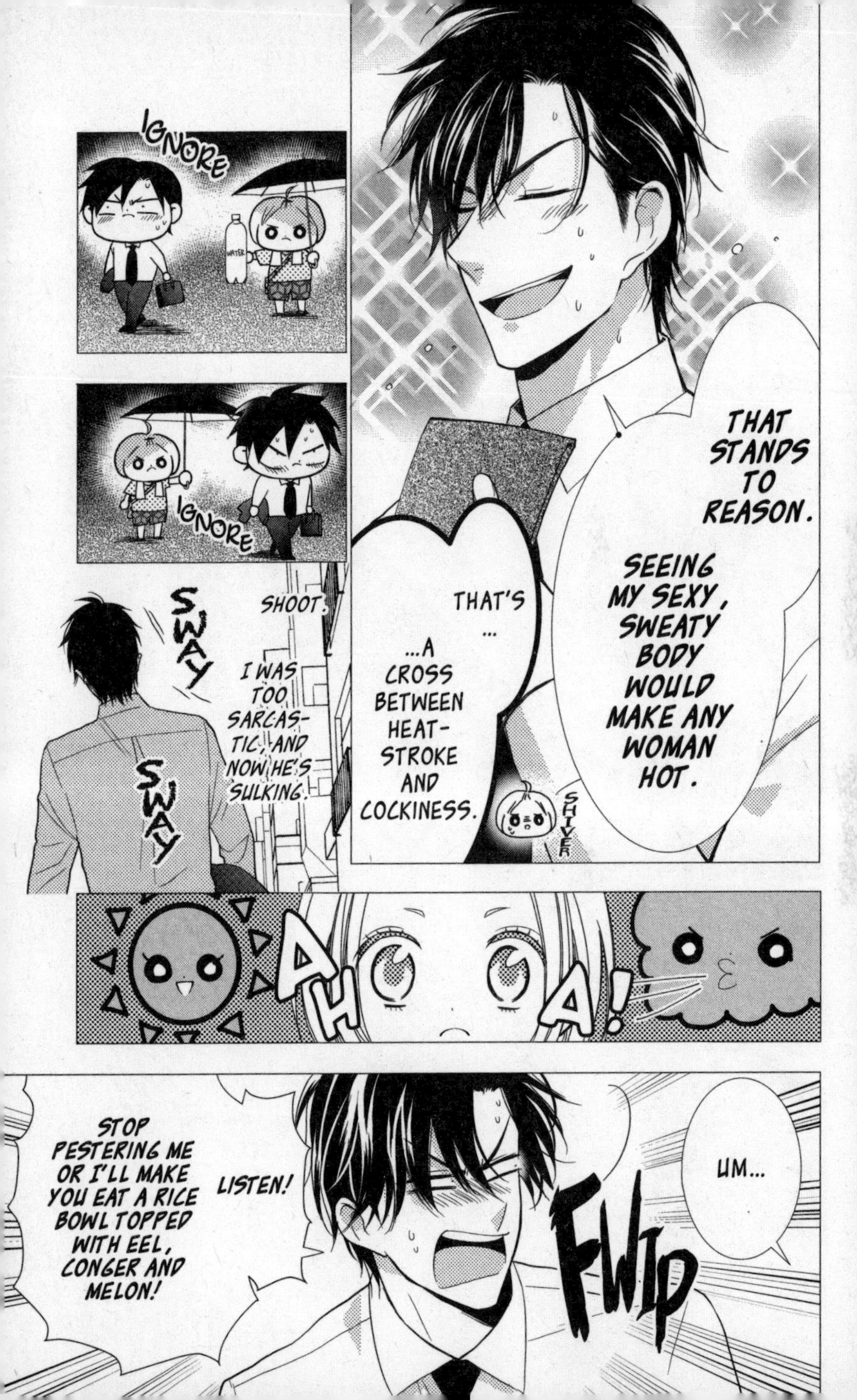
THAT STANDS TO REASON.
SEEING MY SEXY, SWEATY BODY WOULD MAKE ANY WOMAN HOT.
THAT'S ...
...A CROSS BETWEEN HEAT-STROKE AND COCKINESS.
SHIVER
IGNORE
WATER
IGNORE
SHOOT.
I WAS TOO SARCAS-TIC, AND NOW HE'S SULKING.
SWAY
SWAY
AHO A!
UM...
FWIP
LISTEN!
STOP PESTERING ME OR I'LL MAKE YOU EAT A RICE BOWL TOPPED WITH EEL, CONGER AND MELON!

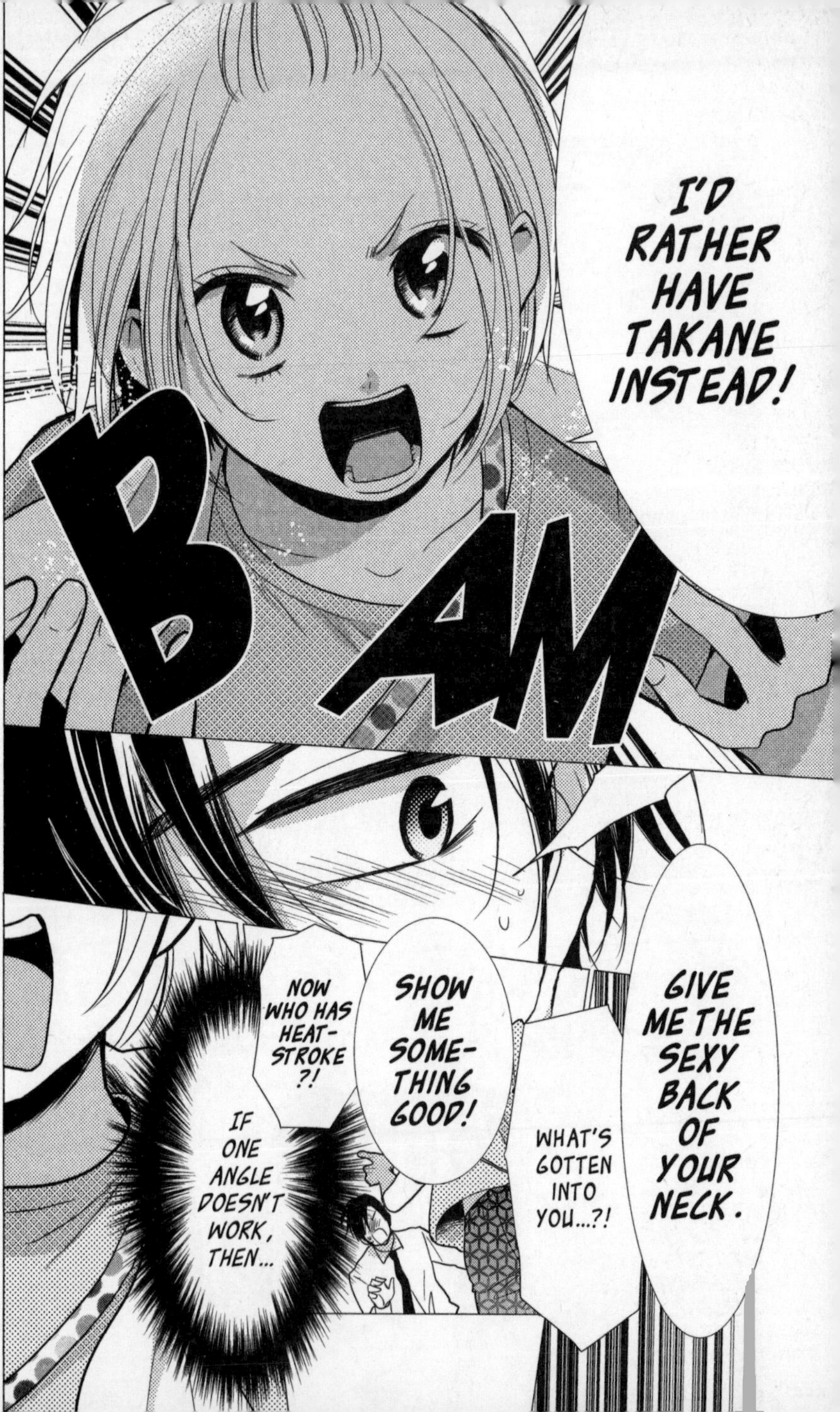
I'D RATHER HAVE TAKANE INSTEAD!
BAM
GIVE ME THE SEXY BACK OF YOUR NECK.
WHAT'S GOTTEN INTO YOU...?!
SHOW ME SOMETHING GOOD!
NOW WHO HAS HEAT-STROKE?!
IF ONE ANGLE DOESN'T WORK, THEN...

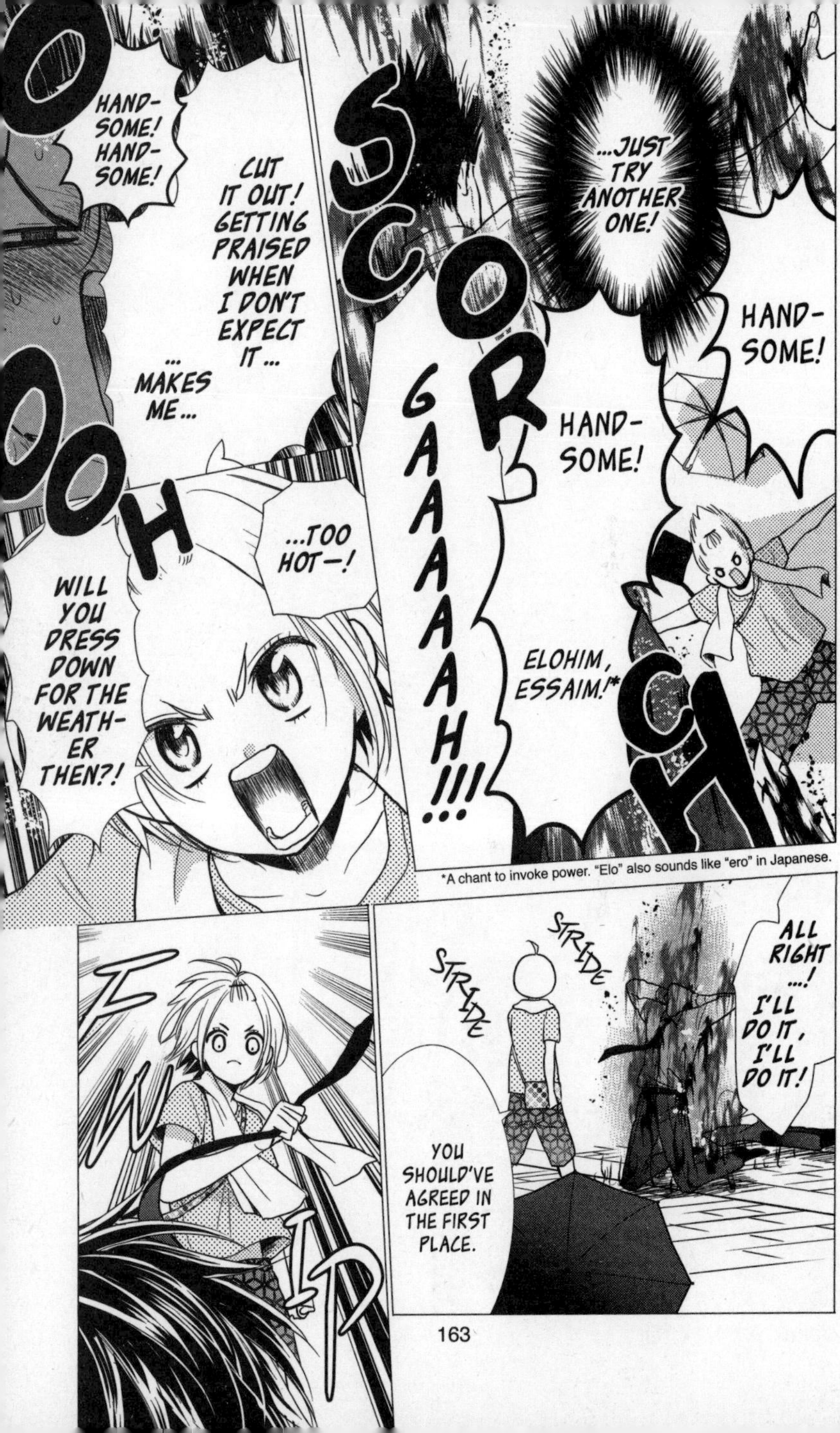
...JUST TRY ANOTHER ONE!
HAND-SOME!
HAND-SOME!
SCORCH
ELOHIM, ESSAIM!*
GAAAAAAAH!!!
OOOH
HAND-SOME! HAND-SOME!
CUT IT OUT! GETTING PRAISED WHEN I DON'T EXPECT IT...
...MAKES ME...
...TOO HOT—!
WILL YOU DRESS DOWN FOR THE WEATHER THEN?!
ALL RIGHT...! I'LL DO IT, I'LL DO IT!
STRIDE
STRIDE
YOU SHOULD'VE AGREED IN THE FIRST PLACE.
FWIP

*A chant to invoke power. "Elo" also sounds like "ero" in Japanese.

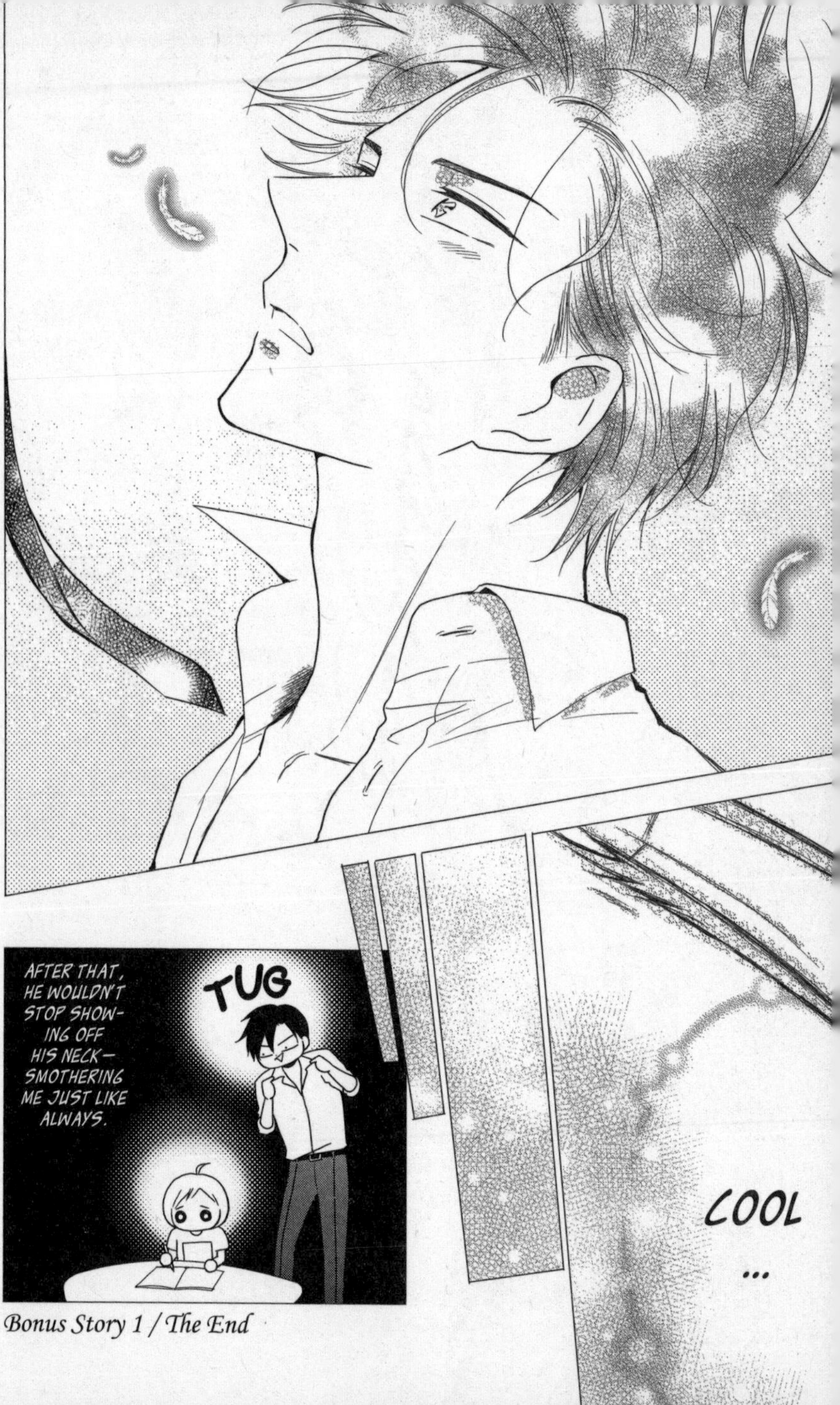
COOL
...
AFTER THAT, HE WOULDN'T STOP SHOWING OFF HIS NECK—SMOTHERING ME JUST LIKE ALWAYS.
TUG

Bonus Story 1 / The End

Bonus Story 2

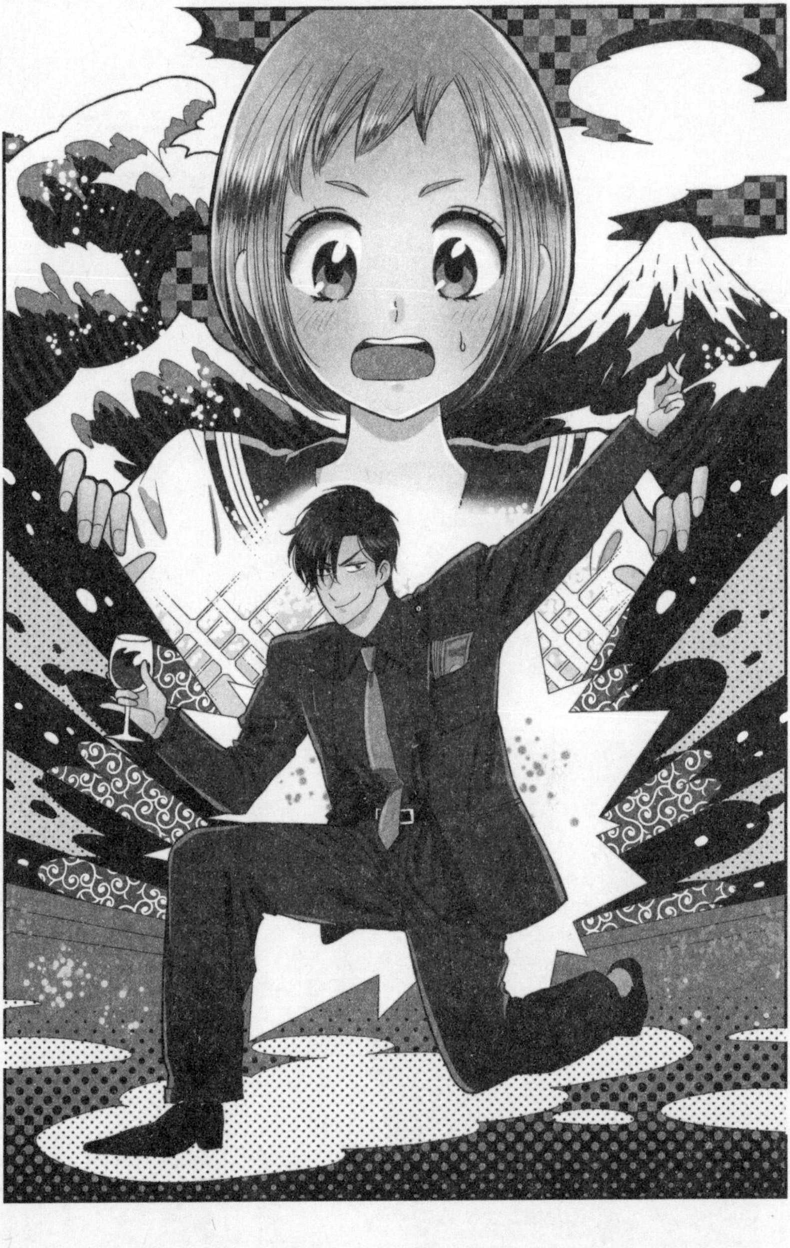

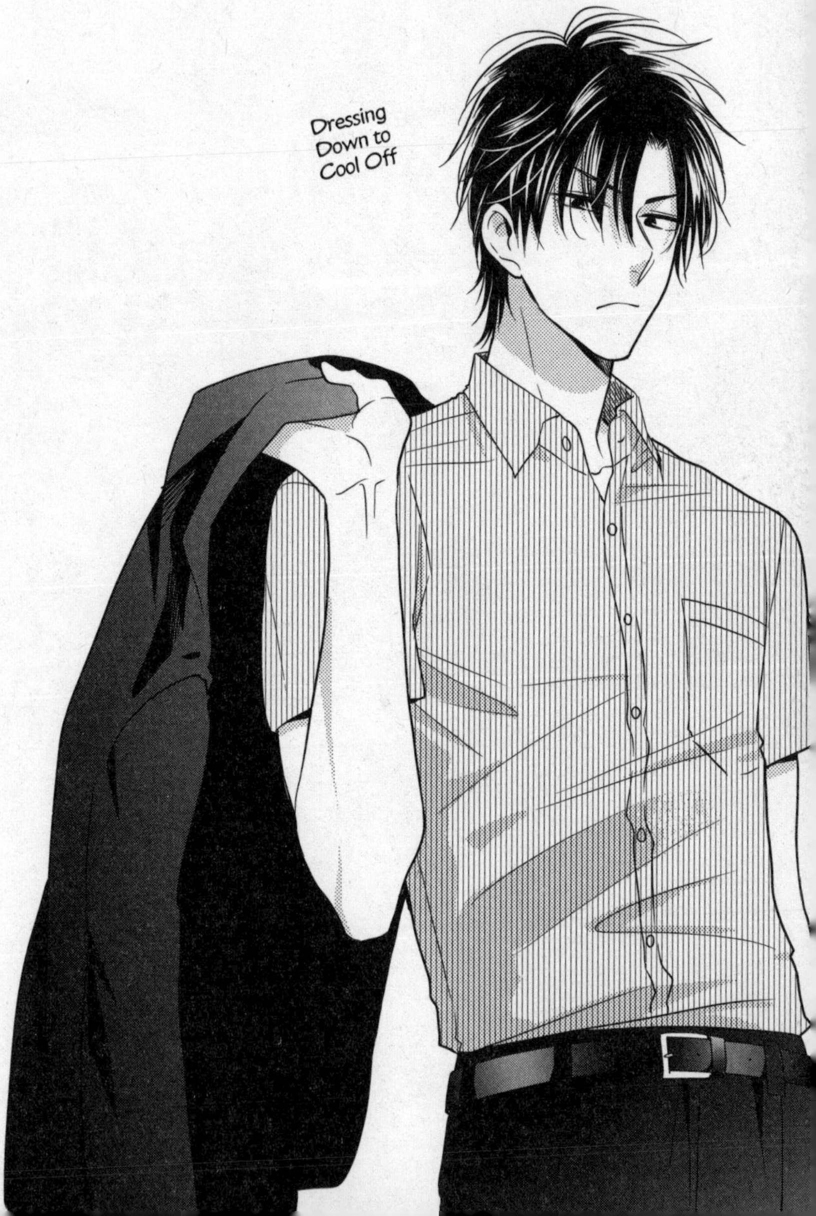
Dressing
Down to
Cool Off

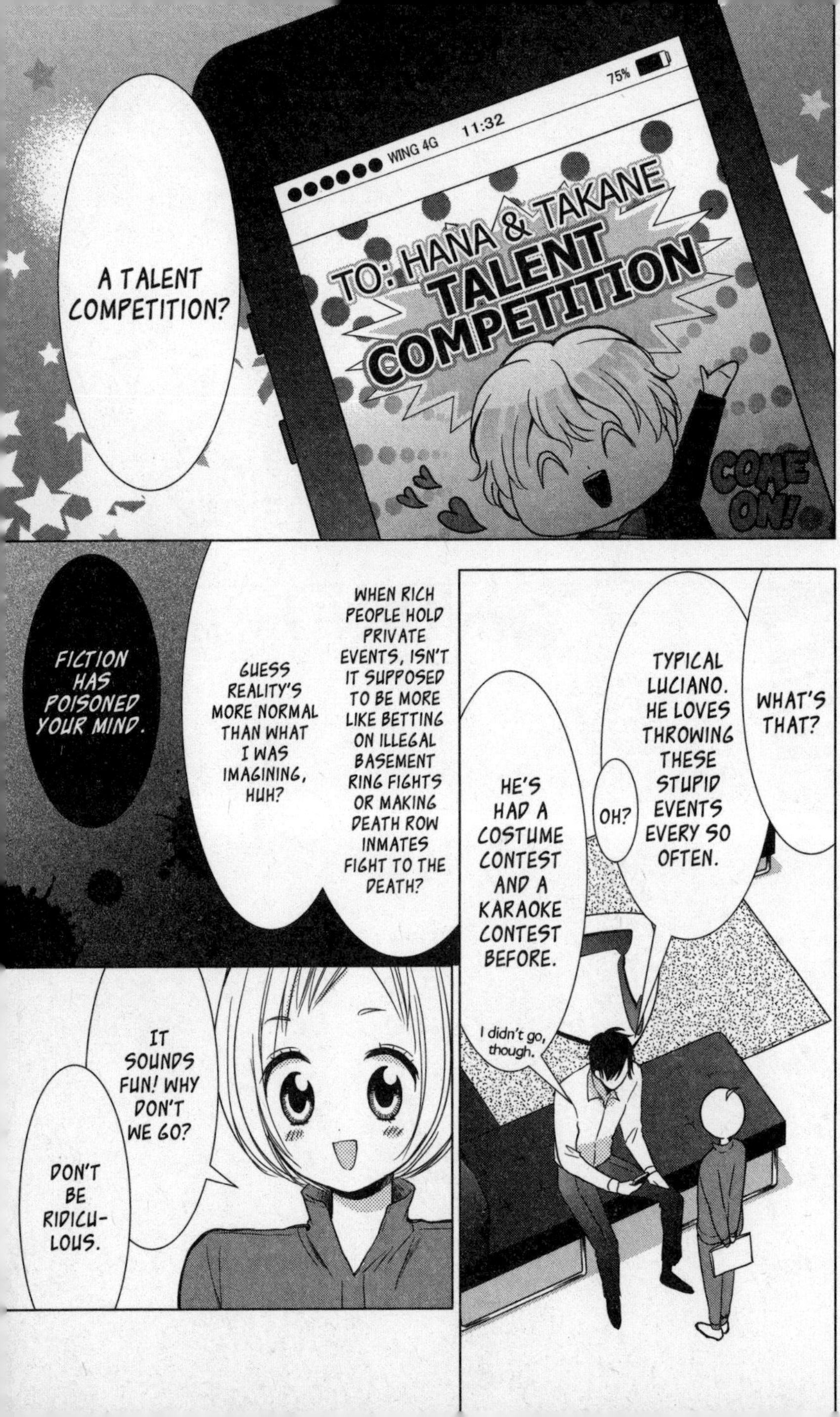
75%
WING 4G 11:32
TO: HANA & TAKANE
TALENT COMPETITION
COME ON!
A TALENT COMPETITION?
WHAT'S THAT?
TYPICAL LUCIANO. HE LOVES THROWING THESE STUPID EVENTS EVERY SO OFTEN.
OH?
HE'S HAD A COSTUME CONTEST AND A KARAOKE CONTEST BEFORE.
I didn't go, though.
WHEN RICH PEOPLE HOLD PRIVATE EVENTS, ISN'T IT SUPPOSED TO BE MORE LIKE BETTING ON ILLEGAL BASEMENT RING FIGHTS OR MAKING DEATH ROW INMATES FIGHT TO THE DEATH?
GUESS REALITY'S MORE NORMAL THAN WHAT I WAS IMAGINING, HUH?
FICTION HAS POISONED YOUR MIND.
IT SOUNDS FUN! WHY DON'T WE GO?
DON'T BE RIDICULOUS.

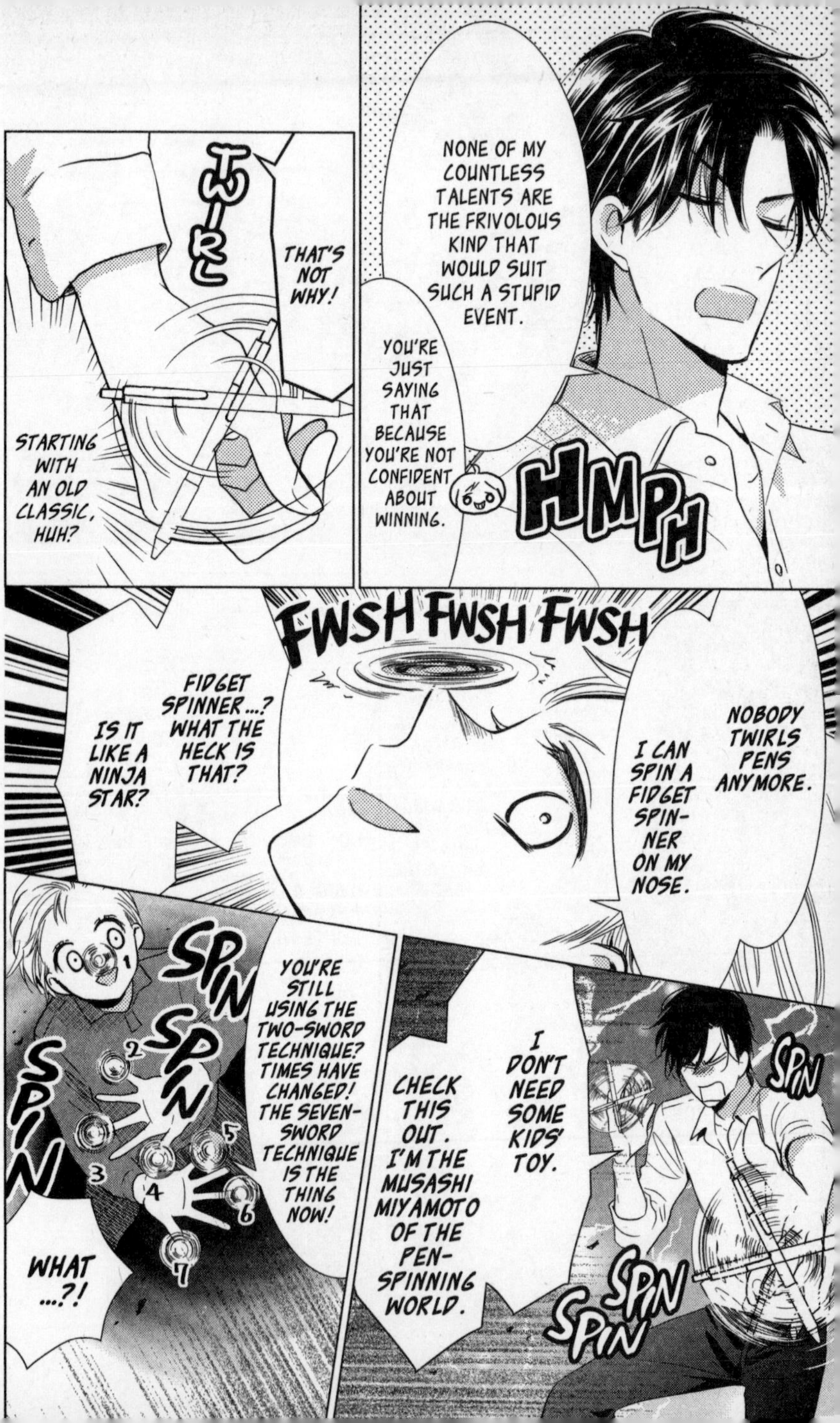
NONE OF MY COUNTLESS TALENTS ARE THE FRIVOLOUS KIND THAT WOULD SUIT SUCH A STUPID EVENT.
YOU'RE JUST SAYING THAT BECAUSE YOU'RE NOT CONFIDENT ABOUT WINNING.
HMPH
TWIRL
THAT'S NOT WHY!
STARTING WITH AN OLD CLASSIC, HUH?
FWSH FWSH FWSH
NOBODY TWIRLS PENS ANYMORE.
I CAN SPIN A FIDGET SPIN-NER ON MY NOSE.
FIDGET SPINNER...? WHAT THE HECK IS THAT?
IS IT LIKE A NINJA STAR?
SPIN
I DON'T NEED SOME KIDS' TOY.
CHECK THIS OUT. I'M THE MUSASHI MIYAMOTO OF THE PEN-SPINNING WORLD.
SPIN SPIN
YOU'RE STILL USING THE TWO-SWORD TECHNIQUE? TIMES HAVE CHANGED! THE SEVEN-SWORD TECHNIQUE IS THE THING NOW!
SPIN SPIN SPIN
1
2
3
4
5
6
7
WHAT ...?!

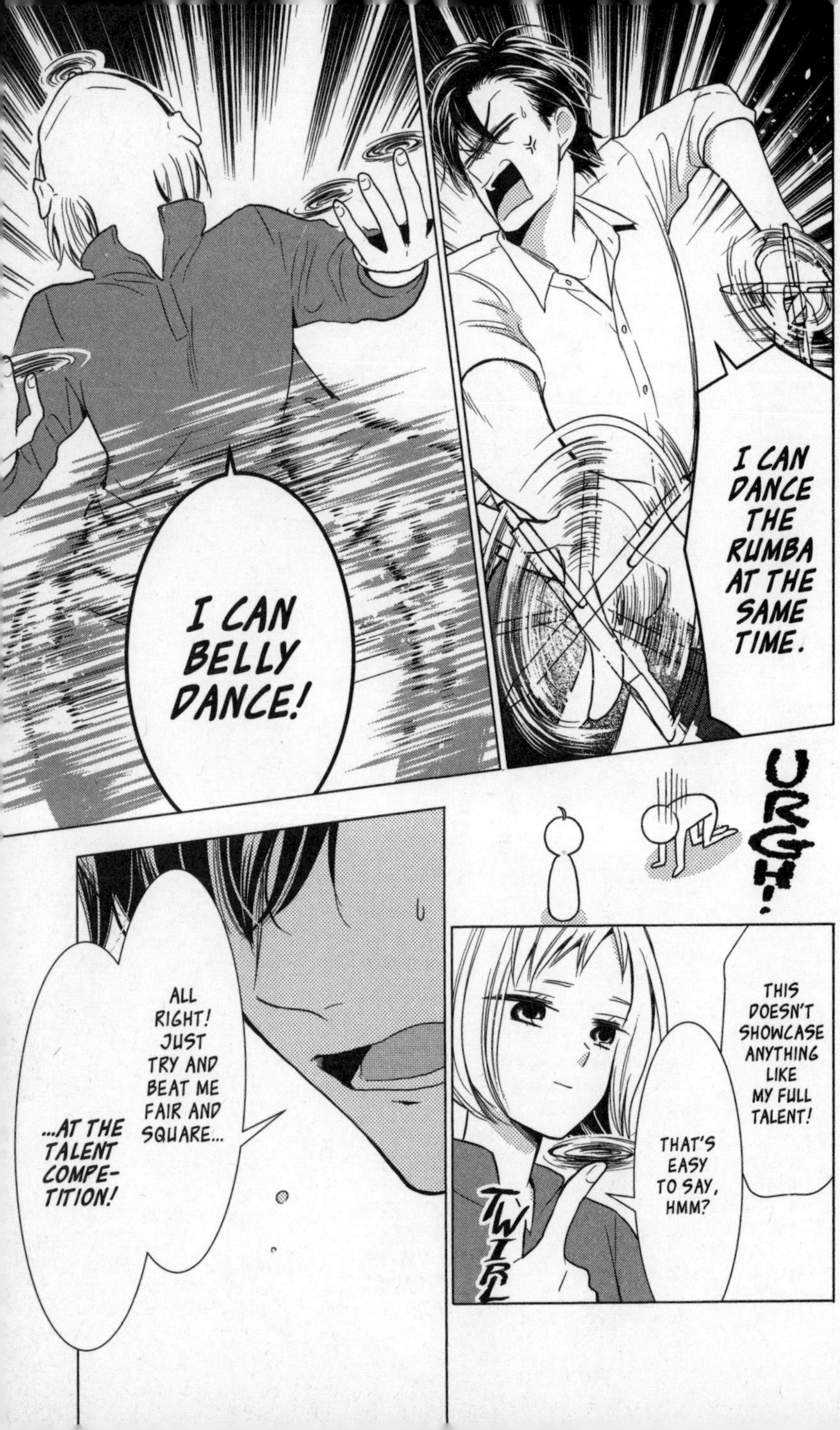
I CAN DANCE THE RUMBA AT THE SAME TIME.
I CAN BELLY DANCE!
URGH!
THIS DOESN'T SHOWCASE ANYTHING LIKE MY FULL TALENT!
THAT'S EASY TO SAY, HMM?
TWIRL
ALL RIGHT! JUST TRY AND BEAT ME FAIR AND SQUARE...
...AT THE TALENT COMPETITION!

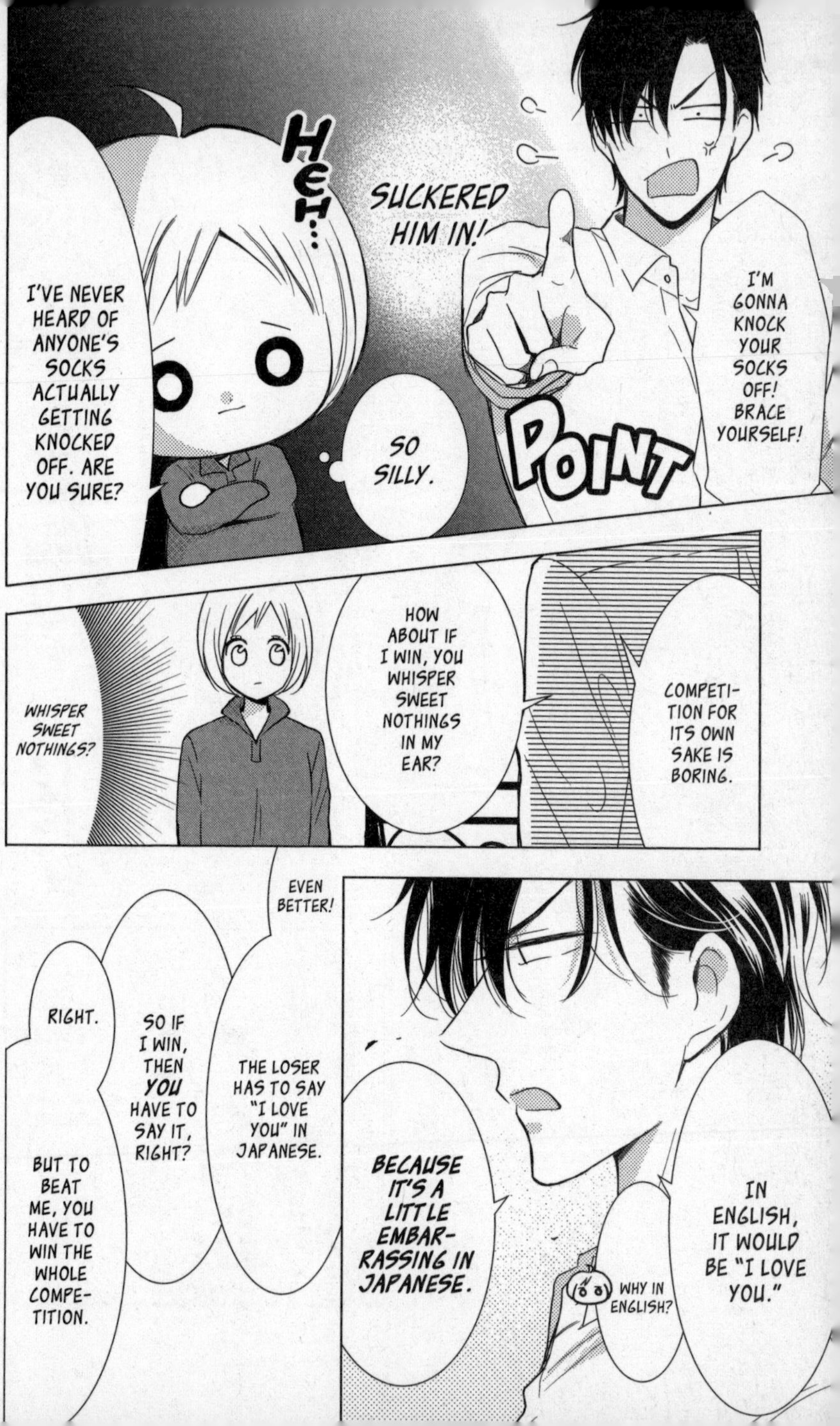
I'M GONNA KNOCK YOUR SOCKS OFF! BRACE YOURSELF!
POINT
SUCKERED HIM IN!
HEH...
SO SILLY.
I'VE NEVER HEARD OF ANYONE'S SOCKS ACTUALLY GETTING KNOCKED OFF. ARE YOU SURE?
COMPETITION FOR ITS OWN SAKE IS BORING.
HOW ABOUT IF I WIN, YOU WHISPER SWEET NOTHINGS IN MY EAR?
WHISPER SWEET NOTHINGS?
IN ENGLISH, IT WOULD BE "I LOVE YOU."
WHY IN ENGLISH?
BECAUSE IT'S A LITTLE EMBARRASSING IN JAPANESE.
EVEN BETTER!
THE LOSER HAS TO SAY "I LOVE YOU" IN JAPANESE.
SO IF I WIN, THEN YOU HAVE TO SAY IT, RIGHT?
RIGHT.
BUT TO BEAT ME, YOU HAVE TO WIN THE WHOLE COMPETITION.

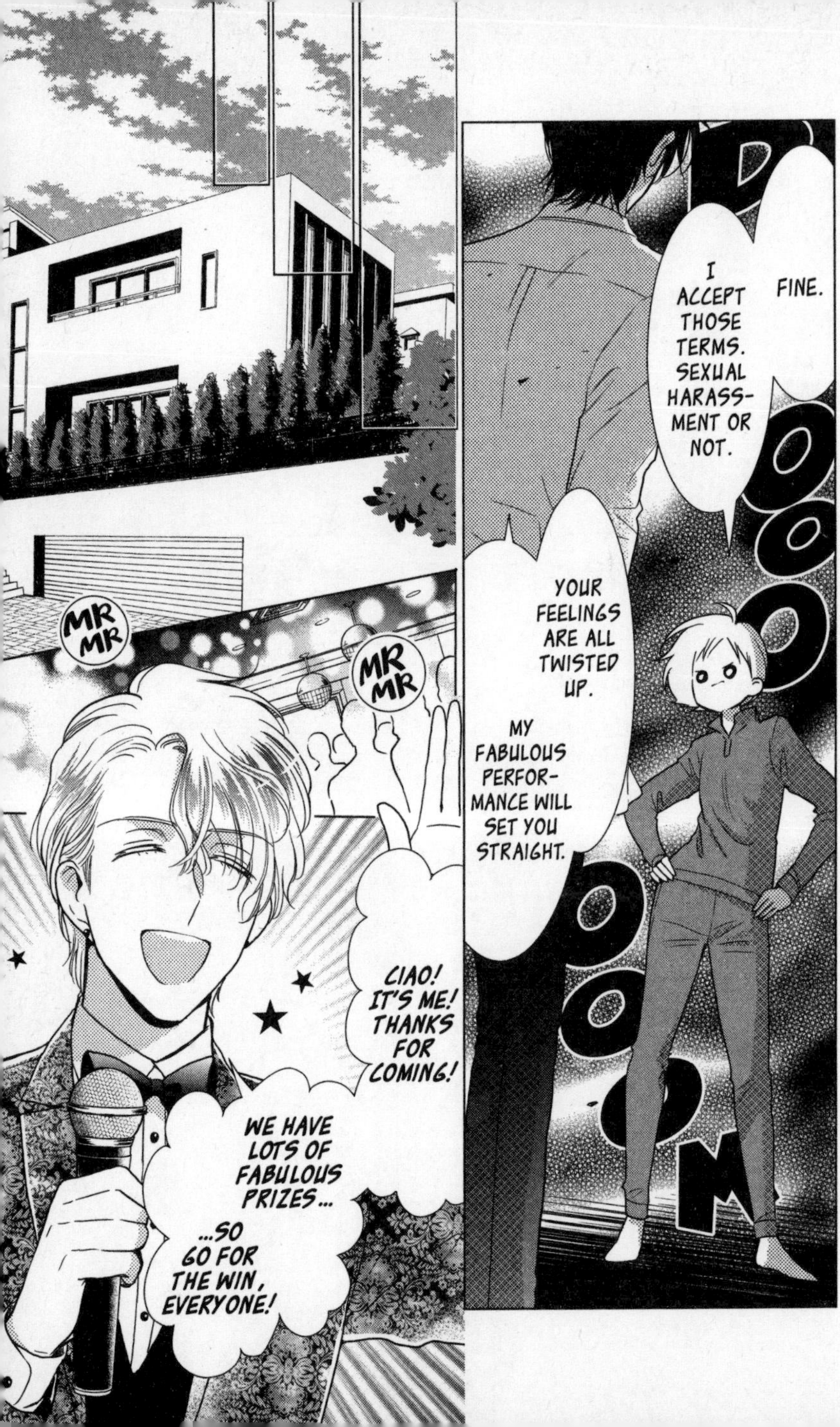
FINE.
I ACCEPT THOSE TERMS. SEXUAL HARASS-MENT OR NOT.
YOUR FEELINGS ARE ALL TWISTED UP.
MY FABULOUS PERFOR-MANCE WILL SET YOU STRAIGHT.
MR MR
MR MR
CIAO! IT'S ME! THANKS FOR COMING!
WE HAVE LOTS OF FABULOUS PRIZES...
...SO GO FOR THE WIN, EVERYONE!

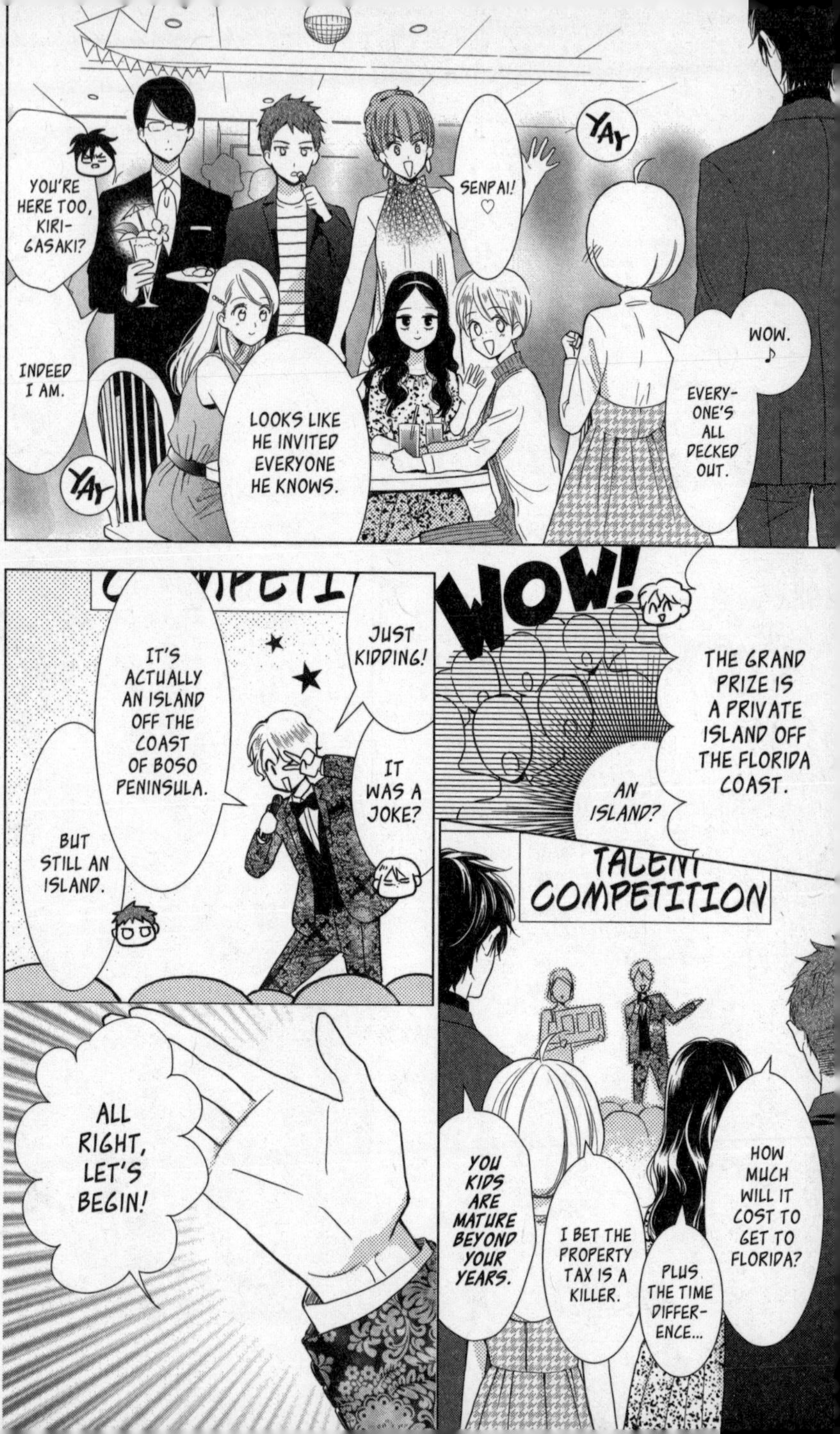

WOW. ♪ EVERYONE'S ALL DECKED OUT.
SENPAI! ♡
YAY
YOU'RE HERE TOO, KIRIGASAKI?
LOOKS LIKE HE INVITED EVERYONE HE KNOWS.
INDEED I AM.
YAY
THE GRAND PRIZE IS A PRIVATE ISLAND OFF THE FLORIDA COAST.
WOW!
AN ISLAND?
TALENT COMPETITION
HOW MUCH WILL IT COST TO GET TO FLORIDA?
PLUS THE TIME DIFFERENCE...
I BET THE PROPERTY TAX IS A KILLER.
YOU KIDS ARE MATURE BEYOND YOUR YEARS.
JUST KIDDING!
IT WAS A JOKE?
IT'S ACTUALLY AN ISLAND OFF THE COAST OF BOSO PENINSULA.
BUT STILL AN ISLAND.
ALL RIGHT, LET'S BEGIN!

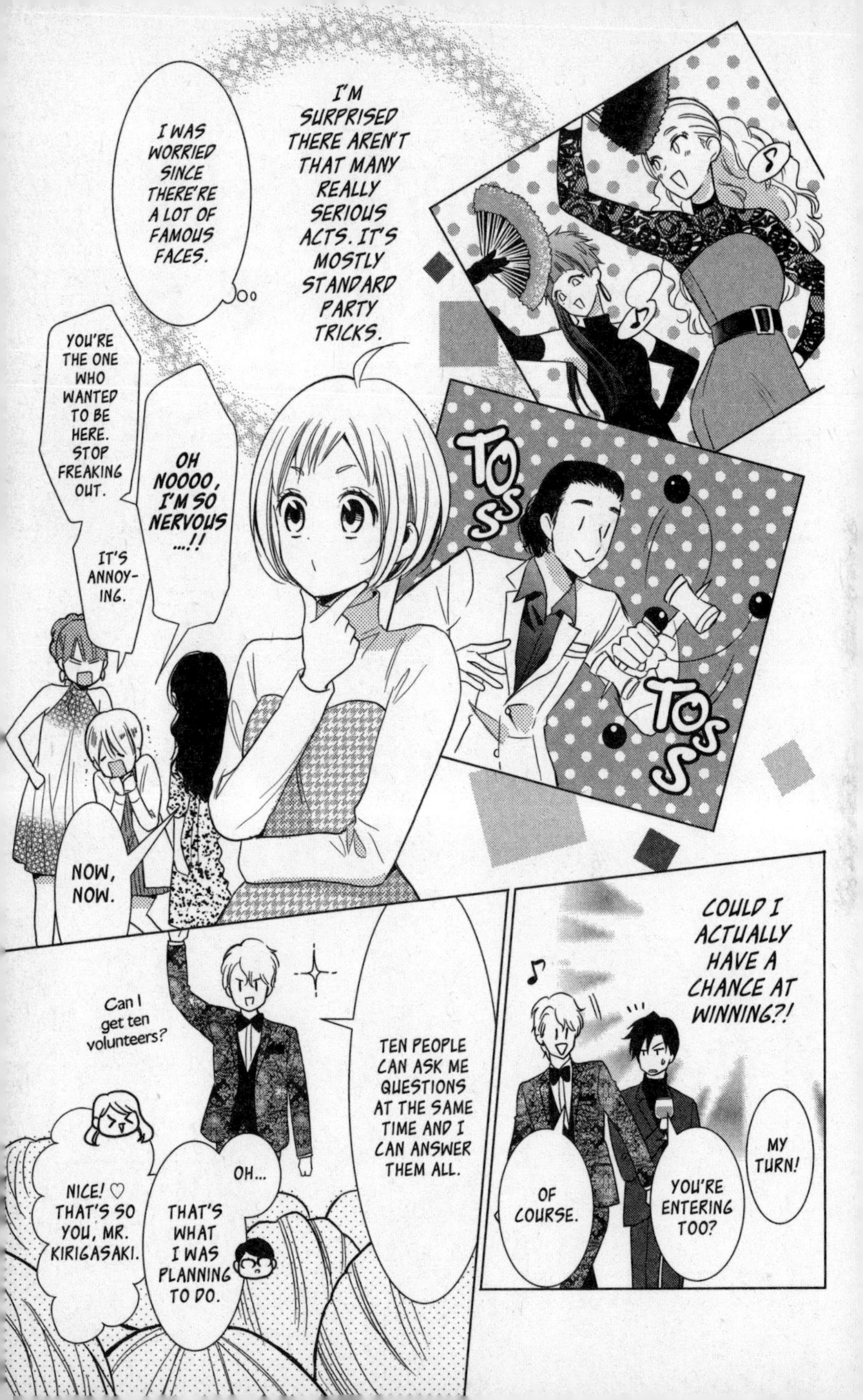
I'M SURPRISED THERE AREN'T THAT MANY REALLY SERIOUS ACTS. IT'S MOSTLY STANDARD PARTY TRICKS.
I WAS WORRIED SINCE THERE'RE A LOT OF FAMOUS FACES.
TOSS
TOSS
OH NOOOO, I'M SO NERVOUS ...!!
YOU'RE THE ONE WHO WANTED TO BE HERE. STOP FREAKING OUT.
IT'S ANNOY-ING.
NOW, NOW.
COULD I ACTUALLY HAVE A CHANCE AT WINNING?!
MY TURN!
YOU'RE ENTERING TOO?
OF COURSE.
Can I get ten volunteers?
TEN PEOPLE CAN ASK ME QUESTIONS AT THE SAME TIME AND I CAN ANSWER THEM ALL.
OH... THAT'S WHAT I WAS PLANNING TO DO.
NICE! ♡ THAT'S SO YOU, MR. KIRIGASAKI.

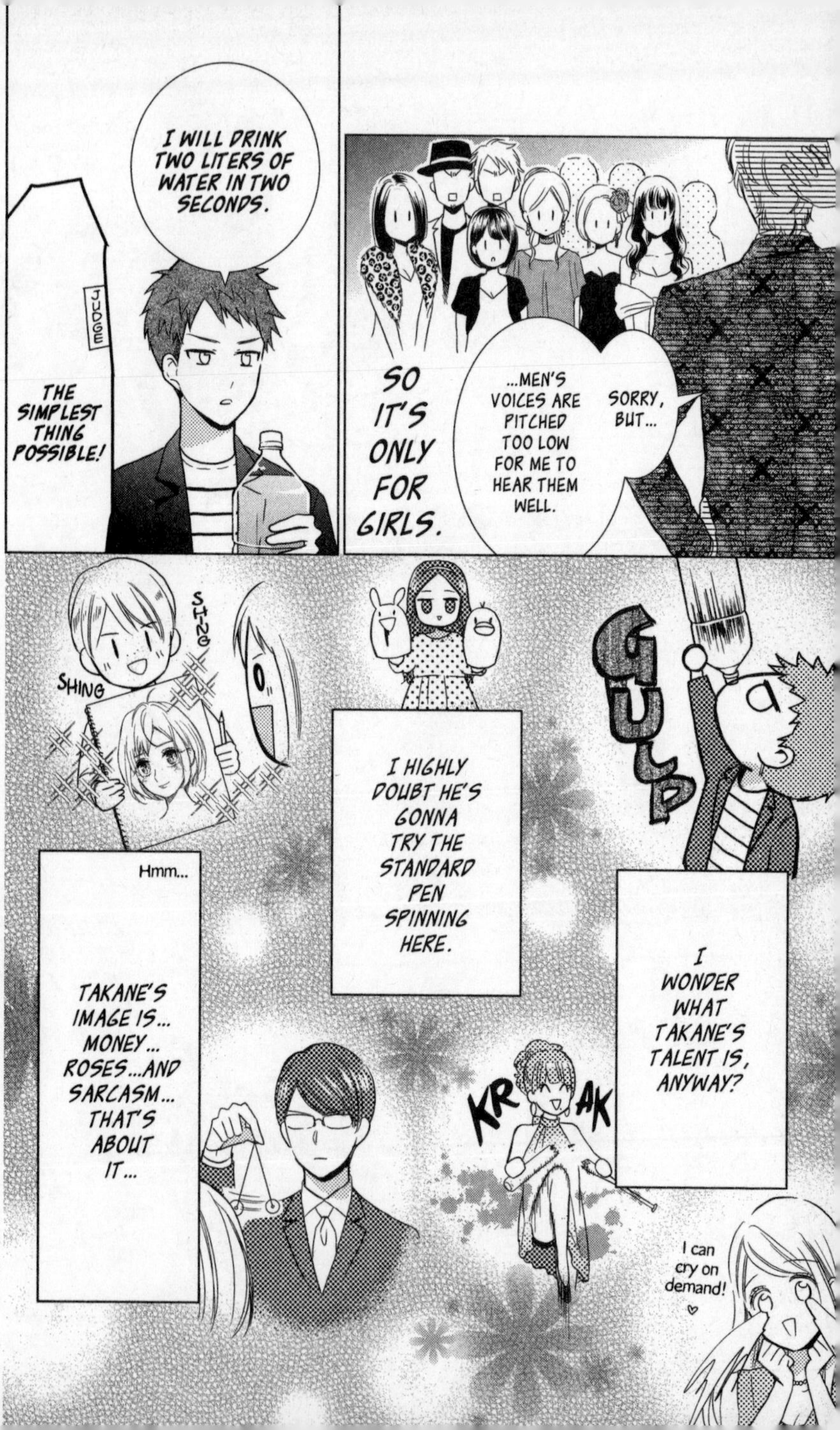
SORRY, BUT...
...MEN'S VOICES ARE PITCHED TOO LOW FOR ME TO HEAR THEM WELL.
SO IT'S ONLY FOR GIRLS.
I WILL DRINK TWO LITERS OF WATER IN TWO SECONDS.
JUDGE
THE SIMPLEST THING POSSIBLE!
GULP
I HIGHLY DOUBT HE'S GONNA TRY THE STANDARD PEN SPINNING HERE.
SHING
SHING
I WONDER WHAT TAKANE'S TALENT IS, ANYWAY?
KRAK
I can cry on demand!
Hmm...
TAKANE'S IMAGE IS... MONEY... ROSES...AND SARCASM... THAT'S ABOUT IT...

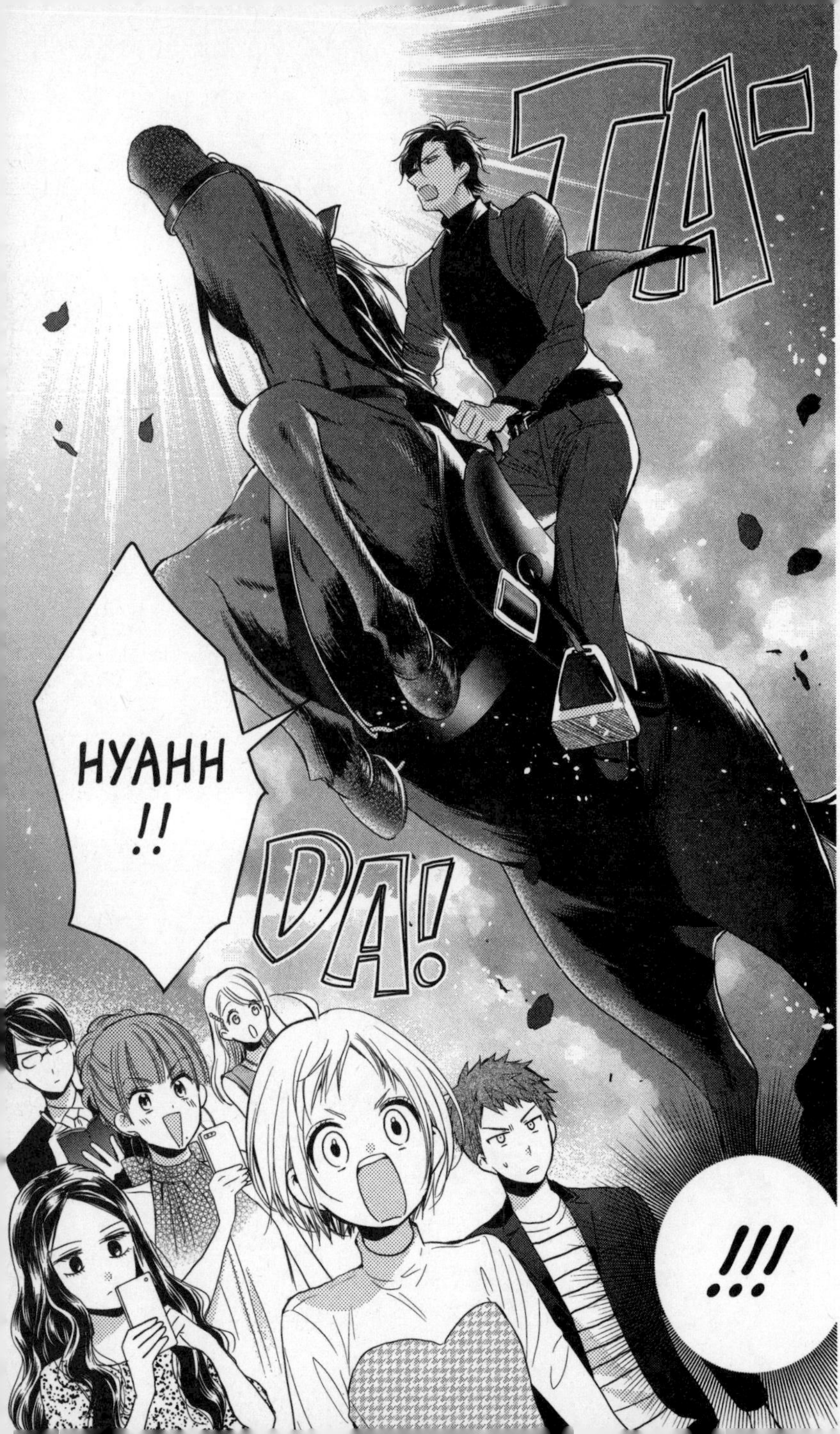
TA-
HYAHH !!
DA!
!!!

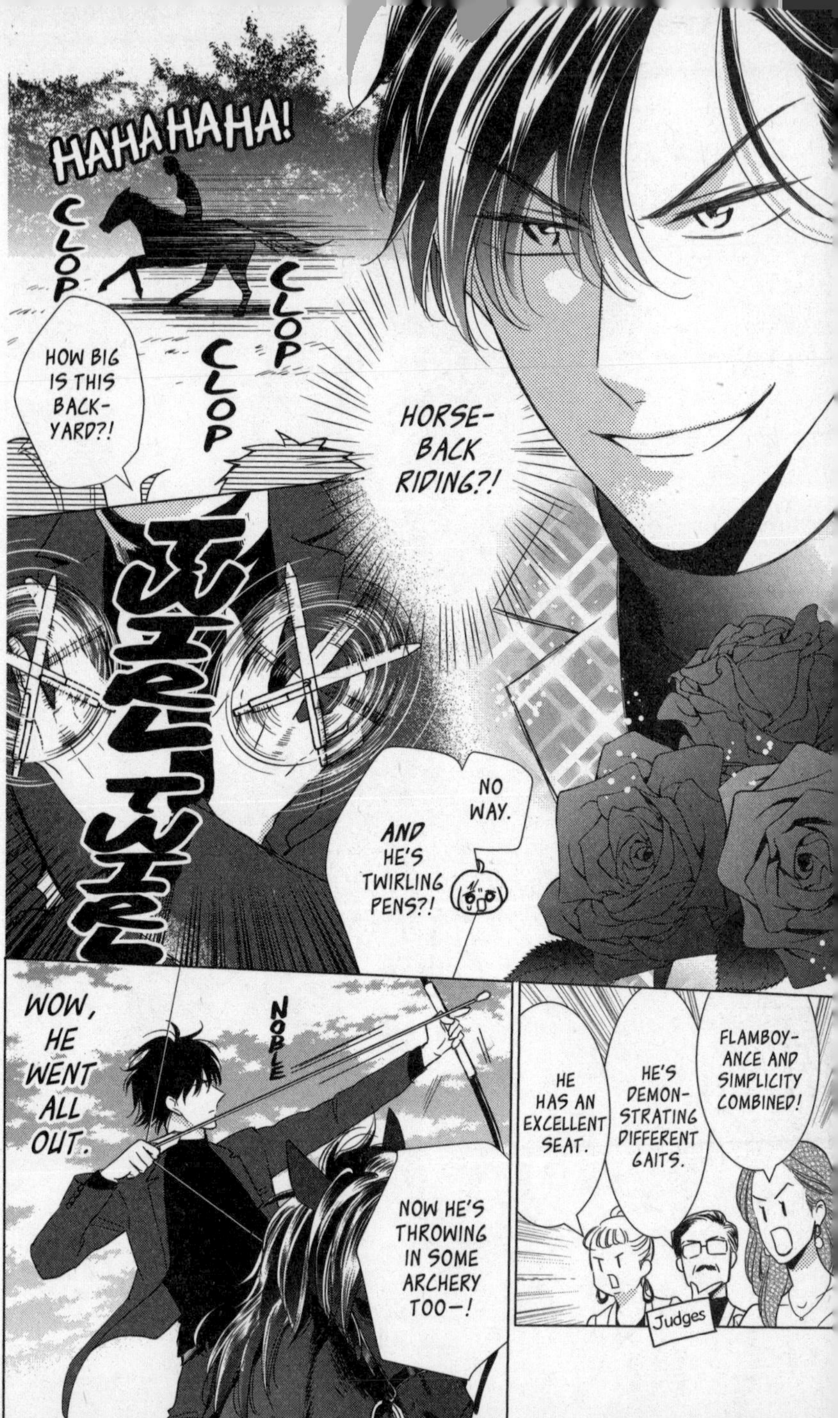
HAHAHAHA!
CLOP
CLOP
CLOP
HOW BIG IS THIS BACK-YARD?!
HORSE-BACK RIDING?!
TWIRL TWIRL
NO WAY.
AND HE'S TWIRLING PENS?!
FLAMBOY-ANCE AND SIMPLICITY COMBINED!
HE'S DEMON-STRATING DIFFERENT GAITS.
HE HAS AN EXCELLENT SEAT.
Judges
NOBLE
WOW, HE WENT ALL OUT.
NOW HE'S THROWING IN SOME ARCHERY TOO—!

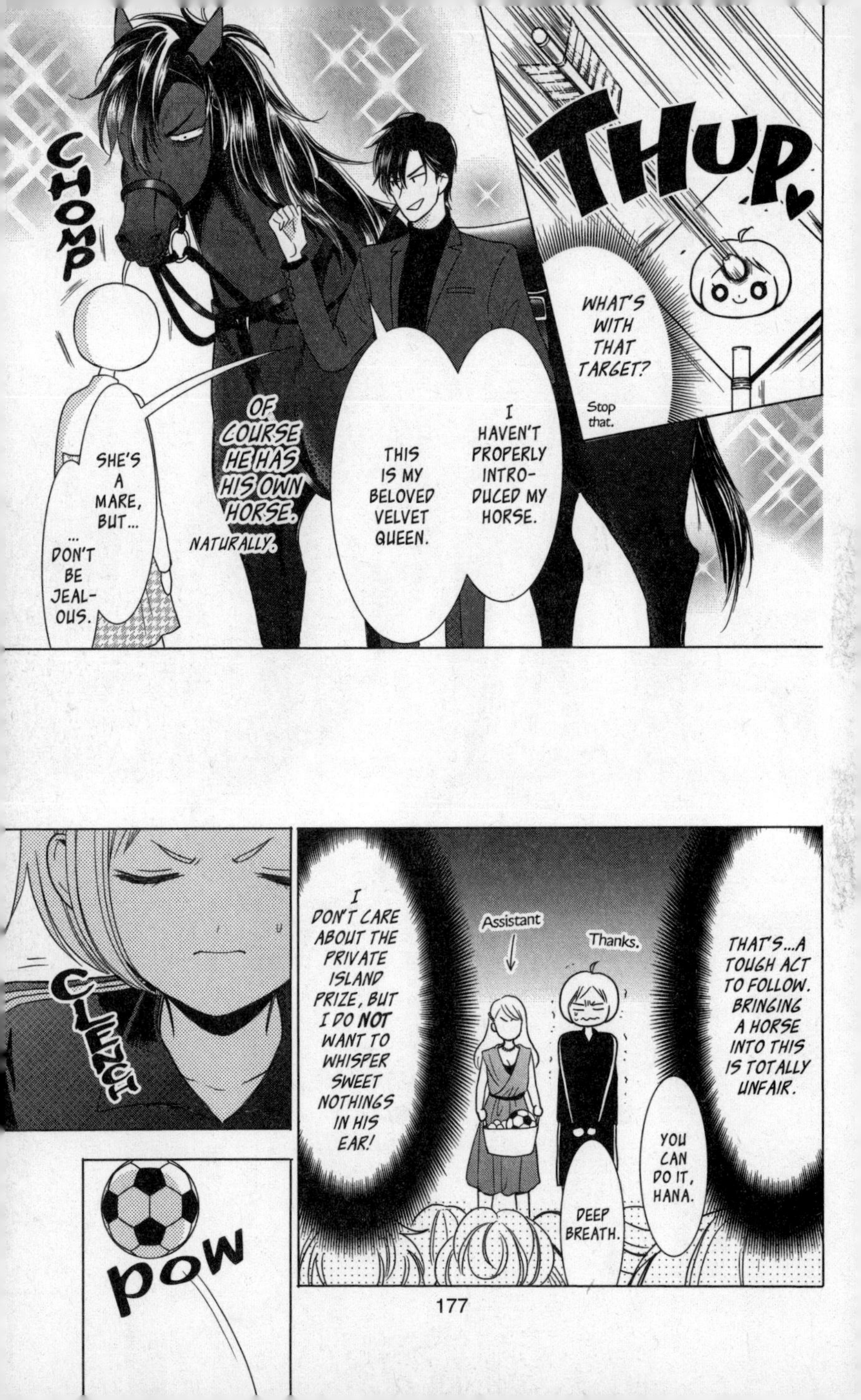
THUP♥
WHAT'S WITH THAT TARGET?
Stop that.
I HAVEN'T PROPERLY INTRO-DUCED MY HORSE.
THIS IS MY BELOVED VELVET QUEEN.
OF COURSE HE HAS HIS OWN HORSE.
NATURALLY.
CHOMP
SHE'S A MARE, BUT...
...DON'T BE JEAL-OUS.
THAT'S...A TOUGH ACT TO FOLLOW. BRINGING A HORSE INTO THIS IS TOTALLY UNFAIR.
YOU CAN DO IT, HANA.
DEEP BREATH.
Thanks.
Assistant
I DON'T CARE ABOUT THE PRIVATE ISLAND PRIZE, BUT I DO NOT WANT TO WHISPER SWEET NOTHINGS IN HIS EAR!
CLENCH
pow

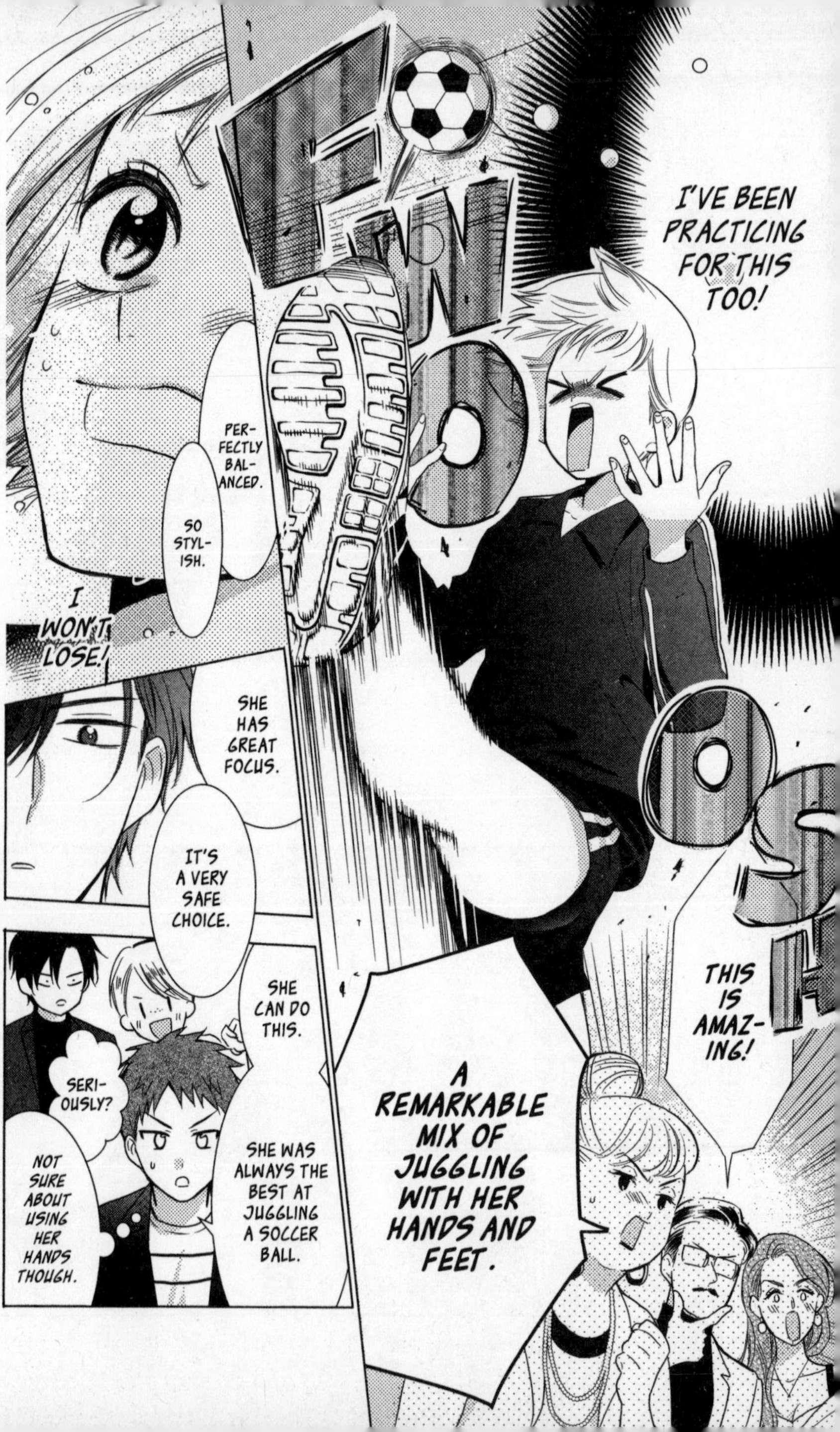
I'VE BEEN PRACTICING FOR THIS TOO!
THIS IS AMAZING!
A REMARKABLE MIX OF JUGGLING WITH HER HANDS AND FEET.
PERFECTLY BALANCED.
SO STYLISH.
I WON'T LOSE!
SHE HAS GREAT FOCUS.
IT'S A VERY SAFE CHOICE.
SHE CAN DO THIS.
SHE WAS ALWAYS THE BEST AT JUGGLING A SOCCER BALL.
SERIOUSLY?
NOT SURE ABOUT USING HER HANDS THOUGH.

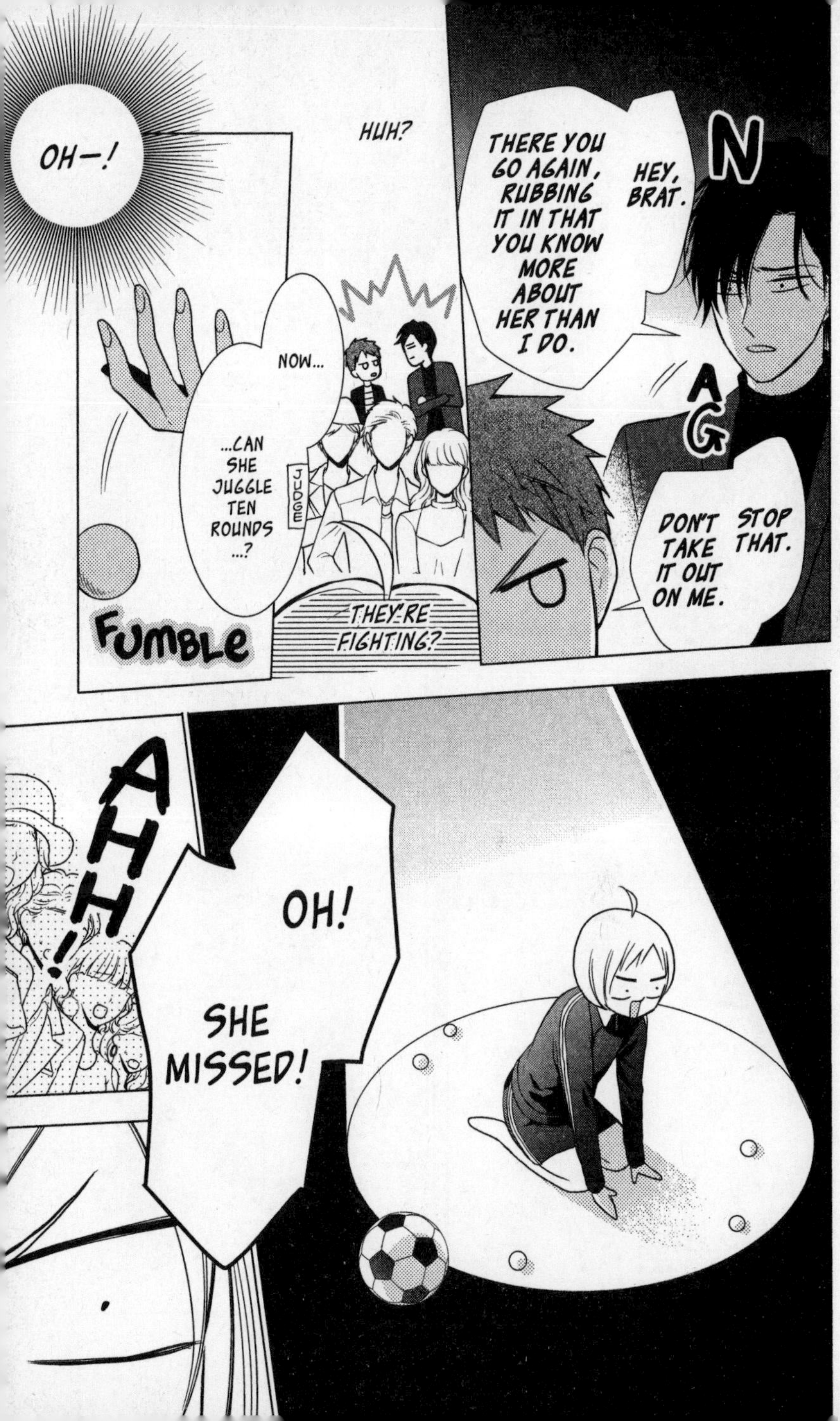
NAG
HEY, BRAT.
THERE YOU GO AGAIN, RUBBING IT IN THAT YOU KNOW MORE ABOUT HER THAN I DO.
STOP THAT.
DON'T TAKE IT OUT ON ME.
HUH?
THEY'RE FIGHTING?
JUDGE
NOW...
...CAN SHE JUGGLE TEN ROUNDS ...?
OH—!
FUMBLE
OH!
SHE MISSED!
AHH!

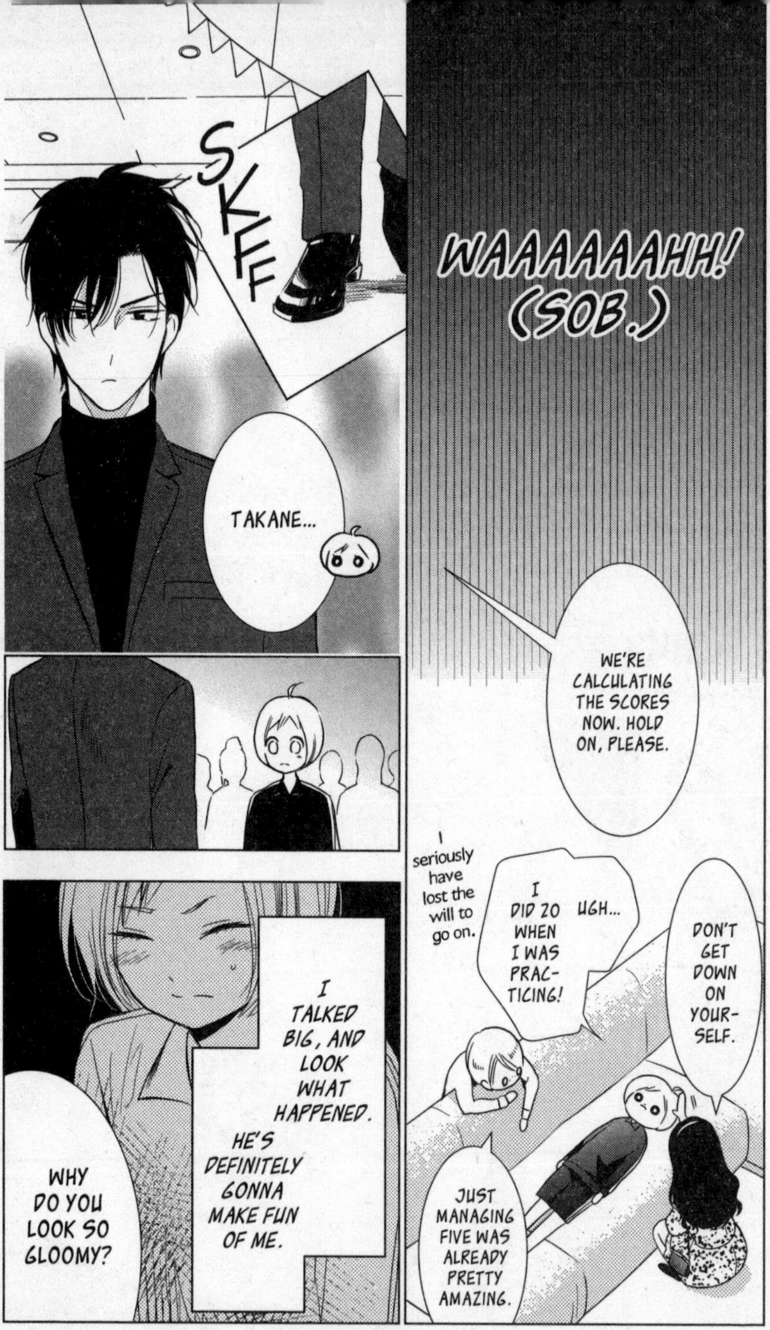
WAAAAAAAHH! (SOB.)
WE'RE CALCULATING THE SCORES NOW. HOLD ON, PLEASE.
DON'T GET DOWN ON YOURSELF.
UGH...
I DID 20 WHEN I WAS PRACTICING!
I seriously have lost the will to go on.
JUST MANAGING FIVE WAS ALREADY PRETTY AMAZING.
SKFF
TAKANE...
I TALKED BIG, AND LOOK WHAT HAPPENED.
HE'S DEFINITELY GONNA MAKE FUN OF ME.
WHY DO YOU LOOK SO GLOOMY?

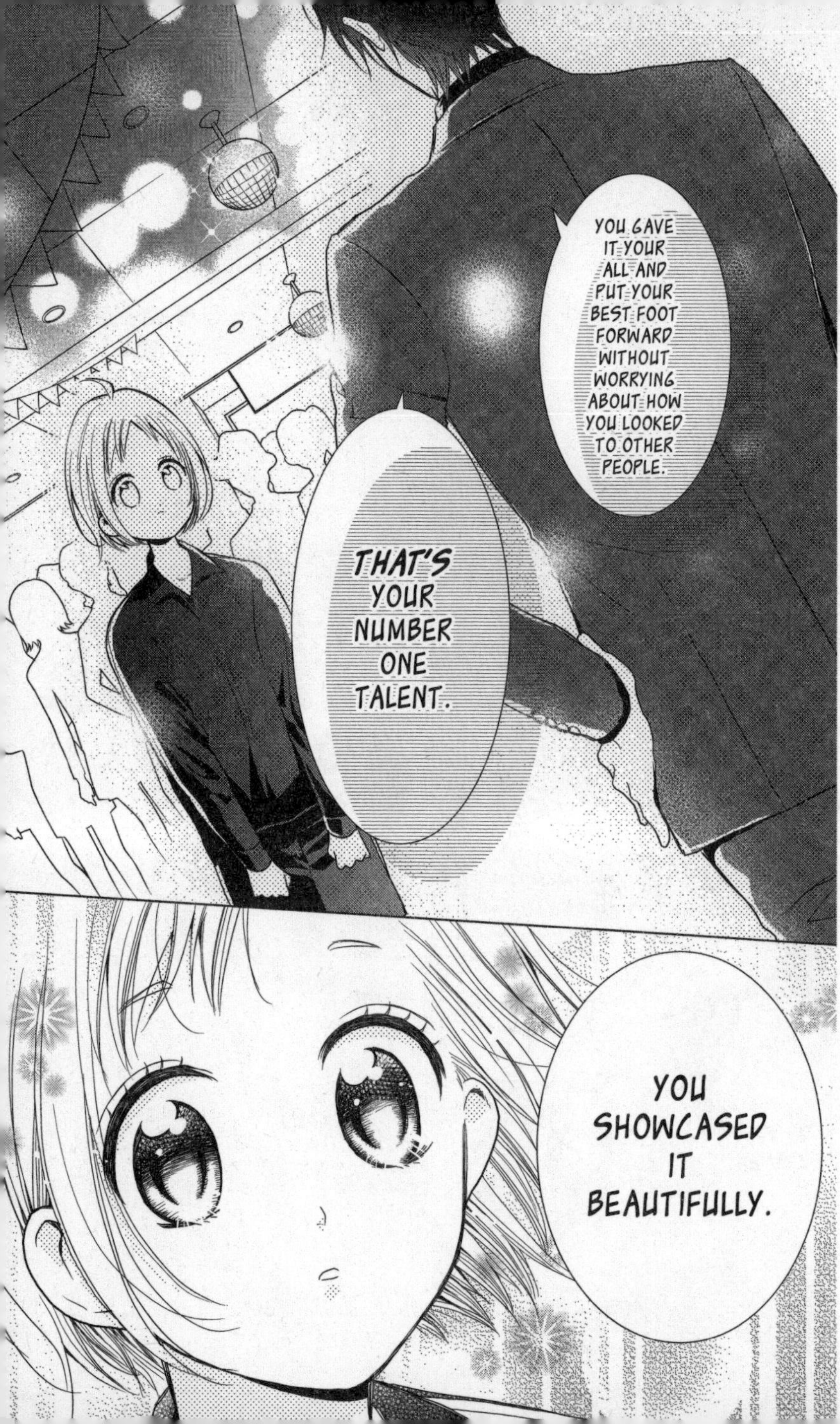
YOU GAVE IT YOUR ALL AND PUT YOUR BEST FOOT FORWARD WITHOUT WORRYING ABOUT HOW YOU LOOKED TO OTHER PEOPLE.
THAT'S YOUR NUMBER ONE TALENT.
YOU SHOWCASED IT BEAUTIFULLY.

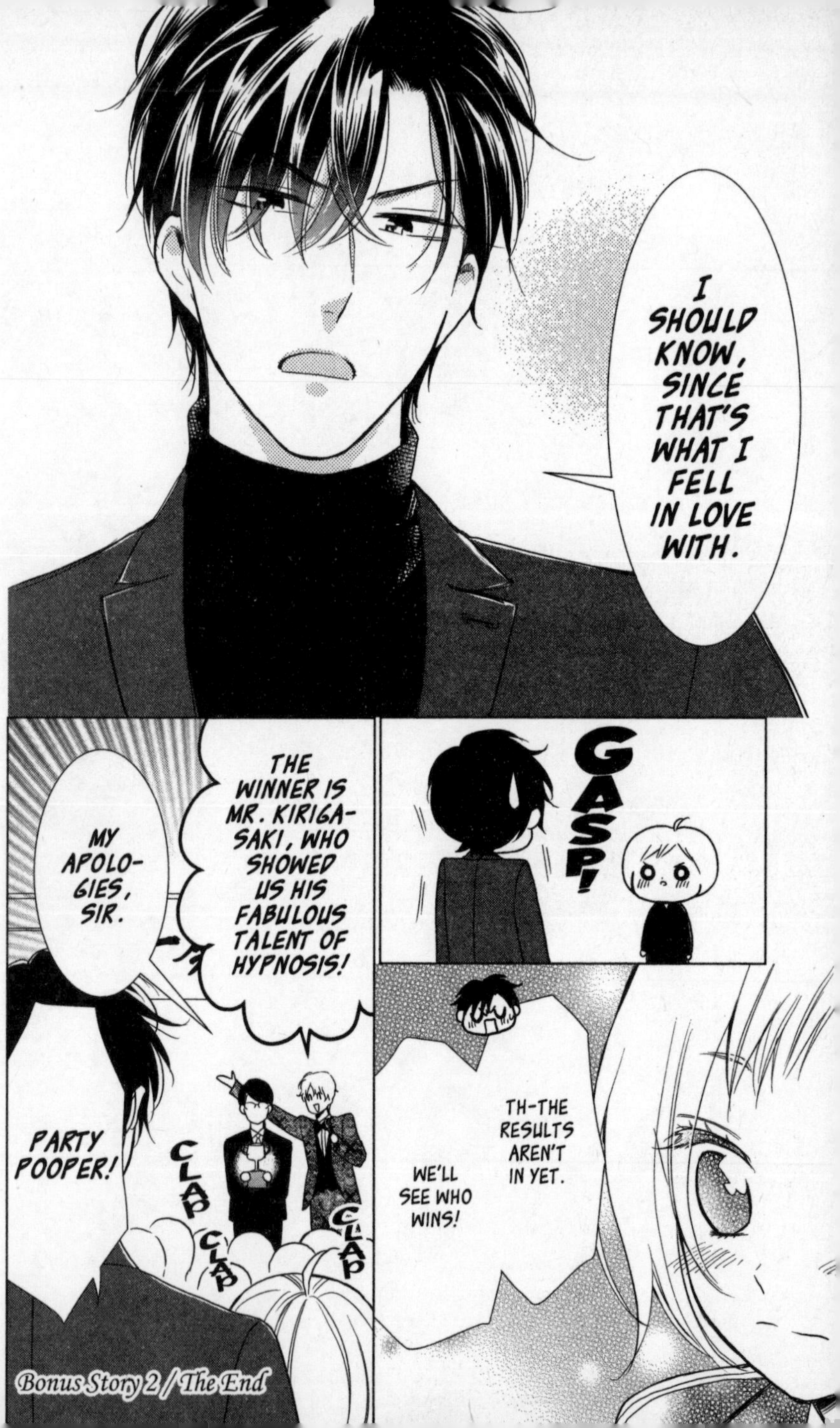
I SHOULD KNOW, SINCE THAT'S WHAT I FELL IN LOVE WITH.
GASP!
TH-THE RESULTS AREN'T IN YET.
WE'LL SEE WHO WINS!
THE WINNER IS MR. KIRIGASAKI, WHO SHOWED US HIS FABULOUS TALENT OF HYPNOSIS!
MY APOLOGIES, SIR.
PARTY POOPER!
CLAP
CLAP
CLAP
Bonus Story 2 / The End

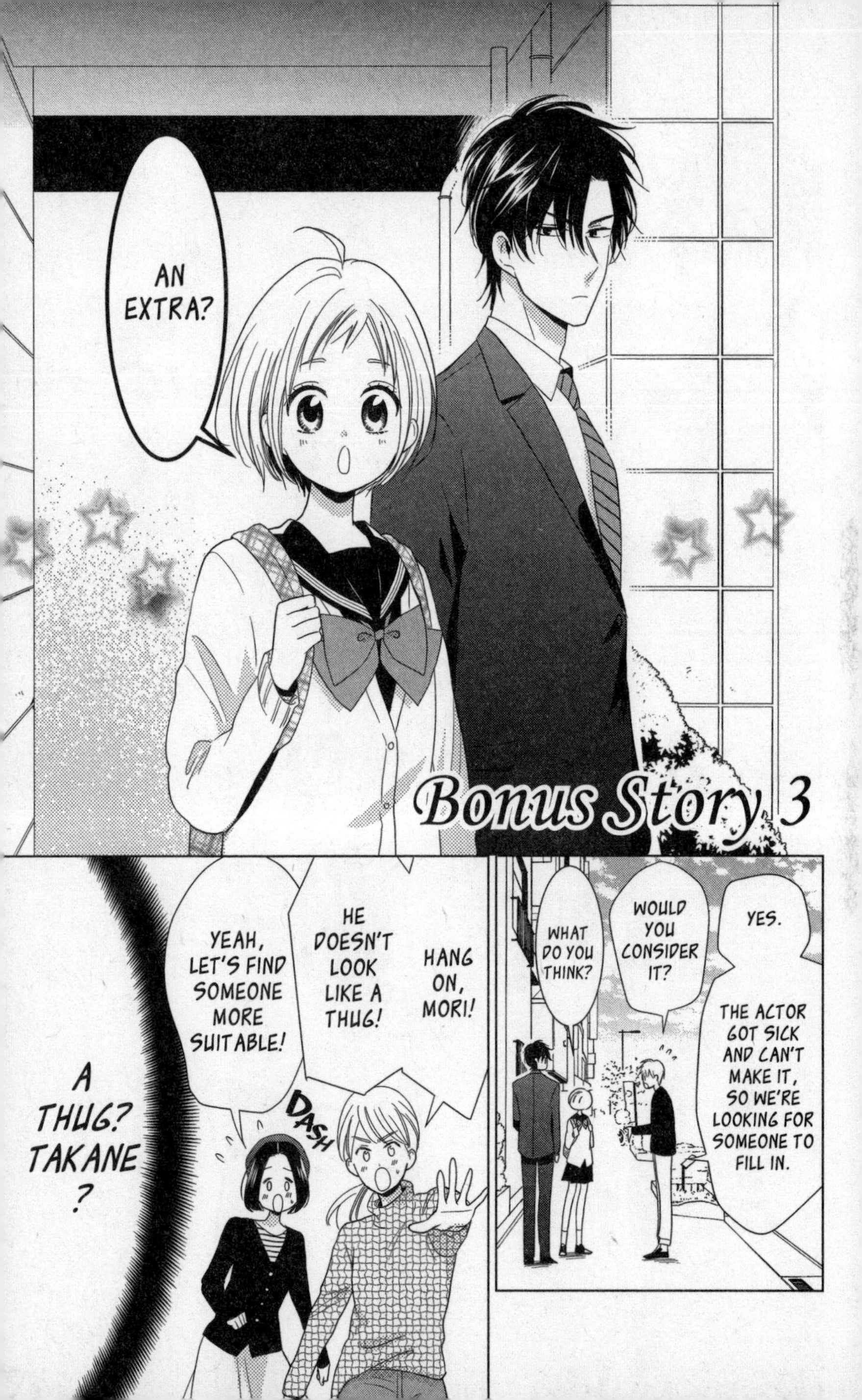
AN EXTRA?
Bonus Story 3
YES.
THE ACTOR GOT SICK AND CAN'T MAKE IT, SO WE'RE LOOKING FOR SOMEONE TO FILL IN.
WOULD YOU CONSIDER IT?
WHAT DO YOU THINK?
HANG ON, MORI!
HE DOESN'T LOOK LIKE A THUG!
DASH
YEAH, LET'S FIND SOMEONE MORE SUITABLE!
A THUG? TAKANE?

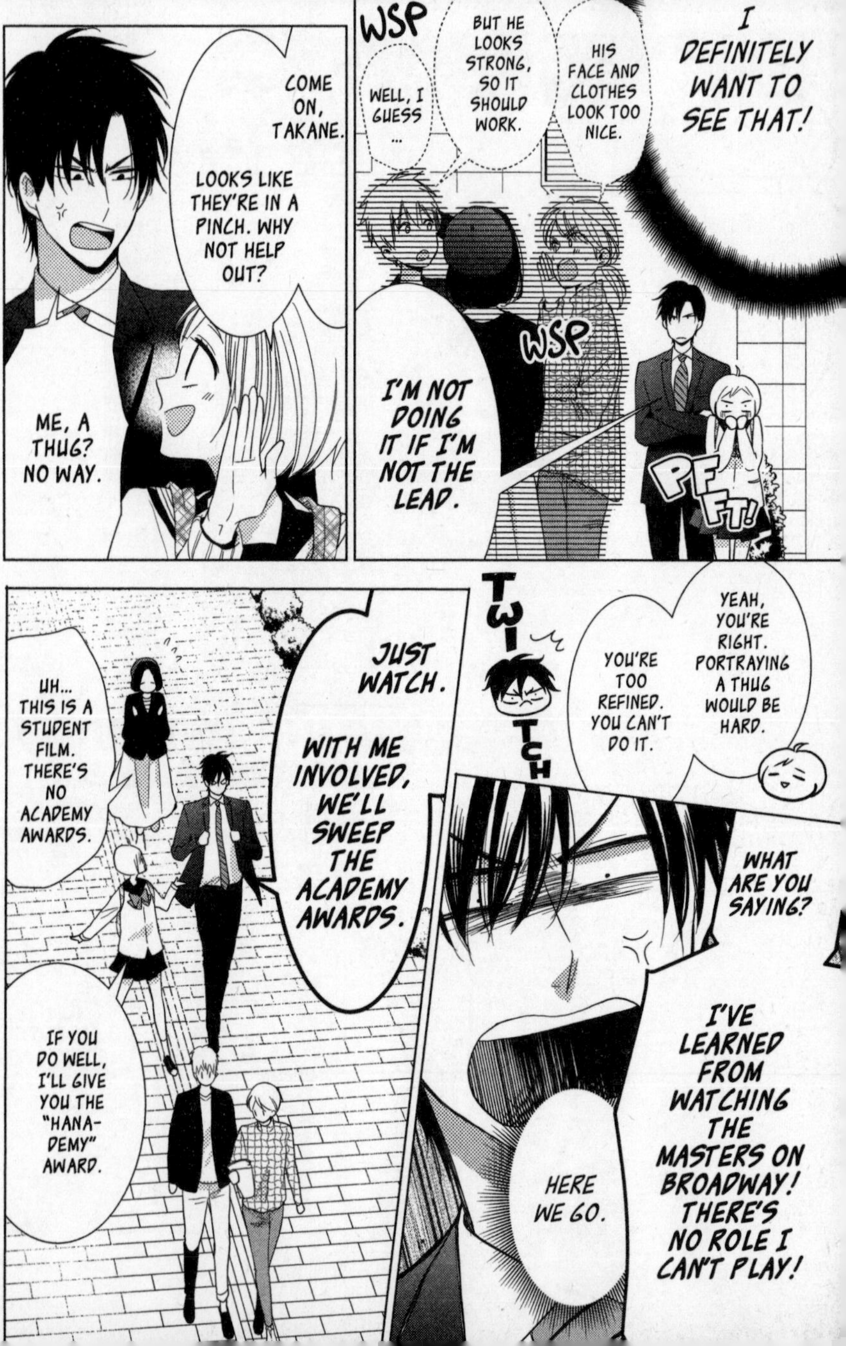
I DEFINITELY WANT TO SEE THAT!
HIS FACE AND CLOTHES LOOK TOO NICE.
BUT HE LOOKS STRONG, SO IT SHOULD WORK.
WSP
WELL, I GUESS...
WSP
I'M NOT DOING IT IF I'M NOT THE LEAD.
PFFT!
COME ON, TAKANE.
LOOKS LIKE THEY'RE IN A PINCH. WHY NOT HELP OUT?
ME, A THUG? NO WAY.
YEAH, YOU'RE RIGHT. PORTRAYING A THUG WOULD BE HARD.
YOU'RE TOO REFINED. YOU CAN'T DO IT.
TWITCH
WHAT ARE YOU SAYING?
I'VE LEARNED FROM WATCHING THE MASTERS ON BROADWAY! THERE'S NO ROLE I CAN'T PLAY!
HERE WE GO.
JUST WATCH.
WITH ME INVOLVED, WE'LL SWEEP THE ACADEMY AWARDS.
UH... THIS IS A STUDENT FILM. THERE'S NO ACADEMY AWARDS.
IF YOU DO WELL, I'LL GIVE YOU THE "HANA-DEMY" AWARD.

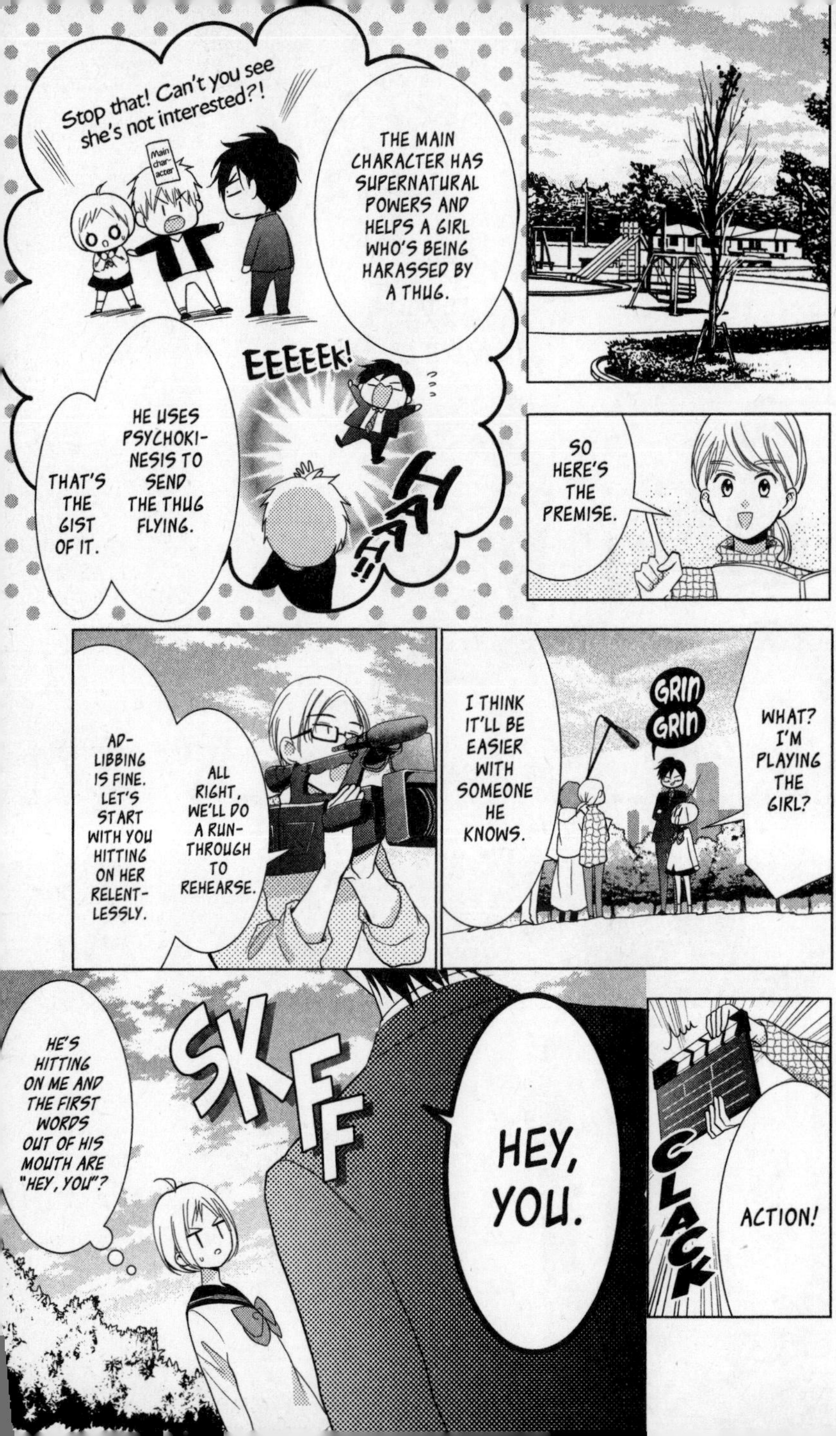
SO HERE'S THE PREMISE.
THE MAIN CHARACTER HAS SUPERNATURAL POWERS AND HELPS A GIRL WHO'S BEING HARASSED BY A THUG.
Stop that! Can't you see she's not interested?!
Main character
EEEEEK!
HAHAH!!
HE USES PSYCHOKINESIS TO SEND THE THUG FLYING.
THAT'S THE GIST OF IT.
WHAT? I'M PLAYING THE GIRL?
GRIN GRIN
I THINK IT'LL BE EASIER WITH SOMEONE HE KNOWS.
ALL RIGHT, WE'LL DO A RUN-THROUGH TO REHEARSE.
AD-LIBBING IS FINE. LET'S START WITH YOU HITTING ON HER RELENTLESSLY.
ACTION!
CLACK
HEY, YOU.
SKFF
HE'S HITTING ON ME AND THE FIRST WORDS OUT OF HIS MOUTH ARE "HEY, YOU"?

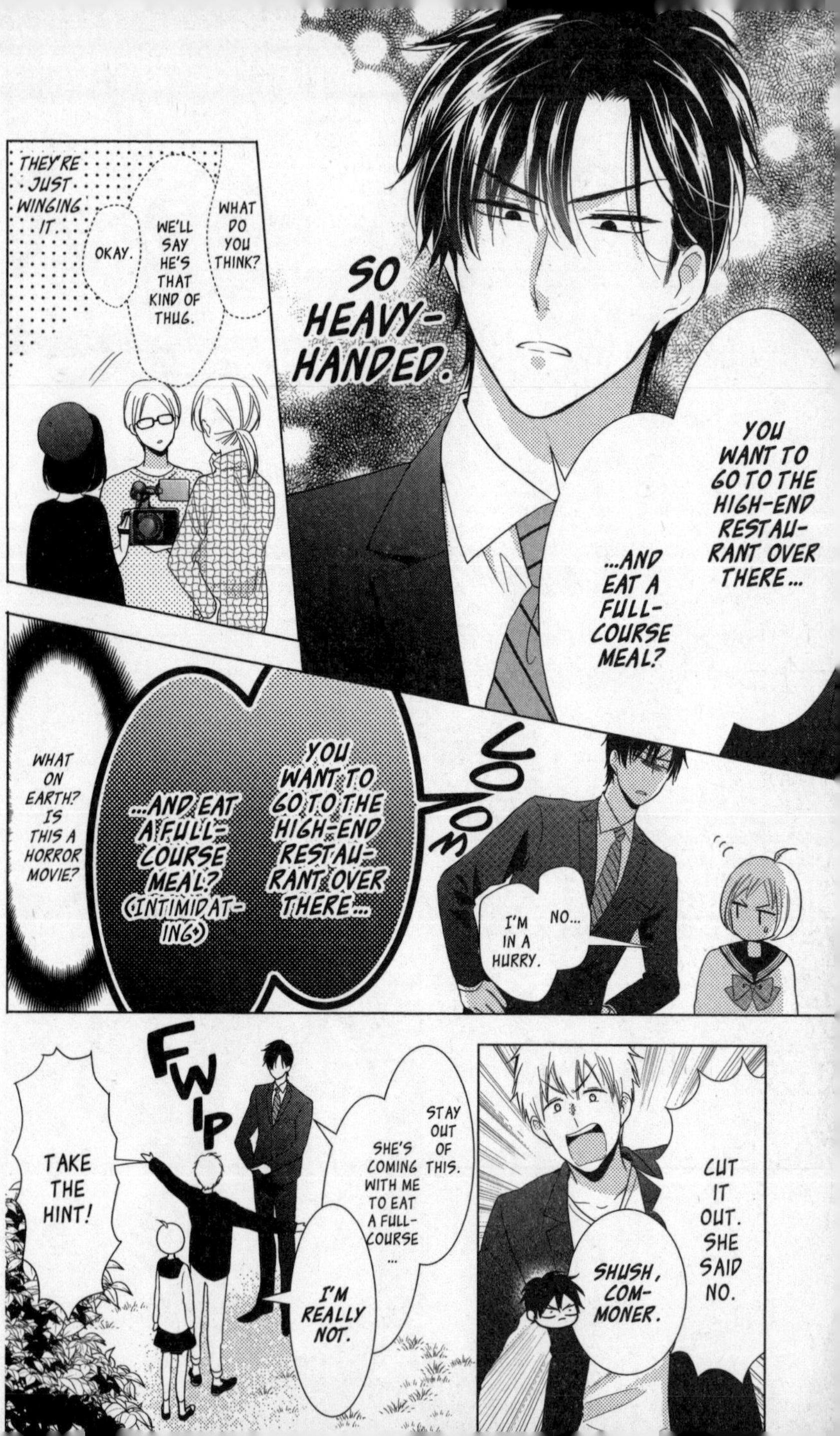
YOU WANT TO GO TO THE HIGH-END RESTAURANT OVER THERE...
...AND EAT A FULL-COURSE MEAL?
SO HEAVY-HANDED.
WHAT DO YOU THINK?
WE'LL SAY HE'S THAT KIND OF THUG.
OKAY.
THEY'RE JUST WINGING IT.
VOOM
NO...
I'M IN A HURRY.
YOU WANT TO GO TO THE HIGH-END RESTAURANT OVER THERE...
...AND EAT A FULL-COURSE MEAL? (INTIMIDATING)
WHAT ON EARTH? IS THIS A HORROR MOVIE?
CUT IT OUT. SHE SAID NO.
SHUSH, COMMONER.
STAY OUT OF THIS.
SHE'S COMING WITH ME TO EAT A FULL-COURSE ...
I'M REALLY NOT.
FWIP
TAKE THE HINT!

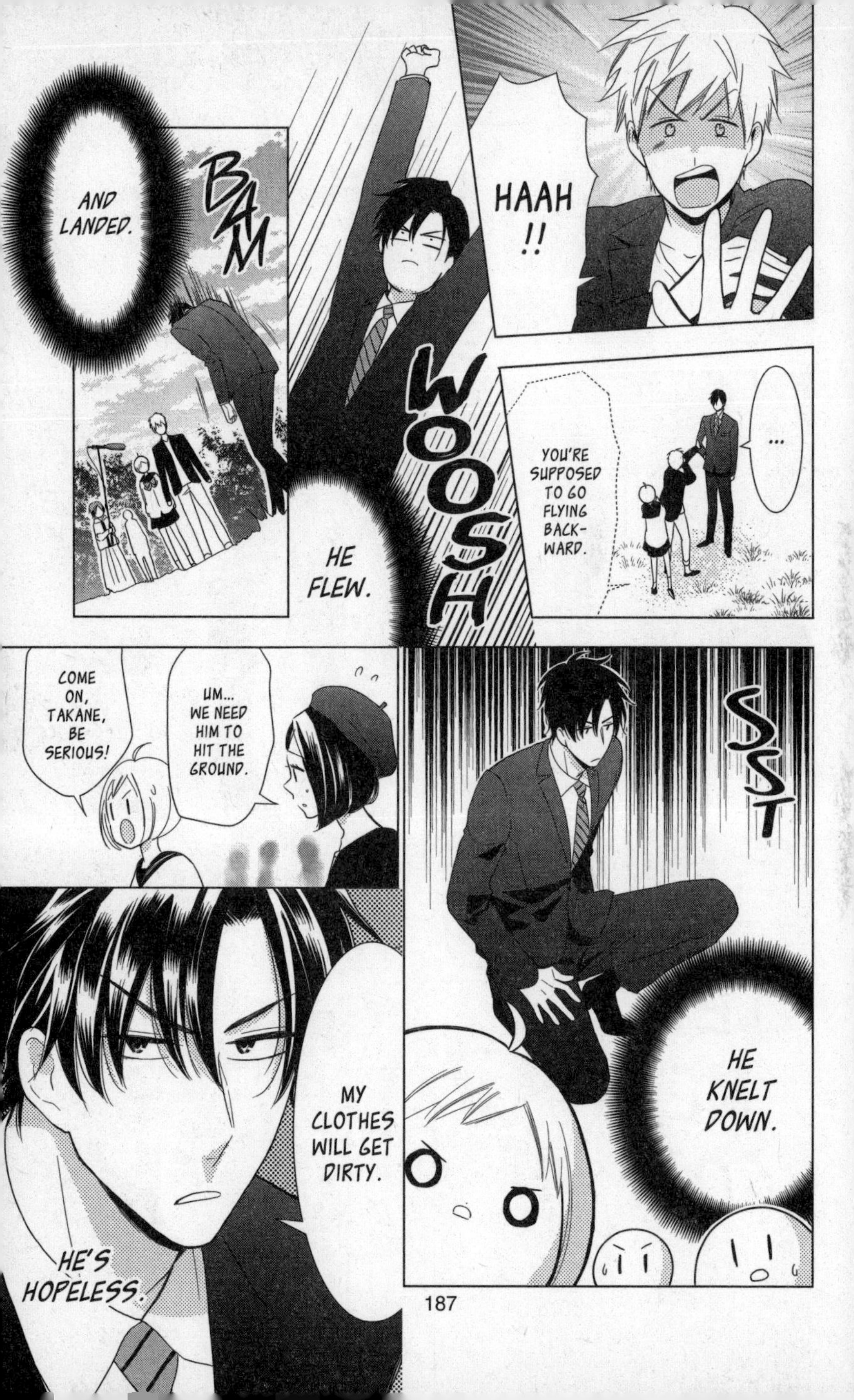
HAAH!!
WOOSH
HE FLEW.
BAM
AND LANDED.
...
YOU'RE SUPPOSED TO GO FLYING BACKWARD.
SST
HE KNELT DOWN.
UM... WE NEED HIM TO HIT THE GROUND.
COME ON, TAKANE, BE SERIOUS!
MY CLOTHES WILL GET DIRTY.
HE'S HOPELESS.

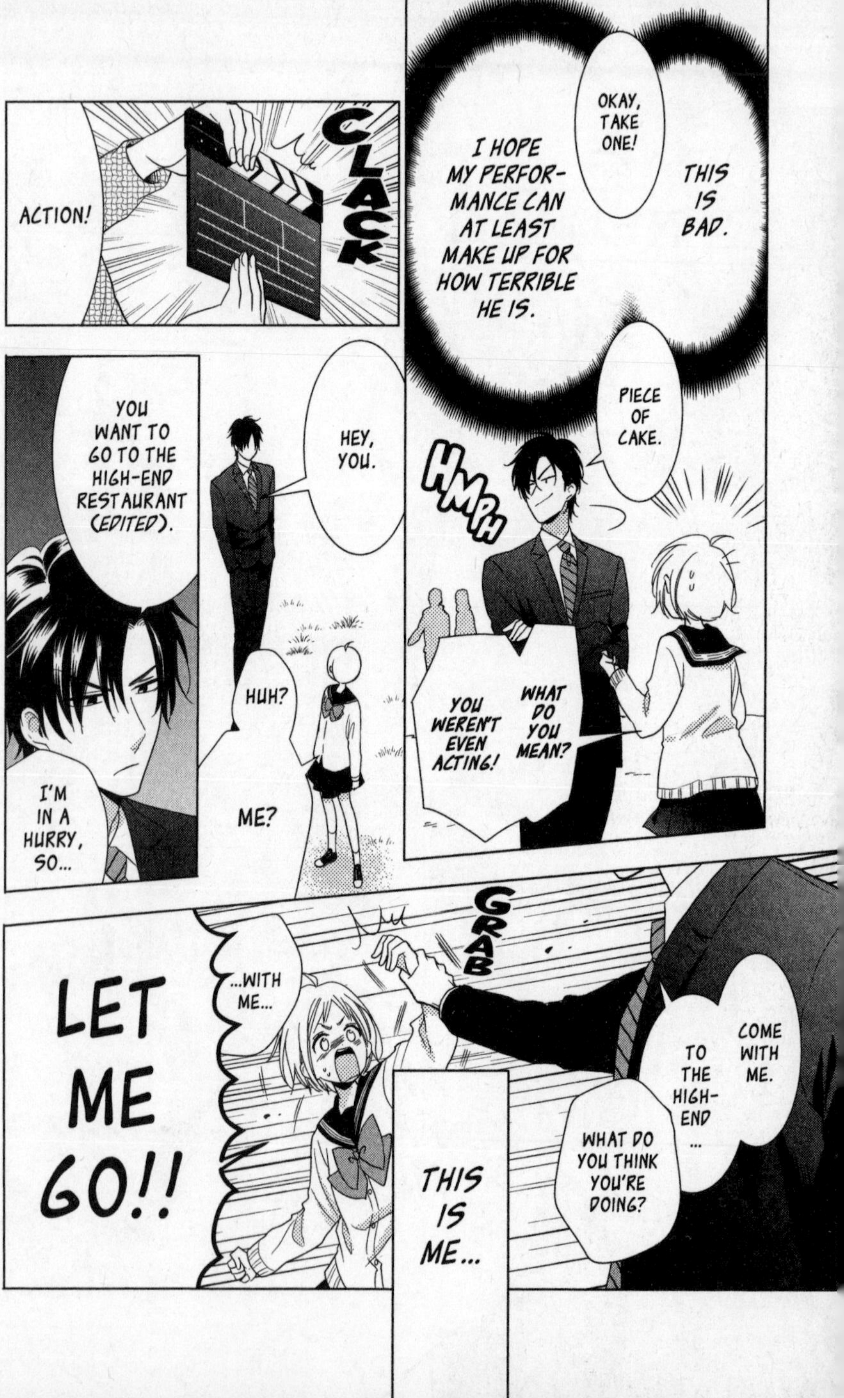
THIS IS BAD.
OKAY, TAKE ONE!
I HOPE MY PERFORMANCE CAN AT LEAST MAKE UP FOR HOW TERRIBLE HE IS.
PIECE OF CAKE.
HMPH
WHAT DO YOU MEAN?
YOU WEREN'T EVEN ACTING!
CLACK
ACTION!
HEY, YOU.
HUH?
ME?
YOU WANT TO GO TO THE HIGH-END RESTAURANT (EDITED).
I'M IN A HURRY, SO...
GRAB
COME WITH ME.
TO THE HIGH-END...
WHAT DO YOU THINK YOU'RE DOING?
THIS IS ME...
...WITH ME...
LET ME GO!!

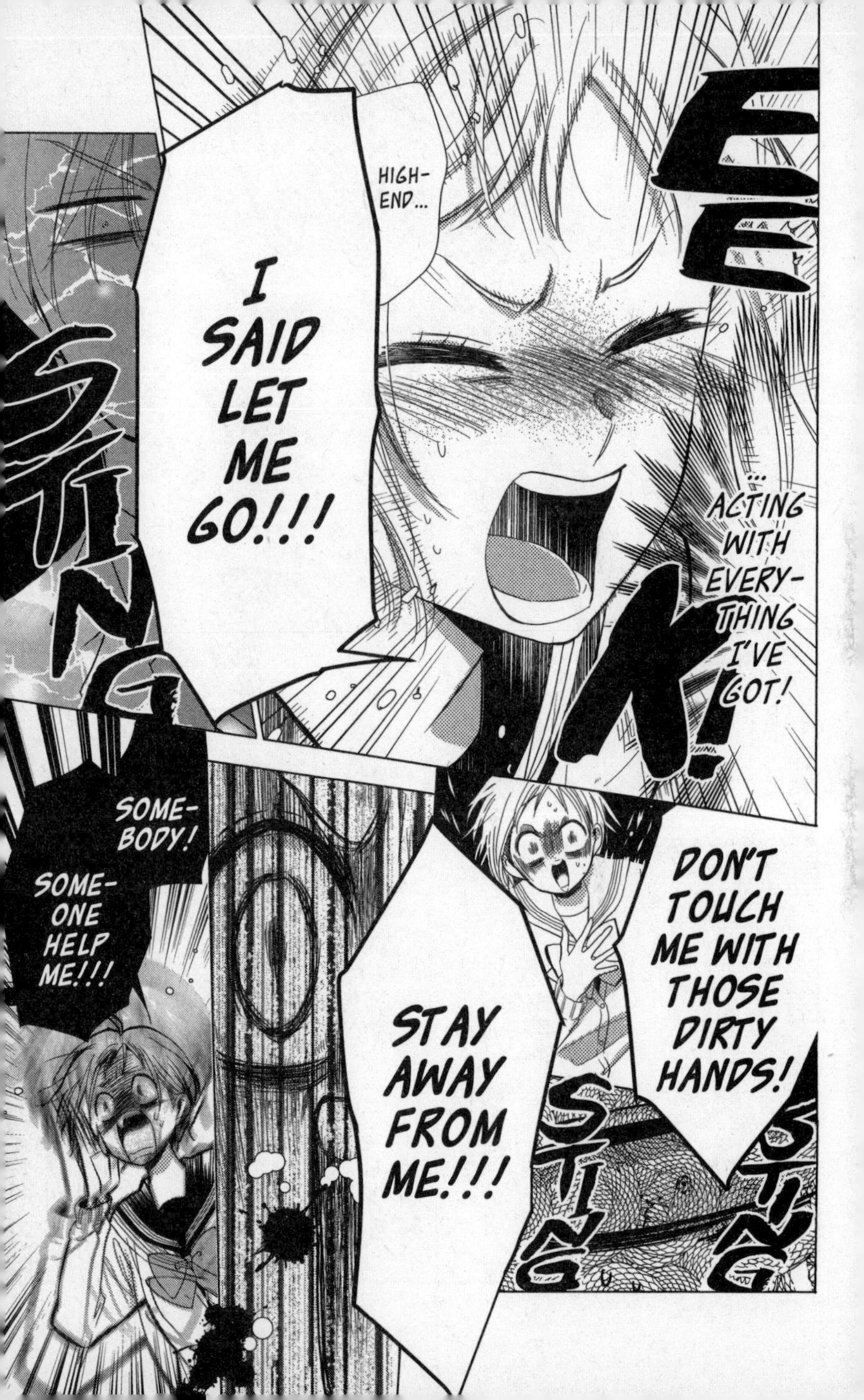
HIGH-END...
...ACTING WITH EVERYTHING I'VE GOT!
I SAID LET ME GO!!!
DON'T TOUCH ME WITH THOSE DIRTY HANDS!
STAY AWAY FROM ME!!!
STING
STING
SOME-BODY!
SOME-ONE HELP ME!!!

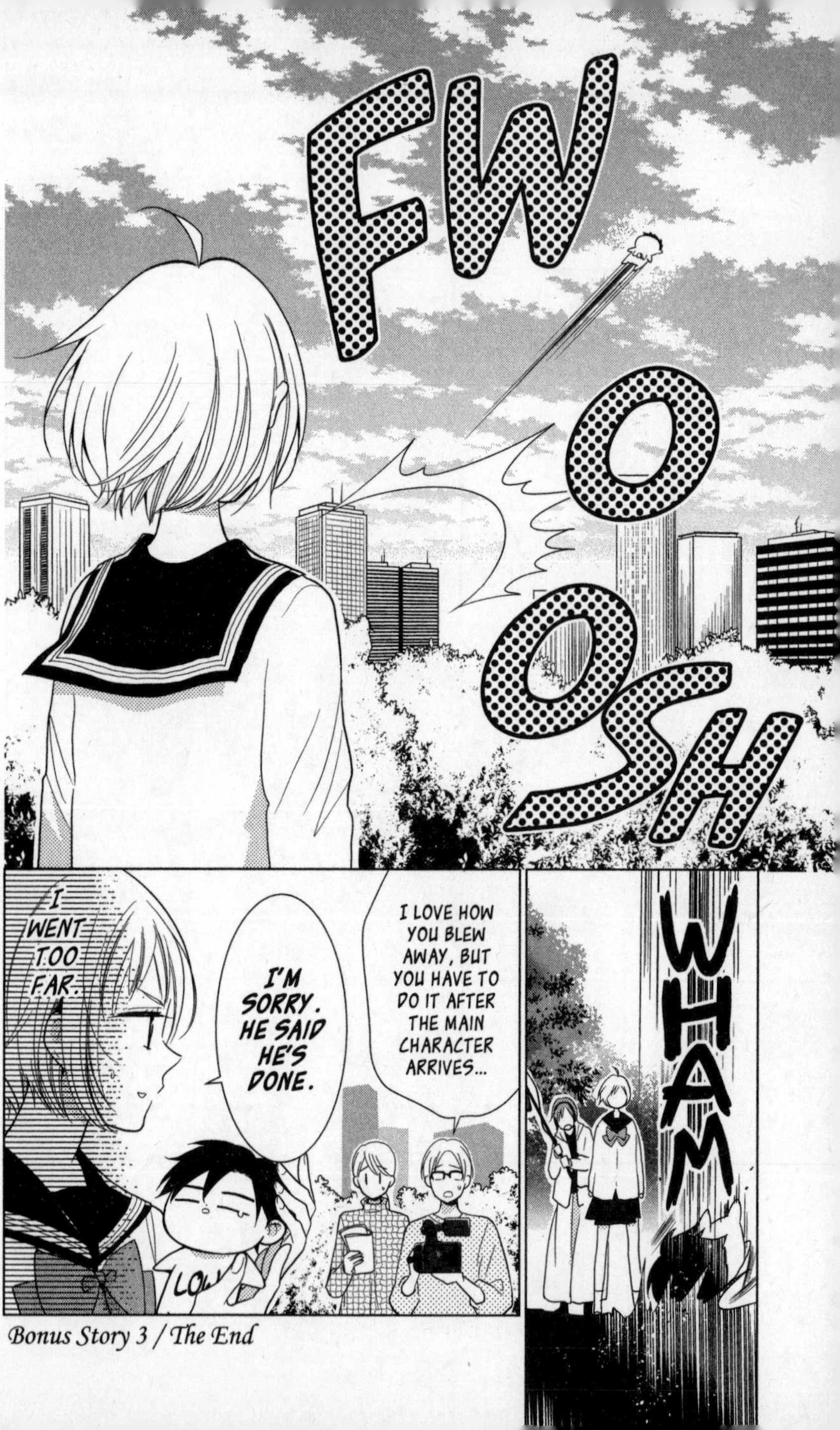
FWOOSH
WHAM
I LOVE HOW YOU BLEW AWAY, BUT YOU HAVE TO DO IT AFTER THE MAIN CHARACTER ARRIVES...
I'M SORRY. HE SAID HE'S DONE.
I WENT TOO FAR.

Bonus Story 3 / The End

The halfway point between Default Takane
and Comical Takane...

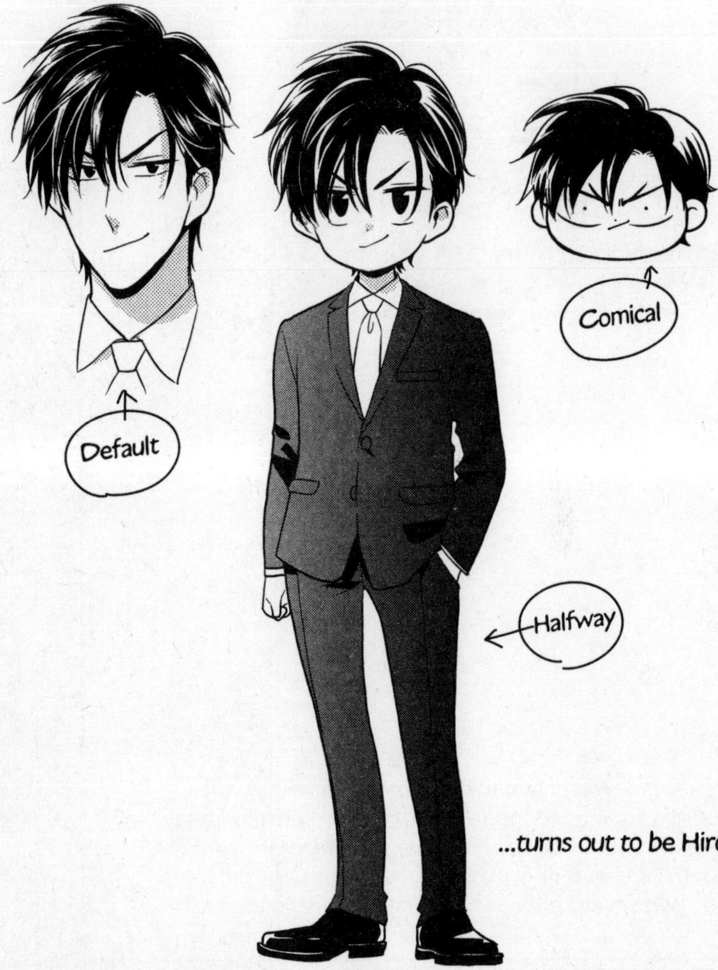
Default
Halfway
Comical

...turns out to be Hiromi.

In keeping with the "falling from the sky" theme, this cover shows drops of water falling from the sky. What you see Hana drinking there is juice.

—YUKI SHIWASU

Born on March 7 in Fukuoka Prefecture, Japan, Yuki Shiwasu began her career as a manga artist after winning the top prize in the Hakusensha Athena Newcomers' Awards from *Hana to Yume* magazine. She is also the author of *Furou Kyoudai* (Immortal Siblings), which was published by Hakusensha in Japan.

Takane &Hana

VOLUME 14
SHOJO BEAT EDITION

STORY & ART BY **YUKI SHIWASU**

ENGLISH ADAPTATION **Ysabet Reinhardt MacFarlane**
TRANSLATION **JN Productions**
TOUCH-UP ART & LETTERING **Annaliese Christman**
DESIGN **Shawn Carrico**
EDITOR **Amy Yu**

Takane to Hana by Yuki Shiwasu
© Yuki Shiwasu 2019
All rights reserved.
First published in Japan in 2019 by HAKUSENSHA, Inc., Tokyo.
English language translation rights arranged with HAKUSENSHA, Inc., Tokyo.

The stories, characters and incidents mentioned
in this publication are entirely fictional.

Printed in the U.S.A.

Published by VIZ Media, LLC
P.O. Box 77010
San Francisco, CA 94107

10 9 8 7 6 5 4 3 2 1
First printing, April 2020

viz.com   shojobeat.com

Snow White
with the Red Hair

Inspired the anime!

STORY & ART BY
SORATA AKIDUKI

Shirayuki is an herbalist famous for her naturally bright-red hair, and the prince of Tanbarun wants her all to himself! Unwilling to become the prince's possession, she seeks shelter in the woods of the neighboring kingdom, where she gains an unlikely ally—the prince of that kingdom! He rescues her from her plight, and thus begins the love story between a lovestruck prince and an unusual herbalist.

STORY & ART BY
ARINA TANEMURA

At age 31, office worker Chikage Deguchi feels she missed her chances at love and success. When word gets out that she's a virgin, Chikage is humiliated and wishes she could turn back time to when she was still young and popular. She takes an experimental drug that changes her appearance back to when she was 15. Now Chikage is determined to pursue everything she missed out on all those years ago—including becoming a star!

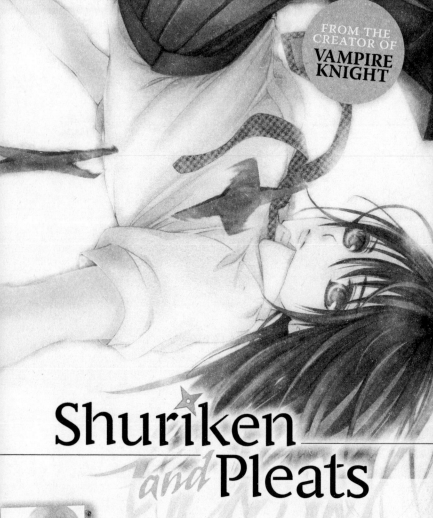

Shuriken *and* Pleats

When the master she has sworn to protect is killed, Mikage Kirio, a skilled ninja, travels to Japan to start a new, peaceful life for herself. But as soon as she arrives, she finds herself fighting to protect the life of Mahito Wakashimatsu, a man who is under attack by a band of ninja. From that time on, Mikage is drawn deeper into the machinations of his powerful family.

www.viz.com

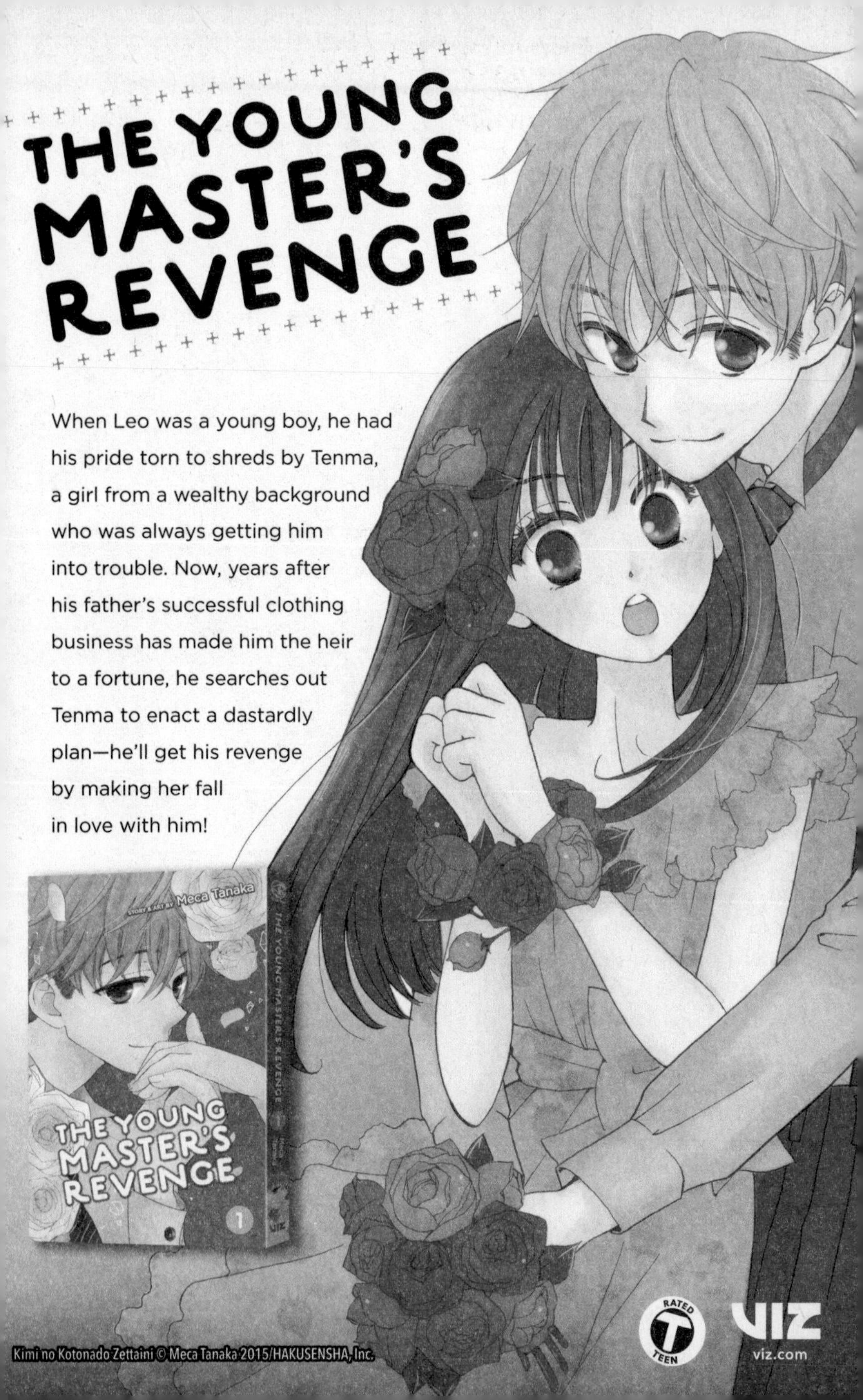
THE YOUNG MASTER'S REVENGE
When Leo was a young boy, he had his pride torn to shreds by Tenma, a girl from a wealthy background who was always getting him into trouble. Now, years after his father's successful clothing business has made him the heir to a fortune, he searches out Tenma to enact a dastardly plan—he'll get his revenge by making her fall in love with him!
STORY & ART BY Meca Tanaka
THE YOUNG MASTER'S REVENGE
1
VIZ
RATED T TEEN
VIZ
viz.com
Kimi no Kotonado Zettaini © Meca Tanaka 2015/HAKUSENSHA, Inc.

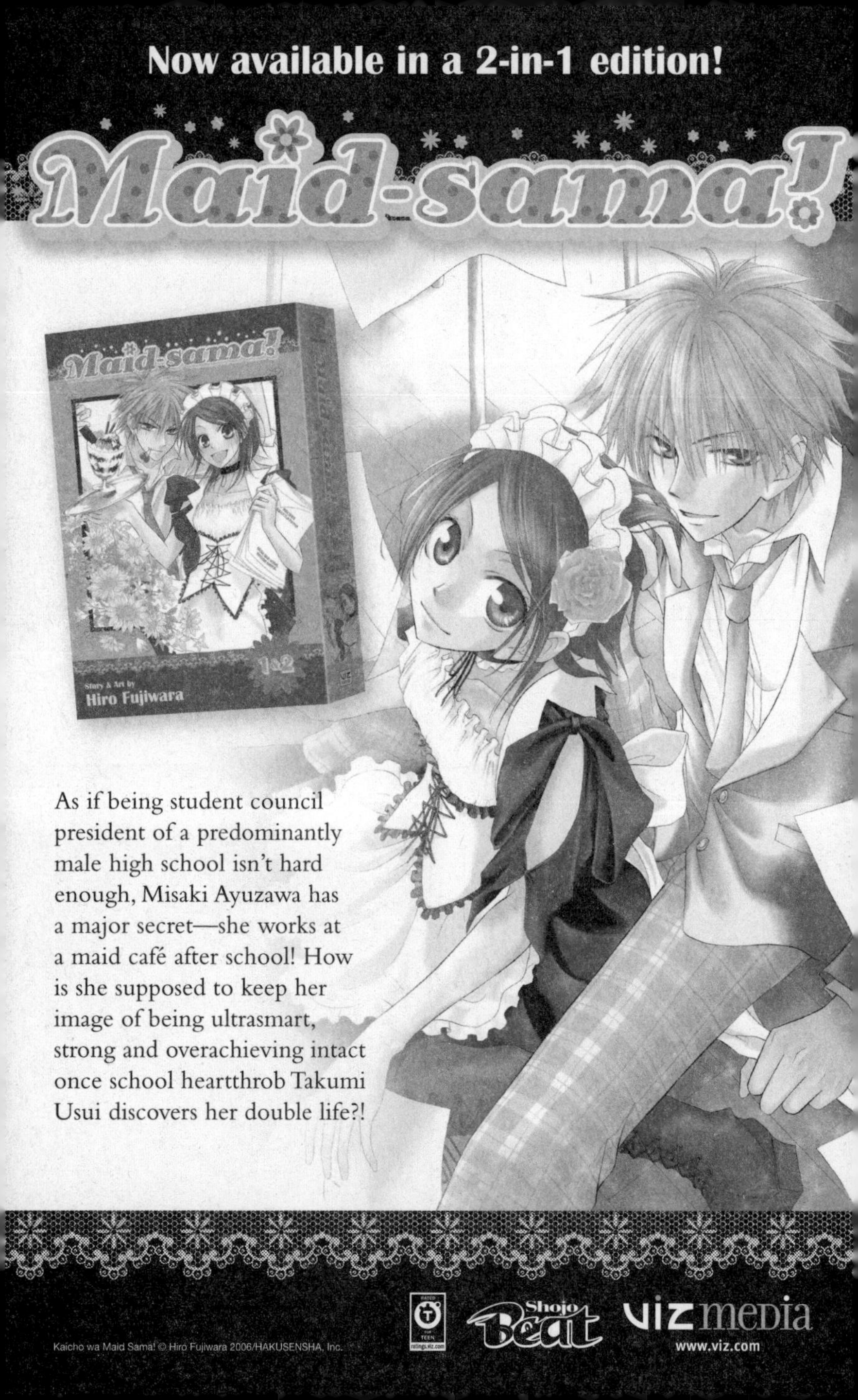

Now available in a 2-in-1 edition!
Maid-sama!
Maid-sama!
1&2
Story & Art by
Hiro Fujiwara
As if being student council president of a predominantly male high school isn't hard enough, Misaki Ayuzawa has a major secret—she works at a maid café after school! How is she supposed to keep her image of being ultrasmart, strong and overachieving intact once school heartthrob Takumi Usui discovers her double life?!
RATED T FOR TEEN ratings.viz.com
Shojo Beat
VIZ media
www.viz.com
Kaicho wa Maid Sama! © Hiro Fujiwara 2006/HAKUSENSHA, Inc.

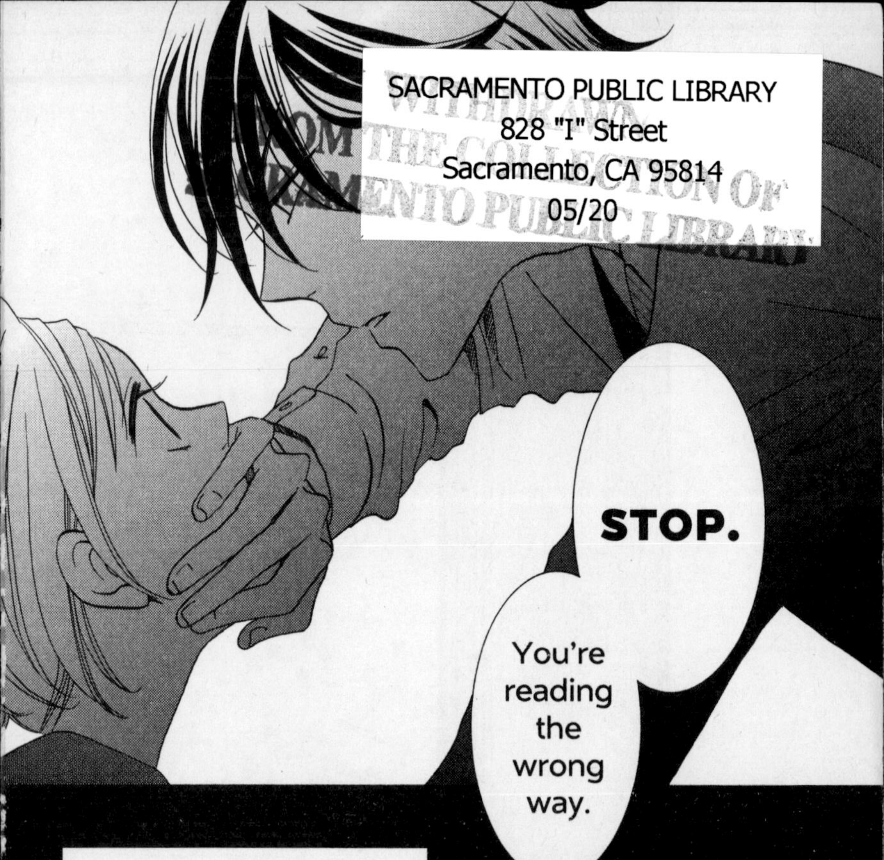
STOP.
You're reading the wrong way.

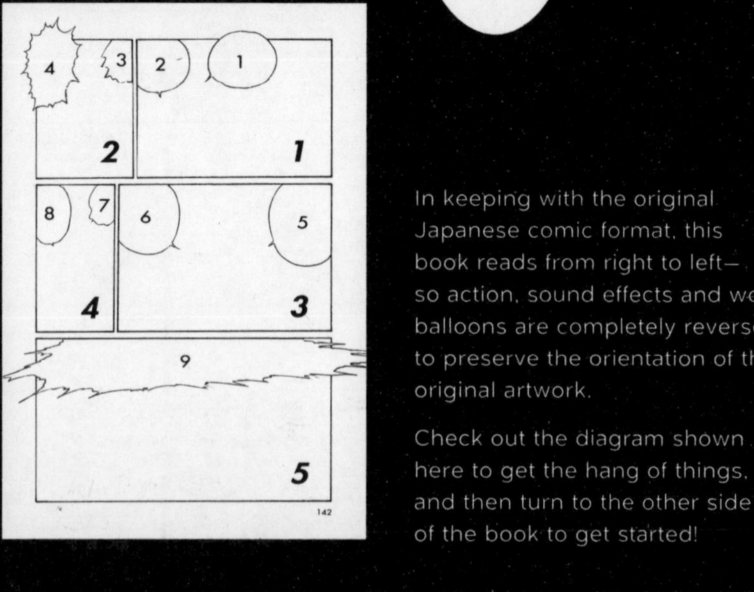

In keeping with the original Japanese comic format, this book reads from right to left— so action, sound effects and word balloons are completely reversed to preserve the orientation of the original artwork.

Check out the diagram shown here to get the hang of things, and then turn to the other side of the book to get started!